URBAN ECONOMICS
AND POLICY
ANALYSIS

URBAN ECONOMICS AND POLICY ANALYSIS

Robert L. Bish
University of Southern California

Hugh O. Nourse
University of Missouri, St. Louis

McGraw-Hill Book Company

New York   St. Louis   San Francisco   Auckland   Düsseldorf
Johannesburg   Kuala Lumpur   London   Mexico   Montreal   New Delhi
Panama   Paris   São Paulo   Singapore   Sydney   Tokyo   Toronto

**URBAN ECONOMICS
AND POLICY ANALYSIS**

34567890KPKP7987

This book was set in English by Black Dot, Inc. The editors were J.S.
Dietrich and Michael Weber; the designer was Joseph Gillians; the
production supervisor was Charles Hess. New drawings were done by
Vantage Art, Inc.
Kingsport Press, Inc., was printer and binder.

Library of Congress Cataloging in Publication Data

Bish, Robert L.
  Urban economics and policy analysis.

  Includes bibliographies and index.
  1. Urban economics. I. Nourse, Hugh O., joint author. II. Title.
HT321.B574   330.9'173'2   74-23913
ISBN 0-07-005388-X

CONTENTS

Costs; Discounting the Future; Project Comparison; Benefit-Cost Analysis and Political Decision Making; Incentives, Professionalization and Unionism; STUDIES OF PUBLIC GOODS PROVISION; Police Services; Fire Protection Services; REFORMING THE URBAN PUBLIC SECTOR; Metropolitan Government: Reform through Consolidation; *The Reform Movement; Metropolitan Governments;* Community Control: A New Reform Tradition; Reconciling Diverse Approaches: Two-Tier Solutions; A Closer Look; *Service Contracting; Rivalry and Cooperation; Understanding the Urban Public Sector;* SUMMARY; SELECTED READINGS

HOUSING SEGREGATION—AN ARBITRAGE MODEL; The Static Model; The Model with Population Growth Included; The Model with Racial Prejudice Included; Some Implications and Modifications; SLUMS; PUBLIC POLICY TOWARD SLUMS; Improvement of Housing Quality; *Public Housing; Rent and Interest Subsidies; Building Code Regulation*; Urban Renewal; Income Maintenance and the Negative Income Tax; Labor Market Policies; *Black Capitalism; Manpower Development and Training Programs; Labor Market Efficiency Programs;* SUMMARY; SELECTED READINGS

RATIONALE FOR ZONING; ZONING CRITERIA; ECONOMICS OF REGULATORY CHOICE; ECONOMIC IMPACT OF ZONING; LEGAL PERSPECTIVE; ZONING PROBLEMS; POLICY ALTERNATIVES; SUMMARY; SELECTED READINGS

BENEFITS FROM EDUCATION; DEMAND ARTICULATION; THE PRODUCTION OF EDUCATION; GROUPING VERSUS SEGREGATION; FINANCING EDUCATION; Current Financing; Equal Opportunity in Education; Financial Reform; *Power Equalizing; Percentage Equalizing; Separation of Residential and Commercial Tax Bases; School District Reorganization; Statewide School Financing; Conclusions on Educational Finance Reform;* RESOLVING MULTIPLE DILEMMAS; School District Consolidations; Performance Contracting; Decentralization, or Breaking Up Large Systems; Voucher Systems; SUMMARY; SELECTED READINGS

PREFACE

The development of urban economics as a new field of economics has paralleled increased interest in domestic urban problems. The features that make the field unique are the addition of location and spatial economic theory to standard microeconomic theory, and the focus on urban problems and policies. Thus it is common to begin courses with location theory and then to analyze problems in housing and renewal, poverty, racial segregation and ghetto development, transportation, pollution, and urban government finance. We believe, however, that to undertake the analysis of urban problems and public policies properly, traditional locational and microeconomic analyses must be integrated with the public choice theory emerging from the study of public finance. Our objective is to provide a beginning synthesis of location and public choice theory for the purpose of analyzing urban phenomena, problems, and public policies. Thus this analysis is much more than a summary of currently taught material in urban economics.

While the integration of location and public choice theory makes the volume more than a text, we have attempted to provide a level of explanation that is suitable for teaching purposes. Our focus, however, is on the application of economic thinking and the logic of relationships among different aspects of the urban economy, not on the development of economic techniques per se. The result is a work that can be used by strong students with only limited familarity with technical economics; but, at the same time, instructors of mathematically oriented undergraduates or graduate students should find the work comprehensive and suitable for use as a major text when supplemented with illustrations from the journal literature of empirical and mathematical applications of the concepts. Many articles suitable for this purpose are listed at the end of each chapter.

We wish to thank our friends and scholars who reviewed earlier drafts of the manuscript. Comments from William Latham, James Little, Stephen Messner, Leland S. Case, Joe Hulett, and John C. Weicher were especially helpful. Comments on closely related work from Robert Kirk, Edwin Mills, Vincent Ostrom, Elinor Ostrom, Richard Pfister, and Dean Worcester were also helpful for this effort. We wish to thank George Hilton for making his study of urban mass transit administration policies available prior to its publication and Elinor Ostrom for making results of studies of police performance available prior to their publication. We also wish to thank Prentice-Hall for permission to use some material from Robert L. Bish and Robert J. Kirk, *Economic Principles and Urban Problems* and McGraw-Hill for permission to use material from Hugh O. Nourse, *Regional Economics.*

We hope that this work will provide firmer conceptual foundations for urban economics than have been previously available and that it will encourage others to undertake further integration of location and public choice theory for the analysis of urban problems and policies.

Robert L. Bish
Hugh O. Nourse

URBAN ECONOMICS
AND POLICY
ANALYSIS

CHAPTER **1**

INTRODUCTION

The development of economics as an independent discipline paralleled the industrial revolution of the eighteenth and nineteenth centuries. Because the industrial revolution represented a significant shift from the traditional relationships of a feudal economy to a predominantly market economy, it is only natural that the study of resource allocation by economists focused primarily on the operation of markets. Even government policies such as taxing and spending have been analyzed primarily for their effects on market operations.

In addition, however, to the rise of markets for allocating resources, another phenomenon, urbanization, has been an integral part of the industrial revolution. Urbanization, the concentration of many people and economic activities in large cities and urban agglomerations, leads to many nonmarket interdependencies that are not understandable within the context of market operations alone. In fact, many problems of urbanization, such as environmental degradation, transportation congestion, and the problems associated with providing public goods and services to urban dwellers, occur precisely *because* markets do not work very well for their resolution. It is primarily in response to interest in contemporary urban problems where markets do not work well that urban economics has emerged as a separate field in the study of economics.

URBAN ECONOMICS AND POLICY ANALYSIS

The major characteristics which differentiate urban economics from other fields in economics are its use of location theory to focus on spatial aspects of the economy, especially the spatial aspects of large urban agglomerations, and its focus on contemporary urban problems which involve nonmarket interdependencies and public policy.

The study of spatial aspects of the economy and development of location theory has a long tradition in economics, both in regional economics which focuses on the location and growth of cities and in real estate economics which focuses on urban land markets and suburbanization. The importance of location and the costs of overcoming spatial separation are crucial elements of location theory. The advantages of proximity among economic activities are the major reason for the development of large urban agglomerations, and the costs of moving goods and people around within urban areas are major determinants of urban land-use patterns. Thus, both of these elements of location theory—agglomeration economies and transportation costs —have been central concepts in urban economics as well, and urban economics has depended heavily on its historical roots in location theory and spatial analysis.

Also important in urbanization, but not central to location theory, are the nonmarket interdependencies that result when many activities are carried on close to one another. Problems such as the negative effects of one land use upon another, or the congestion of traffic and environmental degradation, for example, can influence site choices by consumers and producers as well as restrict the achievement of economic efficiency through market transactions. Still another consequence of urbanization results when many consumers or producers are located closely together. In such circumstances it may be more efficient to provide goods and services collectively through government instead of through private markets. Goods such as police protection, fire protection, and streets, for example, may be supplied more cheaply by providing them for groups of individuals instead of single individuals one at a time. These goods, when provided by a governmental unit for a specific geographic area, also enter into location choice calculations and affect spatial patterns. Both the existence of nonmarket interdependencies and the provision of public goods by political units are important considerations in urban economics, although neither of these issues has received the same emphasis as has agglomeration economies and transportation costs.

Because the study of urban problems requires the analysis of nonmarket interdependencies, the governmental provision of goods, and the impacts of public policies, urban economists have become increasingly concerned with the operation of the public sector. Questions of which laws or policies most effectively will force taking non-market interdependencies into account in resource allocation choices and what size government can most efficiently meet demands for urban public goods and services are examples of the questions asked about the public sector by urban economists. It has become apparent that if urban problems and policies are to be analyzed, the operations of governments themselves must be included in the analysis. This realization that economists must analyze the behavior of governments in the same way that they have traditionally analyzed the behavior of firms is in striking contrast to an older tradition in economic analysis in which governments were viewed as outside the scope of economics. Then economists limited themselves to the consequences of government activities on consumers or producers, or to recommending policies to the government on the assumption that some government official would omnisciently, omnipotently, and benevolently implement the correct policies. The new approach to analyzing government is much different. The behavior of governmental units and public officials is viewed within the same theoretical framework as consumers and private firms are viewed—as individuals who either individually or in their capacities as public officials have specific preferences and face choices in allocating scarce resources. When this approach is taken, the public sector, with its several hundred independent political units and innumerable quasi-independent departments, boards, and commissions, appears extremely complex. While the complexity is very real, an increasing number of analysts are finding that the complexity is subject to systematic analysis. Detailed analysis of the functioning of the public sector by economists, however, has been undertaken primarily by public finance economists who have developed concepts and a theory called the theory of public goods and collective action, or public choice theory. Only limited use of this theory has been made by urban economists. Yet the theory of public goods and collective action is the most appropriate body of theory for the analysis of non-market interdependencies and the provision of public goods—two of the most important elements of the study of urban economics.

We believe that considerable insight can be gained by adding the theory of public goods and collective action to location theory for analysis of urban problems and policies. In fact, we believe that after readers are introduced to the contribution the theory of public goods and collective action makes to the analysis of urban problems and policies they will conclude as we have: that this body of theory is not only useful but, like location theory, is indispensable to the field of urban economics. Thus, we have made the thrust of this analysis the integration of location theory and the theory of public goods and collective action for the understanding of urban problems and policies. Since there has been only a modest literature combining spatial and public goods theory, we have only made a start at their integration. We look forward to future contributions that readers of this analysis may make by building on our efforts.

POSITIVE AND NORMATIVE ANALYSIS

Our approach to urban economics and policy analysis is to focus first on *predicting* the consequences of particular public policies and the kinds of policies likely to emerge under alternative public sector organizational arrangements. Our focus first on predictive or positive analysis is based on the assumption that we must be able to predict the consequences of policies and organizational changes before we can recommend policies or organizational changes to achieve particular, normative objectives with any confidence that desired objectives will in fact result.

While we stress predictive analysis, all of our work is not confined to positive economics. The very definition of urban problems implies normative concern. In general, however, we take a restrained approach toward advocating our own preferences. We accept the philosophy that the economy and polity should be organized to meet individual preferences *as perceived by the individuals who make up the society*, not the preferences of third-party "experts," and we remain suspicious of any "social-welfare function" approach for both empirical and philosophical reasons. Since policies and organizational changes are likely to affect each individual differently, we believe it is useful to view recommended policies and organizational changes as hypotheses whose first validation is their acceptance by concerned parties.[1]

As a consequence of our perspective, we have tried to limit expressions of strong, normative content to areas where we have concluded that the possibility for widely shared gains exists or where current policies or institutional arrangements are not responding to the preferences of consumer-citizens. Where our analysis indicates that proposed solutions to problems would result in a very uneven distribution of costs and benefits, we attempt to pinpoint the crucial factors of the dilemma in the hope that other analysts may perceive solutions of a more mutually satisfactory nature. While some analysts will be disappointed that we do not take stronger advocacy positions, we be-

---

[1]Normative criteria for evaluating public policies are examined more fully in Chapter 5.

lieve modesty is a good approach to the social science analysis of urban problems. After all, it has yet to be demonstrated that social scientists have reached the turning point achieved by physicians in the early 1900s—when they began to do more good than harm.

ORGANIZATION OF THE STUDY

Our analysis begins with a brief survey of world urbanization and the relationship between the industrial revolution and urbanization. This overview is followed by an analysis of the concepts and definitions used in gathering data to describe urbanization in the United States. Trends in the rise of large cities, suburbanization, and the growth of large urban agglomerations are examined. A description of the parallel growth and increasing complexity of the urban public sector concludes the chapter.

In Chapter 3 we provide the framework for analyzing the existence, location, size, and growth of urban areas. The relationship between economies of scale in production, transportation costs, population density, and market size is developed, followed by the use of theory to construct a model of a system of cities that is equivalent to a statistical description of cities relating their sizes and ranks. The model is then expanded by introducing unequal natural resource distributions, problems of industrial location choice, and the role of agglomeration economies in urban growth. Issues of urban growth and decline are analyzed in terms of the migration of capital and labor from declining to growing areas. Finally, we consider the policy alternatives open to a community which wishes to alter its size or enhance the income and employment opportunities of its citizens.

Land-use patterns within urban areas are analyzed in Chapter 4. Determinants of urban property values are examined. The uses of a single, centered land-use model in explaining general land-use patterns, population density, the location of high- and low-income families, and the relationship between declining transportation costs and suburbanization are analyzed. Deficiencies in explanations provided by the single centered model are examined, especially in relation to the functioning of urban land markets, nonmarket interdependencies among land uses, and the relationship between location and public sector activity. Chapters 3 and 4 present the most important elements of location theory used in urban economics.

In Chapter 5 we discuss the basic theory of public goods and collective action. The problem of obtaining efficient resource allocation where nonmarket interdependencies exist is explored, followed by an analysis of the problems of providing public goods and managing common pools and natural monopolies. These analyses lay the basis for the economic theory of collective action. Within this framework, issues of the size and scope of political units for urban areas, including considerations of demand articulation, participation, political leadership, and economies of scale in production, are treated. Because nonmarket interdependencies and public goods have geographically defined attributes and political units are defined by geographic boundaries, the relationship between problems of efficient resource allocation and political organization is specifically examined. The residential and business location choice factors presented in Chapters 3 and 4 are also reexamined in light of public goods provision and government regulation. Chapter 5 provides much of the basic theory that is used to examine the public sector and urban problems and policies.

Financing of the urban public sector is the subject of Chapter 6. Alternative revenue sources, including property, sales, and income taxation, user charges, functional grants, and revenue sharing, are examined. Urban fiscal issues such as the perpetual financial crises of large-city governments, the effect of suburbanization on the central city, and fiscal inequality among citizens in different governmental units are analyzed.

Chapter 7 is devoted to the analysis of special problems in the urban public sector. Concepts developed in previous chapters are applied to examine the role of benefit-cost analysis in improving decision making, the incentives generated by different organizational structures, and professionalization and public sector unionism. Empirical studies of the provision of police and fire services are presented to relate concepts developed in theory to the actual provision of public goods and services. The final section of this chapter examines urban government reform with a discussion of consolidated metropolitan governments, neighborhood governments, and rivalry and cooperation among different jurisdictions in the urban public sector. Special emphasis in this analysis is placed on the problems of minorities and the poor.

In Chapters 8 to 12, topical problems and policy analyses are explored. The problems we have selected include housing, segregation, poverty and race, zoning and land-use control, education, environmental management, and urban transportation. The analysis of each topic involves the analysis of market outcomes, related nonmarket effects, the potential for public provision or regulation to achieve preferred resource allocation patterns, and the effects public policies will have on spatial patterns and other urban problems. Elements of location theory and the theory of public goods and collective action are used throughout the topical analyses to diagnose problems and forecast consequences of alternative policies proposed as solutions.

In the final chapter we examine the relationships among the previously analyzed topical areas and the future of urban areas. Questions examined include the potential role of a national urban policy, optimal city size, new towns, the role of collective action, and the importance of political organization in urban areas.

Upon mastering the contents of this analysis, readers should have a good grasp of the elements of location theory and the theory of public goods and collective action and be familiar with their application in a variety of problem situations. Readers should also be able to extend the use of these theoretical frameworks to analyze new problem areas and evaluate the potential for success of new policies. We also believe that upon completing this analysis the usefulness of the theory of public goods and collective action as an integral part of urban economics will be recognized, and that this integration of location and public goods theory will foster and promote even better analyses of urban problems and policies than we have been able to accomplish in this initial effort.

CHAPTER **2**

URBANIZATION

URBANIZATION

Urbanization, or the concentration of population and economic activity in cities and large urban agglomerations is a recent phenomenon in the history of man.[1] In earlier times some cities such as Athens, Rome, and Constantinople had populations over 100,000, but prior to the nineteenth century no more than 1 or 2 percent of the world's population lived in towns of more than 5,000 people.[2] Instead, the vast majority of people lived and worked in rural agricultural settings, and the task of producing sufficient food for survival occupied most of everyone's time. Prerequisites for urbanization—high agricultural productivity to free some men from the agricultural work force, good transportation from farm to market, and a developed market system— were lacking.

In the sixteenth and seventeenth centuries changes began in

[1]Excellent discussions of early urbanization are presented in Kingsley Davis, "The Origin and Growth of Urbanization in the World," *American Journal of Sociology*, 60 (March 1955), pp. 429–437. The classic study on the period of most rapid urbanization is Adna F. Weber. *The Growth of Cities in the Nineteenth Century* (Ithaca: Cornell, 1963, first published in 1899).

[2]Glenn T. Trewartha, *A Geography of Population: World Patterns* (New York: Wiley, 1969), p. 147.

the conditions of life that would eventually result in urbanization. Horse-drawn machinery for agriculture was developed, and productivity increases were achieved through cultivation of large fields instead of small individual plots. The increases in agricultural productivity created excess labor in rural areas and encouraged migration to towns and cities. Town and city growth, however, was very slow because the high disease-related city death rates equaled migration and birthrates in most cities until the eighteenth or nineteenth centuries.

While the countryside was changing, cities also began to change, especially in the nineteenth century. The cottage industry was declining and being replaced by early factory systems. The steam engine was invented and provided power for mechanized factories on a scale previously unknown. There was also a considerable increase in foreign trade as manufacturers sought markets for their products and imported food for their work force and raw materials for the new industrial processes. It was during the nineteenth century that large cities emerged. Some, like Manchester, England, grew from a population of 5,000 in 1700 to over 100,000 in 1800. London, Europe's largest city, reached a population of nearly 900,000 by 1800. Even with the emergence of large cities, however, there were fewer than fifty cities with populations over 100,000 at the beginning of the nineteenth century.[3]

The nineteenth century was the century of industrialization, urbanization, and market trade expansion. Agricultural productivity was increased with the development of chemical soil analysis, commercial fertilizers, and improved seed strains. McCormick's reaper and other labor-saving machinery were invented and mass produced. The final stages of the enclosure movement[4] in Europe forced many workers off the land and into the growing cities. The movement of produce from agricultural areas to emerging cities was facilitated by major improvements in transportation. Steamboats, railroad (including refrigerated rail cars), and, toward the end of the century, automobiles and trucks were some of the transportation innovations of the nineteenth century. These improvements permitted the importation of food and raw materials from as far away as Australia, New Zealand, the United States, Eastern Europe, and Russia to supply England and Western Europe's industrialization. At the same time inventions such as the electric motor and generator permitted the development of still

[3]Davis, "The Origin and Growth of Urbanization in the World," p. 434.

[4]In the enclosure movement small plots worked by tenants and common land used for grazing were consolidated under single ownership. While the process displaced tenants whose families had worked the plots for generations and was often of questionable legality, it did foster the introduction of more efficient large-field agriculture, prevent overgrazing of common pastures, and permit landowners to shift pasture lands to the production of corn and grain as the prices of those commodities increased.

larger factories, and the electric streetcar facilitated transport of workers from larger and larger residential areas to factory concentrations in larger and larger cities. It was also in the nineteenth century that public health measures reduced the high death rates long associated with city life, and city populations grew rapidly.

By the end of the nineteenth century, the large city and laissez faire markets were dominant in the economy and society of Western Europe, of increasing importance in the United States and other industrializing areas, and emerging throughout the rest of the world. Urbanization and the rise of large cities has continued into the twentieth century. By 1950 there were close to 900 urban areas with populations over 100,000 and 79 with populations over 1 million. By 1970 the number of areas with over 100,000 people had risen to nearly 1,600, and the number of areas with 1 million or more people had risen to 164. There were three urban agglomerations with populations in excess of 10 million, and 40 percent of the world's population resided in urban areas.[5] The trends toward urbanization and concentration of population and economic activity within large urban areas are continuing, and it now appears that between the years 1800 and 2000 a majority of the world's population will have shifted from being a rural, agriculturally oriented people dependent primarily on their own farming efforts to a people residing in urban agglomerations completely dependent upon specialization and trade for their survival.

URBANIZATION IN THE UNITED STATES

The United States has undergone the same process of urbanization and development of large cities as has the rest of the world. Before examining urbanization in the United States, however, it is useful to become familiar with the definitions used in collecting data describing urban phenomena.

Definitions of Urban Areas

The United States census is the major source of data on the distribution of population and economic activity in the United States. The census definitions are the definitions most commonly used in research and descriptions of urbanization. The census itself provides several definitions of "urban." Some are based on economic relationships and population densities, others are based on political entities such as

[5]Kingsley Davis, *World Urbanization 1950–1970*, vol. 1: *Basic Data for Cities, Countries, and Regions* (Berkeley: Institute of International Studies, University of California, 1969).

cities and counties, and still others combine aspects of political boundaries with economic characteristics and population density. The major definitions used in the study of urban economics include place, urbanized area, urban population, standard metropolitan statistical area, central city, central business district, suburban ring, and standard consolidated area.[6]

Place The census publishes data for all incorporated places with populations of 1,000 or more. These data on the population of incorporated areas (cities, towns, municipalities), however, do not correspond to a concept of urbanization defined by high population density because areas outside an incorporated place's boundaries may be as densely populated as the place itself. Furthermore, the individual place populations do not provide an indication of the total population within an urban area when many incorporated places are located next to each other. In addition to incorporated places, the census lists unincorporated concentrations of population over 1,000 outside of urbanized areas and unincorporated places within urbanized areas if their population exceeds 5,000 and if they possess a separate identity.

Urbanized Area The census concept which comes closest to an integrated, densely developed area is the urbanized area. An urbanized area is an area containing a central city of 50,000 or more population (or contiguous twin cities totalling 50,000 population with the smaller city containing at least 15,000), the surrounding closely settled territory which includes incorporated places of 2,500 or more, incorporated places of less than 2,500 if they contain one hundred housing units in a 5-square-mile area, and unincorporated territory containing over 1,000 inhabitants per square mile. Other small areas are included to eliminate enclaves, round-out boundaries, and link areas less than 1½ miles apart. This concept provides a good definition of an urban area for any given year although it may include some low-density areas. The major problem with the definition is that it is only available for the last three census years (1950, 1960, and 1970), so there is no consistent historical record. Furthermore, the physical boundaries of urban areas change over time, which makes time comparisons difficult, and other information such as employment and income data are not available for these areas.

[6]Definitions are from U.S. Bureau of the Census, *1970 Census of Population*, vol. 1, *Characteristics of the Population* (Washington, D.C.: Government Printing Office, 1972).

Urban Population The urban population consists of all the inhabitants of urbanized areas plus the inhabitants of incorporated or unincorporated urban places of over 2,500 population in the rest of the United States. The main purpose of this concept is to separate urban or city dwellers from the rural population. The geographic boundaries of the urban population vary from one census to the next, but other data such as income and employment, are available for the urban population within states and counties.

Standard Metropolitan Statistical Area (SMSA) Standard metropolitan statistical areas combine the stability of political unit boundary definitions with concepts of urbanization. SMSAs are defined (except in New England) as counties or groups of contiguous counties that contain at least one city of 50,000 inhabitants (or contiguous twin cities totalling 50,000 with the smaller city containing at least 15,000). (In New England, SMSAs consist of towns and cities rather than counties.) In addition to the county containing the large city or cities, contiguous counties are included in the SMSA if 15 percent of the workers living in them work in the central county of the area, or 25 percent of those working in the contiguous county live in the central county of the area.

SMSAs include most urbanized areas. But because they are defined by county boundaries, they also include very large land areas that are agricultural, forested, or unused. The concept is advantageous because most other economic and demographic information is available on a county basis, and county boundaries are more stable over time than city or urbanized area boundaries.

Within SMSAs it is common to identify the *central city, central business district,* and *suburban ring.* The *central city* is the large city within the SMSA from which the SMSA takes its name. The area outside the central city is called the *suburban ring.* Most SMSA population, income, and employment data are available for the central city and the suburban ring as well as the entire SMSA. Within the central city, data are often provided for the *central business district* (CBD) as well as the entire city. The CBD is the few square miles of downtown area characterized as the center of the city's business activity.

Standard Consolidated Area Since even the SMSA is inadequate to describe the urbanization of some areas, the designation standard consolidated area is used when several contiguous SMSAs make up one continuous urban complex. So far there are only two standard consolidated areas in the United States: the Chicago–Northwest Indiana area and the New York–Northeast New Jersey area.

Trends

In 1790, at the time of the country's first census, the United States contained a population of nearly 4 million, only 5.1 percent of which resided in urban places of over 2,500 population. The largest cities were Philadelphia and New York, with populations of 42,444 and 33,131 respectively. The only other cities with over 10,000 people were Boston (18,088), Charleston (16,359), and Baltimore (13,503).[7] By 1970, 73.5 percent of the nation's total population of 203 million people resided in urban areas, and nearly 35 percent of the population resided in the twenty-five urbanized areas of over 1 million population.[8] The most important trends in the urbanization of the United States from 1790 to the present have been the increasing percentage of the population residing in urban areas, the rise of large cities, and the suburbanization or spread of economic activity and population around large cities to create huge urban agglomerations, the largest of which in 1970 contained over five times the entire population of the United States in 1790.

The urbanization of the population and the rise of large cities in the United States has followed the experience of Western Europe.[9] The earliest cities were small port cities, whose main function was to serve as collection points for the export of raw materials and agricultural products from the colonies to the industrializing areas of Europe and as distribution points for European manufacturers. Following independence some manufacturing began, and during the nineteenth century the United States fully entered the industrial revolution. Trading areas were expanded through the building of canals and railroads, and large cities served both as trading centers and as sites for emerging manufacturers. During the latter half of the nineteenth century industrialization increased rapidly and city populations were swelled by immigration from abroad. By the beginning of the twentieth century nearly 40 percent of the population resided in urban areas;

[7]U.S. Bureau of the Census, *A Century of Population Growth in the United States, 1790-1900* (Washington, D.C.: Government Printing Office, 1909), p. 11.
[8]*1970 Census of Population,* vol. 1. p. 1–43.
[9]One of the best histories of urbanization in the United States is Charles N. Glaab and A. Theodore Brown, *A History of Urban America* (London: Macmillan, 1967).

Table 2-1 Urban Population in the United States

Year	Total		Urban		Rural	
	Population	% Increase per Decade*	% of Population	% Increase per Decade*	% of Population	% Increase per Decade*
1790	3,929,214	—	5.1	—	94.9	—
1800	5,308,483	35.1	6.1	59.9	93.9	33.8
1850	23,191,872	34.3	15.3	62.6	84.7	22.6
1900	76,212,168	27.0	39.6	54.1	60.4	18.7
1950	151,325,798	14.8	59.6	24.9	40.4	5.9
1970	203,211,926	15.9	73.5**	24.3	26.5	-0.6

*For multidecade intervals percent increase is average of all decades during the interval.
**New definition of urban population used. If 1960 definition used the percent of population urban would be approximately 68.
Source: U.S. Bureau of the Census, *1970 Census of Population, Characteristics of the Population*, vol. 1, *Number of Inhabitants*, p. 1-42.

Table 2-2   Large Cities in the United States

Size	YEAR					
	1790	1800	1850	1900	1950	1970
Over 1 million	—	—	—	3	5	6
500,000 to 1 million	—	—	—	3	13	20
250,000 to 500,000	—	—	—	9	23	30
100,000 to 250,000	—	—	5	23	65	100
50,000 to 100,000	—	1	4	40	126	240
25,000 to 50,000	2	2	16	82	252	520
10,000 to 25,000	3	3	36	280	778	1385

Source: U.S. Bureau of the Census, *1970 Census of Population, Characteristics of the Population*, vol. 1., *Number of Inhabitants*, table 7.

three cities had populations in excess of 1 million and another thirty-five cities had populations over 100,000. By 1970, 73.5 percent of the population was classified as urban, six cities contained populations over 1 million, and another one hundred and fifty cities exceeded 100,000 population in size.[10]

Data on the growth of urban population are presented in Table 2-1. These data indicate that the percentage of the population residing in urban areas has continually increased and the growth rate of the urban population has consistently exceeded both total United States population growth and population growth in rural areas. Furthermore, after 1950, not only has the percentage of population residing in rural areas decreased, but the absolute number of inhabitants of rural areas has declined.

Table 2-2 provides data on increases in the number of large cities in the United States. In early years city boundaries did encompass most of the urban or developed area, partially because annexation of developing areas beyond the city's boundaries was common. We must remember, however, that a city is defined by its boundaries of incorporation, and in later years, especially in the twentieth century, city boundaries have generally *not* encompassed the area of urban activity. At the same time, many of the smaller cities are contained within the urbanized area of a large city and are not really independent urban centers. Thus, data on city sizes as presented in Table 2-2 does not provide as accurate a picture of the rise of urban centers as is desired, but it is our only data source of this kind with reasonable historical continuity.

The spread and growth of fringe areas at lower densities have

[10]See Tables 2-1 and 2-2.

Table 2-3   SMSA Growth in the United States

	Unadjusted Growth Rates		Growth Rates Corrected for Annexations*	
	1950-60	1960-70	1950-60	1960-70
SMSA	26.4	16.6	26.4	16.6
Central cities	10.8	6.5	1.5	0.1
Suburban rings	48.5	26.7	61.7	33.1

*Correction involves using beginning year boundaries for allocating growth throughout the decade.
Source: *1960 Census of Population,* vol. 1, p. 1-192; *1970 Census of Population,* vol. 1, p. xxv.

gradually replaced the growth of the older centers of business and population in large cities. Earlier analyses, based on retrogressing the SMSA concept developed in 1950 back to 1900, concluded that the rate of suburban ring growth did not exceed the rate of central-city growth until the 1930s and proceeded to attribute the rise of suburbanization to the automobile.[11] However, subsequent analysis has indicated that falling land-use densities in the oldest parts of a city and more rapid growth rates of fringe areas tend to occur within fifty years after a city reaches a size of 50,000 and thus occurs at different times for different cities. New York City, for example, was undergoing this process by 1850. Albany, Baltimore, Boston, Cincinnati, Duluth, New Haven, St. Louis, San Francisco, and Scranton were all decentralizing prior to 1900.[12] It now appears that the automobile was just another transportation innovation like the horse-drawn street railway, electric streetcar, and interurban in facilitating the growth of suburban residential areas around older central cities.

The erroneous conclusions of earlier analyses regarding suburbanization appear to be based on the use of a political unit definition of a central city without accounting for the fact that much of the city's population growth resulted from the annexing of suburban territory and not from growth within the boundaries of the older central city. Examples of this problem are illustrated by 1950, 1960, and 1970 data on central-city and suburban-ring growth rates in SMSAs. (These are the only two decades where data on annexation are readily available.) Table 2-3 indicates the population growth rates of SMSA.

[11]For a classic example see Donald J. Bogue, *Population Growth in Standard Metropolitan Areas 1900-1950* (Washington, D.C.: Housing and Home Finance Agency. 1953).
[12]Leo F. Schnore, "The Timing of Metropolitan Decentralization: A Contribution to the Debate," *Journal of the American Institute of Planners,* 25 (November 1959), pp. 200-206.

central-city, and suburban-ring populations for each decade based on unadjusted census data and data adjusted to show the effects of central-city annexations. The adjustment decreases the central-city growth rate from 10.8 to 1.5 percent between 1950 and 1960 and from 6.5 percent to 0.1 percent between 1960 and 1970. Thus, most central-city growth was due to annexation of suburban territory, rather than growth within the older central city. Furthermore, if we used a time span longer than ten years for adjusting city boundaries, we would further observe a reduced rate of central-city growth compared to suburban-ring growth. For example, most of the growth in Los Angeles between 1930 and 1970 was within the boundaries of the city as of 1930, but between 1915 and 1927 Los Angeles added approximately 325 square miles, much of it agricultural land that is still being filled in.[13]

While we have used data from 1950 to 1970 to indicate the bias introduced by utilizing unadjusted city size data compared with suburban-ring data to draw conclusions on the decentralization of central cities, data from earlier decades, if available, would be still more striking. This is because expansion through annexation occurred much more often prior to the 1930s than afterwards. Thus, it is not surprising that the 1930 to 1940 decade was the first decade to show a higher rate of suburban-ring than central-city growth, even though the process of decentralization had been occurring for many years before.[14] Analyses which place the beginning of the decentralization of economic activity away from the older centers of business and population as late as the 1930s are a product of reliance on political unit definitions of population and do not describe the actual decentralization that occurred. Data on land-use density gradients, which better describe decentralization, are presented and analyzed in Chapter 4.

Since the slow-down in annexations it has become obvious not only that central cities are growing slowly but that many are losing population.[15] Of the twelve largest central cities, only New York and Los Angeles did not lose population between 1960 and 1970. Smaller

[13]Robert Warren, *Government in Metropolitan Regions: A Reappraisal of Fractionated Political Organization* (Davis, California: Institute of Governmental Affairs, University of California, 1966), pp. 71–75.

[14]An additional problem that appears in aggregated SMSA, central-city, and suburban-ring data is that as new SMSAs are added (because their central cities reached a population of 50,000) to the totals each decade, more people are added to the central-city population than to the suburban-ring populations. This inflates the growth rate of the central cities relative to the suburban rings, obscuring the fact that older, larger central cities may be growing very slowly or even declining. Only if one holds the area of the *earlier* measurement constant when comparing growth rates can rates of change be determined.

[15]Glaab and Brown, op. cit., pp. 270–275, and Kingsley Davis, "The Origin and Growth or Urbanization in the World," p. 436.

Table 2-4 Urbanized Areas by Size

	Year		
Size	1950	1960	1970
Over 10 million	1	1	1
5 to 10 million	0	2	2
2.5 to 5 million	4	4	5
1 to 2.5 million	7	9	17
500,000 to 1 million	13	22	21
250,000 to 500,000	24	30	35
100,000 to 250,000	69	85	91
Under 100,000	38	60	76
Total	157	213	248

Source: *1950 Census of Population*, vol. 1. p. 1-29; *1960 Census of Population*, vol. 1. p. 1-50; *1970 Census Population*, vol. 1. 1-87.

central cities such as Seattle, Akron, and Buffalo also declined in population.[16] As urbanized areas continue to grow, the older central cities are declining both as economic and as population centers. Urban America is becoming more and more a nation of suburbs.

Although suburban growth has supplanted central-city growth, urban areas themselves continue to grow. Good data on early urban-area growth are lacking. In some places the growth of urban concentrations is reflected in city growth because city boundaries were regularly expanded to annex adjacent developing territory. In the 1930s, however, central-city annexations began to decline, with the result that city population sizes became less and less reflective of the size of the urban agglomerations that have developed. The size classes of urbanized areas for 1950, 1960, and 1970 are presented in Table 2-4. The greater number of large urbanized areas compared to the number of large cities indicated in Table 2-2 clearly illustrates the inadequacy of city boundaries for defining the large urban agglomerations which characterize twentieth century America.

THE PUBLIC SECTOR

Accompanying urbanization and the rise of markets is the need for collective or governmental action. The interaction among many people

[16]U.S. Bureau of the Census, *1970 Census of Population and Housing, General Demographic Trends for Metropolitan Areas, 1960 to 1970* (Washington, D.C.: Government Printing Office, 1972), table 10.

undertaking their daily activities in close proximity creates a need for regulations regarding public health, sanitation, housing, and public safety. It is also often more efficient to provide "public"[17] goods such as streets, sidewalks, and parks, and it may be efficient to provide other services such as water, libraries, schools, and transportation services through government rather than privately. The need for regulation and the advantages of providing goods and services collectively have been reflected by the increasing numbers and importance of local governments in urban areas.

Local governments preceded both state and national government in the United States. Early local governments, however, carried on few of the functions we expect of them today. In New England they were more religious than secular; those in the South were created primarily to serve as administrative arms of British mercantilist policy, and those in the middle colonies often undertook commercial functions such as managing trade fairs, public markets, and docks.[18] It was only as cities began to grow that local governments took on other important functions, including the provision of a city surveyor, courts, street construction and repair, street drains, and pumps and wells. Toward the end of the 1700s, providing night watchmen and street lights became municipal functions, and by 1810, New York City was spending approximately $1.00 per capita on municipal services for its 100,000 citizens. Services noticeably missing included public education, welfare, police, libraries, and parks.[19]

It was not until the middle of the nineteenth century that municipal governments significantly began to expand their activities. Uniformed police were provided in New York City in 1845 and the practice spread to other large cities. Public schools, libraries, welfare, and parks became common municipal services, as did increased regulation of private activities, especially sanitation and, through code regulations, building practices in the larger cities. Improvements in sanitary conditions were probably local government's most important achievement, because it was only through reducing high city death

---

[17]"Public" goods are goods or services that when provided are available to everyone, and one person's consumption of them does not reduce the consumption of others. Mosquito control and military security are two common examples of public goods. The term "public" characterizes the consumption attributes of nonexclusion and joint-consumption, not the nature of the producer who may be either a private firm or a government. Public goods are analyzed in Chapter 5.

[18]The history of local government in the United States is presented in Anwar Syed, *The Political Theory of American Local Government* (New York: Random House, 1966); Glaab and Brown, op. cit.; and in chapters of early local government texts such as Herman G. James, *Local Government in the United States* (New York: Appleton, 1921). Most recent texts on local government neglect its history.

[19]James, ibid. pp. 371–372.

rates that large cities could develop. It was also common for many of these services, especially schools and parks, to be undertaken by special boards or districts instead of the city government proper. Finally, between 1870 and 1900 local governments nationwide greatly expanded their functions and expenditures. By 1900 a pattern of expenditures similar to today's had appeared.

The largest categories of local government per capita expenditures for 1902, 1942, 1967, and 1972 are presented in Table 2-5. The percentage of the gross national product accounted for by local government spending is also indicated to put the expenditures in perspective. One must recognize that the data in the table are for *local* governments only and will vary from state to state, not only because of different local conditions or preferences, but also because different states have different divisions of responsibility between state and local governments. For example, in some states all public welfare may be run by local governments, but in other states all public welfare may be directly administered by the state government. In spite of these differences, however, the data provide an indication of the relative importance of different functions of local governments and their expansion over time.

As the data in Table 2-5 indicate, local government spending as a proportion of the GNP has been increasing. In 1972 it accounted for over 9 percent of the GNP and employed 9 percent of the nation's labor force.[20] In addition, approximately 69 percent of local government expenditure and over 62 percent of local government employees were within SMSAs. Because SMSAs contained only 52 percent of the United States population, this indicates that local governments spend more in large urban areas than in other places.[21] The observation that local governments in urban areas spend more than local governments elsewhere is consistent with the conclusions of economists who have worked on identifying the "determinants" of expenditures by state and local governments. The most common factors "explaining" expenditures, population density, and income or wealth[22] are an integral part of the process of urbanization.

When we think of local government we usually think of cities, counties, school districts, and perhaps townships in some Eastern and

---

[20]U.S. Bureau of the Census, *The Statistical Abstract of the U.S.* (Washington, D.C.: Government Printing Office, 1972), calculated from appropriate tables.

[21]U.S. Bureau of the Census, *Local Government Finances in Selected Metropolitan Areas and Large Counties: 1970–71* (Washington, D.C.: Government Printing Office, 1972), p. 1.

[22]For examples see R. W. Bahl, *Metropolitan City Expenditures: A Comparative Analysis* (Lexington: University of Kentucky Press, 1969), and A. K. Campbell and S. Sacks, *Metropolitan America* (New York: The Free Press, 1967).

Table 2-5 Per Capita Local Government Expenditure

	1902	1942	1967	1972
Direct general expenditure	$11.00	$47.61	$298.70	$503.39
Education	3.00	16.28	144.21	229.23
Highways	2.16	5.19	22.79	30.08
Public welfare	.34	5.20	19.85	42.37
Health and hospitals	.35	2.17	16.84	32.93
Police	.63	2.62	13.19	24.38
Fire	.51	1.75	7.58	12.38
Sanitation	.64	1.70	12.75	22.71
Parks and recreation	.37	.95	6.52	11.16
Housing and renewal	—	1.75	7.28	13.19
Direct general expenditure as a percentage of GNP	3.63	4.07	7.48	9.10

Source: U.S. Bureau of the Census, Census of Governments 1967, *Historical Statistics on Governmental Finances and Employment* (Washington, D.C.: Government Printing office, 1969), pp. 45–47; U.S. Bureau of the Census, *Governmental Finances in 1971–72* (Washington, D.C.: Government Printing Office, 1973), p. 23.

Midwestern states. The complexity of local government in urban areas, however, is seldom recognized.

The 1972 Census of Governments identified 78,218 units of local government in the United States, 22,185 of which were in SMSAs. Table 2-6 indicates the numbers and types of units for 1942, 1957, 1967, and 1972. As the table shows, there has been a decline in the total number of units caused by the large decline in the number of school districts. There has been a large increase in the number of special districts and a moderate increase in the number of municipalities. These changes in the number of units reflect both rural-urban migration and suburbanization. Much of the decline in the number of school districts is due to a consolidation of rural districts, since population has declined and improved highways have permitted students to travel greater distances to fewer schools.

Special districts, the kind of government increasing in number most rapidly, are usually single purpose political units with boundaries arranged to fit the particular function undertaken. They are created when the boundaries of previously existing units are not suitable for the new functions. This occurs when rural areas around a city are built up. The most common kinds of special districts are for managing natural resources, such as soil conservation, drainage, irrigation, and

Table 2-6 Governmental Units in the United States

Type of Government	Number of Units				Percent Change 1942–72
	1942	1957	1967	1972	
Total	155,115	102,391	81,298	78,269	−49.5
States	48	50	50	50	—
Local	155,067	102,341	81,248	78,218	−49.6
Counties	3,050	3,050	3,049	3,044	—
Municipalities	16,220	17,215	18,048	18,517	+14.2
School dist's.	108,579	50,454	21,782	15,781	−85.5
Special dist's.	8,299	14,424	21,264	23,885	+187.8
Townships	18,919	17,198	17,105	16,991	−10.2

Source: U.S. Bureau of the Census, *1972, Census of Governments*, vol. 1, *Governmental Organization*, p. 23.

flood control, and for fire protection, urban water supply, housing and renewal, cemeteries, sewage disposal, school buildings, parks and recreation, highways, hospitals, and libraries.[23] The increase in the number of special districts reflects trends toward suburbanization, and in 1972 over one-third of all special districts were in SMSAs.[24] In most cases, after the area reaches urban densities, a new city government is created and it absorbs most of the functions formerly provided by the special districts.

Large-scale special districts covering several counties and often crossing state boundaries, such as air pollution control districts and water pollution control districts, have also been created to deal with problems that need larger boundaries for their solution. As concern for the management of environmental consequences increases, we may expect to see even more large districts, because their boundaries can be designed to encompass specific problem areas. Existing political units may be either too large or too small.

There is considerable variation in the number of local governments within single metropolitan areas—ranging from four in Honolulu to 1,172 in the six-county Chicago SMSA. The populations and numbers of local governmental units for a sample of the larger SMSAs are presented in Table 2-7. Nearly all United States citizens are members of from five to fifteen local governmental units.

Local governments themselves comprise a complex public sector in urban areas, and since the 1960s both the state and the national governments have become increasingly involved in urban programs. States have assumed increased responsibility for financing welfare

[23]U.S. Bureau of the Census, *1972 Census of Governments*, vol. 1, *Governmental Organization* (Washington, D.C.: Government Printing Office, 1973), p. 10.
[24]Ibid.

Table 2-7 Population and Local Governments in Selected SMSAs

SMSA	Population (1970)	Local Governments (1972)
Phoenix, Ariz.	967,522	112
Sacramento, Calif.	800,592	210
Hartford, Conn.	673,891	68
Miami, Fla.	1,267,792	33
Honolulu, Hawaii	692,176	4
Chicago, Ill.	6,978,947	1,172
Indianapolis, Ind.	1,109,882	296
Detroit, Mich.	4,199,931	241
St. Louis, Mo.	2,363,017	483
New York, N.Y.	11,571,899	538
Fort Worth, Tex.	762,086	87
Seattle-Everett, Wash.	1,421,869	269

Source: U.S. Bureau of the Census, *1972 Census of Governments*. vol. 1, *Governmental Organization*, table 19.

and education services, and the national government provides grants for literally every public service including housing, transportation, public health, welfare, education, environmental management, law enforcement, and the provision of parks and recreation. Thus, even an awareness of the complexity of local governments is only a beginning in understanding the operation of the public sector in urban areas.

SUMMARY

While it has been generally recognized that urbanization accompanies industrialization, and increased public sector activity accompanies urbanization, there has been relatively little examination of the direct relationships between urbanization and suburbanization and public sector organization and operation. Our study is not the place for a historical examination of these relationships, but we believe them to be more important than is commonly recognized. In the following chapters we will attempt to provide historical background for these important relationships where possible, even though the thrust of our study is to utilize location theory and the theory of public goods and collective action to analyze contemporary urban problems. Our detailed analysis of the urban public sector will begin with Chapter 5, following our more detailed examinations of urban growth and urban land-use patterns.

SELECTED READINGS

Davis, Kingsley: "The Origin and Growth of Urbanization in the World," *American Journal of Sociology*, 60 (March 1955), pp. 429–437 (Bobbs-Merrill Reprint, S-66.)

Glaab, Charles N., and A. Theodore Brown: *A History of Urban America* (London: Macmillan, 1967).

U.S. Bureau of the Census: *1970 Census of Population*, vol. 1, *Characteristics of the Population* (Washington, D.C.: Government Printing Office, 1972).

U.S. Bureau of the Census, *1972 Census of Governments*, vol. 1, *Governmental Organization* and vol. 4, no. 5, *Compendium of Government Finances* (Washington, D.C.: Government Printing Office. 1973 and 1974).

Weber, Adna F.: *The Growth of Cities in the Nineteenth Century* (Ithaca: Cornell, 1963, first published in 1899).

CHAPTER **3**

LOCATION
AND GROWTH

In the first two chapters we stated our purpose of attempting to integrate spatial analysis and public goods theory for understanding urban problems and evaluating alternative policies. We have also outlined the rapid growth of urbanized population, the dispersion of population within cities, and the resulting complexity of political organization. In this, the first analytical chapter, we will explore the reasons for the existence of cities and the rationale for the distribution of size and location of cities. After exploring the fit of theory to reality, comparative cost and agglomeration economies will be shown to explain much of the difference. Agglomeration economies will cause further reduction in costs for continued concentration of firms in the same place and add a momentum to growing areas that will cause people to anticipate further growth. We will explore why such growth does not automatically bring about the appropriate migration of capital and labor and we will then indicate a potential role for public policy to influence urban growth and change.

CHOICE AND CHANCE

By choice or chance towns and cities are established. In the uncertain world that we live in people do not have all of the information necessary to make optimal decisions as to where to locate stores, plants, cities, or even whether to invest at all. Initially, a town site was determined by whether it was easily defended from attack, had a special religious significance, or was a convenient trading place. Or perhaps a particular individual found the site attractive and thought he could establish a profitable business there.

It is sometimes argued that economic theory is of little help in understanding the location of people and businesses. Surveys in which people are asked why they selected a particular place for business reveal that personal reasons or chance were the dominant factor.[1] Actually, the goals attributed to the decision maker in economic theory are maximization of utility or profits. Obviously, if a person sacrifices monetary profit in order to reap the nonpecuniary gain of a particular site, he is being rational. His decision would conform to a broader definition of profit that would include both pecuniary and nonpecuniary gain.

There is a more fundamental problem, however, in attributing maximization behavior to people selecting locations for businesses and residences. The fundamental problem is that these decisions are long-run decisions involving expectations about future costs and returns at alternative sites. To evaluate such alternatives, future values must be discounted into present values. Consider the problem of whether to invest in a machine that is expected to yield a net income of $100 per year above operating costs for ten years. At the end of ten years the machine is expected to have no scrap value. An alternative way of spending our money is to buy certificates of deposit at the bank yielding 6 percent interest. To find out the worth of an income in each of the next ten years, we must calculate how much it would cost to obtain a bond that would yield the same income, that is, how much it would cost to buy a bond that would yield $100 in each of the next ten years. The cost of the bond depends upon the interest rate, which is dependent upon the alternative yield that could be earned, 6 percent.

The present value of the first year's $100 is found by solving for P in the following equation:

$$P(1 + r) = \$100$$

That is, what sum plus the interest on it for one year will equal $100? If the interest rate is .06, the value of P is $100/1.06, which is $94.30. Note that at the end of the year we receive our capital expenditure of $94.30 plus 6 percent in interest—the alternative cost of the capital.

[1]Eva Mueller, Arnold Wilken, and Margaret Wood, *Location Decisions and Industrial Mobility in Michigan* (Ann Arbor, Mich.: Institute of Social Research, The University of Michigan, 1961), p. 16.

Remember, too, that the $100 is the expected *net* income, receipts less operating costs.

The present value of the expected net income received in the second year is found by solving for P in the following formula:

$$P(1 + r) \times (1 + r) = \$100$$

That is, what sum plus the interest on it for the first year plus the interest from the first to the second year on the sum of P and the first year interest will equal $100? If the interest rate is .06, the solution is as follows:

$$P = \frac{\$100}{1.06^2}$$

If we can get an annual yield of 6 percent on a certificate of deposit, the $100 from this particular activity coming in two years must pay off the equivalent.

By now we should expect the present value of the $100 in the third through tenth years to be solved by using the following equation:

$$Pn = \frac{\$100}{(1 + r)^n}$$

where Pn = the present value of the $100 received in the nth year
n = the year of receipt of the $100
r = the interest rate

The total present value of the expected net income stream of $100 in each of the next ten years is the sum of the present values of the income received in each of the ten years. This can be expressed in the following way:

$$P = \frac{\$100}{1.06} + \frac{\$100}{1.06^2} + \frac{\$100}{1.06^3} + \cdots + \frac{\$100}{1.06^{10}} = \$736$$

If alternative opportunities to invest money yield 6 percent, the investor would not spend more than the present value of the expected net income stream for the machine. As long as the present value of a possible activity or investment is greater than the cost, the activity should be undertaken. If the cost is greater than the present value, that is, if the machine costs more than $736 to acquire in the above example, then the activity is not worth undertaking. It would be more profitable to put money into the certificates of deposit.

There is no way for us to know for sure what the income for the next ten years will be. We can only know what we expect the income to be. Since expected income is only vaguely known, it is very unlikely that fluctuations in that income will be known. Therefore, we often only indicate that the same income is expected each year for the expected life of the activity. We, in fact, did this in the above calculations. When the annual income is expected to be constant for the entire period of the investment, the present-value calculation collapses to the following multiplier:

$$P = \left[\frac{r(1 + r)^n}{(1 + r)^n - 1} \right] a$$

where a is the annual expected income. When a is \$100, r is 6 percent, and n is ten years, the present value is 7.36 × \$100, or \$736, which is the same amount obtained in the previous calculation.

In the face of uncertainty, it is unlikely that people can choose the business site that would maximize profits. They can, however, choose the best of the alternatives available to them in the light of their own expectations. Some will have better foresight than others. Large firms and very large enterprises establishing branch plants do tend to use economic considerations in location decisions more than small firms.[2] Still, it is likely that optimism about expected net income and chance will play a great role in initiating new ventures.[3]

In recent years the point has been made that even if individual decision makers did not choose to maximize profits or even utility broadly defined but acted randomly, economic constraints would force them to make choices conforming to theory based on maximizing behavior. If an individual chose a bad location, he would incur losses and go out of business. If the choice was a good location, he would profit and survive.[4] Thus, even if people choose their locations for reasons entirely unrelated to economic factors, economic constraints will force patterns of location related to them.

The argument that competitive survival leads to economic determination of business location requires two qualifications. First, economic theory is a theory of how markets operate and not how an individual firm might operate. The theories are simplifications of reality to determine how groups of firms will operate on the average, so that market response to changes in public policy and to changes in demand, technology, etc., can be determined. If institutions generating the same

[2] Ibid.

[3] John Maynard Keynes, *The General Theory of Employment, Interest and Money* (London: Macmillan, 1936), pp. 161–163.

[4] E. M. Hoover, *An Introduction to Regional Economics* (New York: Knopf, 1971), pp. 60–62; Armen Alchian, "Uncertainty, Evolution, and Economic Theory," *Journal of Political Economy*, 58 (June 1950), pp. 211–221; Charles M. Tiebout, "Location Theory, Empirical Evidence, and Economic Evolution," *Papers and Proceedings of the Regional Science Association*, 3 (1957), pp. 75–82; and Gary Becker, "Irrational Behavior and Economic Theory," *Journal of Political Economy*, 70 (February 1962), pp. 1–13.

services are few with relatively little competition, decision makers will have relatively more latitude and it will be more difficult to predict outcomes than if the institutions are more competitively organized. Second, although economically efficient location patterns may emerge from competitive survival, there is surely the possibility that wasteful mistakes might be made along the way. Firms may be established in very unprofitable places. The first owner may be the only one to suffer losses for his mistake. Subsequent owners would only pay the present value of the enterprise to take over and would not necessarily change to more optimal uses.

In searching for reasons for the establishment and growth of cities we will concentrate on the location of businesses, both commercial and industrial. The reason for this is that most people must locate near their employment. There is always an exception, and in this case it is that retired persons may locate where amenities provide an easier life. Nevertheless, a recent survey shows that most people indicate job-related reasons for their moves.[5]

In this chapter we will develop three concepts that will help explain the economic reasons for the location, size, and specialization of cities. First, the hierarchical ordering of cities will be shown through explanation of the concept, "specialization is limited by the extent of the market." Second, the specialization of small and middle-size places will be explained through use of comparative cost analysis. Third, the continued momentum of growth and the similarity of larger cities will be shown to be a result of agglomeration economies. These three sections will be followed by a section on the implications of the equilibrating mechanism of migration and capital movements for growth. The last section will explore policy alternatives for alleviating problems caused by unemployment and low incomes.

SPECIALIZATION IS LIMITED BY THE EXTENT OF THE MARKET[6]

In this section we want to show how purely economic factors could lead to cities and to a hierarchical ordering of cities. We will neglect those many factors often thought important: a good view, harbor,

[5]John B. Lansing and Eva Mueller, *The Geographic Mobility of Labor* (Ann Arbor, Michigan: Institute for Social Research, The University of Michigan, 1967), pp. 58–68.

[6]The material for this section is from Hugh O. Nourse, "An Alternative to Central Place Theory," in *Studies in Regional Structure*, edited by Rolf Funck, forthcoming. It is a synthesis of A. Lösch, *The Economics of Location* (New Haven: Yale, 1954), pp. 103–134, and George J. Stigler, "The Division of Labor Is Limited by the Extent of the Market," *Journal of Political Economy*, 59 (June 1951), pp. 185–193.

crossroads, special resources, etc. Lösch first led the way in thinking about this problem by imagining a flat plain with uniform distribution of resources and people. If we can show how cities may arise on such a plain using economic concepts, we can later bring in less restrictive assumptions to show how the ideal may be modified.

Why should manufacturing production be unevenly distributed over the imagined homogeneous plain, and why should cities arise? Imagine that the homogeneous plain is uniformly occupied by self-sufficient farms and consider the production of beer. Why should nearby farmers buy from one of the farmers who decides to produce beer? They might do so if he could sell it to them for less than it would cost to produce it by themselves. The farmer producing the beer could achieve lower unit costs if economies of scale were obtained in the production process, that is, if the average cost of production fell with increases in the rate of production.

Economies of scale may be the result of a number of factors. A greater rate of production allows more specialization of labor functions. As each worker repeats a narrow range of tasks he becomes more proficient. The fuller use of some inputs with a large fixed capacity will reduce the average cost of using such inputs. The less than proportionate increase in reserves required for unexpected interruptions in supply, increases in demand, or production breakdowns by large plants will reduce the average cost of inventories. Finally, purchases of some inputs in large quantities often reduce input prices by quantity discounts.

There is, however, a limit to the scale of operations that the farmer producing beer can undertake. That limit is determined by the population density surrounding the producer and the transportation costs of shipping the beer. Assume that prices are set for sales at the production site, that consumers pay transportation costs, and that transportation costs are the same per mile in any direction. The delivered price of beer, then, is the price at the producer site plus the cost of transporting the beer to the consumer. At some distance from the producer the delivered price will rise to equal the cost of making beer at home. At that distance beer will no longer be demanded from the producer. At each possible price the producer could charge there will be a quantity demanded. The maximum distance the beer can be shipped will, of course, increase with decreases in the producer's price, so that the quantity demanded will increase with decreases in price. There is another dimension to demand, the density of population. For each price the producer sets, the quantity demanded will be greater as the density of population is greater. More consumers will be within the area in which delivered price is less than the cost of homemade beer.

These ideas can be illustrated in Figure 3-1. *OA* is the average cost of beer made at home by each family. The average cost declines as the rate of production increases. D_1 is the demand curve for alternative prices with a low population density. D_2 is the demand curve for alternative prices with a higher population density. D_3 and D_4 illustrate still higher densities. As yet, we are assuming no competing producer exists in the area or on the fringe, so that the producer is a monopolist. Thus, the producer would not produce at a rate that would equalize average cost and price. He would establish monopoly profits by selling less than the maximum that he could. Still, the graph amply demonstrates that the possible economies of scale are limited by the extent of the market, where extent really indicates depth or density of the market subject to travel cost constraints.

One point not covered so far is that more people would move to live near the beer producer. There are two reasons for this. As more beer was produced, employment would increase. Employees would tend to live closer to their source of employment. Since the transporta-

FIGURE 3-1   Economies of Scale and the Extent of the Market

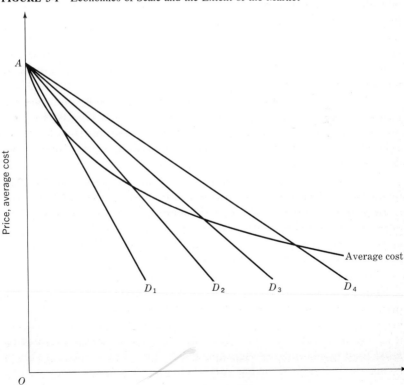

tion cost of the product would be reduced for consumers located near the production site, consumers would also prefer to live near the producer. Whereas before beer production, land rents were equal throughout the plain, rents would now rise close to the producer because individuals would be willing to pay more for a closer location. The amount individuals would be willing to pay would reflect the value they place on the closer location. After the payment, however, the welfare of consumers and workers, whether they lived close or far from the producer, would be the same. There would no longer be an incentive to move. As population density increases, it would, of course, cause the demand for the product to shift to the right on Figure 3-1. Such shifts would yield further economies of scale, increased production, and further incentive for concentration of population.

On our infinite plain occupied by self-sufficient farms scattered uniformly throughout the plain, other beer producers would be established. Each would occupy a site away from other producers until the marketing areas of each producer were contiguous. There would be an incentive for entrepreneurs to enter the industry so long as the present value of the expected net income was greater than alternatives. So long as monopoly profits existed in the industry, returns greater than the opportunity cost of capital would be earned. Notice, however, that part of the profits would be absorbed by increases in rent for the sites occupied. The increase in rents would cause the average-cost curve of the producer to shift upward. At the same time the demand curve might begin to shift down because of the entry of new firms on the edge of existing producers' markets. Part of each firm's market would be lost because another firm could sell to that part of the market at a lower delivered price even though both firms were selling at the same price at the plant. The reduction in the market area would cause the demand curve to shift to the left.

Simultaneously, then, producers are seeking to locate near groups of people, and people are adjusting to the producer locations, so that around each producer we have the beginning of a town development. Scale economies may be so great that the number of workers for each producer would by themselves create a town. Other business activities will find it feasible to locate in the town.

Nevertheless, it is important to see that employees can not gather around the producer unless some further specialization is also taking place. If the employees are to spend their time making beer, someone else must be growing food, making cloth, etc., to support the specialized group of workers. This means that nearby farmers are producing more food by not making their own beer. Furthermore, there are fewer farms so that each farm has more land. Specialization in agriculture now allows economies of scale in that production, and the farmer can supply himself plus the beer producers. Specialists in distributing the beer and other products will appear because there are also economies of scale in distributing goods to many people, rather than each person seeking out his own supply of goods.

At any moment in history there are products that can be made with varying degrees of scale economies. Changes in technological knowledge can allow the average-cost curve for any product to shift down, so that the same population can support even greater specialization. For the time being, however, consider the state of technology unchanged. There are average-cost curves with varying downward slopes and heights. If demand were large enough, some products could be produced with very large scales of production and others with only very small scales because of the relation of cost to demand. Thus, concentrations of population around production centers would be of different size because the employment necessary for different scales of production would vary. Therefore, towns of different sizes could be created.

In a place with a very small concentration of population there would be insufficient demand to support a large supermarket, but a general store selling clothes, food, hardware, etc., would be supported. As the size of place increased, separate stores could develop for selling clothes, food, and hardware. The shift of the demand to the right in these larger places makes it possible to utilize greater economies of scale in each function—the selling of food, clothing, and hardware. Thus, as one compared places with small populations with those of very large populations, one would find workers becoming more and more specialized as the increase in demand allowed it. There would also be more diversity in ways to satisfy particular needs as population increased. Goods or services that represent the tastes of only a small proportion of any population cannot appear until the population includes enough people to support a person specializing in the service or product, such as bookstores, opera, exotic restaurants, professional theatre, specialized medical facilities, etc.

Systems of Cities

Models of specific systems of cities have been developed by making more specific assumptions about the size of markets and the number of activities located at the center of each market. Usually, these models begin with a farm-market town, which is the smallest market size allowing some businesses to exist. They are usually thought to include a service station, general store, and a few other activities. Each of these places serves a specific number of farms uniformly distributed over a homogeneous agricultural plain. The next step is a larger city that has for its market a specific number of farm-market towns and the farms included in each hinterland. The larger city also provides the activities of the farm-market town. For example, there might be three farm-market towns included in each larger-city center hinterland. These larger cities would include added businesses that need the larger market size to survive. They might include banks, department stores, auto dealers, etc. The system of cities can be enlarged by adding larger cities to include added activities that require larger markets for survival. Each larger city includes a specific number of the next smaller size cities in its market area or hinterland. The system would have one largest city and specific numbers of cities of each smaller size. The size distribution of cities in such a system would be a step function. As one moved from the largest city, the number of smaller cities would always be some multiple of the larger city determined by the number of cities included in each market. Furthermore, there would be only a limited number of city sizes.

Geographers have found that systems of cities in some places fit this model. In particular researchers have found systems like this in the Dakotas, Iowa, China, and southern Germany.[7] The model, however, does not fit all systems of cities in all places. Beckmann has shown that if the multiplier in the above model relating the number of smaller cities to a larger one is not constant, but varies randomly about a mean value, the size distribution of the system would be continuous rather than a step function and the product of the rank and population size of a city would be a constant.[8]

The theoretical hypothesis that the product of the rank (number of cities with equal or greater population) and city size is a constant in a system of cities has also been empirically generated. The relation is known as the "rank-size" rule, and may be stated as follows:

$$Rs = A$$

where s = population of an urbanized area
   R = number of cities with population s or more. This is the same as the rank of the cities with populations s.
   A = constant

[7]For a summary of the literature see Brian J. L. Berry, *Geography of Market Centers and Retail Distribution* (Englewood Cliffs, N.J.: Prentice-Hall, 1967).

[8]Martin Beckmann and John McPherson, "City Size Distributions in Central Place Hierarchy: An Alternative Approach," *Journal of Regional Science*, 10 (1970), pp. 25–33.

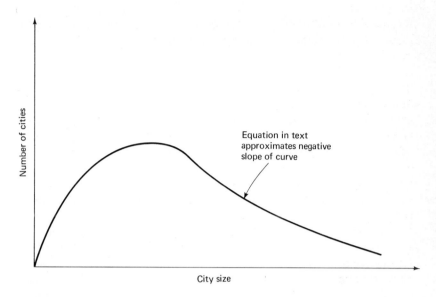

FIGURE 3-2   Typical Pareto Distribution

Researchers have tested this hypothesis in a number of countries and for a number of time periods and have claimed it to be true.[9]

The above equation can be rewritten as follows by dividing both sides of the equation by s:

$$R = As^{-1}$$

This is a special case of the formula describing many other types of size distributions in economics, including the distribution of income and firm sizes. The general formula describing these distributions is called the Pareto distribution and can be written as follows:

$$R = As^{-a}$$

where all the terms are the same as before, except that a is an empirically estimated constant. The distribution is skewed with a long tail toward the high values of the size being considered. In the case of cities we could graph the distribution as in Figure 3-2.[10]

[9]A convenient annotated bibliography of the literature has been compiled. See Brian J. L. Berry and Allan Pred, *Central Place Studies: A Bibliography of Theory and Applications*, Bibliography Series no. 1 with supplement (Philadelphia: Regional Science Research Institute, 1965).

[10]For a useful description of the Pareto distribution see Edwin S. Mills, *Urban Economics* (Glenview, Illinois: Scott-Foresman, 1972), pp. 104–105.

The rank-size rule is a special case of the Pareto distribution in which $-a = -1$. In logarithms the Pareto distribution is linear:

$$\log R = \log A - a \log s$$

Before the spread of knowledge and skill in testing such relations using regression techniques, researchers graphed distributions on double logarithmic paper and pointed out how close the curve fitting the dots was to a straight line. No one seems to have any systematic idea of which definition of the city is the best to use in these calculations. All the ones described previously—places, urbanized areas, and SMSAs—have been used. Since places are usually legal boundaries and SMSAs are county-bounded areas, they would not be expected to work as well as urbanized areas, which are closest to the definition of what a city is. A further difficulty has been the choice of an appropriate group of cities. Should we include those cities in a state, region, country, or group of countries? Many groups have been tried and found to work.

To illustrate the evidence, we have taken a random sample of thirty urbanized areas in the United States in 1970. They are shown in Table 3-1. The product of rank and population size is certainly not a constant, varying from 14.2 million to 24.4 million. Using regression techniques we fitted the data from the thirty urbanized areas to the Pareto equation in logarithms. Our estimate was as follows:

$$\log R = 4.08848 - .92177 \log s$$
$$(.02025) \qquad R^2 = .987$$

The number in parenthesis is the estimated standard deviation of the coefficient, $-a$. The equation explains 99 percent of the variation in rank. Furthermore, the probability is .95 that the true value of the coefficient, $-a$, would lie within two standard deviations of .92 with repeated sampling. Thus our estimate is that the Pareto distribution is a good fit, but that the coefficient, $-a$, is not equal to -1. It is more likely to be $-.92 \pm .04$. Thus, the evidence would indicate that the Pareto distribution applied, but that the rank-size rule is not as good. Still the consistency of the findings is remarkable and indicates that any theories of cities should take it into account.

So far we have found that the concept that specialization is limited by the extent of the market leads to useful models of systems of cities. Nevertheless, the two models, a step function of city sizes and the rank-size rule, are only imperfectly observed in the world.

There are several reasons for the difference between these market systems and reality. There is no guarantee that every activity with the same size trading area will find it profitable to locate in the same place. While retailers selling convenience goods or groups of retailers selling

Table 3-1 Random Sample of Urbanized Areas in U.S., 1970

Urbanized Area	Rank	Pop. Size (in Thousands)	Rank × Pop. Size
San Francisco–Oakland, Calif.	6	2,988	17,928
Cleveland, Ohio	9	1,960	17,640
San Diego, Calif.	19	1,198	22,762
Louisville, Ky.	33	739	24,387
Bridgeport, Conn.	56	413	23,128
Tucson, Ariz.	71	294	20,874
Worcester, Mass.	83	247	20,501
Colorado Springs, Colo.	103	205	21,115
Lorain-Elyria, Ohio	106	192	20,352
Utica-Rome, N.Y.	111	180	19,980
Savannah, Ga.	119	164	19,516
Ogden, Utah	133	150	19,550
Fall River, Mass.–R.I.	140	139	19,460
New Britain, Conn.	148	131	19,388
Springfield, Ill.	157	121	18,997
Port Arthur, Tex.	161	116	18,676
Portland, Maine	165	107	17,655
Provo-Orem, Utah	168	104	17,472
Meriden, Conn.	175	98	17,150
Johnstown, Pa.	177	96	16,992
High Point, N.C.	182	94	17,108
Seaside-Monterey, Calif.	183	93	17,019
Wheeling, W.Va.–Ohio	185	93	17,205
Muncie, Ind.	190	90	17,100
Sioux Falls, S.Dak.	212	75	15,900
Vineland-Millville, N.J.	214	74	15,836
Lima, Ohio	220	70	15,400
Gadsden, Ala.	225	68	15,300
Lewiston-Auburn, Maine	228	65	14,820
Nashua, N.H.	234	61	14,274

Source: U.S. Bureau of the Census, 1970.

shopping goods may locate together because these goods may be purchased by the buyer on the same shopping trip, manufacturers with the same size market areas may not find any advantage in locating with other activities with the same size market areas. To show that activities with the same market areas do not necessarily locate in the same place we need look at only a few cases. For most activities New York is the center of a trading area including the whole set of cities in the United States. International banking, publishing, national advertising, and corporate finance are activities centering in New York City. The national political administration, however, is in Washington, D.C.; Detroit has in the past served a national market for automobiles; Chicago has provided the nation with meats and televisions; and Los Angeles has provided the nation with motion picture entertainment.

The reasons why these activities with the same market size may not be located in the same center are that resources are not uniformly distributed, that labor productivity is not uniformly distributed, and that some activities will be drawn to the same center even though they do not have the same market size. Furthermore, some locations are historical accidents. They are accidents in the sense that factors other than those of economics created them. A good example would be the site of the nation's capital, Washington. From the point of view of minimizing transportation costs for the national population, a point in the Midwest just east of St. Louis would be a better site.[11] The site, of course, was selected before the final size of the nation was known, and it was, indeed, central to the thirteen colonies.

Resources may draw plants away from the center of their markets because lower input prices will cause the average-cost curve of the firm to shift downward. It will be profitable for the plant to be located nearer materials if this reduction in the cost schedule is greater than the possible downward shift of the demand curve facing the firm, since its site is farther from the market center. Thus, some places that would be smaller because of their trading area position become larger places as activities with much larger market areas are drawn to them because resources are near or labor productivity is greater.

Another reason why activities with the same market size may not be located in the same place is the existence of agglomeration economies. In particular it may be profitable to locate a plant adjacent to other plants in the same industry because they have common inputs, or it may be profitable to locate adjacent to plants in supplying or buying industries. The reasons why firms can profit by locating adjacent to each other are called agglomeration economies. These will be discussed later in this chapter.

The surrounding area of a central place is a supply area and a market area. The city is a production center buying inputs locally and from a wide area and the city is a trading center selling its products to the city and a wide area. The supply area depends upon the commodities and services produced in the city. A large center may require

---

[11]Chauncy D. Harris, "The Market as a Factor in the Localization of Industry in the United States," *Annals of the Association of American Geographers,* 44 (1954), pp. 315–348.

a very large supply area. At the same time the commodities and services provided by the center are determined by the resources available in the hinterland. The supply areas, market areas, and products of a center are interdependent and depend also on the transportation connections of the center.

Therefore, a group of cities, such as the group in the United States, is really several systems rather than one. Wholesaling, retailing, banking, professional services, and other services to households that are relatively free of input constraints and are tied to markets fit into a hierarchical system such as the simple one presented previously. This simple system, however, is overlaid by the more complex development of places dependent exclusively or partially upon manufacturing industries. The supply and trading areas of these manufacturing places will depend upon the scale of production that is profitable in the city. The supply area may be a region and the trading area may be the entire nation, as in the case of cottonseed-oil processing in Memphis and canning in New Orleans and San Diego. On the other hand, the trading area may be only a region and the supply area the world. Many combinations are possible.

Extent of Market Used to Explain Cases of Urban Growth

The notion of the market area and the limitation of specialization and growth by the possible extent of that market provides an incisive way of contrasting the relative growth of urban places. It can perhaps be best illustrated by relating the story of the differential growth rates of Chicago and St. Louis during the 1800s.

Before the railroad, St. Louis was the largest city in the upper Midwest. It served as a distribution and exporting point for trade between the upper Midwest via the Missouri, Mississippi, and Ohio Rivers, and the rest of the world. Agricultural products were collected at St. Louis and shipped to Europe and New York via New Orleans. Manufactured products from New England were distributed to the region from St. Louis after being shipped up the Mississippi River from New Orleans. Even the Erie Canal did not make Chicago a better transshipment point to the East because there was no good transport link between Chicago and the entire upper Midwest. The river system was St. Louis's great advantage. The development and construction of railroads provided a way for Chicago to develop a transport link with the upper Midwest. In the 1850s the construction of railroads connecting Chicago to Missouri, Illinois, Iowa, Minnesota, Wisconsin, Indiana, Ohio, and the South, as well as with New York, made Chicago the cheapest transshipment point for exports from and imports to the upper Midwest. Because transportation costs were less from the hinterland to Chicago than to St. Louis, Chicago became the place for activities requiring the larger market size. By 1870 population statistics confirmed that Chicago was the largest city of the region.[12]

In the same way the ultimate ascendancy of the port of New York over Boston, Philadelphia, Baltimore, Norfolk, and Charleston had much to do with its access to a richer hinterland. In the colonial period New York was second in importance because it had only the second richest hinterland with which to trade. Later, however, the Erie Canal and railroads gave New York access to greater markets than either Philadelphia or Boston. The South was at a disadvantage not only because of its smaller population, but because part of that population included slaves who had little buying power.[13]

The growth of these cities was not a result of the farm to city migration that was previously discussed. Immigration from outside the United States and the natural increase in population was the source of population growth. Farm to city migration became more important in the twentieth century.

COMPARATIVE COSTS

If resources are distributed over an area unevenly, input prices will not be uniform throughout the plain. Although the average-cost curve may be declining as we have previously described it, the curve may shift up or down depending on the abundance of needed inputs in each location. Prices for materials, such as coal, lumber, and mineral ores, will increase because of the added cost of transportation.

The transportation cost in producing goods from these materials may be reduced by locating near the materials source because there is considerable weight loss in the production process. For example, ore smelting, sugar refining, and operations requiring a great deal of fuel tend to locate near the source of materials. Production processes using fuels that are burned up in the process, or causing waste that is discarded in the process and does not become a part of the final product to be shipped, tend to be attracted to material sources. On the other hand, some production processes are weight-gaining rather than weight-losing and thus tend to raise the transport cost on the final

[12]Wyatt Winton Belcher, *The Economic Rivalry between St. Louis and Chicago, 1850–1880*, (New York: Columbia, 1947); Lewis F. Thomas. "Decline of St. Louis as Midwest Metropolis," *Economic Geography* (April 1949), pp. 118–127; W. H. Bishop, "St. Louis," *Harpers New Monthly Magazine* (1884), p. 501.

[13]Allan R. Pred, *The Spatial Dynamics of U.S. Urban-Industrial Growth: 1800– 1914: Interpretive and Theoretical Essays* (Cambridge, Mass.: M.I.T., 1966), pp. 186–196.

product. For example, a soda-bottling plant combines a soft-drink syrup with water, bottles the product, and distributes it. In this process, water, a ubiquitous material, adds weight to the final product to be shipped. Water has relatively the same price in most locations. Thus the transport cost on the final product can be avoided, and the delivered price can be lowered by locating at the market center. Ink and beer production also add ubiquitous materials and tend to be located near the center of the market.

A process requiring large numbers of man-hours of labor in a scarcely populated area would have to pay a higher wage rate to attract workers to the area. Higher wages would also have to be paid in areas with a higher cost of living. Furthermore, if there were uncertain fluctuations in the demand for labor, as in the case of fashion clothing, the costs of hiring would be greater in areas with few workers. The cost of labor is higher in areas where there is not a concentration of workers in the specific industry. This is a point we will expand on later in the chapter. In any case, the prices of inputs will not be equal thoughout the plain. They will now rise with distance from sources.

Let us go through an illustration of the way in which variations in input prices could affect the average and marginal-cost curves of an enterprise in order to see what impact these variations may have on the location of the firm. Consider a process in which only man-hours of labor and tons of material per unit of time are needed in production. Figure 3-3 illustrates the case. Z_0 and Z_1 are isoquants for two rates of production, Z_0 and Z_1. At one site the price of material is such that the least-cost combination of inputs to produce Z_0 is M_1 and L_1. At another site the price of material is lower because the site is closer to the source. For the same outlay as AB, the firm could produce Z_1 with least-cost combination L_2 and M_2. At this second site, however, the rate of production Z_0 could have been produced with less cost. By shifting the isocost line AC to $A'C'$ so that it is just tangent to the isoquant representing the rate of production, Z_0, we find the least-cost combination of inputs at the second site for the same rate of production. The input combination would be L_3 and M_3. It is a smaller outlay than required at the first site; therefore, the average cost is less. In this situation all costs are variable costs because we are considering alternative locations. Furthermore, the marginal costs of producing at rate of production Z_0 are less.

The marginal cost is less for the following reason. At the least-cost combination of inputs, the ratio of the price of inputs to their respective marginal products are equal, and equal to marginal cost:

$$\frac{P_m}{\mathrm{MP}_m} = \frac{P_1}{\mathrm{MP}_1} = \mathrm{MC}$$

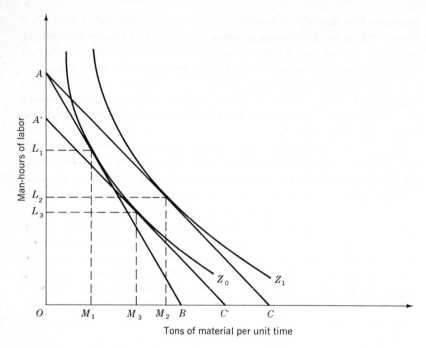

FIGURE 3-3 Input Combinations at Alternative Locations

where P_m = the price of material
  P_l = the wage rate
  MP_m = the marginal physical product of material
  MP_l = the marginal physical product of labor
  MC = marginal cost

In moving from the first to the second site, P_m decreased, but P_l remained the same. Keeping output constant, less labor and more material is being used. Assuming decreasing marginal productivities, the marginal product of labor would increase and that of material would decrease. Since the wage rate remains the same and the marginal product of labor increases, the marginal cost at rate of production Z_0 decreases. It would decrease at every rate of production. Thus, both the average-and marginal-cost curves shift down at the site with the cheaper input price. In Figure 3-4, this is shown by the shift of the average-cost curve AC to AC′ and the shift of the marginal cost curve MC to MC′.

It is tempting to argue that this is the reason for many firms being located near resource sites, but it is not a complete argument because not all resource sites are utilized. The reason is that we must also consider the demand conditions. Consider the demand curve D in Figure 3-4. It is constructed in the same manner as the demand curves in Figure 3-1. If this were the demand curve at both sites, either site would be feasible, but the low-cost site would be the most profitable. It is conceivable that the low-cost site was so remote, however, that the demand curve would shift to D' in which case the firm would not choose the low-cost site because there are fewer people and the population is sparsely distributed over the market area, or because the transport cost of shipping to market is so great that demand shifts, or both.

Our first step in relaxing the assumption that resources are evenly distributed was to show that production processes would be attracted to resource sites so long as demand would enable the producer to make a profit. Thus resource sites become more likely sites for town beginnings for some operations. The expansion of the town around such a center would occur in the same manner as we previously described.

As firms begin to fill up a region, however, the analysis changes from that of the homogeneous plain. One reason is that a new firm might not be able to establish a production center on the fringe of an-

FIGURE 3-4 Pricing and Rate of Production at Alternative Locations

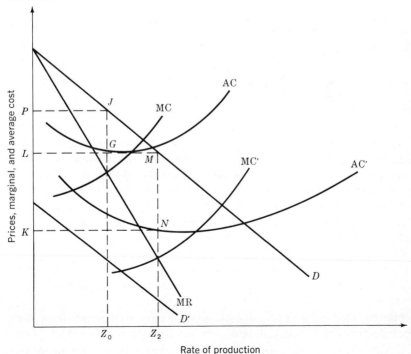

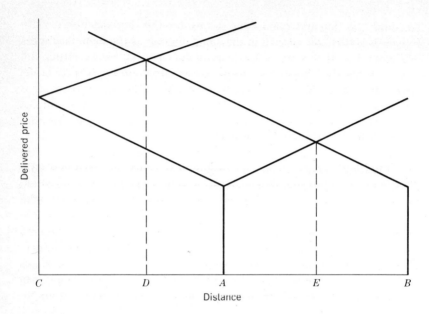

FIGURE 3-5 Delivered Price at Alternative Locations

other firm's market to cut into his demand. There is obviously incentive if excess profits are being made, as illustrated in Figure 3-4. Nevertheless, the cost may be so high that the original seller can undercut the new producer even several miles from the source of material.

This point can be illustrated in Figure 3-5. The height of the vertical line at points A, B, and C represents the price at the producer sites. Consider the low-cost producer at A and the high-cost producer near the edge of his market at C. A's price plus transportation cost is represented by the height of the line rising from A toward C. The slope of the line is the increase in delivered price due to the increase in transportation cost with each increase in distance the product has to be sent. In this situation, C has no chance to produce. New firms would concentrate at A. If, however, the low-cost producer were located at B, and there were sufficient density of population around C, C could carve out a market up to point D.

Consider what would happen if there were excess profits at the low-cost sites of production. The firm illustrated in Figure 3-4 at the low-cost site would produce Z_2 rate of production for a price OL and make profits $KLMN$. Surely an incentive for new firms! New firms could crowd into the low-cost area. As they do so, of course, pricing policy becomes oligopolistic. Each firm's price is dependent upon what the others do. Nevertheless, it is clear we now have another reason for why more people move into the vicinity of production. Low-cost sites may attract a large firm whose employment will be sufficiently great to start a town. Furthermore, low-cost sites may attract several firms in the same industry, attracting still more employment.

AGGLOMERATION ECONOMIES

So far we have explored the location and reasons for town and city settlement on a homogeneous plain with a uniform distribution of resources and on a plain with uneven distribution of resources. There is one more step to explore. Once a place is founded and expands to a fairly large size, it tends to attract new industry relative to rural undeveloped places. We have already discussed part of this cumulative effect resulting from increased population. Another cause is often termed agglomeration economies. Agglomeration economies can be described more precisely as external economies of scale to firms in the same or different industries. Mobile external economies occur wherever firms are located. Immobile external economies only occur if the plants locate in the same place. We will deal only with the latter. These immobile external economies of scale are really an extension of the idea that specialization is limited by the extent of the market.

Consider the case of a center in which many firms in a single industry concentrate because the site is a low-cost location. It turns out that the average-cost curve of each may shift down because of this concentration.

One of the most common reasons given for external economies to the firm is a large and skilled labor pool available to each firm in an area in which the industry is concentrated. Other examples include the possibility of firms existing to process waste materials, which may not be possible without a large industry, the facilitation of research, and the development of markets for raw materials with resultant savings in cost. Concentration, however, is only enhanced if these economies accrue to firms locating in the same place (immobile economies). Some economies of scale to each firm in the industry could accrue just from the expansion of the industry whether or not it was concentrated in one place (mobile economies).

There is another reason for average-cost curves to shift down because of external economies of scale to firms. As firms concentrate in one place, whether they are in the same or different industries, specialized inputs may be produced by a separate operation that services each of the other firms. In that way the firm does not have to provide the service to itself, but can buy it more inexpensively from the new operation. The new operation can produce the service or input more inexpensively because it can achieve economies of scale by selling to many firms. A carburetor manufacturer could sell to all automobile assembly plants, or trucking services could be provided to many firms rather than each providing its own trucking facilities. These specialized services could be provided publicly, and may have to be in some cases. Examples are transport terminals, water supply, sewage disposal, police, and fire protection.

We can illustrate this in Figure 3-6. If a firm operated at rate of production OE, its total average costs would be OA. One of the services or inputs costs OC per unit of final product. We are assuming that the ratio between the input and a unit of output is constant over the ranges of production considered. If the firm produced a rate of production OF, the cost of the given service—trucking, water, electric power, etc.—would only be OD per unit of final product. Limitations of the size of the market, however, prevent the firm from expanding beyond OE. If many firms in the same industry were located in the same place,

FIGURE 3-6   Specialization Limited by the Extent of the Market

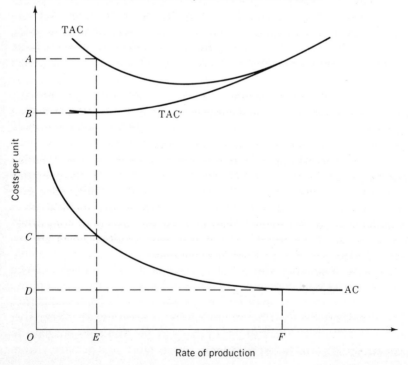

or if many firms in different industries using this same service were located in the same place, a specialized operation could be started that would have sufficient scale because of the size of its market to reduce the average cost of the item to OD. The total average cost of each firm would shift down to TAC'.[14]

Thus, the larger a city becomes the greater the degree of specialization and the more interindustry sales that would be expected. Furthermore, there would tend to be firms of many different sizes.

An interesting sidelight on this question is the size or scale of the first few firms in a place. If they were very large, so that they could provide their own services at low costs because of their own scale, these input services do not get performed by separate organizations, either public or private. This in itself could slow down the further agglomeration of firms attracted by inexpensive services which they would not have to provide for themselves.[15]

As we pointed out at the beginning of the chapter, firms locate on the basis of expectations. Expectations are usually based on some kind of weighting of past experience. Therefore, those places in which population is increasing would attract new investment, whereas in an area in which population is declining expectations will have to be unusual for investment to be encouraged.

Such a momentum would appear to give growing places an advantage for all time. Increasing population density, however, not only brings with it agglomeration economies. There may be diseconomies as well. With few people, waste disposal into the air or water is small in amount and easily diffused. The exhaust from one car does not bother anyone and is soon dissipated. On the other hand, as the number of people in one place increases, pollution and congestion become costly. They are the prime examples of the economist's concept of external costs. A firm may pollute the air or streams with emissions from its production process. Individuals may pollute through disposal of household wastes or operation of their automobiles. The pollution will cost others in the economy but will not be reflected in the operating costs of the polluter. Air pollution increases the maintenance cost of buildings on surrounding lots and increases the medical costs of individuals. Water pollution may increase the costs of treating drinking water for downstream cities. Since these external costs are not borne by the polluter, he does not take them into account when considering profitability. Similarly, congestion in city streets causes travel costs to rise.

---

[14]George J. Stigler, "The Division of Labor Is Limited by the Extent of the Market," *Journal of Political Economy*, 59 (June 1951), pp. 185–193.

[15]Benjamin Chinitz, "Contrasts in Agglomeration: New York and Pittsburgh," *American Economic Review*, 51 (May 1961), pp. 279–289.

As these costs rise in larger cities, they may cause migrants and investors to decide to locate in a smaller place where these costs are less. The present value of future earnings to both migrants and to investors would be reduced by the increased costs. At some point expectations of future earnings would be insufficient to offset the increased costs from congestion and pollution. It must be admitted, however, that although pollution is a "hot" issue, people still are migrating to jobs in metropolitan areas. The opportunities still seem to be located in the big city. There has been dispersal of jobs and residences within the metropolitan areas, but this is a topic for the next chapter. Externalities are central to understanding public goods and will be covered in more detail in Chapters 5 and 11.

MIGRATION OF CAPITAL AND LABOR

Those areas gaining momentum attract resources and those declining cause them to leave. On the other hand, a very simple view of labor and capital markets suggests a reason why relative growth rates may be an irrelevant consideration in understanding the welfare of people in different cities. If capital is earning a higher rate of return in city A compared to city B, capital should shift to A and be withdrawn from B. If wages in a particular occupation are higher in A than B, workers should migrate from B to A, and investors should be attracted to low-wage area B. Migration should continue until returns were equalized in each area. But empirical studies of migration have not been successful in documenting such equilibrating action. Wages and returns to capital *do* tend to remain higher in growing areas.

Although the simple view of the allocation of resources among spatially separated markets may be correct for commodity flows, it is not the best theoretical framework for understanding labor and capital movements. The reason is that it does not account for expectations and the fact that these moves require estimates of what will happen for the remaining life of the worker or for the duration of the capital investment. Small differences in real wages in different cities in any year may not precipitate moves because they are expected to be only temporary. An investment-decision approach that compares the present values of alternative decisions with their costs will take into account expectations.

To apply the investment approach to a worker's decision on whether he should migrate we need to estimate the costs of migration, the returns (which are the increase in real earnings), and the appropriate interest rate. The costs of migration for a family include the costs of moving household belongings, the personal transportation costs, earnings lost while in transit, extra living costs while in transit, the cost of retraining for a new job if required, and the psychic costs of leaving familiar surroundings. If one member of the family worked at the old location but would not be able to do so at the new location, the present value of the lost earnings is an additional cost of migration.

The returns to investment in migration include the present value of the expected increase in earnings in future years and the psychic benefits, if any, in the new place. Expected increases in earnings for other family members would count as returns, whereas the present value of decreases in their earnings would be considered a cost. The expected earnings in the new place do not have to be in the same occupation. The increase in earnings should be deflated by any differences in the cost of living since only differences in real earnings should be estimated. It would not pay to move for a higher nominal income, when in fact the two incomes were equal in buying power.

The rate of interest used in discounting should be the rate that the migrant would receive for alternative investments, if he did not spend it on migrating. This would most likely be the rate of interest for a certificate of deposit in a local bank or for shares in a savings and loan association.

What, then, are the implications of the investment approach for generalizations about migration? First, migration is more likely to be profitable for the young. The life span over which the increase in earnings may be earned is greater for younger than for older workers. Seniority yields increases in pay, but if the worker moves to another place, and in particular if he changes occupations, he may lose the pay gain of seniority and not receive the same wages as men of comparable age and skill in the new place. Empirical studies have indeed shown that the number of people migrating per 1,000 population is much greater for the age group 18–29 than for any other.[16] In fact, this propensity by age is common for all places. Even fast-growing places show outmigration in this age group. Nevertheless, those places showing better opportunities will attract migrants.

The second generalization is that since the cost of migration is less for shorter moves, migration will be more common for shorter distances. A job move is easiest to carry out when no residential move is required. In general, empirical studies of frequency distributions of moves show that most moves are short.[17] Many of the longer moves are made by military pesonnel and their families and by corporate executives.

Even if migration is profitable, that is, if the present value of the

[16]John B. Lansing and Eva Mueller, *The Geographic Mobility of Labor* (Ann Arbor, Michigan: Survey Research Center, 1967), pp. 39–40.
[17]Ibid., pp. 26–29.

increase in earnings is greater than the cost of migration, there may be further hindrances to moving. People cannot borrow money without collateral. Thus, even if the investment would be profitable, the move might not be made because the worker could not borrow the necessary money. When workers have been unemployed for some time, it is unlikely that they will have the necessary cash to make the move, or that they will have the collateral to borrow the necessary funds. Another hindrance may be that the potential migrants do not have the information to know about their alternatives.

To apply the investment approach to the movement of capital from one place to another we need to elaborate the costs and returns from the shift. For a lender in a financial institution—banks, life insurance companies, and savings and loan associations—the costs of lending in another place are the additional costs of handling the loan once it is made. For an entrepreneur, transferring capital or property wealth is more difficult. Suppose that market and supply conditions have changed since the initial location of the establishment. Where initially the establishment was optimally located, assume that the site is no longer optimal for the particular product. What is the cost of shifting resources? The plant and equipment cannot be moved. The entrepreneur can sell them and use the funds to move to a new site. The cost of shifting capital will be the actual transportation cost—a small amount—plus the loss on his investment. If he continues to operate the plant in the old suboptimal site, profits will not be maximized. If the sale of plant and equipment is less than the present value of earnings from the plant at the suboptimal site, the loss is a cost of moving the capital. In particular, entrepreneurs of retail and manufacturing plants in a declining area are locked in. They cannot find buyers for their present establishments because investment returns in the same activity are greater elsewhere. If the place becomes an optimal location for another activity, the establishment might be sold for closer to its present value, or the entrepreneur could shift to a new product while in the same location. If the plant and equipment are torn down and abandoned, the cost of moving capital is the demolition cost plus the loss of the present value of the enterprise had it remained in operation at the old site.

The returns from moving to a new site are the expected increase in earnings per invested dollar in the new site. The interest rate used to calculate the present value of the increase in earnings is the rate of return that it is possible to receive by investing the money in financial institutions or other companies.

The implications of this analysis for the mobility of capital are that the shifting of capital from one place to another is not the costless proposition often assumed in economic analysis. In particular, investments in retail enterprises and in manufacturing plant and equipment are extremely difficult to shift out of when located in declining areas. The cost of shifting the location of an enterprise will decrease as its remaining life shrinks. The lower the present value of an enterprise, the less the cost of selling out and shifting its location. For these reasons, production increases in a new place because of lower costs or larger markets will more often result from the establishment of new firms than from the shift of older firms in the industry from less profitable locations. Branch plants of older firms, of course, are an obvious answer to new and larger market areas.

The formation of loanable funds in undeveloped or partially developed areas lags behind that of the more developed areas. In the United States there is a tendency toward a surplus of loanable funds in the Northeast and a deficiency of funds in the South and West. Shifting these funds is not costless. In particular a greater risk factor is included the farther away the funds will be invested. This is particularly true for real property investment since, as we shall see in the next chapter, the expected returns depend so much on local conditions. To invest wisely one must know a great deal of information. That costs time and money.

Moreover, consider the case of an area whose population increases proportionally more than the increase in jobs available for those who want to work, so that the rate of unemployment increases. With the lag in migration predictable from our analysis, wages should begin to decline. If wages were lower, we would expect new firms to be attracted, particularly because we would also expect increased wages in the expanding areas because of the lag in migration of workers to those places. The lower-wage sites might allow lower costs than the higher-wage areas. Nevertheless, the declining area must overcome the pessimism that makes investment difficult. Myrdal argues that once an area begins to decline other costs rise. The maintenance of public goods that are part of the economic structure of an area—the roads, water systems, schools, hospitals, etc.—will require higher tax rates as the overall income of the particular area declines.[18] Public expenditures do not decline much when income is falling, making the tax rate per dollar of income rise. Thus, lower wages could be offset by higher tax rates, as well as dismal expectations. Therefore, automatic adjustment in areas of unemployment is likely to be slow. Nevertheless, the empirical evidence shows that high taxes are not related in any systematic way to slower growth.[19] The analysis in the previous sections of this chapter indicates why there is not a simple one-to-one relation

[18]Gunnar Myrdal, *Rich Lands and Poor* (New York: Harper & Row, 1957), pp. 23–38.

[19]John F. Due, "Studies of State-Local Tax Influence on Location of Industry," *National Tax Journal* 14 (June 1961), pp. 279–289.

between taxes and the location of industry. A firm could locate in isolation where taxes would be low, but it would have to produce many of its own inputs which could have been bought more cheaply from other firms in an urban agglomeration. Only a very large operation would have the scale to be able to do this. Furthermore, there would have to be an accessible market area to support the operation.

On the other hand, we can also see why differential tax rates for different jurisdictions within one metropolitan area might cause firms to locate at different places within the agglomerative center. Firms would still be able to obtain many savings on input costs and to pay lower taxes. They would also be near their markets. Nevertheless, they would still want to compare the kinds of services provided in the jurisdiction against taxes. It might still pay to be in a higher taxing jurisdiction if significant public service differentials existed.

GROWTH AND POLICY ANALYSIS

As we argued in the last section, growth or lack of growth in numbers of businesses or population should not be the primary concern of the economic analysis of cities. The real problem is that because of hindrances to migration differential growth rates lead to unemployment and to lower real wages and income in some cities.

If in a community the rate of unemployment rose relative to other communities, or if wages for given occupations fall, or both, would there be any mechanism to alleviate the problems indicated by these indexes? In a free market, we have already seen that there is no automatic market response, except after a long period of time. An alternative would be for the community to agree through voluntary cooperation to help those in need. But there are two reasons why voluntary action would probably not be undertaken in appropriate amounts. First, if every worker is unemployed or has a reduced income, there is little to share with others. Second, if only some are unemployed or suffer reduction in income, the well-off workers, even if they would feel better if the suffering were alleviated, would have an incentive to let their neighbors take care of the problem. In Chapter 5 we will describe this problem more analytically. In any case, the only way the community will undertake sustained action is by joining together in a government which coerces all to contribute. This is not a completely satisfactory solution; its problems are outlined in Chapters 5, 6, and 7.

Even if the local community through its political organization decided that some action should be undertaken to correct the rising unemployment or falling wage rate, it may not have the power to do so. First, as above, if all wages are falling, no one group in the community would be in much of a position to transfer income to others. Second, if a tax were used to subsidize the poor or unemployed, there would be an incentive on the part of those taxed to find a new place to live. Nonetheless, if people living in the community prefer the area to others with greater job opportunities, they would be willing to earn less than they could in other locations, if they could stay and find a job. Under these circumstances, it might be possible to tax the earnings of these workers to subsidize the location of a business that could not otherwise consider this location because of its unprofitability.[20]

The community does have other alternatives. One of the reasons why businesses might not have relocated or been established in the area is that an information search is costly and imperfect. The businesses that may find this a profitable location have not found out about the site. Thus, the community can undertake an information campaign so that potential businesses will learn more quickly of the advantages of the location.

Since the local community may have difficulty bringing about change by itself, a more inclusive level of government, state or federal, may be convinced by the representatives of the declining place that it must do something. Because the geographic area of the more inclusive government is wider than the community, the imposition of taxes to make transfer payments to the unemployed and poor can not be resisted as well by migration. Obviously state government would be less able to establish transfer payments than the federal government. The voters from other districts, however, would not be so ready to subsidize a group's preference for a remote location with permanent transfers of income.

The voters of the more inclusive government would prefer to find some way of temporarily subsidizing the declining community which has promise of alleviating the problem of unemployment and poverty in the future. There are two options open to them. They can encourage or subsidize a migration of people *from* the declining place, or they can encourage or subsidize migration of business *to* the declining place.

Several states have established ways of subsidizing the location of businesses in particular declining places within their borders by allowing the issuance of tax-exempt municipal bonds to construct production facilities that can be leased at low rents to business. Care is taken that businesses not be attracted from other parts of the same state, but from other states. These schemes have indeed attracted

---

[20]John E. Moes, *Local Subsidies for Industry*, (Chapel Hill, N.C.: The University of North Carolina Press, 1962).

businesses to many small communities. Nonetheless, the agglomeration economies of location in larger metropolitan places would require large subsidies to attract many firms to very small places. Another possibility is that the taxes of the firm would be reduced for some long but specific period of time. In this case, however, the location must appear to be profitable without subsidy in some future time period, or the site will not be considered with only the temporary subsidy. Of course, information services for plant relocation or initial location would help reduce search costs and perhaps reveal sites that businessmen may have overlooked otherwise.

The more difficult side of this issue is the need to prohibit new plant locations or relocations in already densely populated areas so that businessmen will have to consider areas that are currently declining. The problem, of course, is that less costly services attract firms to the expanding agglomeration, but that if firms did indeed locate there and add their demands to those of others, congestion and pollution would so greatly increase that the area would not be better off. Long-time residents would consider themselves worse off. In England such location was prohibited to prevent further congestion in the London area. In the United States, similar positions have been adopted only by small residential suburbs, in the form of zoning ordinances. Questions of urban growth and zoning will be further discussed in Chapters 9 and 13.

In a democracy the notion of telling people where they should live is abhorrent. Thus, federal and state policies encouraging people to leave declining areas for expanding ones have followed two courses. Employment services providing information on jobs throughout the state and nation have been established to lower the search cost for the individual so that he or she might be better prepared to leave a current location. Secondly, the federal government, through several manpower retraining acts, has established subsidies to help people move to new jobs and new locations and to retrain for skills more in demand. These provisions will be covered again when we discuss poverty within the metropolitan area.

Although expanding cities have always grown through migration, there have been times, such as during the Revolutionary War, when the flood of migrants was greater than they could assimilate in a short period of time. The governments of these areas had to deal with increasing unemployment and poverty. During the Revolutionary War they protested against carrying the burden of the nation's poverty.[21] The same warning has been stated for our time by Kain and Persky.[22]

---

[21]Carl Bridenbaugh, *Cities in Revolt* (New York: Knopf, 1955), pp. 122–128.
[22]John F. Kain and Joseph J. Persky, "Alternatives to the Gilded Ghetto," *Public Interest*, 14 (Winter, 1969), pp. 74–87.

They were concerned that poor areas within expanding cities might be made so attractive by migration subsidies, retraining, and housing programs that migration from less developed areas of the South could exacerbate the problems of metropolitan areas without improving the lot of the migrants. We will return to this question in Chapter 8.

Policies by the more inclusive government which deal exclusively with facilitating the migration of people or businesses, however, may not solve the problems of poverty and unemployment. The economic development of an area beyond geographic reallocation for greater productivity still requires measures that improve the productivity of the labor force and industry through education, improved transportation, pollution control, and many services that must be provided by the public sector. At this point we cannot cover the whole spectrum of policies that encourage the development of a place. We have touched on them throughout this chapter and they will be discussed in almost every chapter in the rest of the book.

Our next task will be to study the internal structure of urban areas. We will approach this through an analysis of urban-property markets and urban land-use models.

SUMMARY

Cities arise and grow by choice and chance. Uncertainty makes it difficult to make rational choices, so that chance may play a large part in site selection. Nevertheless, competitive survival will make it possible to make predictions using economic theory. The first consideration in analyzing the growth of cities is that specialization of labor is limited by the extent of the market. Cities may develop and grow at places central to the transportation network of a large market area. The larger the extent of the surrounding market, the larger the city is likely to be. Nevertheless, markets are not the only explanation for the growth of cities. Using a market model only, one could generate specific hierarchical systems of cities. In reality, the distribution of size and location of cities is more like a system of systems of cities in which the market model may be considered a base. Since resources are unevenly distributed geographically, costs of production will also vary geographically. Therefore, cities may arise near resource sites or low labor cost places, even when the market model does not indicate such a large place.

In all cases, once a place begins to grow there is an internal momentum built into growth because of agglomeration economies. At the same time, external diseconomies may eventually limit that momentum because of the increased cost from congestion and pollution caused by the crowding of more people and industry into the same city.

Another equilibrating mechanism that economists have often used in the analysis of growth is the theory that labor and capital would migrate from areas where they were earning less than average returns to those areas in which they would earn greater than average returns. In practice the mechanism is not as simple as the static supply and demand concepts indicate because migration decisions require estimates of long-run uncertain changes in both geographic areas. It is likely that these decisions would not be precipitously made, so that resource adjustment through migration is unlikely to occur rapidly. Taxes would not appear to cause differences in growth because they represent payments for services, and low-tax areas may also not provide the kinds of services that lead to agglomeration economies.

Resource migration may be brought about by government action. The type of action possible depends upon the inclusiveness of the political organization: community, state, or federal. Most measures that can be undertaken require encouraging or subsidizing the migration of people or jobs. It may be possible to encourage so much migration from depressed areas that expanding areas will be unable to assimilate them, and thus, the migrants will not be better off.

In general, however, development requires policies more comprehensive than just smoothing the process of the reallocation of resources to more productive locations. Education, control of pollution, transportation, and the provision of public services are all important in improving the productivity and welfare of an area. This whole book may be considered a study in the economic development of cities.

SELECTED READINGS

Chinitz, Benjamin: "Contrasts in Agglomeration: New York and Pittsburg," *American Economic Review,* 51 (May 1961), pp. 279–289 (Bobbs-Merrill Reprint, Econ-66).

Lösch, August: "The Nature of Economic Regions," *Southern Economic Journal,* 5 (July 1938), pp. 71–78 (Bobbs-Merrill Reprint, G-135).

Moses, Leon: "Location and the Theory of Production," *Quarterly Journal of Economics,* 72 (May 1958), 259–272 (Bobbs-Merrill Reprint, Econ-222).

Pred, Allan R.: *The Spatial Dynamics of U.S. Urban-Industrial Growth* (Cambridge, Mass.: M.I.T., 1966), pp. 12–86, 143–217.

Stigler, George J.: "The Division of Labor is Limited by the Extent of the Market," *Journal of Political Economy,* 59 (June 1951), pp. 185–193.

APPENDIX:

Location of
the Individual
Producer[1]

The profits of the individual producer are his receipts minus his costs. Consumer tastes, income, and the prices of substitute products affect the receipts of an industry and the individual producer. Improved organization, new technology, and a more skilled work force affect costs. Changes in location, however, may also affect the receipts and costs of the producer. Since the producer's primary goal is to maximize his profits, and since some places will yield greater profits than others, his location is as important as his price and output. This Appendix will attempt to explain how various factors affect the profitability of sites through use of the theory of the firm.

MAXIMIZING PROFIT

To maximize profits the producer selects the product and the rate of production that will yield the maximum excess of receipts over cost. Cost will increase with increases in the rate of production. But cost may vary for a particular rate of production because of the production method—the combination of inputs used. Obviously, the producer will combine inputs in the most efficient way for the rate of production that is selected. For exposition purposes it is assumed that the choice of product has been made. The minimum-cost combination of inputs will be explained first. Then the relationship of cost and receipts to rate of production will be analyzed in separate sections. Minimum cost, rate of production, and receipts will be integrated in the final section on the conditions for the optimal (most profitable) location.

MINIMIZING COST

A labor force equipped with different skills is combined with other resources such as materials, equipment, buildings, land, and manage-

---

[1]The material in this appendix has been reprinted from Hugh O. Nourse, *Regional Economics* (New York: McGraw-Hill, 1968), pp. 9–30.

ment to yield an output. For example, a producer can use many semi-skilled workers and a large amount of machinery in an assembly-line process, or he can hire highly skilled workers and use less machinery. The economist calls this relationship between the inputs and the rate of production the production function. The production function, thus, describes the possible combinations of resources for producing any particular output per hour, day, week, or other unit of time.

The particular combination chosen depends upon the relative prices of each of the inputs. Usually, no one producer is sufficiently large to effect changes in prices of resources that he must purchase. Thus, prices of inputs are thought of as being fixed to the producer. Nevertheless, they are fixed in particular places, and he may be able to reduce the price paid for land, labor, or materials by considering alternative locations. Therefore, to find the least-cost combination for any rate of production, the producer must calculate the minimum-cost combination at each alternative site.

These concepts and relationships can be made more explicit by the following graphical analysis. In Figure 3-7, physical quantities of one input are measured along the vertical axis, and physical quantities of another input are measured along the horizontal axis. Assume that only two inputs are required in the production process. One might be tons of material; the other might be man-hours of labor. Assume also

FIGURE 3-7

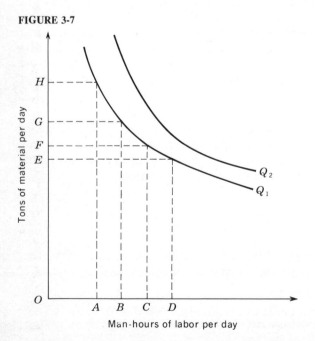

that the state of technological knowledge allows the producer to make the product, perhaps some kind of toy, in many ways, so that continuous infinitesimal changes, substituting labor for materials or materials for labor, can be made while maintaining the same rate of production. The curve Q_1 represents all combinations of labor and material that will produce a particular rate of production. Such a curve is an isoquant. The figure illustrates that the rate of production Q_1 can be achieved using OA man-hours and OH tons of material, or OB man-hours and OG tons of material, or one of the many other combinations traced out by the isoquant Q_1. Isoquant Q_2 represents the possible combinations of labor and material to produce a greater rate of production.

Both isoquants are convex to the origin. Over the relevant range of possibilities a reduction in man-hours of labor requires an increase in tons of material to maintain the same rate of production. Furthermore, while labor and materials may be substitutes, they are not perfect substitutes. As fewer man-hours and more tons of material are used, it becomes more difficult to substitute additional material for man-hours. Therefore, equal reductions in man-hours from OD to OC, from OC to OB, and from OB to OA require increasing increments of tons of material, EF, FG, and GH, to maintain the same rate of production.

The least-cost combination depends upon the prices per ton of material and per man-hour of labor. Suppose prices are given for one of the alternative sites. If the prices were $2 per man-hour and $1 per ton of material, $1,000 could buy either 500 man-hours or 1,000 tons of material. It would also be possible to buy 800 tons of material and 100 man-hours, or any other combination of material and labor the cost of which sums to $1,000. In Figure 3-8, the line XY shows the combinations of material and man-hours that could be bought with a constant sum of money, given prices. Such a line is an isocost line. OY shows the tons of material that could be purchased if the whole sum were used to buy materials. OX shows the man-hours that could be bought if the whole sum were used to buy man-hours. The line XY traces out the combinations of purchases of both inputs that could be made with this sum.

If the price per man-hour of labor should be higher at a second site, say $2.50 per man-hour, fewer man-hours (only 400) could be purchased with the $1,000 if it were all spent on labor. Suppose the price per ton of material is the same at the second site, so that 1,000 tons could still be purchased if the sum were all spent on material. If $800 were spent on 800 tons of material, 100 man-hours of labor could be bought at the first site with the remaining $200, but only 80 man-hours could be bought at the second site. The possible quantities

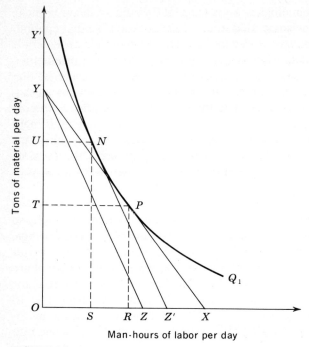

FIGURE 3-8

of inputs that could be purchased at the second site with an outlay equal to that of XY are shown in Figure 3-8 by the isocost line YZ. The vertical intercept OY is unchanged since the price of material is the same. The horizontal intercept OZ is less than OX since fewer man-hours can be purchased with the outlay at the second site.

Parallel shifts of the isocost line represent changes in the total outlay without changes in the relative price of the inputs. A shift away from the origin, as from YZ to $Y'Z'$, represents an increase in total outlay. The line $Y'Z'$ shows the quantities of material and man-hours that could be purchased at the second site with a greater outlay. Similarly, parallel shifts toward the origin represent lower total outlays. Since XY and YZ represent the same outlay with different sets of prices, and $Y'Z'$ represents a greater outlay than YZ, $Y'Z'$ also represents a greater outlay than XY.

Given the prices of inputs, say as they are at the first site, the isocost line XY bounds a triangular area OXY that includes all the combinations that it is possible to buy with the given outlay or less outlay. The question of finding the least-cost combination of inputs to produce an output is the same as asking which combination of inputs with a given outlay will produce the largest output. For the outlay represented by XY in Figure 3-8, the highest output obtainable is Q_1. This is the highest isoquant that XY touches. XY is tangent to Q_1 at P. Higher outputs are represented by isoquants farther from the origin than Q_1. Higher outputs would require combinations of inputs represented by points outside the triangle OXY, and thus could not be obtained with the given outlay and prices. This also means that XY represents the least cost for which output Q_1 could be produced. Greater outlays could be used to produce Q_1, but lower outlays could not purchase enough inputs for producing output Q_1.

In Figure 3-8, the least-cost combination of man-hours and material to produce output Q_1 at the first site is OR man-hours of labor and OT tons of material, as shown by point P. The least-cost combination of man-hours and material to produce Q_1 at the second site is OS man-hours of labor and OU tons of material, as shown by the point N. At N, the isocost line $Y'Z'$ is just tangent to the isoquant Q_1. The first site requires less cost to produce output Q_1 than the second site since, as noted above, $Y'Z'$ represents a higher outlay than XY.

COST AND SCALE OF OUTPUT

So far, we have held the rate of production constant. The next step is to vary the rate of production and relate it to the changes in cost that are incurred. In Figure 3-9 we can trace the least-cost combinations of

FIGURE 3-9

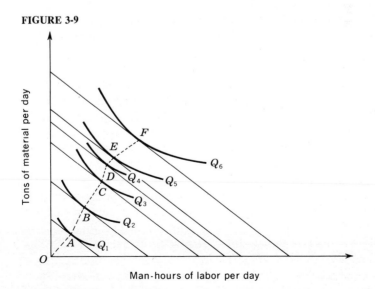

man-hours and material at the first site given the input prices described in the previous section.

The points A through F represent the least-cost combinations for each of the rates of production Q_1 through Q_6 respectively. The line connecting these points, OF in Figure 3-9, is an expansion path. The cost of producing a level of output is determined by the value represented by the isocost line tangent to the appropriate isoquant. In Figure 3-10 the total cost at each rate of production is shown as the height of the curve at a given output. For example, the total cost for the rate of production Q_3 is Q_3C. The curve OF in Figure 3-10 traces the total costs at all the alternative rates of production.

In Figure 3-10, total cost is zero when the rate of production is zero. This would not always be the case. If the planning horizon of the firm is only a few years, and the questions being asked are only about output and pricing, there would be no question of building another plant. During such a period, the firm incurs fixed costs, costs incurred whether it produces or not. Economists describe this situation as the "short run." For a longer planning horizon, however, there may be a question whether the plant should be producing at all, or whether it should be producing in another place. Economists describe this situation as the "long run." The location decision is a long-run decision in which all costs are variable costs. There are no fixed costs incurred if production is completely stopped and the investment is sold. The long-run total-cost curve, such as OF in Figure 3-10, shows the least cost for achieving each rate of production with the most efficient size of plant. There would be a separate long-run total-cost curve for each alternative site.

Total cost divided by the rate of production yields average cost.

FIGURE 3-10

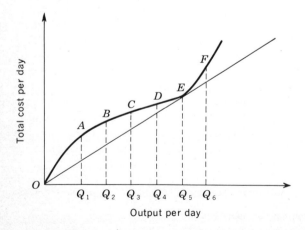

In Figure 3-10, the slope of OE is Q_5E divided by OQ_5. Since Q_5E is total cost and OQ_5 is the rate of production, the slope of OE is the average cost of producing OQ_5. In Figure 3-10, the slopes of lines from the origin to points on the cost curve decrease until OE is reached. After point OE the slopes increase. Thus, as the rate of production increases to OQ_5, average cost decreases. This is the economies of scale condition.[2] As the rate of production increases to rates greater than OQ_5, average cost increases.

Long-run average costs may increase with increased rates of production, as they do in Figure 3-10 for rates of production greater than OQ_5, mainly because of limitations in flexibility, adaptability, and managerial capacity. Flexibility and adaptability are lost in very large operations. Furthermore, some operations require rapid changes in rates of production or in product (to meet changes in seasonal demand and in tastes of the consumer), so that these diseconomies occur with relatively small size. For example, high-style clothing could not be mass-produced. On the other hand, the production of cloth can utilize larger and less flexible facilities because the demands for the basic product do not change rapidly either in kind or in quantity. In any operation managerial capacity becomes less efficient with greater rates of production because the coordination of all activities becomes more difficult. The elaborate forms of coordination required may cause average costs to rise.

RECEIPTS AND LOCATION

Cost information is insufficient to determine the most profitable rate of production or the most profitable site. The potential receipts of the plant at each site and for each rate of production are needed. Total receipts are price per unit times the total quantity sold. The total quantity sold depends on the number of customers and the quantity each customer purchases. The number of customers and the quantity each customer purchases depend on their incomes and taste, the prices of other commodities and the price of the product in question, and the distance between the customer and the seller.

Consider the quantity of a product one consumer will purchase as its price varies. None of the other factors are assumed to vary. During any specified time period the quantity demanded by the consumer would be more if the price were lower and would be less if the price

[2]For further elaboration on economies of scale and the diseconomies of the next paragraph, see E. A. G. Robinson, *The Structure of Competitive Industry* (Chicago: The University of Chicago Press, 1958).

were higher. One reason is that a lower price increases the real income of the consumer. He can buy everything he had purchased before and still have income left for other expenditures. Another reason is that if the price of the product is lower and all other prices remain the same, as assumed, the product in question is more attractive and the consumer will reduce purchases of some other items in his budget in order to buy more of the product. This relation between the quantity demanded and the price of a good is the demand for a product. An illustrative demand curve XY is drawn in Figure 3-11. In this figure the curve is assumed to be linear. The line XY traces the quantity demanded by an individual consumer per unit of time for alternative prices. For example, if the price were OP, the consumer would purchace OQ units per day; if the price were OR, the consumer would purchase OS units per day.

The farther a consumer is from the point of sale, the less he will purchase at a given price. If the price were OP, and the consumer were adjacent to the producer, he would purchase OQ units per day. If the price were OP, and he were k miles from the producer, he might only purchase OU units per day. The price to him would no longer be OP, but OP plus the transportation cost of moving the product from the producer. If the cost of transportation were T per unit per mile, the price to the consumer would be $OP + kT$, and the quantity that he would demand would be OU, as stated. On the other hand, if the producer pays the transportation cost of shipping the product to the

FIGURE 3-11

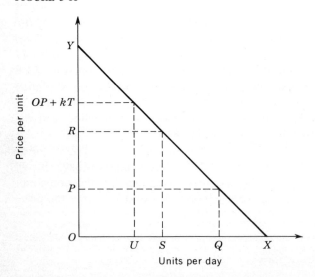

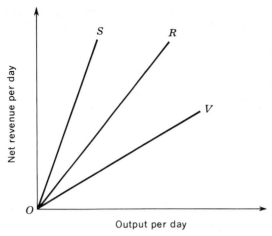

FIGURE 3-12

consumer, the price he receives is $OP - kT$, and the consumer purchases OQ units of the product.

A useful distinction can be made between enterprises that sell to a geographically dispersed market and those that sell to one centrally located market.[3] Manufacturers, retailers, and local service enterprises tend to sell to consumers dispersed throughout a geographic area. Farmers and mining enterprises tend to sell their products in one central market. Those enterprises selling to consumers in a spatial market tend to have control of their price because of their isolation from other competitors. For the present assume that these enterprises establish prices at the plant and each consumer pays this price plus the transportation cost of shipping the product from the seller to buyer.[4] An enterprise that sells to one central market is forced to accept the market price of its product because it is one of many sellers in the same market. The net price that it receives is the price at the market less the transportation cost of shipping the product from seller to market.

Analysis of receipts in the latter case is simpler. To the producer the net price will be the same no matter how great is the rate of production. Therefore, total receipts will increase proportionately with the rate of production. The relation between total receipts or revenues and the rate of production is the net-revenue line, illustrated by line

[3]August Lösch, *The Economics of Location* (New Haven, Conn.: Yale University Press, 1954), pp. 63–66.
[4]The student versed in price theory should wonder why the monopolist does not split the burden of the transportation cost with the consumer. Because price discrimination is complex to handle, and because it would not contribute much to the essential problem of the individual producer's location, it is neglected here.

OR in Figure 3-12. If the production site were shifted to a different location, the producer's net-revenue line would rotate up or down depending on whether the alternative site were closer to or farther from the market. For example, a site closer to the market would cause the net price to be higher because the transportation cost to market would be less, and the net-revenue line would rotate upward to OS. A site farther from the market would cause the net price to be lower because the transportation cost to market would be more, and the net revenue line would rotate downward to OV.

The relationship between revenue and the rate of production for the enterprise with a spatial market is more complicated because price and the extent of the market are also related to the rate of production. Assume that consumers are uniformly distributed spatially, say one per acre, that each consumer has the same taste and income, and that each consumer has the same demand, as represented by line XY in Figure 3-11. With these conditions, the quantity of product demanded by each consumer would depend on the price of the product at the plant and the distance the consumer was from the plant. This relation can be made more explicit. If the price at the plant were OP, the consumers adjacent to the plant would purchase OQ units per day. As demonstrated in Figure 3-11, customers farther from the plant would demand less because the transportation cost would be increased. At the distance where $OP + kT$ was equal to OY, consumers would purchase no units.

The total quantity demanded from the producer for any price, say OP, can be best illustrated by the demand cone, as in Figure 3-13.[5] The two lines EF and GD intersect at O on a plane to represent the north-south and east-west directions of geographic space. OQ is the quantity of the product that is demanded by the consumer adjacent to the plant. Consumers farther from the plant demand less per day: OU units per day by the consumer k miles from the plant. At location D, the consumer would purchase none of the product. If transportation is equally difficult in every direction from the plant, the quantity demanded by consumers at alternative distances from O will be the same in every direction as in the easterly direction. Thus, the triangle OQD can be revolved on the axis OQ to generate a cone. The height of the surface at any point shows the quantity demanded by the consumer at that location, given that the plant is at O, that the price at the plant is OP, and that the transportation cost is T per unit per mile. With uniform population density, the quantity of output that would be sold is the volume of the cone times the population density. The total revenue received would be price, OP, times the quantity demanded.

There is a different demand cone for every price established at

[5]Lösch, op. cit., pp. 105–108.

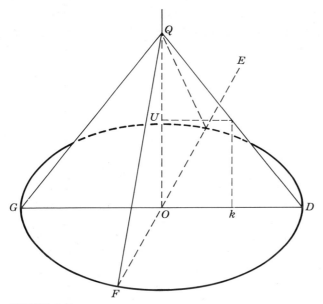

FIGURE 3-13

the plant. If the price at the plant were greater than OP, fewer units per day would be demanded adjacent to the plant. The height and base of the cone would be smaller, and the volume would be less. Thus, with an increase in price the total quantity demanded would decrease. If the price at the plant were less than OP, more units per day would be demanded adjacent to the plant. Demand would vanish farther from the plant. The height and base of the cone would be larger, and the volume would also be greater. Thus, with a decrease in price the total quantity demanded would increase.

For each rate of production, then, there is one price at the plant at which the total output level can be sold. Assume that a price is established such that the output of each period is sold during that period, so that the number of units produced equals the number of units sold. Low rates of production are associated with high prices, and high rates of production are associated with low prices. Whether revenues will be higher as the rate of production is increased depends on whether the percentage increase in production is greater than the percentage decrease in price necessary to sell the greater output. The total-revenue curve OR in Figure 3-14 shows one possible relation between revenue and rate of production. In this example, percentage decreases in price are less than percentage increases in production as the rate of production increases to OQ_6 units per day, and revenues increase. As the rate of production increases beyond OQ_6 units per day, however, percentage decreases in price are greater than percentage increases in production, and revenues decrease.

The responsiveness of changes in the quantity demanded by consumers to changes in price is measured by the elasticity of demand. Elasticity is simply the percentage change in demand divided by the percentage change in price causing the change in demand. Thus, if the elasticity is greater than one, revenues will rise, as from O to Q_6 in Figure 3-14. If the elasticity is one, revenues will be unchanged, as at output OQ_6 per day. If the elasticity is less than one, revenues will decrease, as for production rates beyond Q_6 in Figure 3-14.

Instead of assuming that consumers are evenly distributed over geographic space, it would be more realistic to assume that they are more densely distributed around some site O, and that their density decreases with distance from that site. If the plant should be located at O, the demand cone would be the same as in Figure 3-13. The total quantity demanded, however, would be different. The quantity demanded by each consumer must be multiplied by the number of consumers at a particular location to arrive at the total quantity demanded at each location. Summing these quantities over all locations would yield the total quantity demanded at any particular price. Total revenue would be the product of price and quantity, such as OR in Figure 3-14.

If, however, the plant should be located some distance from O, the demand cone at each price would be the same, but the total quantity demanded would be less. Consider Figure 3-15. This figure is a cross section of the situation. Site O is the center of density of population on

FIGURE 3-14

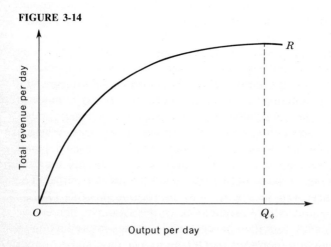

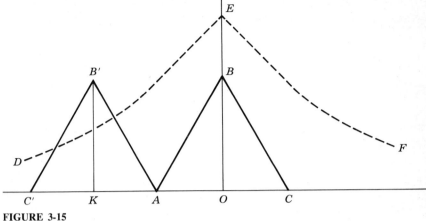

FIGURE 3-15

the plain. Curve *DEF* plots the density of population at each place along a straight line in the plain running through *O*. The triangle *ABC* is a cross section of the demand cone (given a particular price) for a plant located at site *O*. The height of line *AB*, for example, shows the quantity demanded per person at each place along line *AO*. To calculate the quantity demanded from the firm at the given price it is necessary to multiply the quantity demanded per person by the number of persons at each site in the market area. As a plant site at alternative locations is considered, such as site *K* in Figure 3-15, the demand cone is shifted to *C'B'A*. It is the same as *ABC* with the same plant price. The quantity demanded per person at given distances from *K* is the same as at the same given distances from *O*. In the market around *K* the number of persons at each site, however, is less than in the market around *O*. Thus, the total quantity demanded is less than in *O*'s market at the same price. If the plant price at *K* were reduced so that the demand cone was higher and included a larger area, the market would eventually be large enough that when quantity demanded per person times density was summed over the entire market the total quantity demanded from the firm would equal that of the market at *O* at the original price. Thus, it takes a lower price to sell a given rate of production at sites away from *O* than at *O*. If the price necessary to sell a given rate of production were lower at such sites as *K*, then the total revenue at each rate of production would be less, and the total-revenue schedule, such as *OR* in Figure 3-14, would shift downward as alternative sites away from the center of density were considered.

Thus, if markets were uniformly dense and unlimited in areal extent, revenues would remain unchanged with changes in plant location, but if markets were not uniformly dense, revenues would decrease as the plant was located farther from the market center.

CONDITIONS FOR OPTIMUM LOCATION

There would be no location problem if consumers were evenly distributed over geographic space, and if input prices were invariant with location. Neither the revenue curve nor the cost curve would shift with changes in plant site. Thus, the firm's problem would simply be finding any site isolated from competitors and establishing the price and the rate of production that would maximize profits. In Figure 3-16, OR is the total-revenue curve, and OC is the total-cost curve. The firm would maximize profits at the rate of production (OQ units per day) and its associated price that would make the difference between total revenue and cost greatest.

As some variables of the analysis are allowed to vary between sites, location does become a problem. For example, if consumers were unevenly distributed over geographic space, the revenue curve would shift down as the plant site was moved from the center of density. If input prices were everywhere the same, the most profitable plant site would be at the center of density of the market, since revenues at every rate of production would be higher. The rate of production and the price at which it could be sold would be established as before.

A more complicated case will illustrate the integration of minimum cost, economies of scale, and demand in the location decision

FIGURE 3-16

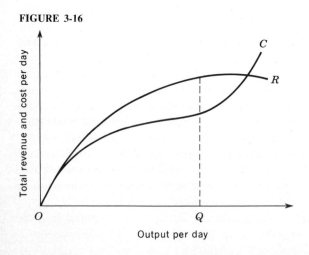

Output per day

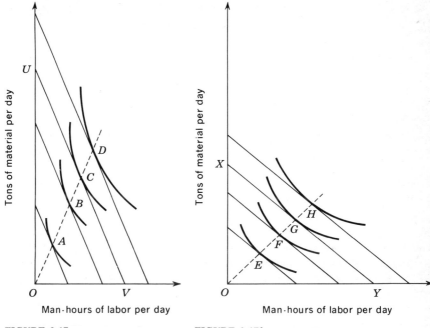

FIGURE 3-17a   **FIGURE 3-17b**

when input prices, scale, and revenues all vary between sites.[6] Assume that a production process requires two inputs: a raw material
found at location M and man-hours of labor. There is an adequate number of workers and they are equally productive at both the raw material
site and the center of density of the market. Nevertheless, the price of
labor is less at the center because the commuting cost of workers to
the plant is less. Materials cost less at the material site than at the
market because the firm would not have to pay the transport cost of
the material from the material site to the market.

In Figure 3-17a the isocost lines, such as UV, indicate the combinations of labor and materials that can be purchased for a given
outlay at the material site. In Figure 3-17b the isocost lines, such as
XY, indicate the combinations of labor and materials that can be purchased for the same given outlays at the market site. Assume that UV
and XY represent the same outlay. The slopes of the two lines are
different because the input prices are different at the two sites. The
slope is steeper at the material site because materials cost less relative

[6]The analysis for this case is essentially from Leon Moses, "Location and the
Theory of Production," *Quarterly Journal of Economics,* 72 (May, 1958), pp. 259–272.

to labor than at the market center. If all a given outlay were spent on material, for example, OU tons could be purchased at the material site and only OX tons could be purchased at the market site, since the price per ton was less at the material site. In the same way, if all a given outlay were spent on labor, OV man-hours could be purchased at the material site and a greater number of man-hours, OY, could be purchased at the market. $ABCD$ shows the expansion path of least-cost combinations at the material site; $EFGH$ shows the expansion path of least-cost combinations at the market site.

These two graphs, however, do not show directly which of the two sites represents the least-cost site for various rates of production. Therefore, in Figure 3-18, the isocost lines for both the material and the market site are shown. Once again, UV and XY are isocost lines for the same outlay at the material and market sites. For combinations of inputs above Z a greater rate of production can be reached along UZ than along XZ for the same outlay of money. For combinations of inputs below Z a greater rate of production can be reached along ZY than along ZV for the same outlay of money. Therefore, the relevant

FIGURE 3-18

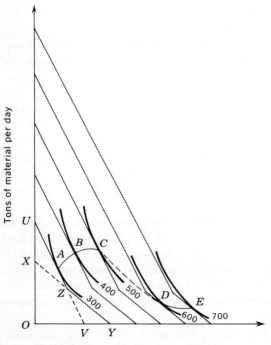

Man-hours of labor per day

segments of each isocost line are UZ and ZY; XZ and ZV will be disregarded in the rest of the analysis.

The least-cost combinations of inputs are the quantities represented by the coordinates of the point at which the isoquant is just tangent to the isocost lines UZY. Since each segment of the isocost lines is associated with a particular site, the site at which a given rate of output can be produced for the least cost is simultaneously determined. In Figure 3-18, for rates of production of 300 to 500 units per day, the least-cost combinations of inputs are located at the material site because the tangencies between the isoquants and isocost lines at A, B, and C are on the UZ segment of the isocost lines that are associated with the relative input prices at the material site. For rates of production above 500 units per day the least-cost combinations of inputs are located at the market site because the tangencies between the isoquants and isocost lines at D and E are on the ZY segment of the isocost lines that are associated with the relative input prices at the market site.

The curvature of the isoquants and the slopes of the isocost lines present two concave surfaces. When the isocost line is a straight line, only one tangency to each isoquant is possible. The similar concavity of the two lines in this case with two sites creates the possibility of two tangencies. If two tangencies should occur, one on each segment of the isocost lines, then that rate of output could be produced for the same cost at both sites. Notice, however, that the least-cost combinations of inputs would be different at the two sites. For example, if the isoquant 300 had been tangent to both UZ and ZY, production would have cost the same at both sites, but more material and less labor would have been used at the material site than at the market site. It is easy to see why. Materials cost less and labor more at the material site than at the market site.

These least-cost solutions determine the least-cost combinations of inputs for each rate of production at each site and at which site costs would be least for each rate of production. Since the actual site depends on profitability, not least cost, the next step is to combine cost with revenues.

In Figure 3-19, TR_p shows the total-revenue curve for the plant, if it were located at the center of density of the market. As noted before, if the density of buyers decreases with distance from some place, the revenue curve will shift downward as the plant is moved from this center because transportation costs increase to consumers. Thus, TR_m, which shows the revenue curve for the plant if it were located at the material site, is lower than TR_p. TC_p is the total-cost curve for the plant if it were located at the market; TC_m is the total-cost curve for the plant if it were located at the material site. For rates

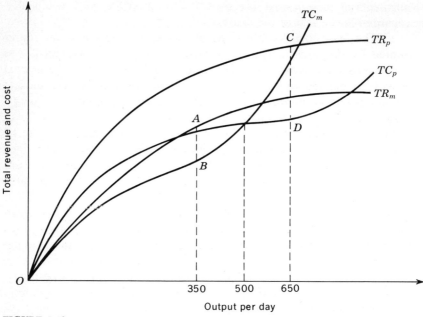

FIGURE 3-19

of production less than 500 units, total cost is less at the material site; for rates of production greater than 500 units, total cost is less at the center of density of the market. This information comes from the isoquant and isocost curves in Figure 3-18.

Subtracting total cost TC_m from total revenue TR_m at the material site at each rate of production reveals that an output of 350 units per day will yield the greatest difference AB. At the market site the greatest difference CD occurs with the rate of production of 650 units per day. Since CD represents a greater profit than AB, the plant would locate at the market. The firm, of course, would have to set the price implied by the revenue curve to sell this rate of production. The most profitable site and rate of production are at the least-cost site in this case, but that would not necessarily be true for every case. The most profitable site might be one at which both costs and revenues were higher and the difference was also higher than at other sites.

So far, the integration of input price, scale, and revenues to determine maximum-profit sites and rates of production has been illustrated with the spatial monopoly case. The same analytical tools can be used to show the most profitable location for a competitive firm selling in a single central market. There are, however, a few differences. The firm must accept the market price since it is unable to influence it, so that revenues are proportional to the rate of production and the revenue curve is a straight line. The net-revenue line would rotate down as sites farther from the market were considered because the firm would have to pay greater transportation costs to ship the product to market. The input prices that would differ at alternative sites would more likely be rents for land than either wages or material prices. Otherwise, the analysis of costs and revenues would proceed in the same way and the maximum-profit site and rate of production would be determined in the same way as in the spatial monopoly case.

UNCERTAINTY

As has already been noted, the plant location decision is a long-run decision, an investment decision. The theoretical determination of the profit-maximizing site assumes that the entrepreneur has perfect foresight: that he can predict the future receipts and costs at each site. The revenues and costs in the previous analysis are the expected receipts and costs that would change in each time period. The receipts and costs have been translated into the equivalent constant receipts and costs per unit time. Nevertheless, the future is so much an unknown that in this case it cannot be treated using probability theory.[7] Thus, the analysis, as stated under the maximizing-profit section, is a tool to use in predicting location patterns, not the behavior of a particular entrepreneur, who may have different goals, or a different assessment of the future course of events.

SUMMARY

By reviewing the analysis to see what factors might change the optimum location, we can find those which are important in determining the site at which the plant maximizes profits. The prices of the inputs and the transportation cost of the inputs to the site of production determine the position of the isocost lines. The least-cost combination depends upon the isocost lines and the production function. Total revenues depend upon the individual consumer demands, transportation costs, and the distance of the plant from the market. These are the basic determinants of the optimum location. No one factor alone is responsible for a particular location, but the combination of all factors determines the location of each plant.

[7]Frank Knight, *Risk, Uncertainty, and Profit* (New York: Harper & Row, 1965, copyright 1921), pp. 197–232.

CHAPTER **4**

URBAN
LAND USE

In the last chapter we explored the existence, location, growth, and size distribution of cities. To complete the spatial analysis of urban places we will explore the internal arrangement of activity within each city. Since the occupancy of each site is determined by that use which can pay the highest price, the chapter will begin with a discussion of the determinants of property values. The possibility for a simple explanation of systematic land-use patterns will be explored with the aid of a single-center land-use model. From this model we will be able to explain the general pattern of land values in a city, the relative location of high- and low-income families, and the population density at alternative distances from the center. The model will be used to explain the trends in suburbanization during the last one hundred years in the United States. Such models do not, however, take account of the lack of competition in real-property markets, the durability of real property, and the interdependencies of demand in these markets. The last section of the chapter will explore these issues.

URBAN PROPERTY VALUES[1]

The first point to understand is that prices for property are really exchanges of money for the rights to the use of the property. The rights to use may be constrained by building codes, zoning laws, and other applications of the police power of the local government. Building codes often determine the materials that can be used in buildings, and zoning laws regulate the types of use to which sites can be put. Often there are also occupancy laws regulating the number of people that can live in certain size units. These regulations come under the police power of local government that permits regulation for the general welfare. Building codes, for example, were originally thought necessary to prevent fire and health hazards. In addition to being subject to regulation, however, property owners and renters are entitled to participate in governmental affairs and receive public goods and services such as schooling, police protection, and park use rights as part of the package of rights in real property.

If you are renting an apartment or leasing office space, it is obvious that the price you pay is for the right to the use of property for a particular period of time, subject to other constraints imposed by the landlord. But even when you purchase a house you are purchasing rights. Obviously you have more rights if you own rather than rent, including the right to resell or rent the property. There may, however, be financial constraints imposed if you borrow to buy the property.

There are two prices for the rights to any property—a ceiling price and a floor price. The ceiling price is the maximum that a buyer will pay for a particular right. The floor price is the minimum that the holder will take to give up his rights. The actual selling price for any right must lie between these prices as long as the ceiling price is higher—otherwise no exchange will take place.

The ceiling price is the present discounted value of the earnings expected from use of the property.

$$V = \sum_{i=1}^{n} \left[\frac{-C_i}{(1+r)^i} + \frac{(R_i - O_i)}{(1+r)^i} \right]$$

where $V =$ ceiling price of property.
   $n =$ life of property, or investment period within which capital is to be recaptured.
   $R_i =$ receipts, which include rents received and expected value of property when sold in n years.

[1]The material in this section is derived from Ralph Turvey, *The Economics of Real Property* (London: G. Allen, 1957), chap. 2.

O_i = maintenance costs, taxes, insurance, and provision of services. Depreciation is not included.

C_i = cost of construction or demolition and redevelopment

r = the opportunity cost of capital, the rate of return on alternative, equally risky investments.

An illustration may help explain the formula. Consider the following case. It takes one year to build an improvement, and all payments for its construction are made at the end of the first year. Construction costs $100,000. Annual receipts from rental will be $40,000 and operating costs including maintenance, insurance, and taxes will be $30,000. The opportunity cost of capital is 6 percent. The above figures, of course, are expected values, and are expected to remain the same over the forty-year life of the building. No scrap value is expected.

$$V = -\frac{100,000}{(1.06)} + \frac{10,000}{(1.06)^2} + \frac{10,000}{(1.06)^3} + \cdots \frac{10,000}{(1.06)^{40}}$$

$$= -94,300 + 140,570$$

$$= \$46,270$$

The ceiling price is the maximum amount that the investor would be willing to pay for the bare site. If there were a building already on it, he would have to include, in the cost of construction, the cost of demolishing the old building and preparing the site for constructing the new building. If a building desired by the buyer was already on the site and suitable for use, then the ceiling price would be for the rights in the property and the cost of construction would be zero. The floor price is determined in the same way, except that it includes the cost of moving from the site plus the present value of alternative properties that will serve the purpose of the present occupant of the property.

If the site is bare or is to be redeveloped, we still need to determine the outlay on building and other investment. While we have discussed these questions separately, it is obvious that construction outlay and ceiling price are actually determined simultaneously. The outlay will depend on the marginal product of capital. This can be seen in the following way. Fix the size of the site. Then increase the outlay on the building. This outlay could be for increasing coverage of the lot or for adding stories. Eventually diminishing returns will occur. By adding an additional story, additional receipts can be earned, but the additional costs may be greater. At least the percentage of net return declines with the increase in outlay.

This can be illustrated by comparing the change in V with the increasing amount of outlay for building improvement. Consider an additional floor in the building. The change in ceiling price would be as follows:

$$\Delta V = \sum_{i=1}^{n} \left[-\frac{\Delta C_i}{(1+r)^i} + \frac{(\Delta R_i - \Delta O_i)}{(1+r)^i} \right]$$

where ΔV = change in ceiling price of property
          n = life of property
        ΔR_i = change in expected receipts from adding one floor
        ΔO_i = change in maintenance costs, taxes, insurance, and provision of services
        ΔC_i = additional outlay being considered
          r = opportunity cost of capital

If ΔV is positive or zero, then the additional outlay will be undertaken. If ΔV is negative, the additional outlay should not be undertaken because it yields less return than alternative investments.

Since we have presented the factors affecting the ceiling and floor prices for a property as an investment problem, it would seem that we have omitted residential choice questions. Residential choice, however, can be presented within a similar but modified investment framework. In the case of residential choice, the buyer would not receive an explicit income. He would receive an implicit income which could be measured by the cost of renting a comparable housing unit from someone else. Whether an investment or residential choice is being made, the implicit or explicit income depends on the bundle of characteristics associated with the property.

In the case of residential choice, the bundle of characteristics includes the physical characteristics of the house, the size of the lot, accessibility to jobs, church, school, shopping, and other activities of the family, amenities (a good view, no pollution), public services, utilities, and taxes, as well as the demographic characteristics of the families on adjacent sites. Accessibility is the key.

Accessibility is also the key to the income that can be generated from commercial and industrial sites. Retail shops will have higher present values if they are in the center of a transportation network of a trade area that includes the people to whom they wish to sell. We could, for this purpose, treat personal services, doctors, bankers, etc., as retailers. Some stores, such as auto dealerships and furniture or appliance stores, increase in value when they are adjacent to other similar stores. The reason is that the products are relatively high in value and consumers can save by comparison shopping. Groups of stores adjacent to each other save travel costs to the consumer.

The present value of sites for manufacturing plants is higher when they are accessible to the local labor market, adjacent to the port, rail facilities, or other transportation mode connecting the city with the firm's markets, or adjacent to a local buyer. The need for accessibility to consultants, legal skills, advertising, and financial experts can be accommodated by splitting the firm into manufacturing and headquarters locations. Each function would be located at its most appropriate site.

The headquarters function is similar to all kinds of administrative, financial, and other office services. The present value of sites for these uses is highest for bundles of characteristics that include accessibility to office worker residential areas, to consultants and customers, and to each other. General accessibility is most important for these uses.

In any economic analysis, it is important to determine how changes in various parameters will affect the results. This is perhaps the most important part of any equilibrium solution. In this case the present value of a site, or the ceiling price, is influenced by changes in expectations about receipts, operating costs, the opportunity cost of capital, and construction costs. Ceiling price will rise if expected receipts rise, operating costs decrease, construction costs fall, or the opportunity cost of capital decreases. Ceiling price will decline if expected receipts fall, operating costs rise, construction costs rise, or if the opportunity cost of capital increases.

There are sales, however, which are not voluntary sales. Prices paid through involuntary sales are likely to be higher or lower than those determined by voluntary buyers and sellers. Lower sales prices are likely to occur in transactions between relatives. Taking property for public use under eminent domain is also considered an involuntary sale.

As we indicated at the beginning of this section, prices for property are really prices for rights in property. There may be many rights in the same property: mineral rights, occupancy rights, rights to land rent. If the value of the property were greater as a whole than the sum of the rights, then it would be profitable to combine them in one ownership. The value of the single ownership, however, cannot fall below the value of the sum of the values of profitable combinations of rights because the single owner can always sell it and lease it back, lease the property right, or mortgage it.

There is a special division of rights that has been often attempted for economic analysis. Many writers divide the total value of the property into building and land value. The division is not useful except for static long-run equilibrium analysis. The argument can be seen using observable values:

where P = market price of a building and site
R = replacement cost of building

P' = market price of property if building were new and represented the best use of the site
C = construction cost of building for best use
$V = P' - C$ = market value of site = land value

If V is greater than P by more than demolition costs, then new construction on a site will occur. If P is greater than V, the difference will
just compensate a building owner for removing the building, but the
difference will not be equal to the replacement cost of building except
when $P = P'$. An alternative division might be to divide the property
price into replacement cost and land value. But subtraction of replacement cost from property price would not equal site value except
under the circumstance when

$$P - R = P' - C = V$$

This condition would hold when the use of the site is the most profitable one ($P = P'$) and the building is new ($C = R$). Thus, total property
value can be divided into land and building values only for new buildings in optimal locations. Land or site value of the best use, however,
can be determined separately from the total value of current real
property on the site. It is the present value of the best use (P') less
construction cost of that building (C). Land value is important for many
real-property decisions.

We have now developed the ceiling and floor price of property
rights, including the additions to structures. We have noted how
accessibility plays a key role in estimating expected receipts when
determining ceiling prices. Other factors were the interest rate and
construction costs. We have also noted the way to estimate land value.
Now, we need to put these pieces together to understand market price.

For a particular urban area, divide the area into land parcels, or
sites, on which there may or may not be buildings. Each user would be
able to indicate a ceiling price for each and every parcel. Occupants,
of course, would have floor prices, but would also bid ceiling prices
on all other parcels. Those users bidding the highest price for a parcel
would obtain it. If parcels change hands, the exchange is a result of a
transaction between individuals and will only occur if the buyer believes that he is gaining more than the money given up, and the seller
believes that he is gaining more in price than the expected value of
holding ownership on the parcel. Thus, although the language used in
explaining the market appears to discuss only demand, there are supply
prices—the floor prices of those occupying parcels and the ceiling
prices of all bidding on the parcel are all opportunity costs to the
eventual owner of a parcel.

One way of envisioning the urban-property market is to draw up a table listing parcels of property across the top as headings to each column, as in Table 4-1. The rows are labeled for each of the bidders on property. Across each row we could insert the ceiling prices that each user, say user one in row one, would bid for each parcel in the area during some specified time period. If the user occupies a site, the bid on that site will be a floor price. Floor prices are shown in parentheses in the table. The highest relevant bid on each parcel is indicated by an underline. For example, user one in this time period occupies parcel six for which his floor price is $7, while that same user would be willing to pay a ceiling price of $10 on parcel five. Since the current occupant is user eight and his floor price is $5 and he will be willing to pay a ceiling price of $10 for parcel six, the two will benefit from exchanging places.

Occupants in parcels two, three, and four have floor prices that prevent anyone else from buying those sites in this time period. Users five, six, and seven, however, would be better off with a three-way trade. User five occupies parcel eight, but will be the highest bidder on parcel one, and user seven will be the highest bidder on parcel seven. User six, like the poor, gets what is left over. Parcel seven is bid away, and user six has the highest bid on parcel eight. Why should that be, since user eight's ceiling price is only $3, which is obviously less than many other bids on that parcel? The reason is that the higher bids on parcel eight are made by persons with still higher bids on other parcels for which theirs was the highest bid. Thus $3 is the highest relevant bid. Parcels three and four are not occupied by the highest bidder for the same reason.

The final market prices are the highest relevant bids on each

Table 4-1 Demand Matrix of Price Bids, Urban Property Market*

Users	Parcels							
	1	2	3	4	5	6	7	8
1	$5	$2	$1	$4	$10	$(7)	$1	$2
2	9	5	(7)	4	8	7	2	6
3	8	(10)	3	9	1	6	4	3
4	3	5	6	(8)	4	1	4	7
5	10	3	6	2	5	3	8	(7)
6	5	2	1	4	4	5	(3)	3
7	(5)	7	6	6	2	8	10	4
8	6	2	8	1	(5)	10	2	9

*Parentheses indicate floor prices by occupant of parcel. Underlined prices are the highest prices offered for a parcel and indicate the market price.

parcel, since everyone would be better off if he made the trades indicated. Thus, the underlined prices in Table 4-1 are the resulting market prices in this time period.

If in subsequent time periods conditions changed, property would change hands again. So far, we have not discussed any possible systematic spatial configurations of use or the impact of durability or interdependency of demand on the resulting market prices and allocation of parcels. We will take these questions up in the subsequent sections of this chapter.

SPATIAL PATTERN OF LAND USE

There have been many attempts to derive general theories of the spatial distribution of land uses in a metropolitan area. None have really been very successful. Early theories have been descriptions rather than explanations. The first was the concentric-zone theory.[2] The city is pictured as a circle with the central business district at the center. In the first ring around the CBD are light manufacturing and warehousing industries. The next ring is for workingmen's houses. There is a ring for upper-income families. Finally, there is a ring for satellite towns. The concentric-zone theory is not really a theory, but more of a broad description of land-use patterns in many cities. Actually, modern spatial equilibrium models lead to the concentric land-use pattern, but the equilibrium models do provide for analysis of change resulting from changes in transportation costs, population, and other model parameters that the concentric-zone theory does not provide.

Another model used in describing land uses in metropolitan areas was Homer Hoyt's sector theory.[3] This too is more a description than a theory. Hoyt made a study of census records in the 1930s and found that sections of a city tend to be wedge-shaped like pieces of a pie. One section includes wealthier families. This high-income sector is usually away from the dust and dirt of the city and located on high ground or with an attractive view, such as of a lake. On either side are wedges or sectors occupied by middle-income families. Industry occupies the sites along rivers and railroad spurs. The central business district includes offices and shopping that require general access to

[2]Chauncy D. Harris and Edward L. Ullman, "The Nature of Cities," in Paul K. Hatt and Albert J. Reiss, eds., *Cities and Society: The Revised Reader in Urban Sociology* (New York: Free Press, 1957), pp. 237–247.

[3]Homer Hoyt, *The Structure and Growth of Residential Neighborhoods in American Cities*, U.S. Federal Housing Administration (Washington, D.C.: U.S. Government Printing Office, 1939). See also Richard M. Hurd, *The Principles of City Land Values* (New York: The Record and Guide, 1924).

the whole city. Finally, the poor occupy the housing in the areas that are left. The wedge-shaped sectors are a result of looking at the pattern at a point of time after development has taken place for many years. An income group is continually moving outward over time; the point of the pie-shaped wedge is the oldest part; and the arc is the leading edge of development. Hoyt presented his theory as a substitute for the concentric-zone theory.

Harris and Ullman developed a different view of uses within the city. Their view was called the multiple-nuclei theory.[4] Instead of describing the city as centered on one focus, they argued that the city has many centers. Uses are attracted to each other or repelled by each other. Once a dominant use develops, other uses arrange themselves around it if they are attracted to it. For example, a university attracts book stores, housing for students, taverns, cultural activities, etc. Other uses would be nuisances in such a district. Notice, however, that this approach does not consider the kind of problems arising when repulsion or attraction are not mutual. The stockyards are an example of an activity that is not attractive to the uses surrounding the university, but there would be no particular reason for the stockyards not to locate near a university if land and transport facilities were available. The theory is merely a description of land-use patterns; it has no predictive power. In fact, the notions of attracting and repelling uses are really externality arguments from economics, although they were not couched in those terms.

A Spatial Equilibrium Model of Land Use

Several spatial equilibrium models of land use in cities have been constructed in recent years.[5] In these models an equilibrium is established by assuming independent demand functions and the location of at least one use. Most models assume a given location for the central business district and assume that all production and exchange take place in that center. Residential demand depends on the trade-off between the journey-to-work costs, the price per square foot of house or land, and the prices of all other goods. The farther away from the center a family locates, the higher are their journey-to-work and shopping costs. For all families to be in equilibrium, then, the price

---

[4]Harris and Ullman, op. cit.

[5]William Alonso, *Location and Land Use* (Cambridge, Mass.: Harvard, 1964); Lowdon Wingo, *Transportation and Urban Land* (Washington, D.C.: Resources for the Future, 1961); Richard F. Muth, *Cities and Housing* (Chicago: The University of Chicago Press, 1969); and Edwin S. Mills, *Studies in the Structure of the Urban Economy*, Resources for the Future (Baltimore: Johns Hopkins, 1972).

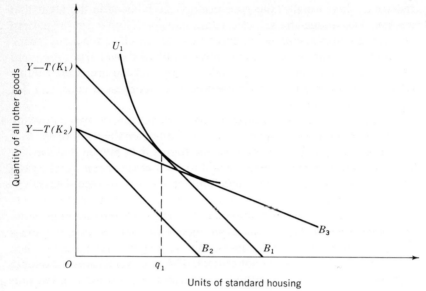

FIGURE 4-1 Consumer Choice, Housing vs. Other Goods

per square foot of house or land must decline as the travel costs increase. When house price is used, land prices are shown to decline
because they are derived from the demand for housing. The amount of
housing purchased at each distance from the center depends upon the
consumer's income and his preferences for travel, housing space, and
other goods; the price of housing; the cost of travel; and the price of
other goods.

We will illustrate more exactly only one of these models, the
Muth model of spatial equilibrium in residential housing.[6] Consider the
preferences of individuals as illustrated in Figure 4-1. At some distance from the CBD, K_1, the consumer's real income can be shown by
the budget line B_1. The budget line shows the amounts of housing and
other goods he can buy, given prices of housing and other goods and
given that his income is reduced by his commuting cost, $Y - T(K_1)$.
$T(K_1)$ is the commuting cost from K_1, and Y is his money income. The
consumer would buy q_1 units of a standard quality house in order to
maximize his utility. If we move that consumer farther from the CBD,
commuting costs increase, and real income is reduced. If the price per
unit of standard quality housing is unchanged, the budget line shifts
to B_2, and the consumer is worse off. Those consumers farther away,
who are worse off, would bid up the price of housing close in and

[6]Muth, op. cit., 21–36.

reduce the demand for housing farther out until prices in each location left consumers indifferent as to where they would live. This effect can be seen by decreasing the price of housing at K_2 in Figure 4-1 until the consumer is once again on the same indifference curve, U_1, as at K_1. The new budget line would be B_3. Since the price of housing is lower relative to other goods, the consumer will purchase more units of standard quality housing.

Muth assumes that transport costs increase at a decreasing rate so that the marginal cost of commuting decreases the farther a consumer locates from the CBD. Since the price of housing is also decreasing, Muth must assume that at any point K_1 the slope of the marginal commuting cost function must be less than the slope of the marginal housing expenditure from increasing distance 1 mile. The reason can be seen in Figure 4-2. T_k is the marginal cost of increasing commuting distance; $-qp_k$ is the marginal saving on housing caused by increasing distance from the CBD. In equilibrium the consumer has no incentive to move farther from the CBD because the marginal increase in commuter cost, T_k, is just equal to the saving in housing costs, qp_k. Remember p_k is declining with distance; q is the number of units of standard housing the consumer purchases, which is determined by taste and income level. In Figure 4-2, the consumer would not move from K_1. Closer to the CBD, qp_k is greater than T_k. The

FIGURE 4-2 Marginal Decrease in Cost of Housing vs. Marginal Increase in Transport Cost

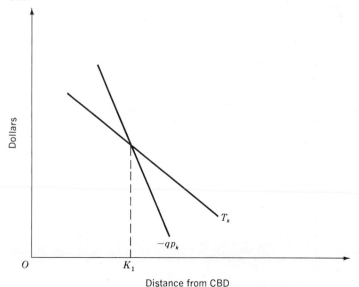

Dollars

T_k

$-qp_k$

O

K_1

Distance from CBD

increase in transportation costs is less than the gains from lower housing expenses.

Would it be possible for T_k and qp_k in Figure 4-2 to be reversed? That is, would it be possible for the marginal cost of transportation to decrease faster than the marginal savings in housing expenditure? T_k would be cut from below by the line $-qp_k$. The answer is that if it did, it would always pay for the consumer to move to the fringe of the city. Since this is not observed, it is assumed that Figure 4-2 shows the correct relation of the rate of decline of the savings and costs.

Thus, the price per unit of standard quality housing would decline with distance from the CBD. This means that the present value of returns for a given building will decline with distance from the CBD. If it costs no more to build the structure in any location, except for the land price, the ceiling price for land will decline with distance from the CBD. This assumes that the prices of materials and labor do not vary throughout the metropolitan area.

Even though land prices have been treated as a residual, they are

FIGURE 4-3 Production of Housing

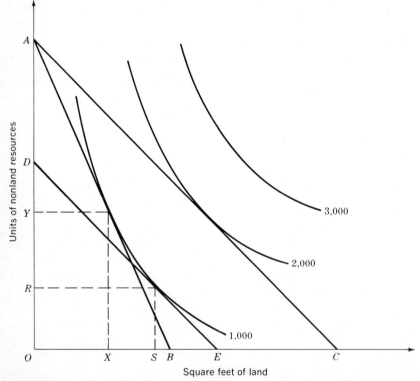

a price of a resource. As the price of land rises and falls, producers of houses and other buildings will vary the amount of land per square foot of building with the price. For example, consider the production function for building a house described by the isoquants in Figure 4-3. The isoquant labelled 1,000 represents the alternative combinations of land and nonland resources that can be used to build a 1,000 square foot house. The isoquant labelled 2,000 represents the alternative combinations that can be used to construct a 2,000 square foot house. The line AB represents a possible level of expenditure and given prices for the land and nonland resources. If the relative prices were as represented by the slope of the isocost line AB, the least cost combination of land and nonland resources would be OY units of nonland resources and OX square feet of land.

Now, suppose that the slope of AB represented land prices at the CBD. If land prices declined with distance as indicated, then the slope of the isocost line would decline too. For the same outlay, the producer could buy more land than before. Since the price of nonland resources has not changed, the isocost line AB would pivot on A to, say, AC. This shift would indicate that more house could be built for the same outlay. As indicated in the diagram, 2,000 square feet of house could be built. More importantly, however, the ratio of land to nonland resources would change. For example, to find the least-cost combination of land and nonland resources to produce the 1,000 square foot house we would have to shift the isocost line parallel until it was tangent to the isoquant for 1,000. The least-cost combination would then be OR units of nonland resources and OS square feet of land. Thus, as land becomes cheaper, the builder is prepared to use more of it for any given size housing space. Put another way, the builder constructs high-rise apartments near the CBD, three-floor walk-ups and duplexes a little farther away, single-family houses at a still greater distance, and finally single-family housing with acre lots at the edge of the city. If there is less housing per unit of land with greater distance from the CBD, then population density will also tend to decline with distance from the CBD.

A more controversial generalization yielded by the spatial equilibrium models is that high-income families tend to live farther from the center than low-income families. The theorists have been anxious to show this, since it appears to be true for the U.S. Nevertheless, it is not so true in other countries, where the slums are often found in shanty towns at the fringe of the city rather than at the center.[7] Since time is a large cost in commuting, one would expect travel costs to

[7]Charles J. Stokes, "A Theory of Slums," *Land Economics*, 38 (August 1962) pp. 187–197.

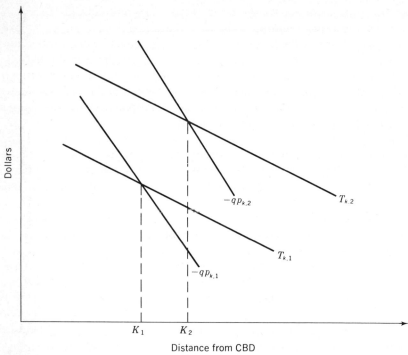

FIGURE 4-4 Marginal Decrease in Housing Cost vs. Marginal Increase in Transport Cost for Poor (*1*) and Rich (*2*)

be higher for high-income families than low-income families. If that were true, high-income families would tend to occupy land near the center, rather than the outskirts. The explanation resolving this paradox is that high-income families apparently have a greater demand for space than for decreased travel time. That is, the value of commuting time as a function of income is proportional to increases in income, but the value of space as a function of income increases more than proportionally to increases in income.[8] Therefore, higher-income families would tend to live farther from the center than lower-income families.

The point may be made clearer by reference to Figure 4-4, which is similar in construction to Figure 4-2. A consumer with a higher income would buy more housing (more *q*) and would have a higher commuting cost, even if he located at the same distance from the CBD as a lower-income family. This is because his high income allows him to buy more of all goods, including housing, and because commuter

[8]Muth, op. cit., pp. 29–34, 99–100; Alonso, op. cit., pp. 108–109.

cost includes the wage value of the time lost in commuting. In Figure 4-4, $T_{k,1}$ and $qp_{k,1}$ are the marginal costs and savings for the lower-income consumer. Assume he is in equilibrium at distance K_1. The higher-income family would be better off at a more distant location, so long as the upward shift in $-qp_k$ was greater than the shift in T_k. It is at this point that Muth argues that the income elasticity of housing expenditure is greater than the income elasticity of commuter cost. This is illustrated by the shift to $-qp_{k,2}$ and $T_{k,2}$. This analysis also indicates why consumers with a greater taste for housing tend to live farther from the CBD. Their savings $-qp_k$ are greater ($-qp_k$ would shift up, holding T_k fixed).

There are other reasons, however, for arguing that high-income families will tend to live in the outer areas of the metropolis. Some hypothesize that the older areas of the city are closer in, while the newer areas are farther out. Because high-income people prefer newer style housing with modern built-in appliances, they therefore live in the newer housing farther out. Another argument, which we will explore further in Chapter 9, is that the outer areas are made up of small, homogeneous suburban governmental jurisdictions in which high-income families can more closely articulate their preferences for public goods. In reality, of course, some high-income families do not have higher preferences for space than for ease of commuting and do locate in housing near the CBD. Large concentrations of such families live in Manhattan, in Chicago's near northside, and in central Philadelphia.

Any economic model is an abstraction from reality. It is hoped that hypotheses, such as those above, that land prices will decline with distance from the CBD, that the ratio of land to nonland resources will increase with distance from the CBD, and that high-income families will tend to live farther than poor families from the CBD, will be validated. The models are most useful if they can explain or predict what factors will cause changes in the above relations.

The most important factor used in analyses has been changes in transportation costs. If transportation costs per mile for commuting to and from the CBD were reduced, the price per unit of house would not have to decline so much to keep households in equilibrium, and if house prices did not fall as much per mile, land prices per square foot would not have to decline so fast. For example, consider the line AB in Figure 4-5 to be land prices per square foot at alternative distances from the CBD. With a reduction in transportation costs of commuting, the gradient AB would tend to pivot on A to AC. The reason, of course, is that sites next to the CBD without commuting costs do not have to change in price. Nonetheless, if the rent gradient AC were to prevail temporarily, all of the land in a circle around the CBD from zero miles to *OC* miles away would be devoted to housing. If there had been no increase in income or change in population at the same time, too much land would be devoted to housing, and land prices would tend to fall until the land available for housing just matched that demanded at current house prices. Thus, not only might the gradient with respect to distance from the CBD become less steep, but the whole gradient could shift down to *DE* so that there would not be too much land available for housing.

So far, economists have been unable to construct a spatial equilibrium model of land use that would also determine a spatial equilibrium if jobs and stores were not fixed in location from the beginning. It is useful, though, to look at a model in which households are fixed in a central location, and in which the location of stores and industry are to be decided. In this case equilibrium is achieved by having the firm pay wages high enough to equalize wages less transportation costs to and from work. The more distant the firm from the clustered,

FIGURE 4-5 Land Price Gradients

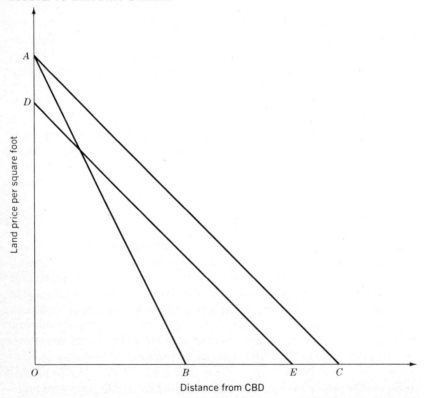

residential area, the higher the wages it would have to pay in order to attract and keep workers. In equilibrium all workers would be satisfied. There would be no incentive to switch jobs for a higher wage, because all differences would be exactly equal to differences in journey-to-work costs.[9] To equalize profits at different locations, land prices would have to decline with distance from workers, *ceteris paribus*.

In reality, of course, both effects operate. In some cases wages compensate for extra long journey-to-work costs. In other cases, residential land rents compensate for differences in such costs. Nevertheless, to the extent that one business center dominates an entire metropolitan area, there will be a tendency for land values to decline with distance from that center. The main reason is the general accessibility of the center. But that does not explain why the center was established where it was.

Thus, the spatial equilibrium models show that land prices decrease with distance from the CBD. They explain why population density also decreases with distance from the CBD, and they explain why higher-income families might locate farther from the CBD than lower-income families. The models could be used to show how these elements of urban structure would change with changes in transportation cost, per capita income, and increases in population. They have not, however, explained the location of other districts in the city: shopping and industrial districts and subsidiary office centers. This is a serious criticism, since one main problem for urban government is how much land to zone for different uses and where each zone should be located.

Furthermore, economic spatial equilibrium models of land use and land value can also be criticized for omitting the important interdependencies of demand prevalent in urban-property markets. Thus, we have no general theory of land use.

Land Prices

Since land price is more often a decision variable than an actual transaction price, as we noted in the first section of the chapter, empirical studies of the relation between land prices and distance from the CBD have been few. One example is a study by Mills using data from Hoyt's classic, *One Hundred Years of Land Values in*

[9]Leon N. Moses, "Towards a Theory of Intra-Urban Wage Differentials and Their Influence on Travel Patterns," *Papers and Proceedings of the Regional Science Association*, 8 (1962), pp. 53–63; and Albert Rees and George P. Schultz, *Workers and Wages in an Urban Labor Market* (Chicago: University of Chicago Press, 1970), p. 11.

Chicago.[10] Land values per acre were estimated for every square-mile grid in the Chicago area. Although the data may be uneven in quality, it is the only historical record available. Several equations were fitted to the data, but the consistently best fit was the logarithm of land values as a function of distance. Table 4-2 shows the results. The constant term is the logarithm of land value at the city center. It shows that the value has increased over time. The second term shows the amount by which land values decrease with each mile from the center. In each case the amount the value decreases with distance is shown to be significantly different from zero. Furthermore, there is a tendency for that term to decrease with time. These results can be explained by reference to Figure 4-5. In the early period *DE* would represent the relation between value and distance. The actual relation for Chicago is a straight line between the logarithm of value and distance. With the increase of population and the decrease in transportation costs for commuting, the price gradient was pushed up to obtain more land for housing and at the same time the gradient became less steep because commuting costs were reduced. Finally, note that the R^2 showing the percent variation of value explained by distance has decreased over time. That, too, would be expected, as the percentage of employment and shopping conducted in the CBD decreased over time.

The spatial equilibrium models do not explain employment and shopping subcenters in the metropolitan area, but they do point out that land values also decline with greater distance from these subcenters as they do from the CBD. An example is the way in which land values declined from downtown Chicago in 1928.[11] The highest land values were downtown. But if one took a north-south street and followed it south, land values would in general, decline, but there would be a relative peak every mile or half mile for a shopping area. Commercial activity would have to pay more for land than builders for residential use in order to bid the sites away from residential use.

In the past few years researchers have shown another reason for the flattening of the land-price gradient. It had always been thought that commercial and industrial firms selected a site in the city that would minimize costs, since their markets probably encompassed a wide hinterland as well as the city itself. Retailing for the local market, of course, was oriented to the best local accessibility. But inter-regional operations were more interested in the lowest cost site in the city.

[10]Edwin S. Mills, "The Value of Urban Land," in Harvey Perloff, *The Quality of the Urban Environment,* for Resources for the Future, Inc. (Baltimore: Johns Hopkins, 1969), pp. 231–253. Homer Hoyt, *One Hundred Years of Land Values in Chicago* (Chicago: University of Chicago Press, 1933).
[11]Hoyt, ibid., pp. 323–330.

Table 4-2 Chicago Historical Data

Year	Constant (log. of land prices/acre at center)	Distance (in miles)	R^2
1836	5.799	−0.3986 (−27.1104)*	.7836
1857	8.792	−0.4874 (−35.3627)*	.8597
1873	10.05	−0.330 (−22.4327)*	.7066
1910	10.84	−0.3275 (−13.2685)*	.5867
1928	11.85	−0.2184 (−11.7969)*	.4985

*The numbers in parentheses under the distance term are *t*-values.
Source: Edwin S. Mills, "The Value of Urban Land," in Harvey S. Perloff, *The Quality of the Urban Environment*, for Resources for the Future, Inc. (Baltimore, Md.: The Johns Hopkins Press, 1969), p. 247.

This was usually the place at which goods could be shipped to other metropolitan areas. It would include a port on the river, ocean or lake, or a railroad terminal. Around such a central core the city developed.[12]

Prior to the development of motor vehicles the cost of moving goods within metropolitan areas was more costly than that of moving workers from home to job.[13] Therefore, firms located near intercity terminal facilities. Even if they had to raise wages in part to pay commuter costs, that cost was less than the increased costs that would have been required to ship goods from locations closer to the workers in the residential areas, because of the high cost of shipping goods from locations within the city to the terminal facilities.

With the development of the automobile and truck, the cost of shipping goods within the metropolitan area was reduced relative to the cost of moving people from residence to job.[14] Furthermore, the truck and improved highways have also freed industry from rail and barge terminals, since overland truck transportation is cheaper for many goods than either barge or rail. Therefore, as new firms started or as existing ones decided to move, they were able to move closer to households and away from terminals because their total costs per unit of output would be reduced.

[12]Raymond L. Fales and Leon N. Moses, "Land Use Theory and the Spatial Structure of the Nineteenth-Century City," *Papers and Proceedings of the Regional Science Association*, 18 (1972), pp. 49–80.
[13]Leon Moses and Harold F. Williamson, Jr., "The Location of Economic Activity in Cities," *American Economic Review*, 57 (May 1967), pp. 211–222.
[14]Ibid.

Since jobs have become more dispersed, workers no longer inevitably journey to the downtown section of the city. The spread of workers, in turn, has meant that the activities relying on accessibility (retailing, medical services, lawyers, brokers, bankers, etc.) could now locate in dispersed locations, as the trade areas on the fringes of the city were now sufficiently large for firms undertaking these activities to break even.

Although all of these factors have led to a decrease in the extent to which land prices are related to distance from the CBD, that relationship still seems to be important. We often think of Los Angeles as the city without a center. And yet, there too, in the 1960s distance from the central business district was an important explanation of residential land values.[15]

Urban Population Density Gradients

Since land prices have been shown to decline with distance from the CBD and since the gradient has become smaller over time, we could also expect population density to decline with distance from the CBD, and furthermore, that the density gradient would become less steep over time. The reason is that as land prices decline with distance from the CBD, the ratio of land to nonland resources increases. Therefore, there are fewer housing units per square foot of land, and population density declines with distance from the CBD. As land price gradients became less steep because commuting costs declined and because industry tended to shift away from the CBD, population-density gradients would also tend to be less steep. As land price differentials decreased, the ratio of land to nonland resources at different distances from the CBD would not be as different, and population density would be more uniform.

Muth has demonstrated that the exponential density function describes the relation of population densities to distances from the city center.[16] Such a curve would look like *AB* in Figure 4-6. We will use this density function to describe changes in population densities within urban areas in the United States over time. As a result of the changes noted, we would expect the gradients to shift from curves like *AB* to curves like *CE* over the time period studied.

[15]Eugene F. Brigham, "The Determinants of Residential Land Values," *Land Economics*, 41 (November 1965), pp. 325–334. For the same point applied to all cities, see Alan R. Winger, "How Important Is Distance from the Center of the City as a Determinant of Urban Residential Land Values?" *The Appraisal Journal*, 41 (October 1973), pp. 558–565.
[16]Muth, op. cit., pp. 141–145.

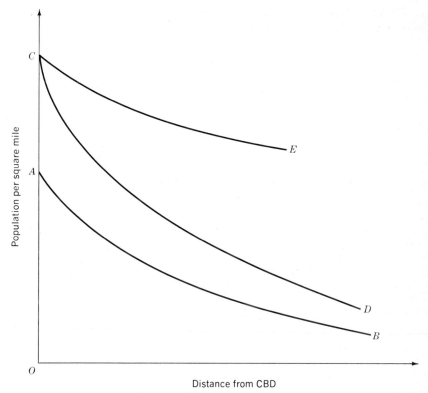

FIGURE 4-6 Population Density Gradients

The density function may be written as follows:

$$D(k) = D_o e^{-bk}$$

where $D(k)$ = population density at distance k from the city center
   D_o = density at distance O
   e = base of the natural system of logarithms 2.71828 . . .
   b = constant estimated from empirical observations
   k = distance from the city center

By differentiating $D(k)$ we find that b is the percentage by which $D(k)$ falls with increasing k.[17] The density function describes a curve that shows how population density will have to decrease with distance from the center in order that the percentage decrease from one mile to the next will be a constant. Thus, the smaller the density gradient, the

---

[17] $dD(k) = bD_o e^{-bk} dk$ $\dfrac{dD(k)}{D_o e^{-bk} dk} = b$

Table 4-3 Averages of Gradients for Population Density Functions, Four Metropolitan Areas

Year	Average gradient	Year	Average gradient
1880	1.22	1940	.59
1890	1.06	1948	.50
1900	.96	1954	.40
1910	.80	1958	.35
1920	.69	1963	.31
1930	.63		

Source: Edwin S. Mills, *Studies in the Structure of the Urban Economy*, for Resources for the Future, Inc. (Baltimore: The Johns Hopkins Press, 1972), p. 49.

more gradually population density declines with distance, and the more spread out the city will be for urban areas with the same population. Two areas of differing population could have the same density gradient, in which case the density at the center, D_o, would be greater in the larger place.[18] Population density, however, would decline by the same percentage with each mile. *CD* in Figure 4-6 would represent the larger area and *AB* would represent the smaller one.

Many estimates of the density gradient have been made for many cities and different times.[19] Estimates covering the longest time period have been made by Mills for four metropolitan areas—Baltimore, Milwaukee, Philadelphia, and Rochester.[20] Originally, Mills purposely selected eighteen metropolitan areas by the following criteria: they should be reasonably close to semicircular in shape so that central city and suburban total populations can be used to estimate the gradients; two or more large cities should not be too close to each other; and they should represent different regions of the country, different sized areas, and different historical growth rates. These eighteen areas were used to estimate population density gradients for the post–World War II period. For estimates back to 1920 Mills had only six of these metropolitan areas because of the lack of data. For estimates back to 1880 he was left with the four metropolitan areas mentioned above.

[18]Edwin S. Mills, *Urban Economics* (Glenview, Ill.: Scott, Foresman, 1972), pp. 95–97; and Edwin S. Mills, *Studies in the Structure of the Urban Economy,* for Resources for the Future, Inc. (Baltimore: Johns Hopkins, 1972), pp. 34–58.
[19]See Mills, *Studies in the Structure of the Urban Economy*, for a review of the literature.
[20]Ibid.

The estimating techniques used by Mills assumed that the density function was appropriate. He did not have data to test the fit. By assuming that the density function was appropriate he only needed information on land areas, population in the central city, and population in the outer suburban ring to estimate the gradient.[21] The averages of the estimates for the four metropolitan areas are shown in Table 4-3. Although the estimates for the density gradients are less for the post-war years for these four metropolitan areas than for the larger group of eighteen SMSAs, the trend from 1948 to 1963 is about the same. Thus, the total picture of the historical trend in suburbanization depicted by the continuous decline in the density gradient from 1880 to 1963 reveals a very dominant change in these cities. These results would be predicted by the spatial equilibrium model.

THE MODEL AND POLICY ANALYSIS

Although the spatial equilibrium model has been shown to yield excellent predictions about land price and population gradients in general, the model does not incorporate many of the idiosyncrasies of the urban real estate market that create the need for public sector action. The model's main assistance is a negative one. Since the trend toward suburbanization has extended over such a long period of time, we should be wary of explanations of recent similar trends that do not take historical continuity into account in designing policies to alter trends. The underlying changes in the transportation costs of moving people and goods appear to go a long way toward explaining the trends.

The difficulties in the functioning of the urban real estate market are the lack of competition, the durability of real property, and the interdependence of demand. Let us now consider each of these problems in turn. The resulting additions to our understanding of these markets will lead to models of more positive use in guiding the evaluation of policy alternatives in later chapters.

Competition[22]

Consider the conditions for a competitive market: perfect knowledge, large numbers, product homogeneity, and divisibility of product. Now, no market can fulfill these conditions, but the real property market fulfills them less than most.

---

[21]For details see Mills, Ibid., pp. 38–39.
[22]Except where noted the material in this section is derived from Ralph Turvey, *The Economics of Real Property* (London: G. Allen, 1957), pp. 25–46.

We may even be able to rank real property markets by the degree to which these competitive conditions are met, and hence to the degree to which prices are determinate and not dependent on the bargaining skills of the transactors. This produces a ranking of markets in real property as follows: housing, office space, retail stores, loft-type buildings, and special-use buildings. The housing market is the most competitive because there are more substitutes and the product is more homogeneous. In each succeeding case substitutes are less available. Special-use buildings are unique and difficult to convert to different uses. For example, old neighborhood movie theaters, bowling alleys, and some of the franchised food stands with special shapes or design are difficult to convert to new uses and may remain empty for a long time after going out of business. Eventually new uses are found. For example, old movie theaters have been converted to churches, bowling alleys, and even hardware stores. Less difficulty would be found in finding new tenants or owners for office space, retail stores, and loft-type buildings than for the special-use property, especially those with good locations and flexibility in size and arrangement of space.

An additional factor that may reduce the number of conversions is the long term of many real-property leases. Thus, even if a property can be more profitable in another use, conversion may not occur because the present tenant does not want to leave. Changes in occupancy usually do not occur unless people have already decided to move. They are not usually moving because of a profitable real estate transaction. Nevertheless, such sluggish responsiveness to market conditions should be somewhat discounted, because with sufficient incentive, such leases can always be bought.

Durability of Real Property

In any analysis of the adjustment process in the real property market, however, we must distinguish two time periods: the market period in which no new building occurs, and the long run in which new construction responds to shortages.

At any given moment there is a standing stock of houses, offices, stores, and other buildings in any metropolitan area or small city. During the market period no new building would be immediately available. The problem, then, is who will occupy which space. Ceiling prices for the residential units will depend upon expectations, incomes, tastes, and size of family. Expected returns will determine the ceiling price of commercial and industrial buildings, as well as of apartments and houses for rent. Those bidders with the highest ceiling price will tend to occupy each building.

With the given population size of the place and income distribution, an array of prices will be offered for the standing stock of facilities. There may be an insufficient number, quality, and size of facilities. If so, a shortage will arise, and prices will rise. As prices rise, users will not use as much space. As long as the ceiling price for any type of standing facility is greater than the cost of building a new one, there will be incentive for new construction. The ceiling price could be higher than the cost of new construction and cause no new construction, if an additional facility of the same kind, such as another supermarket, would so reduce revenues to all such stores that no one could make a profit.

If there are too many facilities for the given population and income of the place, vacancies will arise. One's first reaction is that this should cause prices to decrease. They may not, however, because owners may be optimistic about the future and expect an increase in population, or income, or both. If population and income remained static, the price of facilities would fall until people were willing to occupy all of the space available. If the price for some building fell far enough, it might pay the owner to abandon it because the present value of expected receipts was less than the present value of expected annual costs, including taxes and insurance.

For each type of building for which there is a lack of demand, it may be possible to convert it to a use for which there will be a positive ceiling price. Conversions or improvements may be no more than adding an additional room in a residence or air conditioning an office building, but it may entail extensive remodeling to convert a large house to an apartment building or rooming house, or to convert a movie theater to a bowling alley. In each case the change will be made so long as the present value of expected net annual returns for the new use is greater than the present value of the expected net annual returns for the old use plus conversion costs.

Long-run equilibrium, given income and population, would occur only when the present value of expected net annual returns from each facility was just equal to the construction and site cost of that facility. Thus, no demand would exist for either additions or subtractions from the building stock.

So far we have shown that urban property markets differ in the degree to which prices are determinate and that this characteristic is important for knowing whether the bargaining strengths of the buyer and seller are more important than broader demand and supply characteristics. For most markets, however, substitution is sufficiently strong that prices are influenced by trends in population, interest rates, and costs of construction and maintenance. We have shown how prices signal and give incentive for new construction when new facilities are needed.

Interdependency of Demand

There is another characteristic of urban real property markets, however, that creates even greater problems in determining equilibrium solutions. Equilibrium can be determined not only over time but in space as well. That is, it would be useful to determine a spatial equilibrium of land uses, such that once achieved, there would be no incentive for change in place. With such a model the impact of alternative policies on land use could be thought through.

The difficulty with the urban property market is, however, that each property user changes his or her value of a particular site with every change in the location of other users. The demand by one person for real property is interdependent with the demand of other people. One of the conditions, however, for an efficient equilibrium in economic models is that consumers' preferences are independent of other consumers. Only then can it be shown that in equilibrium no one can be made better off without making someone else worse off. Koopmans and Beckmann have shown that when interdependencies exist no set of individually bid prices will allocate land efficiently.[23] Consider a fixed number of houses and an equal number of families to occupy them. Each family will occupy that house for which it can pay the highest price. However, the price is a function of the house's distance away from other people in the community with whom the family has a large number of contacts. In such a situation there is no array of prices that will enable each family to minimize its transportation cost. There would always be at least one person who would be better off moving closer to some other family. As our description of the location of all activities in the metropolitan area indicated, all uses in the city are dependent for their location on other uses. That is, the ceiling price that each user can afford to pay depends on the location of other uses in the city.

One spatial housing market model that does try to incorporate the impact of demand interdependency is a model by Bailey. Bailey assumes that some people prefer not to live near others whose habits,

[23]Tjalling C. Koopmans and Martin Beckmann, "Assignment Problems and the Location of Economic Activities," *Econometrica*, 25 (January 1957), pp. 58–76. For a more accessible description see Martin Beckmann, *Location Theory* (New York: Random House, 1968), pp. 94–96.

tastes, and income are markedly different from their own.[24] People generally consider it unpleasant to live near groups of people with lower incomes and with tastes and habits they consider inferior. If the group considered to be a nuisance felt the same way about the others, people would live in homogeneous neighborhoods and would not live in heterogeneous areas. It may not be true, however, that the feeling is mutual. Although high-income families may find it beneath them to live near lower-income families, the reverse may not be the case.

Bailey demonstrates the implications of the above situation with the following simplified model. Assume that there are two groups of people: high-income people and low-income people. Low-income families, however, prefer to live in areas adjacent to high-income families rather than in areas where they would be surrounded by other low-income families. Assume that parallel streets A, B, C, and D are occupied entirely by low-income people, and that streets E, F, G, and H are occupied entirely by high-income people. Also assume that all the houses are of the same size and type. Furthermore, assume that only the people occupying streets D and E consider themselves affected by proximity to the other group. If people do not anticipate any changes in the boundary on D and E streets, properties on D street will sell for a premium over properties on A, B, and C streets because low-income families will pay a premium to live near high-income families. On the other hand, properties on E street will sell for less than properties on F, G, and H streets because high-income families will pay the premium to be surrounded by others of their same group.

It may seem incongruous that both the poor and the rich can or will live in comparable structures, or that the same price may be paid for comparable structures occupied by families with two different income levels. However, the incongruity is resolved once we consider that the structure is occupied by a single family, if that family has a high income; and that the structure is occupied by several families, if they are low-income families. The price being discussed is the price of the real property, and not necessarily the expenditure of a family for housing. Nevertheless, conversion costs may be generated in converting a structure from use by high-income families to use by low-income families, or even to make the reverse conversion.

If the prices for properties on streets A, B, and C were the same as comparable properties on streets F, G, and H, prices for properties on D street would be higher than prices for comparable property on E street. It would therefore pay the owners of property on E street

[24]Martin J. Bailey, "Note on the Economics of Residential Zoning and Urban Renewal," *Land Economics*, 35 (August 1959), pp. 288–292.

occupied by high-income families to sell or convert their properties for occupancy by low-income families. For example, suppose prices on streets A, B, and C were P_l, and prices on streets F, G, and H were P_h. Prices on street D would be $P_l + p$; prices on street E would be $P_h - d$. If $P_h = P_l$, $P_l + p > P_h - d$. So long as $(P_l + p) - (P_h - d)$ were greater than the cost of converting property in high-income use for low-income use, owners of property on E street would convert. Properties would continue to be converted to low-income use until the difference between $P_l + p$ and $P_h - d$ was equal to conversion cost:

$$(P_l + p) - (P_h - d) = c$$

$$P_l + p - P_h + d = c$$

$$P_l - P_h = c - p - d$$

That is, conversion would occur until the interior price P_l so decreased and the interior price P_h so increased that P_h was greater than P_l by the quantity $(c - p - d)$.

The above conclusion holds so long as the properties are individually owned. If, however, the properties were all owned by one person, they would not have been converted. The reason is that when street E is converted to use for low-income families, properties on street D lose their premium, properties on street E gain the premium, and the discount is transferred to properties on street F. Therefore, the profit to one owner, taking into account the external effects, is $(P_l + p) - (P_h - d) - p - d - c = P_l - P_h - c$. If P_l equals P_h and c is zero, then there is no profit, and no conversion will take place.

Therefore, since separate ownership of properties does not take into account the impact of preferences on surrounding property, the conversion from high-income to low-income use will go too far. It would proceed until P_l was less than P_h by the sum of premiums and discounts, less conversion costs. This would in fact reduce the total welfare of interior families because the interior prices would not be equal in each use. Total welfare would be greatest when the interior values in each use were equal, or more generally, when their difference $(P_l - P_h)$ was equal to c. That is to say, the interior price for low-income use should be greater than that for high-income use by the amount of the conversion cost.

Thus, as we shall see again and again, the definition of property rights is often the culprit in causing losses to the community from external social costs, such as the premiums and discounts caused by preferences. After we discuss the public sector, we will return to this problem. The Bailey model demonstrates in a nonmathematical way the point that Koopmans and Beckmann proved mathematically—that a competitive land market may not lead to efficient allocation of land when demand interdependencies exist. This point is essential to understanding the uses of public policy, especially in the areas of zoning, poverty, and race.

SUMMARY

In general, land use depends upon who can bid the highest price for each site. These prices, however, are prices for the rights to the use of property, and these rights may be constrained by local public regulations, such as zoning, building codes, and occupancy permits. Since land or property prices are for the return on the use of property for long periods of time, the prices themselves are determined by capitalizing the expected returns and costs for the expected life of the investment. If a new building is to be constructed, the outlay will be increased until the present value of the additional net revenue is just equal to the present value of the additional costs incurred.

For residential choices, the expected returns are the amounts that would have to be spent for alternative places to live. The expected returns depend upon the amenities, housing structure, public goods, services, and accessibility of the site to jobs, friends, and shopping. Accessibility is also the key to the expected value of returns for other types of property.

Theorists have tried to construct spatial equilibrium models of urban land use. In general they have succeeded in explaining the decrease in land prices with distance from the central business district, the decrease in population density with the increase in distance from the central business district, and why higher-income families tend to live farther from the central business district than lower-income families. They have not been successful in handling the problem of interdependency of demand or the location of industrial, commercial, or other nonresidential-use districts outside the central business district. Nevertheless, these models are helpful because they show the way in which changes in population, income, and transportation costs will affect land prices and population density.

Real property markets fit the ideal description of competitive markets imperfectly. The numbers of buyers and sellers are often small, information is difficult to obtain, the properties are not homogeneous, and demands by individuals are often interdependent. Competitive determination of prices is more effective if more substitutes are available. We can indeed show how the markets lead to increases in construction when shortages exist, or to decreases in prices when vacancies occur. Nevertheless, there is no assurance that land prices or property prices lead to efficient land-use allocation, if interdependencies among land uses are prevalent.

SELECTED READINGS

Bailey, Martin J.: "Note on the Economics of Residential Zoning and Urban Renewal," *Land Economics*, 35 (August 1959), pp. 288–292 (Bobbs-Merrill Reprint, Econ-22).

Fales, Raymond L., and Leon N. Moses: "Land-Use Theory and the Spatial Structure of the Nineteenth-Century City," *Papers and Proceedings of the Regional Science Association*, 18 (1972), pp. 49–80.

Moses, Leon, and Harold F. Williamson, Jr.: "The Location of Economic Activity in Cities," *American Economic Review*, 57 (May 1967), pp. 211–222 (Bobbs-Merrill Reprint, Econ-233).

Muth, Richard F.: *Cities and Housing* (Chicago: The University of Chicago, 1969).

Turvey, Ralph: *The Economics of Real Property* (London: G. Allen, 1957), chaps. 1–4.

CHAPTER **5**

PUBLIC GOODS AND POLITICAL ORGANIZATION[1]

The importance of the public sector has been noted in earlier chapters. The location of businesses and residences is influenced by the accessibility to schools and parks, by the availability of such public services as police and fire protection as well as utilities, and by taxes. Improvements in accessibility (highways and public transit) are usually provided through government. In addition, governments generally resolve problems of land-use interdependency, pollution, and congestion, which occur in densely populated areas.

In this chapter we present analyses of the rationale for collective action in an essentially market economy. We also take up the problems inherent in political or governmental decision making and the variety of governmental goods and services available in urban areas. These analyses provide the conceptual framework within which issues such as the following will be examined: urban public finance; improving the functioning of the public sector; policies in the areas of housing, segregation, race, and the ghetto; zoning and land-use control; education;

[1]Some of the material in this chapter is parallel to the analysis presented in Robert L. Bish, *The Public Economy of Metropolitan Areas* (Chicago: Rand McNally/ Markham, 1971), chaps. 2 and 3.

the urban environment; urban transportation; national urban-growth policy; and the future of urban areas.

THE ECONOMIC BASIS OF COLLECTIVE ACTION

The treatment of government within economics is inconsistent. Most economic analysis treats government as exogenous and in the abstract, as if "government" existed apart from individuals. In the most extreme form, government is treated as if it could be taken for granted that when economists recommend a policy, the "government" will wisely and immediately introduce that policy. Another approach is to treat government within the same framework as the economic analysis of markets—as if it were composed of individuals who simply allocate resources in such a way as to improve their condition. Thus, individuals who make demands on political organizations, politicians who try to get elected, and bureaucrats who make decisions are all treated in the same framework as are businessmen who locate and operate firms and residents who locate and purchase consumer goods.[2]

The analysis here will proceed within the framework of microeconomics. However, it will depart from traditional analysis in some important ways, especially with regard to assumptions of perfect information and lack of nonmarket interdependencies. An assumption of perfect information is often used in abstract models of perfect competition. However, a basic assumption about a market system is that it produces information on a low-cost, decentralized basis. We, on the contrary, will assume information to be scarce and expensive like any other economic good. We will also take account of nonmarket interdependencies, because a basic rationale for collective action is related to production and consumption processes affecting individuals other than those directly responsible—especially in densely populated urban areas. Information regarding the magnitude of external effects is also a problem in collective action because it may be in an individual's interest not to reveal his preferences if others will resolve the problem without his contribution.

The basic concepts underlying an economic approach to collective action are externalities (also called neighborhood effects), public or collective goods, common pool resources, and natural monopolies.

[2]A good discussion of this issue is contained in James M. Buchanan, "Positive Economics, Welfare Economics and Political Economy," in *Fiscal Theory and Political Economy* (Chapel Hill, N.C.: University of North Carolina Press, 1960), pp. 105–124. The same dichotomy occurs in political science and public administration. For an analysis in those disciplines, see Vincent Ostrom, *The Intellectual Crisis in American Public Administration* (University, Ala.: University of Alabama Press, 1973).

Each of these concepts is important for understanding the organization and functioning of the public sector in urban areas.

External Effects

During the fifties and sixties, an extensive literature on externalities or neighborhood effects emerged. Our concern here, however, is with only a few of the issues raised elsewhere; namely, whether externalities are pecuniary or technological, what their magnitude and geographic scope may be, and how many individuals are affected.

Externalities are the results of action that affects individuals not directly involved in the transaction. The effects may be either beneficial or harmful. Many external effects are transmitted through the market system. For example, the introduction of automobiles and their purchase had direct effects on the demand for horse-drawn carriages and hence on carriage makers. This effect, however, was transmitted through market transactions and was part of a process which improved the allocation of resources to meet individual demands. This kind of effect is called a pecuniary externality. Pecuniary externalities, which may result in income redistribution, are not an economic efficiency problem.

External effects not transmitted through markets are of a fundamentally different kind in economic analysis. Where these externalities, called technological externalities, exist, economic inefficiency may occur; by taking the externality into account, net gains may be possible. For example, when each of several adjacent residents maintains his house and yard in good condition, the benefit enjoyed by all represents a technological externality. On the other hand, the costs to residents affected by air pollution and noise from a nearby freeway also exemplify a technological externality. In each of these cases, the consumer's interests are directly affected by another's actions, but the effects occur outside the market framework.[3]

Not all technological externalities are economic efficiency problems. The economic inefficiency exists when the benefits gained by removing a negative externality are outweighed by the cost of reducing the external effect, or when additional positive external benefits could be obtained for less than their cost. In other words, economic inefficiency exists when gains from trade are unrealized because the benefits or costs associated with the externality are not taken into account by the generating party. One classification of the

---

[3]Tibor Scitovsky, "Two Concepts of External Economies," *Journal of Political Economy*, 62 (April 1954), pp. 70–82.

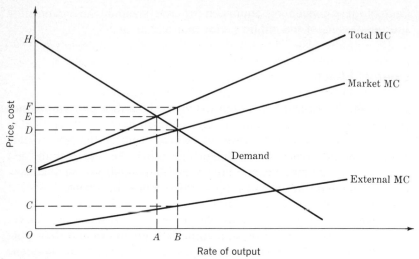

FIGURE 5-1 Production with an External Effect

magnitude of externalities is whether they are trivial, relevant, or Pareto relevant.[4] Trivial externalities are those which the affected party finds so insignificant that he has no desire to do anything about them. Relevant externalities are those where the affected party has an effective demand to have them taken into account; i.e., he is willing to pay to reduce negative external effects or enhance positive external effects. Pareto relevant externalities exist when the amount the affected individual is willing to pay to reduce negative effects or enhance positive effects exceeds the amount the generating party is willing to accept to reduce negative effects or increase positive effects. Thus, only with Pareto relevant externalities are gains from trade possible.

The economic efficiency problem with external effects can be shown graphically. Figure 5-1 illustrates a case where use of a resource generates negative externalities for individuals not involved in the transaction. The consumer's marginal value in use (demand), the market marginal cost (market supply), and external marginal costs are all shown on the figure. In market equilibrium, the consumer will choose output B where marginal value equals perceived marginal cost. At the output, however, external costs equal to OC are generated and total marginal costs (OF) exceed the marginal value in use (OD). The economic efficiency problem is to get the user to select output A where

[4]James M. Buchanan and William Craig Stubblebine, "Externality," *Economica*, 29 (November 1962), pp. 371–384.

total marginal costs are equal to the good's marginal value in use. At any output below A, a relevant externality would still exist, but there would be no opportunity for net gains because external marginal costs are less than the difference between marginal value in use and market marginal costs. One should note that activities generating negative externalities are likely to be carried on at too high a level, but at the same time complete elimination of the use and its externality is not efficient either.

A modification of Figure 5-1 can be used to better illustrate the situation of the consumer and recipient of the externality, provide additional insight into why A is the most efficient output, and indicate some of the implications of potential solutions to the problem.

In Figure 5-2 the net marginal benefits (that is, the surplus of marginal value in use over market marginal cost) is line MB. For example, net marginal benefits at an output just greater than zero is equal to GH in Figure 5-1 and OM in Figure 5-2. At output B, net marginal benefits are zero because market marginal costs equal the marginal value in use. The net marginal benefits are actually the sum of consumer's and producer's surpluses. Also shown in Figure 5-2 is the external marginal cost function—the same as on Figure 5-1.

Assume the consumer has the right to consume the good produced regardless of external costs generated and that no bargaining

FIGURE 5-2 Optimal External Effect

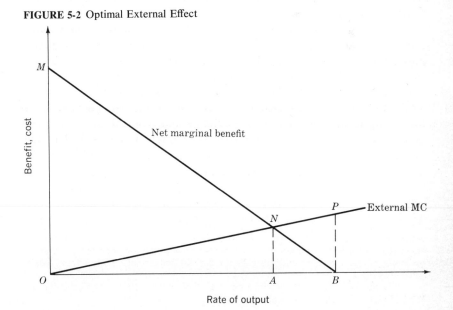

takes place between the consumer and the damaged party. He would then consume at output B, where his net benefits are exhausted. At B, the consumer's total benefits would be equal to area OMB. At B, the marginal external costs are BP; total external costs are the area OPB. Now assume the same benefit-cost structure but that the damaged party has the right to prevent any damages imposed on him and that no bargaining takes place. In this situation, the potentially damaged party could demand zero consumption by the potential consumer. At zero consumption level, the consumer would forego potential net benefits and no damages would be generated.

However, neither zero output nor output B are optimal. At consumption levels up to A, the maximum amount of damages (shown by the marginal-damage curve) is less than marginal-consumption benefits (shown by the marginal net benefits curve). Thus, net gains are possible by increasing consumption to A. At consumption levels greater than A, marginal damages exceed net marginal benefits, so that net gains are possible by reducing consumption from B to A. Consumption level A is the consumption level generating the greatest amount of benefits for both parties combined; i.e., the consumer gain minus damages is maximized. The net benefits at A over zero output are equal to total benefit $(OANM)$ minus total damages (OAN), or ONM. The net benefits at A over consumption level B are total costs eliminated $(ABPN)$ minus benefits eliminated (ABN), or BPN.

Can one expect consumption level A and thus efficient resource use to emerge from the workings of a voluntary exchange economy? Yes, under certain conditions.

If the consumer and damaged party can bargain with one another without incurring excessive transaction or decision-making costs,[5] output B will be achieved no matter whether the consumer has the right to consume or the damaged party has the right to resist costs generated by another's consumption.[6] If the consumer has the right to consume at any level of activity greater than A, the damaged party will be willing to pay the consumer to reduce consumption a sum greater than the net benefits the consumer could receive by continuing consumption at that level. The precise amount of compensation is not determinable. For a reduction in consumption from B to A, the

[5]Decision-making costs, also called bargaining costs, are all the costs borne by individuals in reaching an agreement on the allocation or exchange of resources. They include the value of time and effort engaged in bargaining as well as any direct outlays. If bargaining costs are zero, in economic analysis it is generally assumed that individuals will continue to bargain until all gains from economic exchange have been exhausted and a Pareto optimal allocation of resources is achieved. A Pareto optimal allocation of resources is one where no one can benefit from additional reallocation without loss to someone else.

[6]For a discussion of legal cases, see R. H. Coase, "The Problem of Social Cost," *The Journal of Law and Economics*, 3 (October 1960), pp. 1–44.

damaged party would be willing to pay a maximum equal to $ABPN$. The consumer would be willing to reduce consumption from B to A for any amount slightly greater than ABN. Thus, the net gains, equal to NBP, would be available for division between the two in some indeterminate manner.

Now if the damaged party had the right to prevent the consumer from generating costs without interaction, the damaged party would simply prevent the consumer from undertaking any consumption. However, at levels from O to A the amount of potential gain to the consumer is equal to $OANM$, and he would therefore be willing to pay the damaged party an amount slightly less than $OANM$ to gain permission to undertake consumption level A. The damaged party, on the other hand, would be willing to accept a minimum of OAN to permit consumption level A. The net gains to both from the undertaking of activity level A are equal to $OANM$ minus OAN, or ONM, so they could divide up the net gains in some indeterminate manner. Thus, it does not matter whether the consumer has the right to undertake the activity or the damaged party has the right to prevent the imposition of costs; both will find it to their advantage for the activity to reach level A as long as bargaining costs are low. If bargaining costs are high but less than potential gains from trade, we would expect bargaining to take place and the consumption level to approach but perhaps not to reach A. This is because as consumption approaches A, additional gains from trade will be diminishing, so that eventually bargaining will cease as its costs exceed potential additional gains.

The existence of externalities has often been presented as a justification for governmental action to supplement private market activity. However, a third party (government) could make no contribution toward achieving economic welfare in the above example.[7] Under the assumptions used, it would be predicted that externalities where both parties can be better off through cooperation will be eliminated strictly through voluntary exchange. However, the crucial assumptions are (1) that one or the other party has a "right" to do something, that is, that a system of law and enforceable property rights exists undergirded by a governmental structure of some type, and (2) that decision-making costs are very low. These conditions are likely to be violated (1) if property rights are not carefully specified (for example, does a city have the right to dump municipal sewage in a river, or do downstream water users have the right to prevent upstream cities from such disposal?) or (2) if a large number of individuals are involved, since decision-making costs are likely to be higher the larger

---

[7] In fact, where bargaining is possible between the two parties, the intervention by a third party may actually result in nonoptimal solutions to the problem. See Buchanan and Stubblebine, op. cit.

the number of people involved. What if the consumer's activity in the above example damaged one hundred individuals instead of just one? Could payments or compensation be arranged among a large number of individuals at a reasonable decision-making cost? The problem of uncertain property rights is likely to increase decision-making costs whether two or two thousand individuals are involved and, conversely, large numbers of individuals are likely to increase bargaining costs whether or not property rights are carefully specified and easily enforced. The highest decision-making costs are likely to accrue when both uncertain property rights and large numbers of people are involved. As we will see in subsequent analysis, many of the most pressing urban problems involve external effects where property rights are unclear and large numbers of individuals are affected.

Recognition that externalities affect large numbers of people leads directly to the introduction of a spatial element and additional complications to the examination of externalities. People are distributed over space, and the number affected by an externality is a function of the distance over which external effects occur (noise pollution from a freeway may carry less than a mile while air pollution may spread over 100 square miles) and the population density within that area. Furthermore, individuals not only may value the same level of external effect differently but the level of external effect is likely to change with distance from the originating source.

The issues surrounding externalities which affect large groups over diverse geographic areas are also the crucial issues in the analysis of public goods and common pool resources, to which we now turn.

Public Goods

Public goods are goods or services that can be consumed by many individuals simultaneously, where one person's consumption does not detract from another's, and where exclusion of potential consumers is not feasible. These characteristics are called joint consumption and nonexclusion. Classic examples of public goods include mosquito control and street lights.[8] It should be noted that the designation "public" in regard to public goods relates only to the good's consumption characteristics and not to its producer, which may be either a private firm or a government.

---

[8] Paul Samuelson, "Diagrammatic Exposition of a Theory of Public Expenditure," *Review of Economics and Statistics*, 37 (November 1955), pp. 350–356, Julius Margolis, "A Comment on the Pure Theory of Public Expenditure," *Review of Economics and Statistics*, 37 (November 1955), pp. 347–349. Other authors often use the terms "social goods" or "collective goods" to designate public goods.

Public goods present special problems in a market economy. First, individuals acting in their own interest will, generally, not voluntarily pay for the production of public goods because if someone else pays to provide them, nonpaying individuals cannot be excluded from consuming them. Thus public goods may not be provided or be provided only at very low levels in a market economy. Second, if public goods are provided collectively, the same level must be made available to everyone, making it difficult for individuals to adjust their level of consumption to meet their own preferences in relation to their consumption of other goods and services. The logic of the under-provision problem is examined graphically in Figure 5-3. The problem of meeting diverse preferences for public goods will be examined later in the chapter in the specific context of organizing to provide public goods collectively.

Public goods are unlikely to be provided at optimal levels without cooperative action among consumers. Only if each individual contributes an amount equal to his marginal evaluation for the last unit of

FIGURE 5-3 Demands for a Public Good

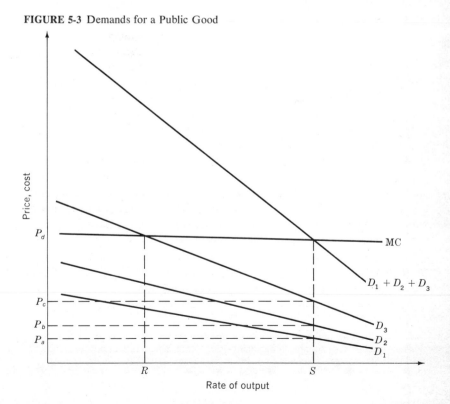

the good produced and if some individuals contribute from their surpluses to pay for the provision of the intramarginal units will an optimal
level of provision be achieved.[9] The optimal level and marginal prices
are illustrated in Figure 5-3. The graph illustrates that the demand
curves for a public good by several individuals are aggregated differently than would be the case with private goods. With the latter, demand curves must be added horizontally, because for each individual
the total amount of the good must be expanded or his consumption
will directly reduce another individual's consumption. With public
goods, demands are added vertically—and the summed demand curve
$(D_1 + D_2 + D_3)$ represents the total amounts all three individuals are
willing to pay to achieve a particular output which they can consume
simultaneously. In Figure 5-3, individual 3 would be willing to provide
output R at price P_d for his own use. If he did this, individuals 1 and 2
would be able to consume R without making any payments. However,
if decision-making costs are zero, there are gains from trade to be made
if individuals 1, 2, and 3 cooperate and provide output S, where the
sum of their demands is equal to the marginal cost. At output S, D_1 is
willing to contribute P_a for the marginal unit and some amount less
than his total benefits (the area under his demand curve up to S) as
his contribution toward payment for the intramarginal units. Individual
2 would be willing to contribute P_b and individual 3 would contribute
P_c for the marginal unit plus some amount less than total benefits for
the intramarginal units. At output S, total costs would be equal to S
times P_d (or the area under the MC curve), and total benefits would be
equal to the area under the summed demand curves $(D_1 + D_2 + D_3)$ up
to S; at this point the total net benefits are maximized. This is so because at any lower output increases would add more to consumer benefits than to total costs and at any higher output reductions would reduce
costs more than the reduction in consumer benefits.

Within small groups, under conditions of zero-cost decision
making and constant costs, we would expect individuals to cooperate
to provide optimal levels of public goods. If bargaining is costly,
output S may be approached, but output will probably be slightly more
or less, with additional decision making ceasing when costs exceed
potential gains (potential gains decline the closer to S they come).
With large groups, decision-making costs may be quite high, leading to
underconsumption or perhaps to no consumption. This is so because
each individual may find it in his own interest to take a let-George-do-it

[9]Actually an optimum level of consumption will be achieved only under conditions of constant-cost supply. For an analysis of increasing-cost situations, see Robert L.
Bish and Patrick O'Donoghue, "A Neglected Issue in Public Goods Theory: The
Monopsony Problem," *Journal of Political Economy*, 78 (November-December 1970),
pp. 1367–1371.

or free-rider attitude, knowing that if the good is provided he can share in its consumption at no cost. Group size, therefore, is extremely important with regard to individual incentives for participating in a group to provide a public good.

Public goods, like external effects, have spatial characteristics. Mosquito control provided by a local government primarily benefits residents of that government (although external costs and benefits may occur from this activity as well as from market-provided goods), and street lights are of use only to those within their range of illumination. Spatial characteristics mean that groups of individuals in different locations may choose to provide different levels of public goods for themselves, even though each individual within a particular group will have available only the level decided upon by that group. For example, residents in some areas may prefer street lights every 300 feet while others will be content with fewer street lights and greater reliance on private porch lights.

Public goods must be regarded as a conceptual, pure type, a pure type at the opposite end of a spectrum from private goods, which possess no external effects. In the real world there are very few pure public goods, but a great number of goods possess significant public goods characteristics over certain geographic areas (flood control, highways, parks, navigation aids). There are many other instances in which the exclusion of free riders would be feasible but where the good may be consumed upon request by an eligible citizen and essentially the same level is available to everyone (fire protection, police services, courts). These also resemble public goods. Most goods provided by government possess some public goods characteristics but at the same time are not generally *pure* public goods.

Externalities and public goods are closely related. Any externality affecting a large number of people may be accruing like a public good (or "public bad" if the externality is negative) in that all are affected simultaneously. Thus problems of undertaking collective action to account for externalities affecting large groups are similar to the problems of undertaking collective action to provide for public goods. Solutions to both problems depend on overcoming the free-rider problem in large groups.

Common Pool Resources

Common pool resources possess characteristics of both externalities and public goods.[10] A common pool resource is one that is available

[10]H. Scott Gordon, "The Economic Theory of a Common Property Resource: The Fishery," *Journal of Political Economy*, 62 (April 1954), pp. 124–142.

for everyone's use; i.e., it is characterized by nonexclusion because exclusion of users or limitations of use are not feasible or legal, but nevertheless one person's use directly reduces the use or value of the common pool to others. The major common pool resources in urban areas are air sheds and water bodies. Clean air and clean water are used by all citizens. Each individual citizen also may find it rational to use air and water for waste-disposal purposes; but when many individuals put wastes into air and water, the assimilative capacity is exceeded and valuable resources are destroyed. Waste discharges which exceed the assimilative capacity of the environment are a crucial problem in densely populated urban areas.

The efficient utilization of common pool resources requires collective action among all users to curtail or ration use to nondestructive levels; yet the number of users may be so large as to make unlikely voluntary agreements to curtail use—the same large-group, free-rider problem as encountered with external effects and public goods.

Common pool resources tend to have specific geographical boundaries determined by physical topography. Air-shed boundaries are determined by prevailing winds and differences in elevation. Watershed boundaries are determined by the shapes of river basins, direction of water flow, or boundaries of bodies of water such as large lakes. Quite often the boundaries of common pool resources do not coincide with boundaries of external effects of other activities or boundaries for efficient provision of public goods, thus adding another complication to the organization of collective action for their regulation and management.

Natural Monopolies

Natural monopolies exist when the market is so small that one firm can service it more economically than two or more firms could do and where the costs of entry for new firms are relatively high. Natural monopolies also exist where the physical nature of the good or service makes provision by a single firm most efficient. For example, a single sewage treatment plant may be most efficient for most cities, and the way in which sewage is collected makes it more efficient for a single collection system to service each area than to have competing collecting systems do so. Other natural monopolies in urban areas include provision of telephone service, cable television, water supply, and electric power distribution. These goods and services may be provided either governmentally or privately, but in cases of private provision, citizen-consumers use collective political action to regulate the producer to prevent exploitation of the monopoly position.

Many public goods and services also possess aspects of natural monopolies. For example, it is more efficient to have each of a number of fire stations serving a distinct area rather than overlapping the stations' territories; also, it has traditionally been felt that a system of neighborhood schools with nonoverlapping service areas was more efficient than one in which children selected from among several schools the ones they wished to attend. Whether or not many traditional government functions are really natural monopolies will be treated in detail in later chapters.

Group Size[11]

The number of people affected by an externality, benefiting from the provision of a public good, using a common pool resource, or purchasing from a natural monopolist is an extremely important determinant of solutions to these resource-allocation problems. In general, if very few people are involved, there is a good chance that they will recognize their interdependency and enter into direct negotiation to take into account external effects, to agree to contribute for the provision of public goods, to limit the use of common pool resources to safe levels, or to bargain with a natural monopolist. However, if large numbers of individuals are involved, it is unlikely that externalities, public goods, common pools, or natural monopolies will be dealt with efficiently. It is in urban areas that large numbers of people encounter these problems.

There are two reasons why large numbers of individuals may fail to deal with resource-allocation problems in purely voluntary exchanges: first, the group may be so large that individuals do not really sense their interdependence; second, even if interdependence is recognized, each individual may not find it in his interest to take the time and trouble to promote cooperative action among such a large group. Groups that are so large that a single individual's contribution makes no perceptible difference to the burden or benefit of other members of the group or to his own consumption of a public good are called latent groups. In latent groups each individual feels that his actions are insignificant in relation to everyone else's actions—and thus being a free rider is the rational action for him to take. One would predict that unless some incentive or sanction is offered in addition to the public good or unless there are benefits from preserving a common pool, latent-group members will not be provided with public goods or

[11]For a comprehensive analysis of group size and public goods, see Mancur Olson, Jr., *The Logic of Collective Action: Public Goods and the Theory of Groups* (Cambridge, Mass.: Harvard, 1965).

preserve common resources. Would mosquito control be provided in the absence of individual sanctions for not paying taxes? Will a large group of homeowners get together and voluntarily contribute to purchase land for a neighborhood playfield, or will individual automobile drivers voluntarily switch to nonpolluting automobiles or other transit modes to improve air quality in a metropolitan air shed? Large-group problems represent the basic problems to be resolved through collective nonvoluntary or political action.

The Logic of Political Organization[12]

Problems with neighborhood effects, public goods, common pools, and natural monopolies have been diagnosed as most severe when a large number of individuals are affected—especially if the group is large enough to be a latent group where no individual feels common interests or perceives net gains from cooperation or from trying to organize the group to articulate its preferences because of the high decision-making costs of dealing with so many people. In general one can expect decision-making costs of group action to (1) increase with the size of the group as a consequence of greater time, effort, and cost to obtain agreement among more and more people and (2) increase with the opportunity one or a few individuals have to prevent action by withholding their consent. These latter decision-making costs are called strategic bargaining costs. They are the time, effort, and cost of bargaining over relative shares of benefits when individuals with the potential to prevent the activity threaten to withhold support unless they receive an especially large share of net gains. Strategic bargaining costs are most likely to occur in very small groups or when unanimity is required.

If decision-making costs increase with group size and are likely to be especially high when unanimity is required, an obvious solution is to establish rules whereby a proportion of the affected group can commit the group to action. For example, 51 percent of a group may be able to approve actions requiring payment by everyone in the group for some purposes. Relaxing the rule of unanimity found in market exchange permits direct saving in decision-making costs and will permit many more neighborhood effects, public goods, common pools, and natural monopolies to be dealt with collectively.

However, relaxing the rule of unanimous consent also has costs, called political-externality costs. External costs were defined as costs

---

[12]The economic logic of political constitutions is developed by James M. Buchanan and Gordon Tullock, *Calculus of Consent: Logical Foundations of Constitutional Democracy* (Ann Arbor, Mich.: University of Michigan Press, 1962).

imposed on individuals by the actions of others undertaking production or consumption. Political-externality costs are costs imposed on individuals because they must participate in or bear the costs of a collective action with which they disagree. Political-externality costs do not exist when unanimity is required for actions, because anyone bearing net costs can refuse consent and halt the activity. Political-externality costs occur only in situations where a proportion constituting less than 100 percent of the individuals involved can commit the group to action.

In general, we expect political-externality costs to increase with a decrease in the proportion of individuals required to agree to group action, because the more people required to agree, the higher the probability of any individual's consent being required. Other factors that affect political-externality costs include the heterogeneity or homogeneity of the group, the likelihood of being included in the decision-making group, and the types of actions the political group can decide. The more homogeneous the group, the lower the political-externality costs, because the tastes of the individuals are similar. The higher the likelihood of being in the decision-making group, the lower the expected political-externality costs. The political-externality costs are also lowered as the importance of the issues the group can decide is reduced. For example, a group empowered only to assess low property taxes for mosquito control can potentially impose much lower political-externality costs than a group with broader taxing and spending authority.

We can compare expected reductions in decision-making costs with increases in political-externality costs resulting from reducing the proportion of a group required to agree to determine the most efficient decision-making rule from the perspective of any particular individual. This is illustrated graphically in Figure 5-4. In Figure 5-4, decision-making costs are shown as an upward-sloping line ranging from close to zero (if only two persons have to agree to commit action on behalf of the group) to very high (under the rule of unanimity). Political-externality costs are shown as a downward-sloping line from very high (where a small proportion can commit the group) to zero (under requirements of unanimity). The total of costs of each decision-making rule are shown by the U-shaped curve labeled social-interaction costs—which is simply the sum of expected decision-making costs and expected political-externality costs at each rule level. In this example, one can observe that the saving in decision-making costs exceeds additional political-externality costs as the decision-making rule is relaxed from unanimity to 55 percent, because to that point the social-interaction costs are declining. A decision-making rule of 55 percent is the minimum social-interaction cost decision-making rule. For decision-

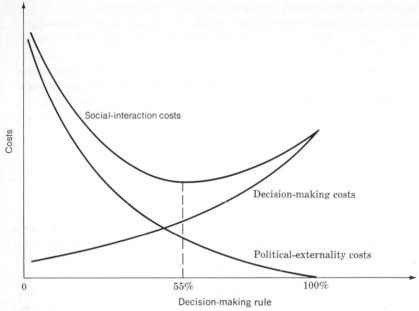

FIGURE 5-4 Costs of Political Decision Making

making rules below 55 percent, social-interaction costs are higher because political-externality costs increase more rapidly than decision-making costs decrease.

We often think 51 percent of an electorate or of representatives in a legislature is an appropriate rule for decision making in the public sector. In fact, however, a variety of decision-making rules ranging from a rule of "anyone" to unanimity are found in different forums. An example of an anyone rule is a citizen's authority to call for services from his fire or police department, with costs of the call financed by taxes paid by everyone in the jurisdiction. When we move beyond the anyone rule, we find situations where a small number of citizens must sign a petition for a candidate to file for office or to obtain preliminary cost estimates for a special improvement district. Decision-making rules above 51 percent include the 60 and 66 percent majority require-ments for tax override levies and rule changes in legislatures. Finally, unanimity is required for conviction in jury trials. Decision-making rules are often more complex than can be expressed by simple per-centages. Concurrent majorities or supermajorities are required for many expenditures, as when a majority of a city council and mayor or a majority of a house, a majority of a senate, and an executive have to agree.

Once we become aware of the range of decision-making rules used in the public sector, we can observe that they are related systematically to two factors—the need for haste and the potential political-externality costs resulting from the decision. Anyone rules for summoning the fire department or calling for police facilitate a rapid response, and costs of any single call are relatively low. Extraordinary majorities are usually required for more costly legislation or changes in the decision-making rules themselves, and of course a trial is a situation where unanimity helps assure that an innocent person is not convicted.

Pareto Optimality

A common welfare economics criterion for evaluating public sector decisions, at least in the abstract, is Pareto optimality. Pareto optimality exists in a situation where no one's position can be improved without loss to someone else. It should be noted that under optimal decision-making rules, individuals expect to be hurt by some political actions—but they still expect to benefit in the course of a series of decisions because of the savings in decision-making costs. Thus the economic logic of dealing with large-group problems implies that the Pareto optimality criterion is irrelevant for evaluating group actions. The decision-making costs of obtaining unanimity, which is essential to Pareto optimality, are so high that individuals are better off by not undertaking them.

The concept that everyone should gain (or at least no one lose) as a criterion for "good" resource allocation may still, however, have relevance for the establishment of decision-making rules, even if it is not relevant for evaluating individual programs. Ideally, everyone involved should agree to the decision-making rules—implying that everyone expects net gains from his participation in the collective decision-making group over time. This makes the welfare economic criterion of "good" resemble the criterion of many political and legal philosophers who stress that the law and institutional structure must be "fair," so that everyone gains from participation even though each individual is not a beneficiary from every action. [13]

THE SIZE AND SCOPE OF POLITICAL UNITS

The concepts of externalities, public goods, common pools, and natural monopolies are all essential for understanding the urban public sector,

[13] For example, see John Rawls, "Justice as Fairness," *Philosophical Review*, 67 (April 1958), pp. 164–194.

as is a recognition that different activities possess different geographic scales. The logic of political organizations operating with decision-making rules of less than unanimity must also be grasped. However, these concepts must be supplemented with analysis of additional relationships and empirical knowledge to be applied to particular problems. A major one of these problems is what kind of governmental structure will best enable individuals in urban areas to resolve problems of externalities, public goods, common pools, and natural monopolies efficiently and fairly.

In treating questions of size and scope, most economists have focused on analysis of supply conditions such as economies of scale or boundary spillovers. These issues are important, but beginning an analysis of the urban public sector with the demand rather than supply side is more in keeping with a focus on meeting individual preferences and provides greater understanding of the public sector.

Demand Articulation

In private markets, demand is articulated by the purchase of products from suppliers. This quid pro quo exchange process is not possible for large-group actions due to the nature of the externalities, public goods, common pools, and natural monopolies, and thus different demand articulation processes are used in political organizations.

Participation, Delegation, and Leadership With the exception of New England town hall meetings, when one thinks of indicating preferences for political action he thinks primarily of voting. Voting is a common preference-indicating mechanism. The major differences between voting and market exchange for preference articulation are that voting usually entails (1) all or none rather than marginal choices, (2) votes are equally weighted rather than weighted by intensity of preference, and (3) voters are often not as careful about their voting choices as their market choices because benefits and costs may be quite indirect and difficult to measure.[14] In addition, in a really large group the rational man may simply decide that the probability of his

[14]James M. Buchanan, "Individual Choice in Voting and the Market," in *Fiscal Theory and Political Economy* (Chapel Hill, N.C.: University of North Carolina Press, 1960), pp. 90–104. Empirical studies demonstrating the usefulness of analyzing voting with this approach include Mark Sproule-Jones and Kenneth D. Hart, "A Public-Choice Model of Political Participation," *Canadian Journal of Political Science*, 6 (June 1973), pp. 175–194, and Rene L. Frey and Leopold Kohn, "An Economic Interpretation of Voting Behavior on Public Finance Issues," *Kyklos*, 23, no. 4, 1970, pp. 792–805.

vote determining the outcome is so low as to make the costs in time and effort of going to the polls higher than potential net benefits.

One can envisage decision making where citizens vote on all government actions directly, but this would entail high costs of obtaining information, making decisions, and voting. Thus it is rational to elect an individual who will make decisions on government activities rather than vote on each activity itself. The delegation of decision-making authority is not unusual in a market economy; individuals are continually hiring lawyers, doctors, landscape architects, interior decorators, engineers, stockbrokers, and many other persons with specialized knowledge to make decisions on their behalf. The major difference with delegation in the public sector is that the delegate is elected by many rather than hired by one in a quid pro quo transaction.

The use of representatives instead of directly voting on each issue involves both costs and benefits.[15] The costs are that an individual has only a single vote to elect a person who, in turn, must represent him on a wide variety of issues; thus it may be difficult for each voter to find a candidate who agrees with him on all issues. This menu problem makes it much more difficult for individuals to use voting to indicate precisely their preferences on important issues. The benefits from electing delegates instead of voting on each issue are that one decision can be substituted for many, and thus voter decision-making costs are reduced; vote trading among delegates in their decision-making process may permit intensity of preferences on different issues to be expressed. Equally important, the election of representatives will allow benefits to accrue from competition among potential delegates. The benefits from competition among delegates include the provision of low-cost or free information on government policies[16] and the search by potential delegates for solutions to latent-group problems in exchange for expected future votes.

Voting, either directly on issues or for representatives, is not the only way in which individuals express preferences for collective action. Lobbying, writing letters, directly contacting officials, contributing to campaigns, and occasionally bribing elected or appointed officials are also ways in which citizens indicate their preferences. None of these methods is as precise as market exchange, but as we have already concluded, market exchange cannot resolve large-group problems, and political organizations with voting and other less precise preference-indicating processes appear to be the best available.

---

[15]Gordon Tullock, "Federalism: Problems of Scale," *Public Choice*, 6 (Spring 1969), pp. 19–29.

[16]The information production resulting from political competition is stressed by Anthony Downs, *An Economic Theory of Democracy* (New York: Harper and Row, 1958).

Residential and Business Location Choices[17]   Accessibility to public facilities and variations in tax burdens are determinants of residential and business location decisions and thus factors to be considered in analyzing urban land-use patterns. Location at a particular site carries with it not only use of the site but the right to utilize publicly provided goods and services and the liability to pay taxes and follow government regulations. We indicated in considering urban land-use patterns that we can generally expect the individual or firm willing to pay the most for a site to occupy that site, and the amount an individual is willing to pay depends on his business needs or preferences for the consumption of government goods and services as well as on site and building characteristics.

In examining the variety of political units in urban areas, one discovers a tremendous diversity in the mixes and levels of public goods available within the different units. Among the seventy-nine cities in Los Angeles County, California, for example, one finds purely residential cities such as Rolling Hills, which feature high natural amenities, very high levels of security, publicly provided riding trails, and the city falls within an excellent school district. Other cities, like Vernon, cater strictly to business and industrial needs. Within Vernon, over one-third of the land area is devoted to rail and roads, and all roads are specially constructed for heavy usage by large trucks. There are also high-capacity sewage facilities for industrial use. Vernon, however, provides virtually no consumer amenities such as parks; the library just meets state requirements, and the city is part of a very large, average school district. The functionally specialized cities found in Los Angeles County and other urban areas provide a spectrum of choices for residential and business location; and location within areas providing goods and services preferred by individuals and firms reinforces the specialization and variety within urban regions. For example, families who place a high value on good schools locate where there are good schools. They then continue to vote, lobby, etc., for the maintenance of good schools. Families who place a lower value on good schools (perhaps preferring lower taxes) will locate where schools are not as good but taxes are lower. In a similar fashion, a trucking firm is likely to find that a location in Vernon will meet its needs much better than one in a city which is more "amenity oriented." Once it locates in Vernon, it will use its political influence to continue the city's business-service orientation. Residents who really have a taste for low taxes but care little for suburban-type residential environ-

---

[17]The implications of the selection of different local governments on the basis of the goods and services they provide is developed in Charles M. Tiebout, "A Pure Theory of Local Expenditures," *Journal of Political Economy*, 64 (October 1956), pp. 416–424.

ments also may locate in Vernon, where, because of the high concentration of business property, tax rates are extremely low.

The rate at which urban land-use patterns change and adjust to new transportation technology or other determinants of land use is reduced by two main factors: (1) site choice in an area already providing the preferred mix of governmentally provided goods and services and (2) continued voting or political demand articulation for those services which attracted the residents or business to the area in the first place. Once a city obtains a strong reputation for a certain mix of services, individuals choosing to locate there can be expected to reinforce the prevailing land-use patterns rather than alter them.[18]

Preference Homogeneity and Functional Specialization   Different levels of taxation and provision of public goods by many different political units in urban areas are continually criticized as undesirable. However, if our interest is in institutional structures which permit individuals to achieve the highest level of welfare, there are distinct advantages to functional specialization and variety among political units. These advantages relate to the facts that (1) governmentally provided goods and services, because of their nature, must be provided in approximately equal levels within the area of production and (2) that different individuals and businesses possess different preferences for governmentally provided goods and services. Figures 5-5 and 5-6 illustrate the basic reason why individuals may achieve higher levels of welfare in homogeneous than in heterogeneous groups.

Figure 5-5 illustrates a normal distribution of demand curves for a particular public good among a randomly selected set of individuals. Figure 5-6 illustrates the distribution of preferences for the same public good among a set of people self-selected through residential site choice. If the political system is functioning smoothly, we would expect public goods provision to approximate that preferred by the median voter. If we assume that each individual pays an equal share of the cost of the good, then each individual's preferred quantity at the observed price would be where his demand curve cuts the price line. We could examine each demand curve to determine the welfare loss because the individual could not purchase the precise quantity he desired at the observed price. If we did so and went on to assume that welfare levels were comparable among individuals, we would conclude that the welfare

---

[18]Sociologists report evidence that supports this a priori expectation from economic theory. For example, Reynolds Farley reports that "once a suburb is established, the population that moves into that suburb tends to resemble the population already living there." "Suburban Persistence," *American Sociological Review*, 29 (February 1964), p. 47.

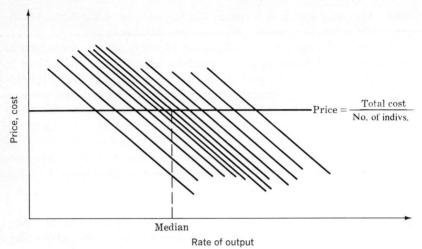

$$\text{Price} = \frac{\text{Total cost}}{\text{No. of indivs.}}$$

FIGURE 5-5 Demands of a Heterogeneous Group

losses from individual optimums was much greater in the heterogeneous than in the homogeneous group.[19]

A second reason why groups of individuals with similar tastes for governmentally provided goods and services may achieve higher levels of welfare is related to decision-making and political-externality costs. Homogeneous groups are expected to have both lower decision-making costs and lower political-externality costs (because of closer basic agreement on objectives); thus a greater number of externalities, public goods, common pools, and natural monopolies can be dealt with collectively without incurring social-interaction costs that exceed gains from the group effect.

If we consider demand articulation conditions only, we must conclude that, in general, preferences may be articulated more precisely and individuals are likely to achieve higher levels of welfare from governmental activities when political units are homogeneous rather than heterogeneous. If we look at the distribution of residents in urban areas, we observe a very high homogeneity in terms of socioeconomic characteristics among residents within individual neighborhoods.[20] Even more homogeneity is usually found within the smaller

[19] For analysis of this issue see Yoram Barzel, "Two Propositions on the Optimum Level of Producing Collective Goods," *Public Choice*, 6 (Spring 1969), pp. 31–37, and James R. Pennock, "Federal and Unitary Government—Disharmony and Frustration," *Behavioral Science*, 4 (April 1959), pp. 147–157.
[20] This is a common observation of sociologists and demographers. For an analysis directly related to different preferences for government goods and services in different neighborhoods, see Charles S. Benson and Peter B. Lund, *Neighborhood Distribution of Local Public Services* (Berkeley: Institute of Governmental Studies, University of California, 1969).

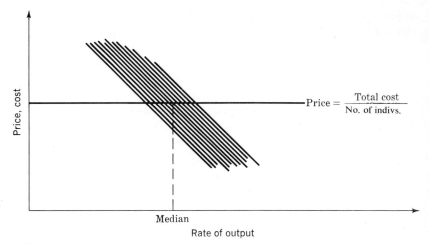

$$\text{Price} = \frac{\text{Total cost}}{\text{No. of indivs.}}$$

Median

Rate of output

FIGURE 5-6 Demands of a Homogeneous Group

political units. The fact that people with similar tastes reside together reinforces the conclusion that smaller rather than larger units may be more desirable because smaller units will contain more homogeneous populations.

Supply

The production of goods and services with public-goods characteristics involves problems of measurement, evaluation, and management not generally encountered in the production of private goods. These problems make analysis of public-goods production much more difficult than the analysis of private-goods production.[21]

    The nature of many governmentally provided goods and services is such that there is no obvious output measuring unit. What units of measurement, for example, accurately indicate the output of police services, education, fire protection, parks and recreation programs, and so on? The lack of good output measures is enough of a problem, but an even greater obstacle is posed by the difficulties of evaluation. Not only are there no output measures to attach valuations to, but the lack of quid pro quo transactions precludes any easy measure of the value of the goods and services provided. Furthermore, if financing is from general funds, direct beneficiaries of particular, governmentally pro-

    [21]Werner Z. Hirsch, "The Supply of Urban Public Services," in Harvey S. Perloff and Lowdon Wingo, Jr. (eds.), *Issues in Urban Economics* (Baltimore: Johns Hopkins, 1968), pp. 477–524.

vided goods and services have the incentive to overstate the value of the output to them because they will not bear the cost of greater production. We will treat problems of both output measurement and evaluation further in Chapter 7 where we deal with empirical studies of governmentally provided goods and services.

The lack of output measures and values for them also makes the problem of managing public organizations more difficult. Managers of private firms can use measures of sales and profits for preliminary estimates of employee performance and then direct specific attention to obvious trouble spots. Public managers—who lack measures of sales, outputs, or values of outputs—must instead concentrate on managing the behavior of employees. This entails setting up working rules and greatly limiting employee discretion. In addition, the face-to-face service nature of many governmentally provided services such as education and police means that the behavior of individual employees is extremely important for determining the value of the service to citizen-consumers. It is extremely difficult, if not impossible, to write and enforce behavioral regulations for every contingency the employee may encounter. The difficulties of measuring, evaluating, and managing goods and services with public goods characteristics are greater than those involving private goods.

Economies of Scale Economies of scale are decreasing average costs as output expands. The presence or lack of economies of scale has been a major focus in economic analysis of local government performance. However, the identification of economies of scale, or the average cost of output over a range of outputs, is not an easy task. The lack of output measurements means that there is often no unit to calculate an average for; what output measurements there are are so crude so that it is virtually impossible to determine if quality is really being held constant over the range measured.

Early economies-of-scale studies in the public sector differ significantly from economies-of-scale studies of private firms, and the functions derived are called "expenditure" functions rather than production or cost functions. The most significant differences are (1) that no assumptions of cost minimization and equilibrium among marginal contributions of factors of production can be made for government production as is done for private firms and (2) that the units of measurement are usually number of people served rather than a unit of good or service output. The expenditure functions tell you what governments serving different numbers of people spent per person—they provide no indication of whether or not the production was efficient or wasteful. A further complication is that conditions beside factor inputs and number of people served influence the expenditure figure. For example, it costs more per person to provide fire protection over exceptionally large or exceptionally dense geographic areas than it does for moderately dense areas. Because of their inherent problems, results of expenditure determinant studies with regards to identifying economies of scale in public services production must be viewed with caution. However, none of the major studies identified any significant economies of scale and some found a significant correlation between city size and per capita costs, implying diseconomies of scale as cities increased in size.[22]

Major attempts to identify production functions for public services were undertaken during the fifties and sixties. These studies are still plagued with the difficulties of output measurement and cannot be used to indicate whether or not the governments analyzed were producing efficiently. The results of different studies, however, have been consistent enough to suggest reasonable conclusions on economies or the lack of economies of scale in public service production. It appears that there are no economies of scale for services such as police, fire, refuse collection, libraries, street maintenance, and primary and secondary education for jurisdictions beyond relatively small size, perhaps as small as 15,000 to 25,000 and certainly no larger than 50,000 to 100,000. The existence of economies of scale in hospitals is uncertain. On the other hand there do appear to be economies of scale for water supply, sewage disposal, and electric power production.[23] The Advisory Commission on Intergovernmental Relations, long an advocate of governmental consolidation to achieve efficiency, has also concluded that "size does not seem to matter in cities of 25,000 to 250,000—neither economies nor diseconomies of scale were significant in number. But in cities over 250,000 population, size does make a difference—the law of diminishing returns sets in and there are significant diseconomies of scale."[24]

Some economists have tried to use concepts of economies

[22]Good examples of early studies include Amos Hawley, "Metropolitan Population and Municipal Government Expenditures in Central Cities," *Journal of Social Issues*, 7 (1951), pp. 100–108; Stanley Scott and Edward Feder, *Factors Associated with Variations in Municipal Expenditure Levels* (Berkeley: Bureau of Public Administration, University of California, 1957); and Harvey Brazer, *City Expenditures in the United States* (New York: National Bureau of Economic Research, 1959).

[23]For a survey of studies, see Werner Hirsch, "The Supply of Urban Public Services." Our conclusions on fire services differ from Hirsch's and are based on the study by Roger Ahlbrandt and discussed in Chap. 7.

[24]Advisory Commission on Intergovernmental Relations, "Size Can Make a Difference. A Closer Look," (Washington, D.C.: Advisory Commission on Intergovernmental Relations, Bulletin no. 70-8, 1970), p. 2.

of scale to define optimally sized governmental units.[25] However, different-sized units may appear "optimal" when one focuses on homogeneous demand-articulating groups, boundary spillovers, or economies of scale. The most important qualification, however, is that there is no special reason why the political unit which serves to articulate demand and collect taxes has to be the same or possess the same boundaries as the producer of the good or service.[26]

It has been traditional for cities, especially those spatially separated from other cities, to be both the demand-articulating and the producing organization. Economists, however, have long recognized that the optimal consuming unit (usually the household) in the private sector is not simultaneously the optimal producing unit for most goods and services. An examination of urban governments indicates that many governments purchase packages of governmental goods or services from other governmental producers and private firms. The possibility of separating demand from supply considerations in determining the boundaries of political units means that economies of scale per se are not an important criterion for determining efficient political unit size (except for isolated cities where deviance from lowest average-cost size is unimportant because nothing can be done about it). Instead, other characteristics of public goods and services can be used to identify efficient political structures. The consequences of separating demand and supply of government-provided goods and services will be explored further in the next chapter.

The Monopoly Problem   Many analysts of the public sector appear to assume that competition should occur in selecting leaders or policies but that the political unit itself should possess exclusive jurisdiction for specified functions within its geographic area. Governments, from this perspective, should be a system of perfect monopolies. Because some public goods possess natural monopoly characteristics, this view is often reinforced by economic analysis of the potential efficiency of governments serving specified geographic areas.

Within economic theory, however, it is not clear why govern-

---

[25]Jerome Rothenberg, "Local Decentralization and the Theory of Optimal Government," in Julius Margolis (ed.), *The Analysis of Public Output* (New York: National Bureau of Economic Research, 1970), pp. 31–64. Also see "Comment," by Gordon Tullock (pp. 65–68 in the same volume). Tullock raises the question as to whether economies-of-scale criteria are relevant for determining optimal size of local government when local governments can contract for their government goods and services with different-sized producing agencies.

[26]Robert Warren, "A Municipal Services Market Model of Metropolitan Organization," *Journal of the American Institute of Planners*, 30 (August 1964), pp. 193–214.

mental administrators will not act like monopolists in terms of being free to pursue their own preferences rather than produce to meet consumer demands.[27] One would not expect public monopolists to try to maximize profits, because if they could obtain surplus revenues it is unlikely that they would be able to put them in their pockets. However, there is reason to expect public administrators to pursue their own objectives, such as a larger bureaucracy or budget; a relaxed, unhurried atmosphere; or any number of other objectives which may or may not coincide with efficient production to meet consumer preferences.

When one examines the structure of government in the United States and especially the logic of the constitutional structure underlying it, he quickly concludes that the designers of the constitution were wholly cognizant of the potential monopoly problem.[28] In fact, they were so cognizant of it that they specifically designed a structure within which pure monopolies are difficult to achieve. Overlapping governments were created both by providing separate branches of the national government and by providing for concurrent state and local governments with considerable overlapping authority. The result is that government officials are constrained not only by political competition for their own offices but also by unsatisfied citizens seeking recourse to overlapping governments for desired public goods and services. In fact, citizens may even force public officials, through the courts, to undertake particular tasks. If local police are corrupt, one goes to the county sheriff, county prosecutor, state attorney general, or even the FBI. If education is poorly provided, one may seek special programs from state legislatures or functional grants from the national government, as well as try to influence local school districts.

In addition to the competition provided by overlapping public jurisdictions, there is competition for providing public-type goods and services in the form of potential private provision (there are more private police in the United States than public). Virtually all types of

[27]Robert L. Bish and Robert Warren, "Scale and Monopoly Problems in Urban Government," *Urban Affairs Quarterly*, 8 (September 1972), pp. 97–122. For an empirical study indicating that competition increases predictability and reduces bureaucratic discretion in the public sector, see Hirschel Kasper, "On Political Competition, Economic Policy and Income Maintenance Programs," *Public Choice*, 10 (Spring 1971), pp. 1–20.

[28]James Madison, Alexander Hamilton, and John Jay, *The Federalist* (New York: Modern Library, n.d.). For an analysis of the logic underlying the Constitution, see Vincent Ostrom, *The Political Theory of a Compound Republic* (Blacksburg, Va.: Center for the Study of Public Choice, 1971). For an application of these concepts to urban governments see Robert L. Bish and Vincent Ostrom, *Understanding Urban Government: Metropolitan Reform Reconsidered* (Washington, D.C.: American Enterprise Institute for Public Policy Research, 1973). The relationships between economic and political competition are also illustrated in George Stigler, "Economic Competition and Political Competition," *Public Choice*, 13 (Fall 1972), pp. 91–106.

goods and services usually provided governmentally in the United States are also made available privately, including education, police and fire protection, parks and recreational facilities, and highway construction and maintenance.

The provision of different mixes and of goods and services by different local governments within urban areas also provides a competitive element. If taxes are high for the services provided, businesses and potential residents will be reluctant to locate in that jurisdiction. As noted in Chapter 3, this reluctance may be directly observed in a reduced demand for (and reduced value of) property in that jurisdiction. In this situation, local citizens might be expected to react unfavorably toward political officials.

Still another type of competition is the use of competitive bidding when political units purchase packages of goods and services from other government or private providers. Contracted provision of goods and services not only permits adjustment of demand and supply boundaries independently but also encourages suppliers to keep prices down, since excessive costs may lead to the loss of a contract. A contract producer faces a real threat of being put out of business, something not faced by most public agencies providing goods for their own governmental units.

While there are few exclusive monopolists in the urban public sector, it is important to recognize the problems that may be posed by monopolies. An institutional design which appears most efficient in the short run may over a longer period of time prove less efficient if monopolies are created. Rivalry achieved through duplication and overlap may be necessary to maintain long-run responsiveness and efficiency.

Spillovers and Intergovernmental Relations

Costs and benefits of government goods and services may accrue to people outside of a governmental unit's boundaries. These effects are analogous to externalities generated in private markets and are generally referred to as spillovers. For example, if a local government maintains a free waterfront park, people from outside the governmental unit who have not contributed to the park's cost through taxation may come and use it, or a local government dumping municipal sewage into a river may provide lower-cost sewage service for its residents while generating higher costs of water purification for downstream users. Individuals affected by governmentally caused spillovers may wish to have their interests taken into account, just like individuals affected by market-generated externalities.

The preferences of individuals affected by government spillovers need to be considered if an efficient allocation of resources is to be achieved. For example, if nonresidents really receive benefits from a local government waterfront park, they should be willing to contribute to the cost of the park. Such funds might be obtained by the imposition of user charges for nonresidents, by the formation of a larger, special park district, which would finance the waterfront park by taxes from a larger area, or by payments from other local governments or from a larger government than the one providing the park. Without some financial contribution from nonresident park users, the local government is likely to provide less than optimal park services. In general, where benefits spill over beyond a government's boundaries, the good will be underprovided; where costs spill over, the activity is likely to be carried on at too high a level. These conclusions are analogous to conclusions concerning positive and negative externalities in private markets.

It is often stated that a government's boundaries should be large enough to include all the effects of its activities. However, that criterion alone may lead to extremely large governmental units, raising the costs of decision making above the gains to be achieved by including all individuals affected within the same boundaries. As indicated in the waterfront parks example, spillovers can be taken into account by intergovernmental agreements as well as by enlarging the boundaries of an existing unit or transferring the function to a larger unit.

The relationships among governmental units, like market relations among individuals, are governed by an extensive body of law.[29] Federal and state consitutions and state-enabling legislation all define the authority and responsibility of political officials acting in official capacities, and intergovernmental agreements, like private contracts, can be enforced in courts of law. The existence of extensive overlapping and recourse by local or state governments to more inclusive levels of government (local to state or state to national) provides a very complex environment for the resolution of spillover problems among governmental units. Very little can be said a priori about the functioning of this very complex system so that "optimum" sizes and scopes of local governments can be determined. Given the diversity among public goods and services and the diversity among citizens' preferences, it would be surprising if many different but relatively efficient institutional structures and agreements had not been created in the urban public sector. It is very unlikely that in such an environment

---

[29] Issues of intergovernmental relations are treated extensively in Bish and Ostrom, op. cit., chap. 5.

there is any one "best way." The issues of spillovers and government organization will be treated in relation to specific problems throughout the book.

SUMMARY

The nature of externalities, public goods, common pools, and natural monopolies creates a need for political organizations to complement markets for allocating goods and services in the economy. The public sector is especially important in urban economies because the high density of population and interaction creates many neighborhood effects that need to be taken into account—many public goods may be desired by urban residents, the population concentrations have the potential for destroying valuable common pools like air sheds and clean water basins, and natural monopolies require regulation. The activities of governments in the urban area are also important because their diversity influences residential and business site choices and thus the urban land-use pattern.

It is impossible to identify a priori an optimal urban public-sector organization. Demand criteria weigh toward relatively small, homogeneous political units. Problems of measurement, evaluation, and management also weigh toward relatively small organizations for management efficiency. Economies of scale appear less important because of the potential for separating political unit boundaries from producer boundaries. The potential monopoly problem may conflict with what appears to be an efficient, nonoverlapping organization structure of public organizations, but a complex structure that limits creation of monopolies simultaneously provides a system for resolving spillover problems through intergovernmental agreement or transfer of responsibility to a larger authority as well as by altering local government size. Economists should not be surprised to find that the urban economy is composed of many political units with different boundaries and different responsibilities.

In this chapter we have summarized a large body of literature which uses the approach of economics to examine public-sector phenomena. In the following two chapters we will look specifically at the urban public sector and bring empirical evidence and descriptive information to bear on its financing, structure, and functioning. Also, throughout the problem chapters in the remainder of the book, careful attention will be paid to the use of the concepts raised in this chapter to understand the urban public economy.

SELECTED READINGS

Bish, Robert L.: *The Public Economy of Metropolitan Areas* (Chicago: Rand McNally/Markham, 1971).

———and Robert Warren, "Scale and Monopoly Problems in Urban Government Services," *Urban Affairs Quarterly*, 8 (September 1972), pp. 97–122.

Buchanan, James M.: *Fiscal Theory and Political Economy* (Chapel Hill, N.C.: University of North Carolina Press, 1960).

———and Gordon Tullock: *The Calculus of Consent: Logical Foundations of Constitutional Democracy* (Ann Arbor, Mich.: University of Michigan Press, 1962).

Coase, R. H.: "The Problem of Social Cost," *Journal of Law and Economics*, 3 (October 1960), pp. 1–44 (Bobbs-Merrill Reprint, Econ.-69).

Downs, Anthony: *An Economic Theory of Democracy* (New York: Harper and Row, 1957; article length summary, Bobbs-Merrill Reprint, PS-378).

Hirsch, Werner Z.: "The Supply of Urban Public Services," in Harvey S. Perloff and Lowdon Wingo, Jr. (eds.), *Issues in Urban Economics* (Baltimore: Johns Hopkins, 1968).

Olson, Mancur Jr.,: *The Logic of Collective Action: Public Goods and the Theory of Groups* (Cambridge, Mass.: Harvard, 1965).

Ostrom, Vincent: "Operational Federalism: Organization for the Provision of Public Services in the American Federal System," *Public Choice*, 6 (Spring 1969), pp. 1–17.

Ostrom, Vincent, Charles Tiebout, and Robert Warren, "The Organization of Government in Metropolitan Areas: A Theoretical Inquiry," *American Political Science Review*, 55 (December 1961), pp. 831–842 (Bobbs-Merrill Reprint, PS-169).

Samuelson, Paul: "Diagrammatic Exposition of a Theory of Public Expenditure," *Review of Economics and Statistics*, 37 (November 1955), pp. 350–356 (Bobbs-Merrill Reprint, Econ.-270).

Tiebout, Charles M.: "A Pure Theory of Local Expenditures," *Journal of Political Economy*, 64 (October 1956), pp. 416–424 (Bobbs-Merrill Reprint, Econ.-307).

Tullock, Gordon: "Federalism: Problems of Scale," *Public Choice*, 6 (Spring 1969), pp. 19-29.

Warren, Robert: "A Municipal Services Market Model of Metropolitan Organization," *Journal of the American Institute of Planners*, 30 (August 1964), pp. 193-214.

CHAPTER 6

URBAN
PUBLIC FINANCE

The need for political units to resolve problems of externalities, provide public goods, manage common pools, and regulate natural monopolies was developed in the last chapter. In that chapter, however, no attention was given to the ways in which political units raise revenue to undertake their activities. In this chapter, we will examine how local governments finance their activities. Financing sources to be examined include property, sales, and income taxes; user charges; functional grants; and revenue sharing. In addition to analyzing the consequences of using different revenue sources, we will examine several fiscal issues that are of special importance. These issues are the chronic expenditure-revenue gap most large city governments face, the issues surrounding tax cooperation and competition among different jurisdictions, the suburban-urban exploitation hypothesis, and the problem of fiscal inequality and income redistribution within urban governmental systems. It will be seen that urban public finance plays an important role in influencing the pattern of land-use development in urban areas.

REVENUE SOURCES

Revenue sources for local governments in 1972 are presented in Table 6-1. Data are provided for the total amount of revenue derived

TABLE 6-1 Local Government Revenue Sources

	Millions	Per Capita	Percent
Property taxes	$40,876	$196	36.1
Intergovernmental transfers	39,017	187	34.5
User charges and fees*	25,215	121	22.3
Sales taxes	4,238	20	3.7
Income taxes	2,241	11	2.0
Other	1,575	8	1.4
Total	$113,162	$543	100.0

*Includes utilities, liquor stores, insurance trust earnings, and other local government fees and user charges.
Source: U.S. Bureau of the Census, *Governmental Finances in 1971–1972* (Washington, D.C.: 1973), p. 20.

from each source, the per capita revenue per source, and the percentage of all local government revenues each source represents.

Before we begin a discussion of revenue sources and their effects, we should remember that each state determines its own local government revenue structure and that there are considerable differences among states. Where states permit local options, there may also be considerable diversity within a state. State-granted local options may range from permission to use virtually any tax to limiting local governments to specific tax sources with maximum (or even exact) rates that can be used. Where rates and sources are very limited, citizens usually grant their local governments authority to levy additional property taxes by a special vote. The special vote often requires a 60 or 66 percent majority to be approved. These restrictions on local governments reduce their flexibility, but at the same time the political-externality costs they can impose on their citizens are also lower than they would be without state-set restrictions.

Property taxes have traditionally been the major source of revenue for all kinds of local governments. With very few exceptions, the property tax and user charges are the only sources of funds for special districts except school districts, which also receive large amounts of intergovernmental transfers. Municipalities have been permitted to expand their taxing authority in some states, and there is some use of sales and income taxes by cities and counties. Most income tax revenue collected by local government is collected by large cities, and two states permit income tax financing of school districts.

Intergovernmental grants are the second largest source of funds for local governments. The largest recipients of these funds in most states are school districts, because state government finances some part of educational expenditures. Most state governments also share revenues from taxes such as liquor and cigarette excises with local governments, often because local governments were the first tax collectors in these areas. The large number of intergovernmental transfers also reflects the fact that many local government activities provide benefits which spill over beyond their boundaries, and state or federal government provides funds to increase the level of those activities.

User charges are a major source of revenue for nonschool special districts and an important source of revenue for municipalities or counties which operate public utilities. Most local governments also impose fees for licenses, permits, copies of documents, and other miscellaneous items, none of which are large but all of which, in the aggregate, may be an important source of revenue. Let us look more closely at the revenue sources used by local governments.

Property Taxation[1]

Property taxation accounted for 83.5 percent of local government *tax* revenue in 1972. This was 55 percent of all local revenue including user charges and 36.1 percent of total revenue.[2] From 1900 through the 1950s, the role of the property tax in the national fiscal scene was declining. This was a consequence of relative expansion of the federal government and greater use of income and sales taxation by state governments. During the 1960s, however, the property tax began again to increase in importance. In 1972 it accounted for 11.0 percent of total government revenues.[3] The relative and absolute increase in the property tax during the 1960s has brought its use into considerable debate, especially since it serves to finance some important activities such as education—a field in which costs have been rising rapidly.

The property tax has three major advantages. First, it can be easily used by very small jurisdictions with overlapping or different boundaries. Each district simply indicates its tax rate to the township or county tax collector, who, in turn, lists it on the annual tax bill of residents within the district's boundaries. The revenues are then passed on to the local units by the tax collector. Second, property, at least real estate, is immobile. This facilitates the use of the property tax

---

[1] For a general discussion of the property tax, see Harold M. Groves and Robert L. Bish, *Financing Government* (New York: Holt, 1973), chaps. 4–6.

[2] Calculated from Table 6-1.

[3] Groves and Bish, op. cit., pp. 80–81; and U.S. Bureau of the Census, *Governmental Finances in 1971–1972* (Washington, D.C.: 1973), p. 20.

by small jurisdictions because property will not get up and leave if a tax is levied on it.[4] Property taxes are very hard to avoid. If one sells his property to avoid paying a tax increase, he can expect to receive a lower sale price because of the higher tax liability the property posesses; thus he has not escaped the incidence of the tax. Third, property taxation may be a benefits-received type of tax to the extent that benefits of government expenditures, financed by the tax, raise the value of property for residential or business usage. This is obvious when revenues are spent for street paving, street lights, sewers, or fire protection, but it may also occur with other services such as education. The issues of tax and benefits capitalization will be examined further after the property tax's major disadvantages are considered.

The disadvantages generally associated with property tax include the fact that it is a burden on housing consumption; that is, housing consumption is reduced relative to the consumption of other goods and services because it is more heavily taxed. Some analysts have concluded that property taxes in large cities may be equivalent to a 25 percent tax on monthly housing expenditures.[5] The property tax is also alleged to be regressive; that is, the tax represents a higher percentage of income for low-income than for high-income people. The property tax also often generates a liquidity crisis for elderly homeowners on fixed incomes. A retired person, for example, may have sufficient income to live satisfactorily in a home purchased and paid for before retirement. After retirement, however, property tax increases cause severe problems because of the relatively low dollar income received. Finally, the property tax is often poorly and inequitably administered because of poor assessment practices. For example, "good" property-tax assessment exists when homeowners pay within 15 percent of what an accurate assessment would require.

The questions of tax incidence, property taxation as a benefits tax, its effect on housing consumption, and its alleged regressivity are all closely related to three issues: first, to what extent property taxes are capitalized into property values; second, what the relation is between housing expenditures and income; and third, to what extent government goods and services are also capitalized into property values.

The more common approach to estimating property tax incidence has been to assume that the proportion falling on land was capitalized into land values and the proportion falling on improvements was entirely passed on to users of the improvements.[6] In Chapter 4 we indi-

---

[4]However, higher property taxes in a jurisdiction, unless offset by special benefits or lower-cost land, may result in a reduced level of new construction in the district.

[5]Dick Netzer, *Economics of the Property Tax* (Washington, D.C.: Brookings, 1966), p. 74.

[6]Netzer, ibid., pp. 32–33.

cated that it was impossible to really separate improvement from land values except for newly constructed property at an optimal location. There is another reason, however, why the traditional view of property-tax incidence is incorrect. This is the durability of real property. If the demand for property is not perfectly inelastic (i.e., the same quantity will be demanded no matter what the price), the tax can only be passed on to users if the quantity of property supplied can be immediately reduced—so the market will clear at a higher price which includes the higher tax.[7] The supply of improvements, however, is primarily made up of buildings already constructed, and new construction seldom exceeds 2 or 3 percent of the building stock. Thus, even a cessation of new construction is unlikely to reduce the building stock sufficiently to permit passing all higher taxes forward to users; some, perhaps most, of the burden is likely to be borne by owners of existing real estate who must now pay higher taxes without being able to raise prices enough to pass the tax forward. Some of the burden is also likely to be borne as reduced earnings in the construction industry as the demand for new construction falls. Construction workers, however, may be able to avoid most of the burden by shifting their efforts to other jurisdictions; owners of real property are likely to realize the burden of the tax increase as a reduction in the capital value of their real property.[8]

Five recent empirical studies bear directly on questions of property-tax capitalization. Larry L. Orr examined effects of different property-tax rates on rents in the Boston area.[9] His conclusion was that *different* property-tax rates on different properties did not significantly affect rent prices. If property taxes were passed on to renters, rents in higher-tax areas, *ceteris paribus*, should have been higher than rents in low-tax areas. Orr's conclusion was that at least differentials in property-tax rates are capitalized into property values rather than passed on to users of the improvements. In another study, John H.

[7]David R. Meinster, "Property Tax Shifting Assumptions and Effects on Incidence Profiles," *Quarterly Review of Economics and Business*, 10 (1970), pp. 65–83; and Frank de Leeuw, "The Demand for Housing: A Review of Cross-Section Evidence," *The Review of Economics and Statistics*, 53 (February 1971), pp. 1–10.

[8]Tax capitalization is a fall (or increase) in the value of real property in response to an increase (or decrease) in taxes. For example, if the market rate of interest for comparable-risk property is 10 percent, real estate producing $10,000 annual net rents would would have a capital value of $100,000 (Value = 10,000/0.10). If a tax increase of 1 percent of capital value is imposed, net rents fall by $1,000 (0.01 × $100,000) to $9,000. At the new level of net rents, the capital value of the building would be only $90,000 (Value = 9,000/0.10). The 1 percent tax increase results in a $10,000 fall in the value of the real estate—a loss which is borne by the property owner at the time the tax is imposed. The return on investment to a new purchaser, who would pay only the capital value of $90,000, remains at 10 percent.

[9]Larry L. Orr, "Incidence of Differential Property Taxes on Urban Housing," *National Tax Journal*, 21 (September 1968), pp. 253–262.

Wicks, Robert A. Little, and Ralph A. Beck analyzed capitalization of a property tax change on residential property in Missoula, Montana.[10] Their conclusion was that the change in property taxes was capitalized into real-estate values, and that the capitalization had to be on structures as well as land because of its magnitude. In another study, R. S. Smith analyzed effects of a property tax change on single-family housing prices in San Francisco.[11] His conclusions are the same as Wicks, Little, and Beck's: the tax change was capitalized into land and structure values. In still another study, Albert M. Church analyzed the effect of property-tax payments on the market price of single-family homes in a small California city.[12] His conclusion was that differences in property taxes on different homes were at least fully capitalized and sometimes overcapitalized[13] in the homes' market value. The only study concluding that differences in property taxes are partially (60 percent) passed on to renters is the study by D. M. Hyman and E. C. Pasour, Jr., of rents paid in different municipalities in North Carolina.[14] Hyman and Pasour attribute their different conclusions to more elastic land and housing supplies in North Carolina than might be found within a single city or metropolitan area.

The extent to which property taxes are capitalized into the value of rental housing and not passed forward in rent prices makes a tremendous difference in the incidence of the property tax on renters, who—on the average—have lower incomes than homeowners. The studies of capitalization all indicate that a high degree of capitalization occurs; thus much less regressivity results from passing property taxes on to renters than has been commonly assumed.

To the extent that property taxes are passed on in rents or property taxes are levied on owner-occupied housing, the relationship between housing consumption and income is crucial to determining the regressivity or progressivity of the tax. The common assumption is that higher-income families spend a lower percentage of their income on housing than do lower-income families and that therefore an equal-rate property tax would be regressive.

This common assumption has been challenged on at least two

[10]John H. Wicks, Robert A. Little, and Ralph A. Beck, "A Note on Capitalization of Property Tax Changes," *National Tax Journal*, 21 (September 1968), pp. 263–265.
[11]R. S. Smith, "Property Tax Capitalization in San Francisco," *National Tax Journal*, 23 (June 1970), pp. 177–193.
[12]Albert M. Church, "Capitalization of the Effective Property Tax Rate on Single Family Residences," *National Tax Journal*, 27 (March 1974), pp. 113–122.
[13]Overcapitalization means that the difference in taxes had a greater effect on market value than the market rate of interest would warrant.
[14]D. M. Hyman and E. C. Pasour, Jr., "Property Tax Differentials and Residential Rents in North Carolina," *National Tax Journal*, 26 (June 1973), pp. 303–307.

bases. One is the fact that most studies of the income elasticity of the demand for housing use short-run income rather than a longer-run permanent income concept. The inclusion of temporary low-income or high-income periods, many of which are not accompanied by changes in housing consumption, makes it appear that lower-income families spend higher proportions of their income on housing and higher-income families spend lower proportions of their income on housing. Use of the short-run income concept biases the income elasticity estimate downward and makes any proportional rate tax appear more regressive than it actually is.

A second problem with most estimates of housing income elasticities is that they utilize monthly or annual expenditures on housing as the measure of housing consumption and assume that there is direct proportionality between monthly or annual expenditures and the capital value on the housing upon which tax rates are based. In fact, the monthly cost of residing in an owner-occupied house increases only about 80 percent as fast as the capital value of the house. This is because mortgage payments and costs of maintenance and insurance are a lower percent of house value the higher the value of the house. Thus, if one moves directly from the observation of monthly housing expenditures to estimates of property-tax payments without correcting for the fact that the ratio of housing expenditure to capital value (and hence property-tax payments) is different at different income and expenditure levels, the resulting estimates will be more regressive than is actually the case. Correcting for transitory income and the changing ratio of housing expenditure to capital value indicates that property taxes may not only be proportional but may be slightly progressive, at least for owner-occupiers.

After analyzing the most significant previous studies of income elasticities for rental and owner-occupied housing, and correcting for permanent income and expenditure-to-value ratios of owner-occupied housing, Frank de Leeuw concludes that the income elasticity for rental housing in the United States is between 0.8 and 1.0 and the income elasticity for owner-occupied housing is between 1.1 to 1.5.[15] This would make property taxes slightly regressive among renters and and progressive among homeowners. When property taxes on rental units are at least partially capitalized rather than passed on to renters, however, as indicated by the capitalization studies, one would expect the overall effect of the property tax to be at least proportional and probably slightly progressive rather than regressive.

The third closely related issue is the extent to which benefits

[15]De Leeuw, op. cit., pp. 9-10.

from government expenditures are also capitalized into land values. It has been indicated several times that the purchase or rental of a site also includes rights to consume certain governmentally provided goods and services as well as liabilities to pay government taxes—and there is every reason to believe that both tax and benefit calculations influence site values. The traditional wisdom on benefits capitalization is that improvements to property (sidewalks, street lights, street paving) will be capitalized into land values but provision of human-type services (such as good schools) will not. This conclusion is inconsistent with theory, where one would assume that individuals with high demands for human-type services would be willing to pay a higher price to reside in a good school district than a poor one. It is also inconsistent with what empirical evidence exists on benefits capitalization.

Wallace Oates, in a study of school districts in New Jersey, concludes that the benefits of residing in a better school district are capitalized into real estate values.[16] In another study, which included both tax and benefits capitalization simultaneously, Edward M. Sabella concludes that increased expenditures on education consistently resulted in higher property values and increased taxes consistently resulted in lower property values.[17] Furthermore, the net effect of tax-financed expenditure increases was to increase the market value of single-family homes. This is what should have occurred if families felt that the benefits from additional educational expenditure outweighed the costs of increased property taxes. More evidence on the capitalization of benefits is needed, but a priori, one would expect benefits from government services as well as taxes—along with other features such as natural amenities, transportation access to employment or shopping, and the usefulness of the site itself—to be a determinant of real estate values. What evidence there is supports this expectation.

Is property taxation benefits taxation? Because property taxes and benefits may both be capitalized into land values, property taxation is not directly comparable to other types of benefits taxation such as user charges. Instead, citizens "buy in" to a local government, and the price they are willing to pay takes into account their estimated value of benefits and costs of residing in that unit. Only if the present value of government benefits was estimated to exactly equal the present value of future taxes would the capitalization of benefits and costs

[16]Wallace E. Oates, "The Effects of Property Taxes and Local Public Spending on Property Values: An Empirical Study of Tax Capitalization and the Tiebout Hypothesis," *Journal of Political Economy*, 77 (November–December 1969), pp. 957–971.

[17]Edward M. Sabella, "The Effects of Property Taxes and Local Public Expenditures on the Sales Prices of Residential Dwellings," *The Appraisal Journal*, 42 (January 1974), pp. 114–125.

cancel each other out, leaving the site price unchanged due to public sector activity. One would expect, however, that as long as demand schedules for public goods and services are downward sloping, there would be some consumer's surplus associated with government goods and services. Thus, a priori, at least, one would expect that on net, property values are higher because of government activity rather than lower.

When it is recognized that property taxation may be progressive rather than regressive[18] and that it may not have heavy excise effects which reduce housing consumption, major objections to its use are greatly reduced. In fact, the property tax would appear to be a very good tax for local governments to use when the goods and services produced are consumed primarily by local residents as long as the tax is well administered and some provision for reducing the burden on elderly low-income residents is built in.[19] This would permit small jurisdictions to provide desired levels of goods and services financed by their own residents or businesses. Sufficient examples of good administration exist to indicate that good administration is possible, and exemptions for low-income elderly are already in use in several states. On the other hand, it would also appear that property taxation may not be as desirable for financing programs whose benefits cannot be captured by local residents, since then capitalization of taxes, but not benefits, would occur.

We will return to questions of benefits and tax capitalization when considering general issues of income redistribution in this chapter and problems of reforming educational finance in Chapter 10.[20]

[18]One analyst who has argued this point for a long time is Mason Gaffney. For a recent statement, see his "The Property Tax Is a Progressive Tax," *Proceedings of the Sixty-Fourth Annual Conference on Taxation, National Tax Association* (Columbus, Ohio: National Tax Association, 1972), pp. 408–426.

[19]States are moving toward property tax relief for owners of low-valued dwellings and for low-income families. Relief for owners of low-valued dwellings comes from increasing the "homeowner's exemption," i.e., the amount of property not taxed at all. Relief for low-income families comes from increasing use of "circuit-breaker property-tax relief." Circuit-breaker programs exist where low-income families receive a credit for property taxes paid on their state income tax. If the property-tax credit is greater than the income-tax liability, a cash refund is received by the family. For a discussion of circuit-breaker programs, see Marc Bendick, Jr., "Designing Circuit Breaker Property Tax Relief," *National Tax Journal*, 27 (March 1974), pp. 19–28.

[20]Specialists in property taxation will note that we have not referred to Peter Mieszkowski's "The Property Tax: An Excise Tax or a Profits Tax," *Journal of Public Economics*, 1 (1972), pp. 73–96, in which he suggests that a perfectly general tax on all property, with total savings in the economy fixed and investments perfectly mobile, will result in a decline in the return on investments on property. Hence he concludes that the property tax is essentially a profits tax. While we agree with Mieszkowski that the property tax is not as regressive as commonly thought, it is not a general tax applying to all kinds of property, and property is certainly not perfectly mobile. For additional comments on Mieszkowski's analysis, see Dick Netzer, "The Incidence of the Property Tax Revisited," *National Tax Journal*, 27 (December 1973), pp. 515–536.

Sales Taxes[21]

Sales taxes are the single most important revenue source for state governments, accounting for 37.8 percent of all state government revenues and 15.1 percent of all federal, state, and local government revenues in 1972.[22] Where food is included and services are excluded from the tax base, the sales tax is estimated to be slightly regressive. When food is excluded and services are included in the base, it comes close to being a proportional tax.

Sales taxes are not heavily used by local governments. In 1971 only twenty-six states permitted their use by local governments, and most states limited the use of sales taxes to municipalities.[23] In 1972 sales tax revenues accounted for 3.7 percent of all local government revenues and approximately 8 percent of the revenue of all municipalities.[24] Where local government sales taxes are used, the local taxes are often collected by the state government at the same time it administers its own sales tax, and the revenue is passed back to the local government.

To avoid severe boundary problems, local government sales tax rates are kept low—usually from 0.5 to 1 percent of the price of the taxed good. The major problem with the use of sales taxation at the local level from an urban economics perspective is the potential lack of fit between any concept of benefits and tax costs. This lack of fit occurs not in areas where shoppers are primarily residents of the local government imposing the tax, as in central cities, but in suburban areas where regional shopping centers have created very concentrated patterns of retail sales. Thus, a local government including a shopping center will need virtually no other taxes—and most of the tax revenue received by the local government will be from nonresidents. One way in which this is taken into account, however, is that citizens in the unit containing the center may have to pay relatively high prices to locate there as the benefits from taxing nonresidents are capitalized into land values. This means that most of the actual gain from the center to the local government was captured by the landowners at the time of the shopping center's location decision. One should not be surprised, therefore, at the time and effort devoted to political activity, especially planning and zoning questions, by large landowners and real estate agents in local governments.

[21]John F. Due, *State and Local Sales Taxation* (Chicago: Public Administration Service, 1971), especially Chap. 10—"Local Government Sales Taxes," by John Miksell. This provides an extensive analysis of local government sales taxation.

[22]U.S. Bureau of the Census, *Governmental Finances in 1971-1972*, pp. 1 and 4.

[23]Due, op. cit., p. 266.

[24]U.S. Bureau of the Census, *City Government Finances in 1971-1972* (Washington, D.C.: Government Printing Office, 1973), p. 5.

TABLE 6-2   City Income Taxes in Relation to City Revenue

City	Percent of City Tax Revenues	Percent of Total City Revenues
Cleveland	47.8	17.3
Detroit	35.1	13.6
New York	21.0	8.1
Philadelphia	62.6	33.0
St. Louis	29.4	17.6
Toledo	74.9	31.8

Source: U.S. Bureau of the Census, *City Government Finance in 1971–1972* (Washington, D.C.: Government Printing Office, 1973), table 6.

One solution to the problem of concentrated retailing is to use a larger geographic area for the collection and distribution of sales tax. For example, the taxes collected throughout a county could be passed back to municipalities on the basis of their population. This would have the effect of enabling local governments to obtain about as much sales-tax revenue as their residents pay in sales taxes. One can argue that the jurisdiction maintaining the shopping center has extraordinary costs that need to be covered and therefore should receive all sales-tax revenue. It is likely, however, that the additional property-tax and business-tax revenues received by the local government within which the center is located is more than sufficient to compensate it for any extra costs.

Income Taxes[25]

Income taxes are the most important federal government revenue source and the second most important source of revenue for state governments. In 1972 income taxes accounted for 56.8 percent of all federal government revenues, 15.5 percent of state government revenues, and 38.4 percent of all governmental revenues.[26] In contrast, income taxes provided only 2 percent of local government revenues during that year. However, local government income taxes are used most by large cities and are more important as a source of revenue for them than national average revenue figures indicate.[27] Data on the percent of city tax revenue and percent of total city revenue for a sample of large cities using income taxes is presented in Table 6-2. From the

[25]Tax Foundation, *City Income Taxes* (New York: Tax Foundation, 1967), provides a useful survey.

[26]*Governmental Finances in 1971–1972*, p. 4.

[27]*City Government Finances in 1971–1972*, table 20.

data, we can see that income taxes are a very important source of revenue for some cities. We must remember, however, that most cities do not use income taxes at all. Only nine states permitted their municipalities to levy income taxes and two states (Pennsylvania and Ohio) also permitted school districts to use income taxes in 1971.[28]

Two characteristics associated with the federal income tax are that it is progressive and that its revenues rise in relation to income growth more rapidly than other tax revenues. These characteristics, however, are limited when the tax is used by local governments because their small boundaries prevent them from using highly progressive taxation. A local government relying heavily on progressive taxation could easily find itself with few high-income taxpayers to tax. Thus, most local government income taxes are proportional flat-rate taxes rather than progressive.

The major boundary problem that occurs with local income taxes arises when individuals work and live in different jurisdictions. Most states require a division of tax revenues if both jurisdictions levy taxes. When a large city utilizes an income tax but surrounding jurisdictions do not, it often taxes commuters at a lower rate than residents. There has been considerable outmigration of jobs and industry in older central cities without income taxes, and adding an income tax differential for employees who commute to the city may increase the the relative advantage of a suburban location for employment and hence of a suburban location for firms as well.

User Charges[29]

User charges accounted for 22.3 percent of local government revenues in 1972, making them the third largest source of local government funds. User charges are also important in the financing of the federal and state governments, for which they provided 31.2 and 21.8 percent of total revenue respectively.[30] Two-thirds of federal user charges and one-half of state charges are trust fund earnings; local government user charges are primarily receipts for goods or services.

User charges are really a price paid to a government for receipt of specific goods and services. User charges cannot be used for pure

[28]Advisory Commission on Intergovernmental Relations, *State-Local Finances and Suggested Legislation* (Washington, D.C.: Government Printing Office, 1970), pp. 100–102.

[29]For a selection of articles on user charges, see Selma J. Mushkin (ed.), *Public Pricing for Public Products* (Washington, D.C.: Urban Institute, 1972). Readers interested in pursuing the traditional issues surrounding average cost versus marginal cost based user charges are referred to this volume.

[30]*Governmental Finances in 1971–1972*, p. 20.

public goods because the exclusion of nonpayers is not possible. User charges are also seldom used for goods and services with significant spillovers, such as education or fire services. Instead, they are restricted to payment for goods and services which provide specific benefit to the payer, such as public utilities, license fees, tolls for bridges or highways, or copies of official documents for individual use. The largest collectors of user charges are public utility districts and municipalities operating public utilities.

User charges which reflect the cost of production can be characterized as equitable, efficient, and information producing. They are considered equitable because the individual benefiting from the good or service provided pays directly for it. The costs are not passed off onto others or to taxpayers in general. User charges are considered efficient because the citizen-consumer pays for the good. Thus, one can be sure that the benefits of the good or service provided exceed the cost. The assumption that benefits exceed costs cannot be made when costs of providing government services are borne by the general taxpayer. Finally, user charges produce information as to what level of service should be provided. The government can produce the quantity where the marginal cost of production equals the price charged for the service. If a government provides, free of charge, a good for which charges could be made, it can expect that the quantity demanded will be at the level where marginal benefits approach zero. This quantity is almost certainly to be one at which marginal costs exceed marginal benefits. Only with charges actually imposed can the producer be assured that users are accurately revealing the value of the good to them. User charges give a government an automatic adjustment mechanism from which to determine the output of its goods and services. This mechanism is lacking when user charges are not used or—as in the case of public goods—when they cannot be used.

Most analysts of user charges by general local governments conclude that much greater use of them could be made. However, while all revenue from user charges, in the aggregate, is a significant source of local government financing, the revenue from any single fee is often very small. Thus, the general taxpayer is relatively unconcerned about additional user charges. But city councilmen can be assured that the particular group to be charged for a service they were formerly receiving free will make their opposition to a user charge known. Thus the easiest path for government officials is to not utilize user charges to as great an extent as would be both efficient and equitable.

Lack of the use of cost-based user charges has been directly related to the spread of urban areas. Because it costs more to provide utilities and public services such as roads to sparsely settled fringe areas than to more densely settled areas, the use of standard fees for everyone or general taxation to provide utilities and services to fringe-area residents provides them with a subsidy that is paid for by other residents. Thus, fringe-area residents do not see the real costs of having utilities and public services extended to them, and they live further away from built-up areas than they would if they had to pay the real costs of their services. This leads to more rapid spread of urban areas and higher public service costs overall. Furthermore, it is unlikely that the fringe-area residents themselves receive the benefit of the subsidy; it more likely accrues to the previous landowner who sold the land for a higher price when it became apparent that public services would be available to the property at less than their real cost.

Some local governments do attempt to alleviate this problem by levying a one-time charge related to the cost of providing services when rural land is subdivided or by using small special assessment districts to finance new services in subdivisions. It is still likely, however, that rural landowners make capital gains and urban areas expand more rapidly than would be efficient as a consequence of the failure to make better use of marginal cost-based user charges for providing utilities and other public services to fringe areas.[31]

In addition to improving the efficiency of public services in fringe areas, user charges have been recommended to help alleviate congestion and ration scarce facilities in our densest urban areas.[32] Many public goods, such as streets and parks, are available to everyone. However, beyond a certain use denisty, one person's use will interfere with another's. After crowding occurs, public goods may resemble common pools and be rendered useless unless access to them is limited. Urban freeways, parks on holidays, and public beaches in many areas are crowded. User charges provide one way to ration use to individuals who place the highest value on access to these facilities. At the same time the revenues derived from the user charges could be used to finance expanded capacity of highways or to purchase more park and beach space until a balance between demand and cost of provision is achieved. Thus user charges may be utilized as a management tool to ration scarce resources such as highways and parks as well as to finance their provision. Further examination of the potential of user charges will be undertaken in later chapters, especially Chapter 11, on the urban environment, and Chapter 12, on urban transportation.

[31]For further analysis of this problem, including differences that may result from different conditions, see Paul B. Downing, "User Charges and the Development of Urban Land," *National Tax Journal*, 26 (December 1973), pp. 631–638.

[32]Wilbur Thompson, "The City as a Distorted Price System," *Psychology Today*, 2 (August 1968), pp. 28–33.

Intergovernmental Transfers[33]

Intergovernmental transfers were the second most important source of financing and provided 35.5 percent of all local government revenues in 1972. Both federal and state transfer programs are large. In 1972 federal government transfers to state and local governments equaled 13.9 percent of all federal expenditure and 16.5 percent of all state and local revenues. State transfers to local governments equaled 33.6 percent of state government expenditure and 32.5 percent of local government revenues.[34]

While the census treats intergovernmental transfers as a single category, there are important distinctions among different kinds of transfer programs. The most important kinds of programs include functional and bloc grants and revenue sharing.

Functional Grants   Functional grants are payments by one level of government to a lower level of government for which the lower-level government undertakes programs agreed upon by the grantee and grantor. While called grants, functional grants are essentially contracts where one government pays another government to undertake specific activities.

The rationale behind functional grants at both the state and federal level is quite clear: the larger unit, representing a larger and different constituency than the smaller unit, has determined that an increased or modified output of some locally produced good or service is desirable. It proceeds to pay the smaller unit to increase or modify its output of that good or service. Local matching funds and conformance to program standards are usually required to ensure a net increase or modification of output rather than simply substitution of federal or state funds for local funds. Thus the financial resources of the larger unit can be combined with decentralized production by smaller units to accomplish policies desired by the larger units.

In 1972 there were several hundred grant programs, but 78 percent of federal functional grant funds were concentrated in education, highways, and public welfare. Housing, urban renewal, and health

---

[33]For a history and analysis of federal grant programs, see Selma J. Mushkin and John F. Cotton, *Sharing Federal Funds for State and Local Needs* (New York: Praeger, 1969). Parts of this section are abstracted or taken from Robert L. Bish and Vincent Ostrom, *Understanding Urban Government: Metropolitan Reform Reconsidered* (Washington, D.C.: American Enterprise Institute for Public Policy Research, 1973), pp. 55–66.

[34]*Governmental Finances in 1971–1972*, p. 20.

and hospitals accounted for another 10 percent. State governments also have a variety of programs, but education alone accounted for 58 percent of the funds. Welfare accounted for 19 percent and highways 7 percent. Thus 84 percent of state grant funds are concentrated in the same areas as federal grant funds.[35]

Education, highways, and public welfare are all areas where benefits from local expenditures spill over the boundaries of local or even state jurisdictions—yet local production of specific services is most efficient. Education spillovers occur because children educated in one district often migrate to other areas. Grants are also made to assure a minimum level of education no matter how poor a school district is. Even though financing is provided by large units, however, small local units still undertake the actual production of educational services.

Highways are another area where benefits spill over to users from outside the jurisdiction undertaking highway construction and maintenance. Thus the federal government finances virtually all expenditures for the construction of the interstate system, with state highway departments responsible for construction and maintenance. Given variations in geographic and climatic conditions, it is doubtful that a federal agency could build and maintain highways more economically than states. Local governments are left to provide their own local roads and streets where benefits are enjoyed primarily by local citizens, with some supplemental funding from state and federal sources. The result is a network of highways, roads, and streets that are financed by different levels of government and serve different communities of interest.

Public welfare presents a somewhat different problem than education or highways. It is in the joint interest of citizens in any single local unit of government to avoid income redistributive policies, even if each individual citizen desires income redistribution, as long as other governmental units provide income redistribution for the poor. Any attempt by a small unit to undertake income redistribution creates the potential for a dual migration problem—high-income families move out to locations where less redistribution is undertaken and low-income families move to areas with high levels of income redistribution.[36] As governmental units become larger, migration becomes more

---

[35]Ibid., p. 22.

[36]It should be noted that families do not have to move in specific response to dissatisfaction with the public provision of services or local government financing of income redistribution. In a society where approximately 20 percent of all families change their residential location each year, all that is necessary is that families take into account public goods and services and local government taxes when selecting a new residential location.

costly. Thus financing of welfare and highly redistributive activities has tended to shift from local to state to national government. The importance of financing income redistributive activities by larger units of government will be developed more fully later in this chapter and in subsequent chapters, especially Chapter 7, on issues in the urban public sector, and Chapter 8, on housing, segregation, race, and the ghetto.

Functional grant programs are often criticized on two bases, and they possess one inherent problem that has not been resolved. The first criticism is that they are extremely complex. The second is that they distort local priorities. The answer to the second criticism is quite simple: of course they distort local priorities. Grants were specifically designed to get local units to undertake actions they would not otherwise have undertaken.

The complexity of the grant programs is a more difficult issue. They were never intended to be an integrated program—they are ad hoc responses to specific problems where different constituencies share different communities of interest by access through different levels of government. From the perspective of any one local government official (or a researcher), the many federal programs can be confusing.

A recent major study of federal grant programs does conclude that some packaging would improve the efficiency of these programs, but it still concludes that many specific programs are needed if national interests are to be properly taken into account.[37] The alternative is either increased national production of public goods and services now produced by state and local agencies or a failure to generate a mix of locally produced public goods and services which meets the preference of national users of those goods and services.

An unresolved problem with grant programs is the same problem that occurs with the creation of any political authority. The authority necessary for public officials to "do good" also permits them to "do bad." Legislative authority to permit efficient achievement of widely shared national or state objectives can also be used to open the treasury to raids by well-organized interest groups. No single interest group will take large enough sums by itself for other legislators or citizens to be greatly concerned. But together, the accumulated raids of all interest groups may involve large sums of money.

The Constitution created a system of overlapping jurisdictions specifically so that minorities within one jurisdiction could carry their case to another jurisdiction reflecting different communities of interest. This was the basis for Madison's solution to the problem of majority tyranny or, as we have called it, the monopoly problem. Func-

[37]Mushkin and Cotton, op. cit.

tional grants have contributed greatly to the openness of the American political system, and it is difficult, perhaps impossible, to conclude that elimination or major reduction of functional grant programs would offer a net improvement.

Bloc Grants and Revenue Sharing Bloc grants are simple cash transfers from one government to another according to a formula that is not related to the performance of a specific service. The recipient government can spend the grant money as it prefers. About 13 percent of state grants to local government are of the bloc grant type. Formulas for bloc grants usually include a per capita component and are sometimes adjusted by income or wealth to achieve some income redistribution.

The federal revenue sharing program introduced in 1972 is like many state bloc grant programs under which an allocated amount is distributed among state and local governments.[38] The amount of the first five-year appropriation is slightly over $30 billion. This will make revenue sharing in 1975, for example, equal to 2 percent of the total federal budget and 12 percent of total intergovernmental transfers to state and local governments.[39] The average per capita share is $29. State shares are calculated from one of two formulas, and whichever provides the higher amount is used. One formula includes population, income, and revenue effort; the other includes population, income, revenue effort, urbanization, and state and federal individual income tax collections in the state. Because there are per capita and income elements in the formula and because higher amounts of income taxes are collected in high-income states, some income redistribution is expected to result.

Once state shares are determined, a proportion is passed through directly to general local governments in proportion to their general tax revenues relative to total tax revenues of all general local governments in the state. By tying allocations to general taxes raised within a state, the formula discriminates against states within which local governments make heavy use of user charge or special assessment areas for financing their services. Furthermore, by allocating funds within states only to general local governments, the use of special districts for functions where boundaries differ from those of general local government, which would be more efficient, is discouraged. For example if taxes collected by a sewage district designed to encompass a

---

[38]Public Law 92–512; 86 stat. 919. *State and Local Fiscal Assistance Act of 1972,* October 20, 1972.
[39]Executive Office of the President, Office of Management and Budget, *The U.S. Budget in Brief,* 1975 (Washington, D.C.: Government Printing Office, 1974), pp. 9 and 48.

drainage area were instead collected by a general local government, that local government's revenue sharing funds would increase. The local government could obtain still more revenue if it financed all sewage facilities from general taxes instead of from user charges.

The original revenue-sharing proposal of the Nixon administration approached a pure no-strings bloc grant. The revenue sharing legislation enacted by Congress added some "strings" but still left revenue sharing more like a bloc than a functional grant. Among the restrictions imposed by Congress are that revenue-sharing funds can be used only for priority areas as determined by Congress. These areas include public safety, environmental protection, public transportation, health, recreation, libraries, social services for the poor or aged, financial administration, and capital construction. Education, highways, and direct welfare, for which considerable functional grant aid is available, are not included on the revenue-sharing priority list. In addition, administration of the revenue-sharing funds must be through a separate trust fund with federally approved administrative procedures—a clause that has resulted in several hundred small governments refusing to accept the revenue-sharing funds because costs of administration exceed the additional revenue.

While revenue sharing in the form of bloc grants has been used by state governments for a long time, federal revenue sharing generated considerable controversy. The major reasons advanced in favor of federal revenue sharing were (1) that it would broaden the use of the rapidly growing and progressive federal income tax so that state and local governments would not have to rely on slow-growing and regressive taxes and (2) that revenue sharing would strengthen state and local governments. Opponents of revenue sharing included those who opposed the heavy use of rapidly growing and progressive taxes. Also included were those who felt that state and local governments needed to be strengthened but who argued that strength comes from efficiently providing goods and services that respond to citizens' preferences as reflected by their willingness to pay. From this perspective, it may be because state and local governments are not responsive to citizens' preferences that citizens do not want to pay higher taxes, and providing funds from the federal treasury will not make these governments any more responsive or efficient. In fact, having federal funds may make the local units less responsive to their own citizens. Some observers have concluded that federal revenue sharing may be just another raid on the federal treasury, this time by state and local government officials who find it easier to convince their congressmen that they need more funds than to convince their local constituents that the benefits from additional taxes would exceed costs.

On balance, we can anticipate that federal revenue sharing will alleviate some fiscal problems by providing additional funds to state and local governments. The administrative requirements may also encourage improved fiscal administration in some smaller units. We doubt, however, that revenue sharing will have a major impact on either strengthening or improving the efficiency of state and local governments. In fact, if the revenue-sharing formula encourages a shift away from user charges, special assessment areas, and special districts where unusual boundaries are needed, its net effects on the efficiency of the local public sector could be negative instead of positive.

URBAN FISCAL ISSUES

We have surveyed the major revenue sources for local governments. Reliance on these sources and their use by hundreds of governmental units within most metropolitan areas introduces problems other than those directly associated with any single source. These problems are the topic of the next section. Analysis of these issues will also indicate how the financing of local governments directly influences the land-use patterns of urban areas, especially the patterns of residential development by high-and low-income groups.

The Revenue-Expenditure Elasticity Gap[40]

A revenue-expenditure elasticity gap exists whenever, as incomes rise, costs of providing a constant level of government goods and services increase more rapidly than revenues from existing taxes. Thus government must either reduce the goods output, raise tax rates, or seek additional sources of revenue. It is the elasticities, or relative rates of growth of costs and revenues, that determine whether or not a revenue-expenditure elasticity gap occurs.

Tax Elasticity Tax elasticity is a measure of the rate of tax revenue growth (with tax rates and base unchanged) relative to the rate of income growth in an economy. The elasticity coefficient is calculated by dividing the percentage change in tax revenues by the percentage change in income.

$$e_t = \frac{\% \text{ change in revenue}}{\% \text{ change in income}}$$

Whenever tax revenues grow more rapidly than income, e_t is

[40]Groves and Bish, op. cit., pp. 342–346.

TABLE 6-3   Tax Elasticity Estimates

		Low	Medium	High
Income taxes:	Individual	1.5	1.65	1.8
	Corporate	1.1	1.2	1.3
Sales taxes:	General	0.9	1.0	1.05
	Motor fuel	0.4	0.5	0.6
	Alcoholic beverages	0.4	0.5	0.6
	Tobacco	0.3	0.35	0.4
	Public utilities	0.9	0.95	1.0
	Other	0.9	1.0	1.1
Property tax		0.4	0.8	1.2

Sources: Advisory Commission on Intergovernmental Relations, *Sources of Increased State Tax Collections* (Washington, D.C.: Government Printing Office, 1968), p. 3. Dick Netzer, *Economics of the Property Tax* (Washington, D.C.: Brookings, 1966), pp. 184–190.

greater than 1 and we call the tax elastic. When tax revenues grow slower than income, e_t is less than 1 and we call the tax inelastic. For example, if revenue growth were 6 percent while income growth were 4 percent, e_t would equal 1.5. Revenue would grow 1.5 times as fast as income and the tax is elastic. If revenue growth were 3 percent and income growth 4 percent, $e_t = 0.75$. Revenue would grow only three-fourths as fast as income and the tax is inelastic.

Tax elasticity estimates for state and local taxes are presented in Table 6-3. Ranges for estimates are provided because of estimating difficulty and because states and local governments often have different bases or rate structures for the same tax.

The elasticities of the different taxes are easy to understand. The high elasticity of the income tax is due to its progressivity and the fact that increases in income are taxed because most exemptions are already accounted for. Sales taxes grow at about the same rate as income, with a lower elasticity when services are excluded from the base and a higher elasticity when food is excluded and services are included in the base. Motor fuel, alcoholic beverages, and tobacco are all slow-growing because as income rises use of these items rises much more slowly. The wide range for the property tax is due to both variations in assessment practices and the fact that property values are strongly influenced by demographic trends within small areas as well as by income growth.

The elasticity estimates indicate that governments relying on income taxes and sales taxes—primarily state governments—can expect rates of revenue growth to be equal or higher than income growth. Governments relying on property taxes and selective excises—primarily local governments—can expect low rates of revenue growth.

Different state and local governments using different taxes or bases may expect different rates of revenue growth.

The Advisory Commission on Intergovernmental Relations has estimated elasticities for state tax structures to range from 0.7 to 1.49, with a median of 1.0 to 1.1.[41] One estimate of overall state and local tax elasticity is 0.9. This would imply that median local government tax elasticity is lower than 0.9, perhaps as low as 0.7 or 0.8. These tax elasticities must be compared with expenditure elasticities to determine the revenue-expenditure elasticity gap.

Expenditure Elasticity Expenditure elasticity is analogous to tax elasticity. The elasticity coefficient is calculated by dividing the percentage change in the cost of providing a constant level of public goods and services by the percentage change in income: that is,

$$e_e = \frac{\% \text{ change in expenditure}}{\% \text{ change in income}}$$

Expenditure elasticity is much more difficult to measure than tax elasticity because of the difficulty of measuring a constant quality and quantity of public goods. Several estimates of expenditure elasticities have been made and all are relatively close to each other. Boyle estimated combined state and local expenditure elasticities from 1956 to 1967 to be 1.1.[42] Bradford, Malt, and Oates estimated that cost increases accounted for 5 to 7 percent of the 9 percent annual growth of local government spending from 1947 to 1967.[43] With annual income growth of 6.1 percent over the same period, this would imply an expenditure elasticity of approximately 1 for local governments only.

The Gap Tax elasticity estimates of approximately 0.8 for local governments and 0.9 for state and local governments combined, and 1 to 1.1 for state governments, compared to expenditure elasticities of 1.1 for the state-local total and approximately 1 for local governments alone indicate that as income rises the costs of providing a constant level of goods and services have been increasing more rapidly than automatic tax revenue growth. Thus many state and most local

[41]Advisory Commission on Intergovernmental Relations, *Sources of Increased State Tax Collections* (Washington, D.C.: Government Printing Office, 1968), p. 3.

[42]Gerald J. Boyle, "The Anatomy of Fiscal Imbalance," *National Tax Journal*, 21 (December 1968), p. 413.

[43]D. F. Bradford, R. A. Malt, and W. E. Oates, "The Rising Cost of Local Public Services: Some Evidence and Reflections," *National Tax Journal*, 22 (June 1969), p. 201.

governments have had to continually raise tax rates or find new sources of revenue just to maintain an existing level of government goods and services. Any increased service levels had to be financed by still higher tax-rate increases and more new revenue sources.

The high cost increases in the public sector have been explained as being the result of their service nature. Labor-intensive services do not have high productivity increases, yet wages must be raised along with productivity increases in the private sector or public employees will shift to private employment.[44] For example, teachers may still teach thirty students in a classroom, but they are paid at much higher rates than they were twenty years ago.

We suspect that the lack of productivity increases in the public sector is due to more than its service nature. It may be equally due to the fact that public employees lack incentives for undertaking innovation in a quasimonopolistic environment. Is it possible that if the proper incentives existed, innovations could be discovered to increase efficiency of public services? We will explore this issue further in the next chapter.

Tax Cooperation, Competition, and the Suburban-Urban Exploitation Hypothesis[45]

Chronic revenue shortages make most local government officials acutely aware of their rivalry with other political units, many of which may be overlapping, for their citizens' and businessmen's tax dollar. This rivalry leads to both tax competition and the need for coordinated policies to prevent problems that occur when a citizen or business undertakes activities in several political units at once.

Tax coordination occurs primarily through the use of credits and deductions, coordinated tax administration, and contracted tax collection. Tax deductions and tax credits[46] are often permitted for taxes paid to another jurisdiction. For example, the federal government permits deductibility of taxes paid to state and local governments, states permit credit for income taxes paid to other states, and local governments permit full or partial credits for income taxes paid to other

---

[44]William J. Baumol, "Macroeconomics of Unbalanced Growth: The Anatomy of Urban Crisis," *American Economic Review*, 57 (June 1967), pp. 413–426.

[45]Some parts of the first two pages in this section are taken from Robert L. Bish and Vincent Ostrom, *Understanding Urban Government: Metropolitan Reform Reconsidered* (Washington, D.C.: American Enterprise Institute for Public Policy Research, 1973), pp. 53–55.

[46]Tax deductions are deductions from income of taxes paid elsewhere in determining the tax base upon which tax liability is calculated. Tax credits are subtractions of taxes paid elsewhere from taxes owed.

local governments. The widespread use of crediting arrangements re-
solves many of the problems of double taxation for persons doing business in two or more jurisdictions or individuals who reside in one jurisdiction and work in another.

Coordinated tax administration occurs when two or more governments agree on rules and regulations, so that an individual or businessman needs to keep only one set of records for two or more governments using the same tax base—as when local, state, and federal
income tax laws require the same information for tax purposes. Further coordination occurs when one jurisdiction contracts with another
for the collection of its taxes. It is common for state governments to
collect income and sales taxes for local governments and for counties
and townships to collect property taxes for state governments and
other local jurisdictions. Since 1972, the U.S. Internal Revenue Service has also been authorized to contract to collect income taxes for
state governments.

Tax competition has two aspects. One is competition for the same
tax base. An implicit assumption exists that the governmental unit that
gets there first preempts the base and prevents the others from using
it. The second type of tax competition is when adjacent jurisdictions
keep taxes low to compete for desired industries or residents. Both
aspects of tax competition may keep taxes down. Both are alleged to
be undesirable by state and local officials and others who advocate
higher public spending.

The heavy use of the income tax by the federal government was
at one time assumed to prevent state and local governments from using
this source of revenue. Thus state and local governments had to resort
to the use of sales and property taxes; hence they derived a lower
revenue growth rate than the federal government. While state and local
governments do rely on slower-growing tax sources than the federal
government, forty-one states and numerous local governments have
adopted income taxes. In spite of heavy federal use, it does not appear
that the income tax has been preempted by the federal government.

Tax competition among adjacent jurisdictions has forced many
local government officials to reconsider tax increases which would
raise taxes to the detriment of local residents or businessmen in competition with those in adjacent areas. This pressure may force local
officials to develop more efficient uses of present revenues in lieu of
tax increases. It would appear that tax competition among adjacent
jurisdictions, like any kind of competition, will limit the discretion
of local government officials and force them to be more efficient than
they might be otherwise. This type of pressure would appear to be
a desirable consequence of tax competition.

One particular problem of competition for citizen's taxes and achieving a balance between taxes paid and benefits received has received considerable recent analysis. This problem is called *the suburban-urban exploitation hypothesis.*

As we discussed in Chapters 2 and 4, population and economic activity have been continually spreading out beyond the boundaries of the older central cities. The movement of high- and middle-income residents and the location of new businesses and industrial plants in suburban areas has left the older central cities with increasing proportions of low-income families and relative and sometimes absolute declines in business activity. These shifts have aggravated the problem of the expenditure-revenue gap by requiring additional expenditures for low-income populations while the tax base was growing very slowly or perhaps even remaining stagnant.

While economic activity in cities has been declining or growing slowly, many suburban areas with their above-average-income families and new business and industry are regarded as affluent. Many suburbanites, however, still commute to the central city for employment and shopping and use its streets, parks, and cultural facilities. These trends have led to the allegation that suburbanites do not pay their fair share of the central-city government costs although they benefit from central-city services. Thus, suburbanites are said to "exploit" the central city.

Several studies have tried to estimate the effect of suburbanites on central city finances. One of the earliest was by Amos Hawley.[47] He demonstrated that the larger the proportion of an urban area's population outside the central city, the higher the central city's per capita expenditures. This study provided evidence that central-city expenditures were higher the larger the surrounding suburban population, and it was concluded that suburbanites caused higher spending by central-city governments. Hawley went on to conclude that because suburbanites were not contributing to city revenues, they were being subsidized by the central-city residents and businesses.

Later studies have confirmed Hawley's observation that central cities do spend more the larger their suburban populations.[48] The later studies, however, also noted that suburbanites must be credited with bearing the burden of a share of central-city taxes because their use of the city raises property values (and hence property-tax revenues),

---

[47]Amos H. Hawley, "Metropolitan Population and Municipal Government Expenditure in Central Cities," *Journal of Social Issues*, 7 (1951), pp. 100–108.

[48]Examples include Julius Margolis, "Metropolitan Finance Problems: Territories, Functions and Growth," in James M. Buchanan (ed.), *Public Finances: Needs, Sources and Utilization* (Princeton, N.J.: Princeton, 1961), pp. 229–270; and Harvey E. Brazer, *City Expenditures in the United States* (New York: National Bureau of Economic Research, 1959), p. 58.

and their purchases from city businesses contribute to businesses' ability to pay taxes and make a direct contribution to sales and excise tax revenues collected by city government. Thus one cannot conclude, as Hawley did, that suburbanites do not pay their fair share of central-city services without an examination of tax incidence and revenue flows to compare with commuter-related expenditures of central cities.

Attempts have recently been made to determine the net effects of suburbanites on central-city expenditures and revenues, but results have not been consistent. Weicher, for example, concludes that taxes paid by suburbanites to central cities outweigh the increase in central-city expenditures. In addition, his analysis points out that because suburban communities differ among themselves, one must know the economic composition of the suburban communities, especially their mix of retailing, manufacturing, and residents relative to the central city, in order to draw conclusions for any particular urban area.[49]

In another study William Neenan examined Detroit's fiscal interaction with six suburban communities.[50] Net fiscal flows between suburban communities and Detroit ranged from $2.22 to $7.24 per capita net subsidy from Detroit for five communities, while Detroit received $1.84 per capita net subsidy from the sixth. Neenan went on to estimate what he terms "willingness to pay" for public services instead of just net fiscal transfers. Willingness to pay is estimated by assuming that higher-income families value public goods and services higher than lower-income families in proportion to their income differences. When the willingness-to-pay factors were introduced to the analysis, Neenan concluded that suburban residents would have really been willing to pay more to Detroit than they did pay; the adjusted "subsidies" from Detroit to suburban communities ranges from $3.96 to $18.22 per capita. Neenan concludes that suburban residents receive considerable welfare gain through the public sector from Detroit.

Neenan's conclusions have been subjected to several criticisms, the most important of which concern the sensitivity of his results to minor changes in some assumptions and his use of the term "exploit."[51] It also appears that Neenan's conclusions are a consequence of Detroit's responsibilities for financing many poverty-linked welfare

---

[49]John C. Weicher, "The Effect of Metropolitan Political Fragmentation on Central City Budgets," in David C. Sweet (ed.), *Models of Urban Structure* (Lexington, Mass.: Heath, 1972), pp. 177–203.

[50]William Neenan, "Suburban-Central City Exploitation Thesis: One City's Tale," *National Tax Journal*, 23 (June 1970), pp. 117–139.

[51]D. A. L. Auld and Gail A. C. Cook, "Suburban–Central City Exploitation Thesis: A Comment," *National Tax Journal*, 25 (December 1972), pp. 595–598; and David D. Ramsey, "Suburban-Central City Exploitation Thesis: Comment," *National Tax Journal*, 25 (December 1972), pp. 599–604.

expenditures and that the conclusions might be reversed if financing of welfare was undertaken on a countywide or statewide basis, as is common in many other states. Thus one must be careful about generalizing from this study to other metropolitan areas.

Kenneth V. Greene, William Neenan, and Claudia Scott have undertaken a study similar to the Detroit study to analyze Washington, D.C.'s relationships with its Maryland and Virginia suburban areas.[52] On a cost-of-service basis, they conclude that suburbanites more than pay for the benefits they receive from the District of Columbia; on a willingness-to-pay criterion, estimated in a manner similar to that of Neenan's Detroit study, they conclude that suburbanites would be willing to pay sufficiently more for the services they receive so that the District of Columbia would receive net benefits.

One important limitation to the suburban-urban public sector flow studies discussed so far is that they make no estimate of gains that accrue to central-city residents in the private sector because the central city is the center of a larger market area than the central city itself. One of the better studies takes this additional income factor into account.

Phillip Vincent estimated the costs generated by commuters in central cities, taxes attributable to commuters, and increased incomes of city residents due to their serving the large urban market area.[53] Vincent's conclusions are that suburbanites may, on the average, generate as much as $39 in additional per capita costs for city residents, but that commuters also generate an increase of $78 in per capita incomes for central-city residents. Thus Vincent concludes that even if suburbanites generate more in additional central-city expenditures than they contribute to central-city revenues, central-city residents are still better off than they would be without the larger commuting population.

In spite of the difficulties of empirically measuring net fiscal flows among citizens of different jurisdictions, some general observations appear warranted. First, the net balance of public sector expenditure benefits and revenues among citizens of different jurisdictions is likely to vary from place to place depending on the ratios of manufacturing, retailing, and people of different income classes in the different jurisdictions. Second, the locus of responsibility for financing poverty-linked expenditures will make a difference in results, with suburbanites benefiting more when poverty services are financed by cities instead

[52]Kenneth V. Greene, William B. Neenan, and Claudia D. Scott, *Fiscal Interactions in a Metropolitan Area* (Lexington, Mass.: Heath, forthcoming).

[53]Phillip E. Vincent, "The Fiscal Impact of Commuters," in Werner Z. Hirsch, Phillip E. Vincent, Henry S. Terrell, Donald C. Shoup, and Arthur Rosett, *Fiscal Pressures on the Central City* (New York: Praeger, 1971), pp. 41–143.

of counties or states. And third, even if net public sector benefit and expenditure flows result in net costs for central-city residents, income increase in the private sector will probably more than make up for the public sector costs. Our general conclusion is that central cities are probably not exploited by their commuters and that the cities would be worse off if commuters found jobs, in addition to residences, in the suburbs.

Fiscal Inequality and Income Redistribution

Suburbanization, the specialization of land uses within small areas and homogeneous population groupings within small jurisdictions, results in different local government units possessing vastly different fiscal resources. Some jurisdictions have high per capita levels of wealth and income while others have low values of wealth and income.[54] Residents of lower-income jurisdictions may also require greater expenditures on some public services, such as education, if they are to participate fully in American society.

It is difficult to obtain agreement on the "proper" amount of income redistribution or reduction in fiscal disparity. Some individuals feel that "equity" is permitting those who contribute the most to the economy, as measured by their earnings, to benefit from their effort. Others feel that equity is best promoted by extensive income redistribution from higher-income individuals to individuals with less income. Still others regard equity as attempting to provide everyone with equal opportunity, and this would require redistributive financing of some public services such as public education. While we cannot treat all aspects of income redistribution questions in this analysis, it is useful to look at the operation of the urban public economy to determine what kinds of income redistribution policies have a greater probability of success if citizens do in fact express preferences for income redistribution through political processes.

Let us begin with the assumption that wealthier individuals do favor some income redistribution, and that some level of redistribution is generally felt to be desirable by sufficient numbers of individuals to permit passage of income redistribution programs in local government decision-making bodies. How might any representative high-income individual analyze his residential location choice? Even a high-income individual, in choosing a residential location, might decide that locat-

[54]For an analysis of fiscal disparity, see Advisory Commission on Intergovernmental Relations, *Metropolitan Social and Economic Disparities* (Washington, D.C.: Government Printing Office, 1965).

ing in a small government composed of other high-income families would best meet his preferences, and his location alone will not make observable differences in the net income redistribution occurring within the metropolitan area. After all, would not the best situation, even for an individual favoring income redistribution, be for others to redistribute their income while he consumes his privately, just as an individual favoring national defense would still be better off if all others paid for national defense and he used his funds for a trip to Spain or a new boat? In other words, it is still rational for any single individual to attempt to be a free rider even if he has a positive, effective demand for income redistribution.

But, we might argue, every high-income family will not choose to live with other high-income families—some will reside in mixed districts and contribute to income redistribution programs. Would this pattern be an equilibrium? If new immigrants to the metropolitan area consider taxes and benefits in their choice of residential site, there will be some tendency for individuals qualifying for redistribution to locate where redistribution programs exist and for higher-income families to avoid such locations. Higher-income families residing in redistributing districts would find that, as more individuals qualified for redistribution moved into the area, the price of maintaining any given minimum income for all residents would rise. This rise in price would then tend to influence higher-income families to move elsewhere or at least not move into an area where redistribution would be very costly to them. This poses a dilemma for governmental policy makers because policies to redistribute income may simultaneously lead to fewer high-income families, and hence reduced fiscal capacity, within the jurisdiction. It is no wonder that central-city governments often demonstrate considerable ambivalence toward proceeding with policies which might benefit a majority of their citizens but discourage higher-income residents or new businesses from locating within the city. It may be very difficult to achieve a stable population mix with high levels of income redistribution within small governmental units, or even governments as large as those of old central cities. This would be the case even if most high-income individuals favored redistribution and were willing to contribute to it.

Furthermore, if high-income people already feel that they redistribute enough of their income through state and federal programs, they may group together in homogeneous political jurisdictions to improve the efficiency of their public goods consumption. In addition, they may specifically support policies such as restrictive zoning and building codes which prevent low-income families from residing in jurisdictions populated by high-income families. At the same time, however, low-income families may prefer to live among high-income families only if benefits, primarily financed from taxes on higher-income families, exceed the lower-income families' tax costs. If lower-income families could receive income redistribution benefits from high-income families without residing with them, the lower-income families might well prefer to reside with others of similar tastes. In this way public sector outputs could also be better designed to meet their preferences. Thus, income redistribution through a larger governmental unit may also reduce some of the tension that exists between groups with homogeneous preferences residing together to efficiently provide public goods and services, and outsiders who could benefit from joining the group, but would simultaneously raise the cost to other group members.

We expect that because of tendencies toward neighborhood homogeneity and the unequal distribution of industry, business, and other elements of fiscal capacity, income redistribution will not be extensive if it is the responsibility of small governmental units. If income redistribution is to be of very large magnitude, it must be undertaken on a large scale, at least on a statewide and probably a nationwide basis. However, financing on a large scale does not imply that actual undertaking of the various programs could be managed on an equivalent scale. It is very difficult for very large public service bureaucracies in welfare or other person-to-person service areas to be run efficiently and also to adjust to unique neighborhood conditions that may be essential for enhancing the life prospects of low-income individuals. Thus, income redistribution may well be an area where intergovernmental grant programs are necessary to achieve a combination of large-scale financing to eliminate the free-rider problem and local government implementation to facilitate the adjustment of programs to meet unique conditions in different communities.[55]

As we indicated in discussing functional grants, grants for education and welfare constitute two of the three areas for which approximately 80 percent of all state and federal functional grants are given. Whether or not the present system is achieving levels of income redistribution that most people would favor is uncertain, however, because the aggregate data cover up the fact that some states leave welfare entirely to local governments while others finance it entirely at a statewide level. Better empirical evidence is needed to identify the consequences of different scales of financing to see if our expectations are borne out.

[55]For an extended analysis of this problem, see Robert L. Bish, "Urban Health, Education and Welfare Programs in a Federal System," in Selma J. Mushkin (ed.), *Services to People: Federal Aids in State Urban Strategies* (Washington, D.C.: Public Services Laboratory, Georgetown University, 1974).

One area where some evidence on redistribution does exist is in school financing. Even though most states contribute significantly to financing local school systems, considerable expenditure disparities due to differences in income and wealth remain. A closer analysis of questions and empirical evidence on this problem will be undertaken in Chapter 10.

IMPROVING FISCAL CAPACITY

Among urban governments, large central cities spend the most per capita, have the highest expenditure increases each year, and are alleged to have the greatest "needs." Most discussions of urban fiscal problems are devoted to how large cities can raise still more revenue.[56]

Before considering questions of more revenue, however, we may well ask whether institutional structures permit citizens to indicate their preferences and receive what they desire for their tax dollars. Thus we need to pay careful attention to the question of whether the "fiscal crisis" is a crisis for bureaucrats desiring larger bureaucracies— bureaucracies that their citizens feel are not worth additional cost— or whether it is a crisis in that citizens willing to pay for more services have no suitable way of doing so. Both interpretations are consistent with a fiscal crisis, but forcing individuals to put more resources into institutions where they feel costs exceed benefits will not improve their welfare. We must remember that in economics, willingness to pay is *the* measure of benefit.

The perspective presented in Chapter 5 raises questions which are directly related to the fiscal crisis. First, how are demands articulated? Are big-city governments too large and heterogeneous to enable diverse neighborhoods within them to indicate their preferences? Second, what incentives exist for producers to be efficient and responsive to citizen preferences? Are they monopolists? Are there gains to be obtained from introducing cost-saving innovations?

Only if demands are articulated effectively and incentives exist to encourage efficient production can we be sure that the solution to a fiscal crisis is more money. If demands are not indicated effectively and incentives to provide and maintain efficient production are lacking, there is no reason to expect additional funds to be spent efficiently for what citizens want.

The popular impression that fiscal problems are more severe in big cities than in the suburbs is consistent with a priori implications of

---

[56]School districts, especially big-city school districts, face similar problems. These problems are analyzed in Chapter 10.

our analysis. It is in big cities, where political units are largest and populations most heterogeneous, that demand articulation is most difficult. Big-city governments are also the most monopolistic, lacking the number and variety of overlapping and competitive political units that the suburbs have. Also, big-city producing organizations are much larger than economies-of-scale criteria warrant—apparently so large as to be extremely difficult to manage efficiently.[57] Thus instead of focusing on the "fiscal crisis" aspect of urban government, perhaps it would be more beneficial to focus on the ways urban governments could be organized to allow for better preference indication by citizens and to provide incentives for government bureaucracies to be more efficient and productive.

If problems of demand and production incentives can be resolved, two serious fiscal problems remain. One is the revenue-expenditure elasticity gap; the other is the financing of welfare or income redistributive services by local governments. To the extent that local governments rely on inelastic taxes and are unable to improve efficiency or introduce cost-saving innovations, they may be forced to continually find additional sources of revenue. One solution would be for local governments to be permitted to levy a broader spectrum of taxes so that the tax elasticity of their combined sources would be equal to expenditure elasticity. If tax and expenditure elasticity were equal, tax rates or new sources of revenue would be necessary only when additional goods and services were provided. At the same time, one might not want local governments' tax elasticity to be much higher than expenditure elasticity, so that goods and services could not be expanded (or at least higher spending undertaken) continually with little public visibility.

One way to balance revenue sources would be for state governments to administer sales and income taxes, with low-rate local options. If most local governments used these sources, then different levels of spending would still be reflected in property taxes, where they enter more directly into location site choices. Local governments could also rely more heavily on user charges, which would provide incentives for efficiency and equity as well as raise additional revenue.

We have concluded that it is not feasible for small local governments to finance welfare or income redistributive expenditures. If this function were shifted to the state or federal level (in the East, states themselves are so small as to make federal redistribution de-

---

[57]These points are developed in Robert L. Bish and Vincent Ostrom, *Understanding Urban Government: Metropolitan Reform Reconsidered* (Washington, D.C.: American Enterprise Institute, 1973); and Robert L. Bish and Robert Warren, "Scale and Monopoly Problems in Urban Government Services," *Urban Affairs Quarterly*, 8 (September 1972), pp. 97–122.

sirable), considerable pressure would be taken off older central cities. Approaches to shifting welfare financing to state or federal levels are explored further in Chapter 8.

SUMMARY

In this chapter on urban public finance we have surveyed the sources of local government revenue, the issues of revenue and expenditure growth, tax cooperation and competition, the suburban-urban exploitation hypothesis, fiscal inequality and income redistribution. When added to the material on the theory of public goods and collective action from Chapter 5, this discussion provides us with essential information and a basic framework for understanding the operation of the urban public sector. Our analysis thus far, however, has certainly not exhausted the issues in which a combination of the theory of public goods and collective action and location theory can contribute significant insight into the problems of urban government organization and urban public policy. In the next chapter we will use our framework to examine additional issues in the urban public sector more closely.

SELECTED READINGS

Bish, Robert L.: "Urban Health, Education and Welfare Programs in a Federal System," in Selma J. Mushkin (ed.), *Services to People: Federal Aids in State Urban Strategies* (Washington, D.C.: Public Services Laboratory, Georgetown University, 1974).

Bradford, D. F., R. A. Malt, and W. E. Oates: "The Rising Cost of Local Public Services: Some Evidence and Reflections," *National Tax Journal*, 22 (June 1969), pp. 185–202 (Bobbs-Merrill Reprint, Econ.-49).

Groves, Harold M., and Robert L. Bish: *Financing Government* (New York: Holt, 1973), chaps. 17 and 18.

Meinster, David R.: "Property Tax Shifting Assumptions and Effects on Incidence Profiles," *Quarterly Review of Economics and Business*, 10 (1970), pp. 65–83.

Mitchell, William E., and Ingo Walter (eds.): *State and Local Finance* (New York: Ronald, 1970).

Mushkin, Selma (ed.): *Public Prices for Public Products* (Washington, D.C.: The Urban Institute, 1972).

Neenan, William: "Suburban-Central City Exploitation Thesis: One City's Tale," *National Tax Journal*, 23 (June 1970), pp. 117–139.

Netzer, Dick: "The Incidence of the Property Tax Revisited," *National Tax Journal*, 26 (December 1973), pp. 515–536.

Oates, Wallace E.: "The Effects of Property Taxes and Local Public Spending on Property Values: An Empirical Study of Tax Capitalization and the Tiebout Hypothesis," *Journal of Political Economy*, 77 (November–December 1969), pp. 957–971.

Vincent, Phillip E.: "The Fiscal Impact of Commuters," in Werner Z. Hirsch, Phillip E. Vincent, Henry S. Terrell, Donald C. Shoup, and Arthur Rosett, *Fiscal Pressures on the Central City* (New York: Praeger, 1971), pp. 41–143.

CHAPTER **7**

ISSUES IN URBAN PUBLIC SECTOR ORGANIZATION

In Chapters 5 and 6 we explored many aspects of public sector operation, organization, and financing. In this chapter we are going to use concepts and conclusions reached in those chapters to focus directly on issues related to organization of the urban public sector. We will devote special attention to proposals for the consolidation of independent municipalities and special districts into a single metropolitan government for an urban area and to proposals to provide neighborhood governments within older central cities.

We will begin with a discussion of the uses of technical analysis for governmental decision making. Our focus will be on benefit-cost analysis, a technique developed by economists for evaluating government investments and programs. Following this analysis we will introduce questions concerning the incentives public officials and employees may or may not have—incentives that encourage them to use technical analysis or to be responsive and efficient in producing municipal goods and services. Next, we will present empirical studies of police and fire protection services to provide a stronger empirical base for our observations on organization of the urban public sector.

The analysis of urban government reform begins with an examination of proposals for metropolitanwide governments. The underlying assumptions of this approach are presented, followed by an interpretation within the framework developed in Chapters 5 and 6. We then summarize studies of the effects of the metropolitan governments that have been created in the United States. Next we will turn to proposals for decentralizing big-city governments. These proposals, we will note, are based on a very different view of urban government than are consolidation proposals. We will also indicate how an understanding of the nature of public goods and services permits a reconciliation of the diverse reform approaches. Finally, we will look again at the complexity of the urban public sector and summarize our conclusions on the organization of government in urban areas. While part of this summary will repeat points made previously, it will serve to focus attention on crucial problems in the public sector that will continually reappear in our subsequent analysis of urban problems. Policies for all our urban problem areas—housing, segregation, poverty, race, zoning and land-use control, education, environmental management, urban transportation, and policies to guide the future of urban areas—are strongly affected by the organization of the public sector in urban areas.

DECISION MAKING IN GOVERNMENT

It may seem unusual to begin an examination of the organization of governments in urban areas with a focus on decision making, but two aspects of decision making are crucial elements in designing effective governmental structures. First is the role of expert technical analysis and second are the incentives offered to individual public officials and employees. Technical analysis is important because, where technical analysis can provide generally agreed upon solutions to problems and where outputs are easy to measure and monitor, citizens would find it rational to rely on relatively simple political structures, perhaps electing a single executive and small council to be responsible for a great number of functions over a large area. The few elected officials could then focus on general policy formation, rely on skilled technical bureaucracies for designing and implementing specific policies, and be able to monitor bureaucratic performance easily.

On the other hand, where technical analysis cannot provide solutions which are generally agreed upon, where large bureaucracies may be difficult to manage, where face-to-face service delivery is important to the value of the service received by the citizen, and where service outputs are difficult to measure and monitor, elected officials have to be closely familiar with the administration of programs as well as the formation of policy if they are to determine what public policies are actually to be followed. Familiarity with program administration would require that the officials limit their scope to relatively small areas and perhaps be functionally specialized, resulting in more smaller governmental units in urban areas. Benefit-cost analysis is one of the most highly developed tools for evaluating public investments and programs. Therefore understanding of its possible uses and limitations is useful for understanding the potential for expert decision making in urban government. Benefit-cost analysis also represents, to as great a degree as possible, the use of economic theory and analysis for decision making.

The analysis of incentives which encourage public officials and employees to try to be responsive and efficient in their provision of goods and services to citizens also represents the application of economics to an understanding of the functioning of governmental organizations. Analysts focusing on incentive systems would stress that no matter how well-developed are expert decision-making techniques such as benefit-cost analysis, unless public officials receive direct rewards (or avoid negative sanctions) for their implementation, the decision-making techniques are unlikely to be used to improve the performance of the public sector. Since different organizations of the urban public sector will provide different incentives to encourage responsiveness and efficiency, these incentives should be considered in all their variety. They must be understood if one is to understand various results achieved by differently organized urban public sectors.

Benefit-Cost Analysis[1]

Benefit-cost analysis appears extremely simple. One simply lists all benefits and costs of a proposed program or project, evaluates the benefits and costs to obtain dollar figures, adjusts costs and benefits occurring in the future by a discount rate to determine their present values, compares the difference between the present values of alternative projects, and finally chooses those projects with the highest

[1]A good survey of benefit-cost analysis is contained in A. R. Prest and R. Turvey, "Cost-Benefit Analysis: A Survey," *Economic Journal*, 75 (December 1965), pp. 683–785. Examples of benefit-cost studies reflecting advances in the state of the art are published annually by Aldine Press and titled *Benefit-Cost and Policy Analysis*.

While our focus is on benefit-cost analysis, the conclusions drawn with regard to the use of technical analysis for decision making would be the same for either cost-effectiveness analysis (the analysis of alternative ways to achieve a given objective), or systems analysis (a more general analysis indicating the relationships among different variables). The weaknesses of technical analysis appear most obvious in benefit-cost analysis because it attempts to accomplish more than the other kinds of analysis. Shifting to other kinds of analysis, however, just makes the problems less visible. It does not solve them.

present values. Each of these steps, however, involves conceptual and empirical difficulty.

Listing Benefits and Costs   Benefit-cost analysis has been developed primarily for application to federal projects or by economists whose perspective was that of the entire society. Thus the recommended practice is to list all benefits and costs regardless of who or where their recipient is. This national perspective presents problems for the use of benefit-cost analysis by local governments. Local government decision makers are primarily concerned with the welfare of their own constituents, not the rest of society. It is rational for them to consider only those benefits and costs that accrue within the local jurisdiction and not to take into account benefits or costs which spill out. Thus the techniques developed to implement benefit-cost analysis may not provide local government officials with the information they are most interested in for their own decision making unless the benefits and costs of the project accrue primarily within the local government jurisdiction. At the same time, benefit-cost analysis which lists only local benefits and costs may neglect important spillovers. This problem is really overcome only when costs and benefits occur within a single jurisdiction or when intergovernmental agreements are utilized to account for spillovers. Generally, however, a listing of benefits and costs is the easiest part of a benefit-cost analysis and is feasible for virtually any kind of project.

Evaluating Benefits and Costs   Benefit-cost analysis was developed first for water-resource investments such as reclamation and irrigation projects, the provision of water supply, hydroelectric power production, and flood control. Evaluation of benefits from these projects is relatively straightforward because, with the exception of flood control, their output is a measurable product which is often sold and for which market values are calculable. It was also possible to make reasonable estimates for the value of flood control by estimating the market value of property protected in relation to the probability of floods of differing levels of severity within the life of the project. The costs of these investments are also reasonably straightforward, with the exception that the value of in-the-channel uses of water for recreation or fish propagation were often neglected or undervalued because those uses lacked market prices.

When we turn to the activities local governments in urban areas undertake, the problem of evaluating benefits and costs, especially benefits, is much more difficult than it was in the case of the water-resource projects. The difficulties exist because (1) the outputs of many government services are not easily measurable; (2) even where they are measurable, a market price may not exist; and (3) the same output may be valued differently by different people.

The outputs of many government services have no simple measures. Services such as police, fire protection, courts, schools, and planning, for example, all lack accepted scales for measuring outputs. Even where we can obtain some measure, such as school attendance, criminals apprehended, library circulation, or park usage, the measure does not reflect all the benefits from the services. Relying on a few simple measures such as these may lead to a neglect of other important characteristics of the service. Furthermore, if measures representing only part of the benefit of a service are used for evaluative purposes, employees may systematically bias their activities to enhance measured performance while overall quality of the service deteriorates. For example, an easy way to reduce crime rates in an area is to undertake aggressive street patrol. Citizens interpret the aggressive patrol as harassment, citizen-police relations deteriorate, and citizens quit calling police to report crimes. The reported crime rate declines and police performance as measured by reduced crime rates improves. However, the value of police services to citizens has actually declined. The fact that most public programs have multiple outputs makes it extremely difficult to rely on only a few measurements for continual evaluation of public programs, even if those few output measures would provide a good picture of service benefits before employees get the chance to bias them.[2]

Lack of measures is enough of a problem, but even where we can get relatively good measures, the lack of a quid pro quo determined price makes it difficult to determine the value of the measured output to the users. The lack of revealed prices may stem from the fact that public sector provision dominates the service—as with education, libraries, and parks—or that the service is a public good. In providing a public good, there is no way to exclude consumers and thus no way to force them to reveal their preferences through pricing. Services such as local parks, streets and roads, public health, police services, fire protection, and court systems are of this nature. Furthermore, even in areas where exclusion would be possible, as with education and libraries, the goods are provided publicly because they are alleged to have external benefits for which preferences are not revealed in any precise manner.

[2]Elinor Ostrom, "Institutional Arrangements and the Measurement of Policy Consequences: Applications to Evaluating Police Performance," *Urban Affairs Quarterly*, 6 (June 1971), pp. 447–475.

Finally, even if average evaluations of public services outputs could be derived, different people are likely to value the outputs differently and one would have to have rather specific information on the consuming group in order to estimate the value of the service to them. Furthermore, the problem of assigning values of services is especially difficult when one has to estimate the value of face-to-face service delivery programs like education. In such areas, the benefits depend on the way a particular public employee treats citizens at some time in the future.

In spite of substantial progress in benefits measurement, the difficulty of measuring and evaluating outputs of public goods and services forces analysts to attribute values on relatively weak empirical bases. Furthermore, differences in values assigned may determine apparent project desirability. For example, the major purpose of investment in streets and public transportation is to reduce the time it takes to go from one place to another. The analyst will be able to make estimates of time saved from the investment, but we have no market where individuals reveal how much they are willing to pay to travel faster in urban areas. Moreover, it is extremely difficult to disentangle revealed values of time saved from cost saving and comfort when we analyze consumer choice of travel routes or modes. Estimates of the value of time saved in transportation studies range from 30 percent of a person's wage rate to his full wage rate, yet because time saving may constitute 50 to 80 percent of the benefits from a transportation investment, an increase in valuation of as little as 20 or 30 cents per hour can change the evaluation of a project from negative to positive.[3] Similar problems arise when we attempt to value such things as park user days or reduction in lives lost from a disease prevention program. Because a service for which we do not have market-revealed preferences is the primary output, a slight change in the value selected may determine the final decision on the project.

The sensitivity of entire project evaluations to slight changes in values placed on major outputs is less important when the purpose of the benefit-cost analysis is to compare several closely related programs. Then the same evaluations can be used for each program, and the relative desirability of programs would usually not be changed if slightly different valuations were used. For example, alternative freeway routes or alternative public transit systems can be compared using the same value—travel time saved—for each. On the other hand, one would feel less confident using benefit-cost analysis to compare a public transit system with a new park.

[3]Transportation studies are discussed more fully in Chap. 12.

Discounting the Future   Most of the benefits from investments and part of the benefits and costs of most public programs accrue in the future. When benefits or costs occur in the future, we need to estimate their present value to be able to compare benefits and costs of a single project or net benefits from different projects. Present-value calculations are made by discounting the net benefits accruing in a future year to the current year. A calculation is made for each year for the life of the project and the present values for all years are then summed to determine the present value of the project.[4] For example, the present value of a project involving an investment cost of $1,000 in the current year, operating costs of $50 annually for the next four years, annual benefits of $250, $300, $350, and $400 in the next four years, and a salvage value of $100 in year five would be calculated as follows:

$$PV = -\$1,000 + \frac{\$250 - 50}{(1 + r)} + \frac{\$300 - 50}{(1 + r)^2} + \frac{\$350 - 50}{(1 + r)^3}$$

$$+ \frac{\$400 - 50}{(1 + r)^4} + \frac{\$100}{(1 + r)^5}$$

If the discount rate, r, used for the calculation was 6 percent, the present value, PV, would be $17.54.

The logic of discounting is straightforward. Benefits or costs expected in the future are not worth their face amount today because a lesser amount, if invested today, would result in the face amount in the future. The choice of a discount rate, however, is not straightforward, and different discount rates may change a project's apparent desirability. For example, if we had used a discount rate of 10 percent instead of 6 percent in our example above, the present-value estimate would be −$24.65 instead of $17.54, a difference of $42.19.

The discount rate is supposed to reflect the opportunities forgone by investing in the project instead of using the resources elsewhere. For the public sector as a whole, that would imply a discount rate equal to the opportunity cost of forgoing either consumption or investments of equivalent risk in the private sector.

There is no market, however, where we observe a private market interest rate that would be appropriate to use because private investor borrowing is complicated by tax adjustments not found in public investments. For example, a private firm may have to return an average of 12 to 14 percent on investments to earn an after-tax return of 6 to 7 percent, but it may be willing to pay 8 to 10 percent to borrow

---

[4]Calculation of the present value of a government investment follows the same procedure as calculation of the present value of real property as presented in Chap. 3.

funds because the interest paid on borrowed funds is tax deductible. The opportunity cost of capital would be the 12 to 14 percent return on the actual investment, not the observed 8 to 10 percent borrowing rate. At the same time, citizens may be forgoing consumption for an after-tax return of 6 or 7 percent.

Selecting a discount rate for use by a local government is still more complicated because the actual cost of funds for a local government is always lower than the cost of funds for a private investor. This is because local governments do their borrowing with the use of tax-free municipal bonds. For example, an investor with a 50 percent marginal tax rate would realize an after-tax return of 5 percent on a private bond paying 10 percent interest, but a tax-free municipal bond at 6 percent would give the investor a real 6 percent return. Given that the before-tax return on private investment is higher than the loan-market interest rate and the cost of borrowing to local government is still lower, local governments will find it rational to undertake investments which provide lower returns than forgone investments in the private sector, even though the return to local government may equal the cost of forgone consumption by purchasers of its bonds.

The use of different discount rates will affect not only the public-private mix of investments but also the relative rankings of public projects. The lower the discount rate used, the greater the bias toward large investments with long payoff periods. If a higher discount rate is used, a low initial investment with shorter payoff periods will appear superior. Different discount rates will have important impacts on the outcome of a benefit-cost analysis, and we know what the differences will be. However, we still do not know precisely how to pick a discount rate that accurately reflects the opportunity cost of forgone consumption and private investment.[5]

Project Comparison   There are two major issues in relying on benefit-cost analysis for selection of public expenditures. First, evaluation of benefits and selection of the discount rate involve considerable discretion on the part of the analyst. Second, no attention is given to the distribution of benefits and costs in standard benefit-cost analysis. The inability to evaluate benefits means that there is no objectively verifiable "right" evaluation, and thus persons may still disagree as to which project is superior. Likewise, people may differ in their idea of

[5]For a good analysis of the discount rate problem and an attempt to resolve it by picking a weighted average of the opportunity costs of forgone investment and consumption, see William J. Baumol, "On the Discount Rate for Public Projects," in *The Analysis and Evaluation of Public Expenditures: The PPB System*, A compendium of papers submitted to the Subcommittee on Economy in Government of the Joint Economic Committee (Washington, D.C.: Government Printing Office, 1969), pp. 489–503.

a proper discount rate, and again no right answer stands out. Hence knowledgeable persons may disagree about even the most carefully done benefit-cost analysis.

Accounting for the distribution of benefits and costs may be even more important than the issue of evaluation in benefit-cost analysis. The assumption in benefit-cost analysis is that a dollar of benefits is worth the same to everyone and that as long as benefits to the group as a whole exceed costs, the project is desirable. Many persons, however, would regard a program providing some benefit to a high proportion of the citizens in a jurisdiction as superior to a program providing high benefits to only a few citizens, even though the total of benefits to the few exceeded the benefits to the many. At the same time, many people may prefer a program with smaller total benefits financed from progressive taxation to a program with greater benefits financed by regressive taxes. Distributional issues are important in public-sector decision making, and ignoring the distributional consequences of public expenditures in benefit-cost analysis greatly reduces the value of the analysis for decision-making purposes. At the same time, the simple inclusion of distributional consequences in an analysis may not make a decision any easier, because different people will place different values on distributional outcomes.[6]

Benefit-Cost Analysis and Political Decision Making Just what is the role of benefit-cost and other technical analyses in political decision making? Some analysts have argued that benefit-cost analysis can be viewed as a substitute for the political processes of demand articulation through voting, lobbying, and bargaining. These analysts assume that the political process stops where general objectives have been determined and that, then, technical decision-making experts take over to define the most efficient programs to achieve specified goals. Other analysts believe that the existence of unmeasurable benefits, the difficulty of placing evaluations on benefits for which there are no quid pro quo demands, the problems of selecting a discount rate, and the importance of distributional consequences make benefit-cost analysis so questionable that they deem it almost useless in decision making.

This is not the place for full evaluation of the role of benefit-

---

[6]The analysis of distributional effects of governmental programs have been undertaken within a benefit-cost framework by a few analysts. For example, see James T. Bonnen, "The Distribution of Benefits from Cotton Price Supports," in Samuel B. Chase, Jr. (ed.), *Problems in Public Expenditure Analysis* (Washington, D.C.: Brookings, 1968), pp. 223–254.

cost or other technical analyses in governmental decision making, but three observations seem warranted. First, the question is not whether benefit-cost represents a perfect decision-making approach; rather it is how it compares with other decision-making processes such as voting, lobbying, and bargaining. Thus to a large extent one's enthusiasm for technical analysis may be a consequence of feeling that political decision-making processes do not work very well and that therefore even a very imperfect benefit-cost or technical approach is superior. A second observation is that benefit-cost and other technical analysis will be much more useful in some areas than others. For example, where outputs are measurable and often sold, as with water supply and electric power production, projects can be evaluated quite well. Where outputs are more difficult to measure, as in police services, fire protection, education, court services, and urban planning, benefit-cost or other technical analysis will be less reliable. Furthermore, when services are of a face-to-face nature, as with police and education, measurement and especially evaluation will be still more difficult. In general, the closer the production process is to transformation of physical resources into measurable products, the more reliable benefit-cost analysis will be; studies of less measurable services will be less reliable; and analysis of face-to-face services—where employee-citizen relations are crucial in determining the value of the service to the citizen—must be regarded as extremely tentative.

The third observation concerning benefit-cost analysis is that even an imperfect analysis forces the systematic thinking through of benefits and costs from a project or program. Thus the very process of undertaking the study produces a higher level of knowledge about the impact of governmental activities. This can make explicit the nature of the opportunities that must be forgone in selecting one program over another, even if the precise value of the alternatives remains unknown. When approached in this manner, benefit-cost analysis can be an important aid to decision making, even though it is inadequate as the only basis upon which public sector decisions are made.[7]

The problem of measuring and evaluating public sector output has plagued administrators for many years. Benefit-cost analysis has forced a more explicit recognition of the difficulties inherent in measuring and evaluating governmental outputs where measurability and evaluation are difficult. Recognition of the importance of these difficulties and the unlikelihood of their being overcome with advances in technical analysis means that demand articulation through political processes has a major role to play in determining the output of goods and services from urban governments.

---

[7]For an analysis of the opportunity cost revealing nature of benefit-cost analysis, see Roland N. McKean, "The Use of Shadow Prices," in Chase (ed.), ibid., pp. 33–77.

Incentives, Professionalization, and Unionism

An important but often neglected issue in public sector analysis is what incentives public officials have to try to be responsive and efficient in meeting their constituents' demands. No matter what decision-making techniques are available, there is no reason to predict their use by public officials unless they are stimulated by rivalry and competition or rewarded for innovation and efficiency.[8] Improved performance may be encouraged by competition among candidates for an office or rivalry among bureaucrats in competing departments or overlapping political units. Only a very small number of political officials are usually subject to these conditions of external competition, and the difficulty of measuring and monitoring the performance of government agencies in many areas may reduce pressures for improved performance. For example, in those areas where failure is easy to identify, as when one's water or power is disrupted, responsible officials face direct sanctions for failure. In other areas, like police protection or education, poor performance may be more difficult to measure and sanctions much less direct.

Where there is only limited external pressure for improved performance, there may also be real negative incentives to undertaking innovations which may improve performance but which also involve some risk. For example, a police chief or fire chief who uses standard procedures is unlikely to be criticized for not innovating; if he does undertake nonstandard procedures to improve performance, there may be little reward. Furthermore, if something goes wrong with a nonstandard procedure, the police or fire chief may find himself without a job. The inability to appropriate gains from improving efficiency, combined with the high risk of mistakes, does not provide top officials with incentives to try to improve public sector performance.

While high-level officials may not perceive net gains from innovations to improve efficiency, they may also discourage innovation among subordinate employees. Innovation may be discouraged because any deviance from standard procedure decreases reliability and predictability in organizational behavior and thus reduces a manager's ability to control a large bureaucracy. At the same time, if subordinate employees have sufficient discretion to utilize nonstandard procedures without possessing the scope of knowledge supposedly held by their superior, their innovations may produce bad as well as good results.

[8]Roland N. McKean, "Property Rights within Government and Devices to Increase Governmental Efficiency," *Southern Economic Journal*, 39 (October 1972), pp. 177–186. A systematic treatment of bureaucratic behavior from the perspective of economic theory is presented in Gordon Tullock, *The Politics of Bureaucracy* (Washington, D.C.: Public Affairs Press, 1965) and William A. Niskanen, Jr., *Bureaucracy and Representative Government* (Chicago: Aldine, 1971).

Therefore managers may prefer to have employees go by the book and avoid risking anything new. Employees will then find that they may advance their careers by following the rules, whether or not the rules result in desired public services efficiently performed. At the same time, deviance from rules may retard promotion. Employees, like high officials, usually face an incentive system in which the risks of error far outweigh any potential gains from improved performance.

To a large extent, it is the nature of public goods whose outputs cannot easily be measured that forces public managers to try and manage the behavior of employees—instead of permitting more employee discretion and managing by output measurement, as is common in the private sector. While the systematic study of innovation (or the lack thereof) in the local public sector is just beginning, what evidence there is indicates that incentives to promote innovation and improved efficiency are severely lacking in large public bureaucracies.[9] Thus the lack of productivity increases—which was identified as the cause of the expenditure-revenue elasticity gap in the last chapter—may be due to the lack of incentives to increase productivity as well as to the labor-intensive nature of public sector production.

One alternative to trying to manage the behavior of employees is to hire only employees who have been indoctrinated into a profession and thus are supposed to have both the knowledge and motivation to deliver public services without supervision. In fact, virtually all studies that aim at improving the efficiency of the public sector include recommendations for more education and training of employees.

Recent analyses of the behavior of professionals vis-à-vis their clients in police work, education, and social work have raised serious questions about the beneficial consequences of professionalism.[10]

[9]For a survey of research on innovation in the public sector, see Victor Thompson, *Bureaucracy and Innovation* (University, Ala.: University of Alabama Press, 1969). For a good empirical study see Martin M. Rosner, "Administrative Controls and Innovation," *Behavioral Science*, 13 (January 1968), pp. 136–143. Also see the November–December 1972 issue of the *Public Administration Review*, which is devoted to the problem of productivity increases in government, and Harry P. Hatry and Donald M. Fisk, *Improving Productivity and Productivity Measurement in Local Governments* (Washington: The Urban Institute, 1971).

[10]For a good analysis of the crisis of confidence in professionalism see Marie R. Haug and Marvin B. Sussman, "Professional Autonomy and The Revolt of the Client," *Social Problems*, 17 (Fall 1969), pp. 153–161. For studies in police, education, and social work, see Robert M. Fogelson, "From Resentment to Confrontation: The Police, the Negroes and the Outbreak of the 1960's Riots," *Political Science Quarterly* 83 (June 1968), pp. 217–247; *Advisory Commission on Civil Disorders Report* (New York: Bantam, 1968), pp. 301–305; Marilyn Gittell, "Decision-Making in the Schools: New York City, A Case Study," in *Educating an Urban Population* (Beverly Hills, Calif.: Sage, 1967); David Rogers, *110 Livingston Street* (New York: Random House, 1968); Frances Fox Piven and Richard A. Cloward, *Regulating the Poor: The Functions of Public Welfare* (New York: Pantheon, 1971); and Neil Gilbert, *Clients or Constituents: Community Action in the War on Poverty* (San Francisco: Jossey-Bass, 1970).

Critics have accused professionals of being more concerned about their own welfare than that of their clients and of not really knowing how to solve problems and improve clients' welfare. Furthermore, studies of police performance have not identified a relationship between additional education and training for policemen and increased police efficiency.[11]

It is difficult to determine why professionalism may lead to consequences that are detrimental to agency performance. It could be that the problems of large-scale bureaucracies are not really overcome by attempting to substitute professionalism for detailed rules of behavior, or perhaps professionals feel constrained by rules because the risks of breaking rules outweigh the potential benefits of doing what they feel is best. It could also be that the very process of professionalization, in which a professional learns to view the world in a particular way, makes him incapable of really understanding the problems of other individuals, especially if those individuals possess backgrounds and socioeconomic characteristics different from those of the professional. Thus far, at least, the professionalization of public employees has not overcome problems of providing labor-intensive services through large bureaucracies. Professionals, however, have been successful in designing physical projects such as water systems, highways, and sewage disposal facilities. These are all areas where professional knowledge is applied to working with materials rather than with people and where outputs are more easily measured. Thus it is in these areas—areas in which benefit-cost and other technical analyses can be utilized—that professionals have performed in the most satisfactory manner. The very fact that it is easy to measure and monitor outputs of professional activity in some areas may account for higher levels of performance in these areas, professionalization itself being a secondary factor. Professionalization may actually reduce the value of a face-to-face service when, in determining what services are to be provided, professionals attempt to substitute their own value preferences for those of their clients.

While government employees, especially those providing face-to-face services, have always exercised considerable discretion and policy-making authority in carrying out their responsibilities, public employees have more recently turned to public employee organizations to strengthen their role in governmental policy formation. By 1970, well over half of all teachers were members of a union or professional association (which may negotiate with employers like a union), and nearly 40 percent of all other state and local employees, including over

[11]Dennis C. Smith and Elinor Ostrom, "The Effects of Training and Education on Police Attitudes and Performance: A Preliminary Analysis," in Herbert Jacob (ed.), *Problems in the Criminal Justice System* (Beverly Hills, Calif.: Sage Criminal Justice System Annuals, vol. 3, 1974).

60 percent of all employees in cities with populations of over 10,000, were members of employee organizations. The public sector has become more unionized than the private sector, where only about 25 percent of all employees are members of employee organizations.[12]

More important for policy purposes, employee organizations have expanded their areas of negotiation beyond conditions of employment to include budgetary allocations to different functions, tax rates, regulations concerning service delivery, reorganization of governmental units, and racial and ethnic issues. Public sector unions have also been active in lobbying and campaigning for national health insurance, against wiretapping, for or against candidates including mayors and local government officials who are their employers, and for tax and bond levies needed for salary increases. Organized employee activiy has become a major factor in the performance of local governments.[13]

Many observers have viewed public sector unions as a simple extension of private market unions to the public sector. There are significant differences, however. The most important difference is that the demands of public sector unions are not disciplined by market competition.[14] In the private sector, union members recognize that their employers must remain competitive to stay in business and that there may be a direct relationship between higher wages and potential unemployment. In the public sector, however, the monopolistic position of the governmental unit is good assurance that it will not go out of business, no matter how high its labor costs. In addition, a strike is potentially much more disruptive in many public sector areas than the curtailment of private firm production. This is because many government functions are of a service nature and cannot be stockpiled or inventoried like steel or automobiles. When there is a strike, services cease. The disruption of service stoppage may make political officials anxious to settle a strike as quickly as possible, and it may not be too difficult to pass the costs of a settlement on in the form of slightly increased taxes. It may be even easier for political officials to give in to union terms on those details of service delivery that do not result in increased costs; this is because they realize that the effects of changes in service delivery may be difficult to perceive, while a strike would cause obvious disruption. Furthermore, given the political strength of public employee unions, their

[12]Jack Stieber, *Public Employee Unionism* (Washington, D.C.: Brookings, 1973), pp. 11–13.
[13]Ibid., pp. 195–196.
[14]Harry H. Wellington and Ralph K. Winter, Jr., *The Unions and the Cities* (Washington, D.C.: Brookings, 1971), pp. 7–32.

support may be highly valued by elected officials for the next campaign.

The long-run consequences of public sector unionism on the performance of local governments is not yet clear. Many unions have abandoned the goal of client-oriented professionalism for union bargaining, and unions have been leaders in fighting moves to give citizens more control over public services. This is evidenced by the United Federation of Teachers' expenditure of $250,000 to $500,000 to defeat the proposal for decentralization of the school system and the strong antivoucher and antiperformance contracting stands taken by teachers' unions and professional associations.[15] There are reasons to believe that public employee unions—because of their control over important public services where strikes are extremely disruptive and because of their political activity vis-à-vis their employers—have the potential for leaving competing groups in the urban public sector at a permanent and substantial disadvantage.

There are no simple answers to the problems raised by public sector unions, but we might expect that problems would be less severe in that public sector which consists of a large number of relatively small political units rather than a large monopoly employer. Multiple opportunities would be advantageous to employees if strikes are prohibited. Moreover, the availability of choice for citizens among many relatively small political units would introduce some market limitation on union power if these units are permitted to develop along the private sector model. While public sector unionism is not commonly an issue in urban economics, it is an example of public employees working in their own self-interest. It needs to be taken into account in examining the consequences of alternative organizations of the urban public sector, so that union activities do not become major barriers to achieving an efficient and responsive public sector.

When analyzing the operation of the public sector, it is important to remember that public officials and employees appear to respond to incentives in much the same way as do persons employed in the private sector. However, the impossibility of capturing gains from innovation or improved efficiency and the difficulty of measuring and monitoring the performance of employees in many service areas creates special problems for the public sector management. These problems must be taken into account when organization of the urban public sector is considered.

[15]Melvin Zimet, *Decentralization and School Effectiveness* (New York: Teachers College, 1973), p. 26; and Ed Willingham, "Education Report/OEO Goes Ahead with Voucher Plans Despite Opposition from Teacher Groups," *National Journal* (May 1, 1971), pp. 939–946.

STUDIES OF PUBLIC GOODS PROVISION

Throughout our discussion of the urban public sector, we have referred to empirical studies of public goods provision. We have also noted that the evidence bearing on economies of scale, incentives to promote efficiency, and citizen satisfaction with public goods and services is relatively weak, a weakness due partially to the difficulty of measuring and evaluating public sector outputs. Several recent studies of police services and one of fire protection services bear directly on these questions. They are also high-quality studies, firmly based in theory and focused directly on questions of public sector performance.

Police Services

A legal system is a basic public good—one that is essential to the functioning of any advanced economy. Concepts of property and exchange are meaningless without some collective agreement and enforcement of property rights and rights to personal safety. Historically, legal systems for enforcing property and personal rights emerged from within the walls of cities. It was easier to provide this public good within a small, confined area than over a large area of countryside. Recently, however, it has become evident that it may be more difficult to provide law and safety in large urban areas and specifically in the most densely populated areas of large, older central cities.

An evaluation of police services is not easy. First, police services are only one component of the legal system, and to some extent measures of police performance reflect the performance of prosecuting attorneys, courts, and correctional facilities as well as police. Second, measures of police performance may also reflect the general attitudes of citizens toward any symbol of authority, government, or the rest of society. These attitudes, in turn, may be influenced by the relationships citizens have with landlords, neighbors, store owners, employers, and other public officials as well as police. And third, while the major service provided by police is generally thought to be preventing crime or apprehending criminals, policemen actually perform a wide range of services. They mediate family and neighborhood disputes, patrol traffic, respond to calls from citizens with a variety of critical problems —from medical emergencies to being locked out of one's home—most of which are not reflected in FBI uniform crime reports or other crime statistics. Furthermore, problems relating to the nature and collection of crime data, especially FBI uniform crime reports, make the data useless and misleading for evaluative purposes.[16]

The variety of tasks policemen are called upon to perform makes the value of police services to a community heavily dependent on face-to-face police-citizen relations. Public alienation reduces not only the value of community and social services rendered by the police but also the police's crime-fighting efficiency. Maintaining low crime rates and safe neighborhoods is much easier when citizens and police have good relations.

All these complications make the evaluation of police services difficult. Aggregate data on service conditions and citizen attitudes for large cross-sectional statistical studies of police performance is limited, and the cost of obtaining detailed survey information is sufficiently high to prevent the collection of data for large sample sizes. One alternative is to utilize a most similar systems research design. This is a research design in which all aspects of the research environment except those differences that one is specifically trying to analyze are similar.

Several similarly designed studies of police performance have produced significant findings on the question of the size of police jurisdictions relative to (1) the cost of providing police services and (2) citizen satisfaction with police performance.[17] In the studies, one or more small cities in the metropolitan area were matched with neighborhoods within the large central city. Matching was on the basis of race, income, age distribution, housing ownership, multifamily housing residents, and population density.

A sample of citizens was then selected from the small jurisdictions and matched areas within the large cities. Each citizen was interviewed to obtain information on police services, citizen attitudes toward safety of their neighborhoods, citizen attitudes toward police, and citizen evaluation of police performance. A variety of items within the interview comprised the measures used to compare police performance. No attempt was made to aggregate the measures into a single index number or place dollar values on them. The results for two of the

---

[16]Albert D. Biderman, "Social Indicators and Goals," in Raymond A. Bauer (ed.), *Social Indicators* (Cambridge, Mass.: MIT, 1966), pp. 68–153; and Elinor Ostrom, "Institutional Arrangements and the Measurement of Policy Consequences," pp. 447–476.

[17]Elinor Ostrom et al., *Community Organization and the Provision of Police Services* (Beverly Hills, Calif.: Sage Professional Papers in Administrative and Policy Studies 03–001, 1973); Elinor Ostrom and Gordon P. Whitaker, "Community Control and Governmental Responsiveness: The Case of Police in Black Communities," in David Rogers and Willis Hawley (eds.), *Improving the Quality of Urban Management* (Beverly Hills: Sage Urban Affairs Annual Reviews, vol. 8, 1974) pp. 303–334; and Samir Twefik Ishak, *Metropolitan Police Departments: The Citizens' Input* (Allendale, Mich.: School of Public Service, Grand Valley State College, 1973).

studies are presented in Tables 7-1 and 7-2. Also presented in the tables are the costs of police services for the matched neighborhoods within the city and the smaller jurisdictions. Costs for the matched neighborhoods were calculated by detailed analysis of the larger-city police budgets and allocation of police manpower.

Table 7-1 indicates comparative performance of police in three independent communities (Speedway, Beech Grove, and Lawrence) and matched adjacent neighborhoods in the city of Indianapolis. The areas are all white, middle-class areas containing single-family homes and a few apartments. The three independent communities were not merged into the new consolidated government of Indianapolis and Marion County in 1970, although Mayor Lugar and other UNIGOV (UNIted GOVernment) officials have indicated a desire to merge the local police forces into the special services area police force of UNIGOV. The arguments of the promerger advocates have been based on the idea that a large consolidated police department can provide better police services at lower cost than the small independent departments.

TABLE 7-1 Comparison of Service Levels and Citizen Evaluation of Police Services in Indianapolis Neighborhoods and Matched Adjacent Independent Communities

Indicator	Independent Communities	Indianapolis Neighborhoods
Victimization	+	−
Willingness to report victimization	+	−
Extent of police follow-up	+	−
Assistance (receipt of emergency aid)	+	−
Promptness of response to call	+	−
Quality of assistance	=	=
Stopped as suspected offender	=	=
*Evaluation of promptness of response to call	+	−
*Evaluation of crime trend	+	−
*Evaluation of potential bribe taking	=	=
*Evaluation of police-citizen relations	+	−
*General evaluation of police performance	+	−
Per capita expenditure on police services	$12.76	$10.72

+ indicates a higher level of police performance
= indicates equivalent levels of police performance
− indicates a lower level of police performance
*Evaluations are comparisons of citizens evaluations of events referred to.
Source: Elinor Ostrom et al., *Community Organization and the Provision of Police Services* (Beverly Hills, Calif.: Sage Professional Papers in Administrative and Policy Studies, 03–001, 1973), pp. 51 and 57.

TABLE 7-2   Comparison of Service Levels and Citizen Evaluation of Police Services in Chicago Neighborhoods and Matched Independent Communities.

	Percentage of Respondents	
Indicator	Independent Community	Chicago Neighborhood
Not victimized in preceding 12 months	75	74
Do not stay at home because of fear of crime	58	45**
Receiving high levels of police follow-up to reported crime	59	46*
Calling police for assistance not related to victimization	19	24*
Reporting police response in less than 5 minutes	60	48
Reporting effective police assistance	95	94
Reporting fair treatment when stopped by own police force	77	70
Evaluating local police-community relations as good	46	44
Evaluating local police response time as very rapid	26	25
Believing local police do not accept bribes	37	21**
Agreeing they have some say about what police do	49	47
Agreeing that local police have the right to take any action necessary	61	38**
Agreeing that redress is possible for police mistreatment	67	66
Agreeing that local police treat all equally according to the law	46	18**
Agreeing that local police look out for the needs of the average citizen	56	36**
Expenditures per area	$40,000	$500,000

*confidence level—0.95
**confidence level—0.999

Source: Elinor Ostrom and Gordon P. Whitaker, "Community Control and Governmental Responsiveness: The Case of Police in Black Communities," in David Rogers and Willis Hawley (eds.), *Improving the Quality of Urban Management*, (Beverly Hills, Calif.: Sage Urban Affairs Annual Review, vol. 8, 1974), pp. 323–325.

UNIGOV's special services area department, which is the old city of Indianapolis department, contains over 1,100 employees serving 485,000 people. The three independent communities have police departments of 20 to 35 persons serving populations of 13,468 to 16,646.

The summary data from the study indicate that citizens rated the independent community departments higher on nine of twelve items and equal on the other three. No firm conclusions on relative efficiency can be drawn, because the per capita cost of police services in the independent communities was $2.04 higher than the per capita costs of police services provided in the matched Indianapolis neighborhoods. One can conclude, however, that small communities can provide police services to their citizens and that bigger, more professionalized departments do not necessarily produce higher levels of service.

Table 7-2 provides comparative performance and cost data for two independent communities outside of Chicago and three matched neighborhoods within Chicago. The areas are all populated primarily by low-income blacks in single-family and apartment residential areas. The Chicago police department had 12,500 men serving 3,378,000 citizens, Phoenix had 4 full time and 15 part-time men serving 3,596 citizens and East Chicago Heights had 6 full time and 5 part-time officers serving a population of 5,000. The Chicago police department is considered to be one of the most professionalized and one of the best in the United States. The police departments in the two independent communities (East Chicago Heights and Phoenix) are, by criteria of professionalization, underpaid and undertrained.

The comparisons of service levels and evaluations of police performance for such different police departments are quite striking. By all criteria of police professionalization, the city of Chicago should be providing superior police services to its citizens.[18] Instead, we observe that on six of fourteen indicators, police performance is higher in the independent communities; on eight indicators there is no difference; and on one attitudinal question, citizens in the independent communities feel more strongly that local police have the right to take any action necessary than do Chicago residents. Citizens in Chicago neighborhoods do, however, call on police for assistance not related to victimization more often than do citizens in the independent communities.

The comparison of costs of police services is even more striking. The independent communities spent an average of approximately $40,000 annually for police services, while the city of Chicago was spending $500,000 to provide police services to each of the three matched neighborhoods within the city.

The results of studies in Grand Rapids and Nashville are also interesting and consistent. In those cases, citizens of the smaller cities, as compared to citizens in matched neighborhoods within the large cities, evaluated their police services at an equal or higher level on all measures of performance. Furthermore, in each case the costs of

[18]Criteria of professionalism are input criteria, including modern equipment, high training requirements for personnel, and high pay.

police services were lower in the small jurisdictions that were providing superior services.

The conclusions from these comparative case studies are consistent with the analysis of aggregative data, collected by the National Opinion Research Center, on crime and victimization for the President's Commission on Law Enforcement and the Administration of Justice.[19] Conclusions drawn from analysis of those data are that (1) crime rates are higher in larger jurisdictions; (2) citizen evaluation of police services is higher in suburban and small jurisdictions; (3) for relatively similar levels of service, the cost of police services is higher in larger jurisdictions; and (4) the larger the number of jurisdictions per 100,000 population, the lower the per capita costs for relatively similar levels of service.

Thus, in this fundamental and very important face-to-face service activity, one can conclude that small jurisdictions may well be able to provide superior services (in terms of citizen satisfaction) than large jurisdictions—a conclusion consistent with the analysis of the nature of public goods and services in Chapter 5.

The comparison of cost differences and production processes between large jurisdictions and small jurisdictions in the case studies provides an explanation for at least some of the results. It appears that large departments utilize a much higher proportion of their manpower in headquarters administrative tasks, presumably trying to manage the police in the field. The smaller jurisdictions, on the other hand, maintained a larger share of patrolmen in the field with fewer assigned to administrative tasks. It appears that police services may well exhibit decreasing economies of scale beyond relatively small sizes because of higher and higher administrative costs.

As a general rule, in those areas of police services where economies of scale are more likely (police training and crime laboratories), only the large central-city departments operate their own facilities.[20] The small departments were served by either state or county facilities, and there is considerable cooperation among smaller police departments for emergency mutual aid. The interdependence of different-sized political units for provision of different services—even within the police protection area—is an indication of how subfunctions of a public service can most efficiently be provided by different-sized organizations.

These analyses of police services are important for two reasons.

[19]Elinor Ostrom and Roger B. Parks, "Suburban Police Departments: Too Many and Too Small?" in Louis H. Masotti and Jeffrey K. Hadden (eds), *The Urbanization of the Suburbs* (Beverly Hills, Calif. Sage Urban Affairs Annual Reviews, vol. 7, 1973), pp. 380–387.
[20]Cost data for the comparative studies were adjusted so that direct comparisons could be made.

First, they do bring relatively strong evidence to bear on questions of governmental size for a very important function. Second, the comparative format may be a useful one for studies of other public goods and services. Conclusions can be drawn in terms that are meaningful to both analysts and citizens, and it was not necessary to proceed to aggregate measures of performance or attempt to put dollar values on them. This makes the studies much more understandable, both in terms of their limits and the information they provide.

Fire Protection Services

Roger Ahlbrandt's study of fire protection services is interesting because it deals with questions of different incentives faced by public monopolies and a private profit-making firm producing on a contract basis for a city.[21] Ahlbrandt's major objective was to derive an empirical cost function for public fire departments that could be used to predict the costs of providing fire protection to Scottsdale, Arizona, and then to compare predicted costs with costs actually incurred in Scottsdale. Scottsdale, however, does not provide its own fire services but instead contracts to a private firm, the Rural-Metropolitan Fire Protection Company.

Construction of the cost function was based on data from forty-four fire departments. They served areas ranging in population from 900 to 536,000 and in size from 1.5 to 102 square miles. Output variables used were population served, area served, and the value of the structures protected. Input and quality variables included firemen's wage rates, number of full-time personnel, number of volunteers, number of aerial ladder trucks, number of aid cars, number of fire stations, fire insurance ratings, and percentage of substandard housing. A least-squares regression analysis in log-linear functional form provided a coefficient of multiple determination of 0.962. That is, the variables included in the analysis "explain" 96.2 percent of the costs of providing fire services by a public fire department. The equation was then used to predict costs for Scottsdale. Predicted costs were $7.10 per capita. Actual costs in Scottsdale were $3.76 or 47 percent lower than predicted.

The predicted costs were, of course, based on the costs of serv-

---

[21]Roger S. Ahlbrandt, Jr., *Municipal Fire Protection Services: Comparison of Alternative Organizational Forms* (Beverly Hills, Calif.: Sage Professional Papers in Administrative and Policy Studies 03 –002, 1973). Summaries of the study are available as "Implications of Contracting for a Public Service," *Urban Affairs Quarterly*, 9 (March 1974), pp. 337 –358; and "Efficiency in the Provision of Fire Services," *Public Choice*, 16 (Fall 1973), pp. 1 –15.

ices rendered by a traditional monopolistic department. Because differences between costs predicted and actual costs under contract to the Rural-Metropolitan Fire Protection Company were so large, Ahlbrandt went to Scottsdale and undertook an on-site investigation of how Rural-Metropolitan's operations differed from those of traditional departments. The major differences identified include the following:

1 The use of "wranglers." Wranglers are fully trained firemen who work full time for a city department, usually in parks or public works. They are on call at all times. They are as qualified as full-time firemen but available to deal with peak-load problems as volunteers would be. They are paid by the fire department only when fighting fires, which compensates them for pay lost when they are absent from their other job.

2 Equipment savings. Rural-Metropolitan builds or directly subcontracts construction of its own trucks at a 40 percent cost saving when compared to the cost of equipment in traditional fire departments. It also uses some smaller trucks. The operations cost saving by using a small instead of a large truck is sufficient to pay for the small truck in six years. The company also uses 4-inch plastic hose with quarter-turn couplings. The hose is less costly and the couplings are much more quickly connected than traditional male-female seven-thread screw couplings. The use of 4-inch instead of 2 1/2-inch cotton or nylon hose also permits hydrants to be spaced 1,300 instead of 500 feet apart, with a considerable saving in installation of water lines. The cost saving on water lines is in addition to the lower cost of fire protection.

3 Innovation. Rural-Metropolitan spends 3 percent of its gross income on research and development. The company has developed a two-pump truck in which the second pump can be hydraulically lifted off the truck at the site of the fire. Thus two pumps can be delivered with a single truck. The company has also developed a "snail" or robot fireman. The snail runs on water pressure and can be radio-controlled to enter buildings, travel down corridors, climb some stairs, and spray water as directed from outside.

4 Spreading Overhead. Rural-Metropolitan also services other areas in Arizona through contracts with other cities, special districts, the Federal Housing Administration, and individual homeowners. Some of the central office costs are charged to these other activities, resulting in some savings for Scottsdale.

5 Information. Although these are not directly a cost savings, Ahlbrandt found significant differences between Rural-Metropolitan's reports on its costs and activities and the reports of public departments. Traditional departments usually present a short description of what a good job they are doing, talk about how much the "need" for their services has increased, and then provide appendixes consisting of unexplained statistical tables. Rural-Metropolitan's reports indicate what it costs to make specific changes in service levels and lay out what costs were incurred for what results. Rural-Metropolitan is especially careful when introducing innovations in fire-fighting technology. To avoid being accused of cutting corners, they carefully explain potential benefits, cost savings, and risks; then they let the city manager or city council decide if they wish to adopt the innovation and the cost saving.

Ahlbrandt found quite a different attitude in traditional departments. There, innovation was simply regarded as too difficult and too risky. The fire chief or firemen could not really capture gains from cost saving for themselves, and they would bear the costs of any failures due to nonstandard technology. This may be one reason why there has been virtually no innovation in fire-fighting technology (outside the military) in public monopolistic departments since the introduction of the truck and gas engine to replace horse-drawn wagons with hand pumps.

Ahlbrandt attributes the cost saving exhibited by Rural-Metropolitan directly to the cost consciousness and profit orientation of the owner and manager. The company is regulated by the Arizona State Corporate Commission and is permitted to earn a 7 percent annual profit on sales. By tying profit to sales, the only way profits can be increased is to expand business. The only way to expand business, according to the company owner, is to do a better job at less cost than traditional departments. Also, 5 percent of all profits are allocated to an employee profit-sharing plan, which the owner feels contributes to company loyalty and effectiveness.

The operation of the Rural-Metropolitan Fire Department provides a good example of what could be done to improve the efficiency of fire protection. There is no reason to assume that any of the techniques developed are so unusual that public departments could not have developed them if they had desired to do so. The difference is in the incentives faced by public monopolies compared to the incentives faced by a profit-making producer. The owner of Rural-Metropolitan, in producing fire services that may make him one of the highest-paid fire chiefs in the country, also saves the citizens of Scottsdale an estimated 47 percent of their fire protection bill.

The studies of police and fire protection services lend empirical support to previous conclusions on public sector organization and operation. Small political units can provide face-to-face services efficiently and incentives may have a significant impact on the behavior and performance of public managers.

REFORMING THE URBAN PUBLIC SECTOR

In Chapters 5 and 6 we examined the choices which result in small, relatively homogeneous and functionally specialized political units within metropolitan areas. We concluded that it would be easier for citizens to articulate demands to smaller, more homogeneous political units than to large, heterogeneous big-city governments. We also found that because economies of scale in the production of public services are exhausted at small sizes, especially for labor-intensive services such as police and education, the suburban governments would be more likely to be efficient producers than big city governments. In addition, we observed that different public services possess different geographic scopes and different economies of scale, so that an efficiently organized public sector would be characterized by a variety of political units—many with overlapping boundaries—and by intergovernmental agreements to account for interdependencies among the political units themselves.

In Chapter 6 we proceeded to examine fiscal implications of complex urban governmental systems, and we observed that much of the homogeneity of small political units was by income class. Further, we found that different political units possessed vastly different fiscal capacities. We concluded that one could not expect much income redistribution within small, local governments. Even large central cities are limited in their ability to redistribute income because such redistribution could encourage the outmigration of wealthier residents, business, and industry, thus reducing the fiscal capacity of the central city. Furthermore, we concluded Chapter 6 by asking whether local-government financial crises, especially in big cities, might not be due to failure to meet citizens' preferences efficiently, implying that fiscal crises could be alleviated with improved efficiency as well as more funds.

In this chapter we observed that the use of benefit-cost and other technical analyses is limited by the difficulty of evaluating public goods outputs, selecting a discount rate, and the problem of taking into account the distributional consequences of public programs. We also observed that unless public officials have incentives to be responsive and improve efficiency, even techniques like benefit-cost analysis will not be used where they would be helpful. Our examination of police and fire services confirmed that small governments can provide face-to-face services as responsively and efficiently as larger governments, and that incentives can be very important in public sector performance. All these observations on public sector operation, organization, and financing need to be taken into account in analyzing the organization of the urban public sector and proposals for change.

Metropolitan Government: Reform through Consolidation

The Reform Movement From the 1920s through the early 1960s, most analyses for improving the urban public economy have recommended the creation of a single metropolitanwide government to take the place of the many existing cities and special districts.[22] The basic assumptions upon which these recommendations are based are that (1) metropolitan areas are really single communities linked by social economic ties but artificially divided by different governmental jurisdictions, (2) the needs of the metropolitan community cannot be met by fragmented governmental jurisdictions, and (3) the elimination of duplication and overlap among governmental units will permit more efficient provision of public goods and services by larger units with greater economies of scale. The recommendations for reform also specify that there should be a single government headed by a single elected executive and a small elected council, and that this should be staffed by professionals and civil servants. The single hierarchically organized unit would then be able to provide equal levels of public goods and services at equal tax rates throughout the entire metropolitan area.

Reformed governmental structures would focus demand articulation on voting for a few top officials who would implement uniform

[22]One of the best analyses of the consistency of reform recommendations is contained in Robert Warren, *Government in Metropolitan Regions: A Reappraisal of Fractionated Political Organization* (Davis, Calif.: Institute of Governmental Research, University of California, 1966), chaps. 1–3. For a recent report on the reform-through-consolidation tradition, see Committee for Economic Development, *Modernizing Local Government* (New York: Committee for Economic Development, 1966). Portions of the discussion of governmental reform are taken from Robert L. Bish and Vincent Ostrom, *Understanding Urban Government: Metropolitan Reform Reconsidered* (Washington, D.C.: American Enterprise Institute for Public Policy Research, 1973). For an analysis of political reform traditions, also see Bish and Ostrom, *Understanding Urban Government*. For an analysis of major points of reform through consolidation from the perspective of economic theory, see Robert L. Bish, *The Public Economy of Metropolitan Areas* (Chicago: Markham/Rand McNally, 1971), chap. 8.

policies throughout the urban area. These top officials and their hierarchically organized delivery systems would also be monopolists, and no overlapping jurisdictions would exist for citizens to have access to if they were unsatisfied with the policies of the single metropolitan government. Differences in fiscal capacity among small governmental units would be eliminated because all taxing and spending would be uniform throughout the area. With uniform tax rates, this would result in income redistribution from high-wealth areas to low-wealth areas.

We would expect that in functional areas where technical analysis can be utilized to achieve generally agreeable solutions to problems, where general policies can be delegated to professionals for implementation, and where economies of scale exist, the consolidated metropolitan government may perform quite well. These areas would include water supply, sewage disposal, and electric power production. On the other hand, where outputs are less measurable and technical analysis is more difficult to utilize, where preferences for levels of goods and services vary among subpopulations within the metropolitan area, and where economies of scale are exhausted at small sizes, we would expect to find the consolidated government performing poorly. Areas with these characteristics include labor-intensive services such as refuse collection, fire protection, and street maintenance. We would anticipate especially severe difficulty with face-to-face services such as police and education for groups of people with preferences different from the average. Furthermore, because of the monopolistic position held by the metropolitan government, citizens would have little recourse to other governmental agencies if they were dissatisfied with the services they received. Given that well over half of local government expenditures are in areas where no economies of scale can be expected beyond relatively small population sizes and that citizens in different areas possess different preferences for public goods and services, it is difficult to anticipate net improvements in public sector performance from reform through consolidation in urban areas.

One of the purposes of a metropolitan government is to equalize service levels throughout the metropolitan area.[23] However, relatively little attention has been given to the problems of minorities and the poor. It is simply assumed that the larger, professionally staffed bureaucracies will deliver the services minorities and the poor desire

---

[23]While equal service levels areawide has always been an element of the reform tradition, there is considerable evidence that different areas within cities do not want the same levels and kinds of services. See Charles S. Benson and Peter B. Lund, *Neighborhood Distribution of Local Public Services* (Berkeley, Calif.: Institute of Governmental Studies, University of California, 1969). Furthermore, it does not appear that big-city governments are able to provide equal levels of services within big cities. G. M. Ratner, "Inter-Neighborhood Denials of Equal Protection in the Provision of Municipal Services," *Harvard Civil Rights-Civil Liberties Law Review*, 4 (Fall 1968), pp. 1-63.

while at the same time diluting their political strength by adding predominantly white middle-class suburbs to the central city, where
minorities and the poor are concentrated. We believe sufficient evidence exists to cast serious doubt on the assumption that minorities
and the poor will be better off under a metropolitan governmental
structure where they are even more dependent on policies designed by
the white middle class than they currently are in big cities.

Metropolitan Governments Well over a hundred recommendations
for reform through consolidation have been made for urban areas in
in the United States.[24] In spite of the long-standing consensus among
reformers, however, very few consolidations have been implemented;
since 1950 there have been four partial consolidations of urban-area
governments in the United States.[25] In 1957, a federated structure was
created in Dade County, Florida. In this reform, Dade County assumed many services formerly undertaken by cities, but cities were
left with authority for some functions. At present, there are thirty-
three governmental units in Dade County, including twenty-seven
independent municipalities and five special districts in addition to the
county government—not exactly a single governmental unit but fewer
governments than one would anticipate in an SMSA of nearly 1.3
million people.

County–central-city consolidations have occurred in three other
areas: Nashville-Davidson County in 1962, Jacksonville-Duval County in 1967, and Indianapolis-Marion County in 1970. In these instances
the county government was consolidated with the government of the
largest central city. In each case, however, smaller independent cities
and most special districts were left intact. The result is that Davidson
County has 15 independent governmental units, 7 of which are independent municipalities, for 448,000 people; Duval County has 9
governmental units, 5 of which are municipalities, for 529,000 people,
and Marion County (called UNIGOV) is left with 52 governmental
units, 5 of which are municipalities, for 794,000 people. In all the consolidations except Indianapolis-Marion County, residents of the unincorporated areas of the county and central city voted for the consolidation. In Indiana, the Mayor of Indianapolis, the Governor, and

[24]Warren, op. cit., p. 24.

[25]Stephen P. Erie, John J. Kirlin, and Francine F. Rabinowitz, "Can Something
Be Done? Propositions on the Performance of Metropolitan Institutions," in Lowden
Wingo (ed.), *Reform of Metropolitan Governments* (Baltimore: Johns Hopkins, 1972),
pp. 7–41. Data on the number of governmental units and population size are from U.S.
Bureau of the Census, *1972 Census of Governments*, vol. 1, *Governmental Organization*
(Washington, D.C.: Government Printing Office, 1973), table 19.

the majorities in the state house and senate were all Republicans—an unusual situation. Therefore the state was able, through legislation, to impose the reformed governmental structure on Indianapolis without a vote by the affected citizens.

None of the reforms through consolidation are true creations of single, areawide governments. Some do not even attempt to integrate internally, as in Indianapolis, where the old city of Indianapolis police department serves a special area with boundaries equivalent to the old city of Indianapolis. The old county sheriff's department, on the other hand, serves a special area encompassing the formerly unincorporated territory.

A large number of articles and books have been published describing the consolidations and the benefits expected to flow from them. For the most part, however, there is little empirical evidence on the basis of which one might determine whether or not metropolitan consolidation has produced the consequences which proponents anticipated. Stephen Erie, John Kirlin, and Francine Rabinowitz have surveyed various writings on consolidated metropolitan governments to determine what the impact has been.[26] They claim only to summarize what others writers have found; they do not critically evaluate the studies they summarize. Their conclusions are that

1 Professionals have increased their impact on policy making.

2 Few economies of scale have been identified outside of large metropolitan districts (serving such functions as water supply, sewage disposal, air pollution control, and mass transit).

3 In the short run, access by minorities is guaranteed by the apportionment of representatives, but in the long run it may well be diluted.

4 Service levels increase, as do fiscal burdens and costs.

5 The emphasis is on tangible, physical goods, not on social problems or social services.

6 There is no immediate short-term impact on the redistribution of power or wealth.

7 Citizen attitudes toward and understanding of local and area wide political processes remain largely unchanged.[27]

These conclusions do not provide as much evidence on consoli-

---

[26]Erie, Kirlin, and Rabinowitz, op. cit., pp. 7–41.
[27]Ibid., pp. 36–37.

dated governments as would be desirable. Many of our expectations are borne out, however. Professionals have increased their role, but, as we previously noted, this need not enhance citizen satisfaction with public goods and services. The lack of economies of scale—except for metropolitan-wide districts performing such functions as pollution control, mass transit, and water supply—is consistent with our expectations. We cannot tell if the efficiency of the governmental system increased because both service levels and fiscal burdens and costs went up. Our expectation would be that costs increased more than service levels. The emphasis on tangible physical goods and not social problems or social services also fits our expectations, because person-to-person services are the most difficult for large organizations to manage.

It is still too soon to determine whether the reformed structures will, over a longer time period, become nonresponsive and inefficient—especially to minority groups—as might be anticipated from their quasimonopolistic position, or whether problems with the delivery of face-to-face services will lead to still further reform, with some decentralization included. In Indianapolis, for example, legislation has been passed to permit the formation of neighborhood governmental units within UNIGOV to provide smaller groups of citizens with greater voice in decisions affecting their areas.[28]

Community Control: A New Reform Tradition

Beginning in the 1960s there has been considerable questioning of the performance of large administrative agencies in the bigger cities of the United States.[29] Citizens' groups have complained about the unresponsiveness of big-city agencies to provide desired police services, perform educational services, get garbage hauled away, resolve traffic problems, and carry out the basic functions for which city governments are responsible. These critics do not attribute citizens' dissatisfaction and rising costs to city government smallness or the existence of overlapping governments but rather to its largeness, cumbersomeness, and its monopolistic position. Proponents of community

[28]A bill permitting the establishment of community governments (called minigovernments) within UNIGOV passed in 1972. Indiana State Legislature, Senate Enrolled Act No. 362 (1973). In areas meeting requirements, election of community board members began in November 1974.

[29]Representative statements of the new reform-community control positions include Milton Kotler, *Neighborhood Government: The Local Foundations of Political Life* (Indianapolis: Bobbs-Merrill, 1969); and Alan A. Altshuler, *Community Control: The Black Demand for Participation in Large American Cities* (New York: Pegasus, 1970).

control argue that public bureaucracies in major cities are so large and rigid as to be unmanageable no matter how well-intentioned top officials and administrators may be. They also argue that voting for a mayor and a few top officials for a large city as a whole is insufficient to indicate the variety of citizen preferences regarding those officials.

Community control advocates argue that citizen preferences, lifestyles, and problems vary from neighborhood to neighborhood and that equal service levels areawide are not wanted. Furthermore, highly centralized governmental units are unable to respond to the variations in conditions and preferences among neighborhoods. The new reform movement has proposed the creation of community councils and neighborhood governments to return greater control over government to the people, so that they will be supplied with the services they prefer rather than an arbitrary kind or level of service that fails to meet their needs. The new reformers also have noted that, for the most expensive functions such as education and police services, cost savings do not occur in cities over 50,000 to 100,000. Thus, there is little reason for not organizing some services in relation to neighborhood conditions and assigning control over their provision to community councils or neighborhood governments.

These new reformers advocate small enough political units so that (1) the different preferences of different groups of people within urban areas can be more adequately known to public officials, (2) public officials will be located close enough to practical problems so that those officials can be forced to respond to the conditions of life in different neighborhoods, and (3) bureaucracies can be kept small enough so that they are manageable.

Traditional reformers see large governmental bureaucracies as directed by enlightened leadership and professional administrators acting efficiently on the basis of a high level of knowledge about their environment. Community control advocates, on the other hand, see large government bureaucracies as unresponsive, unmanageable, lacking knowledge of the varying conditions existing among different neighborhoods and of the different lifestyles existing among different communities of people in large urban areas. Traditional reformers attribute rapidly rising costs to overlapping jurisdictions and duplication of services; the new reformers attribute those cost changes to bureaucratic inefficiencies in the larger consolidated units of government.

The new reformers demanding community control over the provision of neighborhood public services within large urban areas clearly reject the proposition that a single, monopolistic, areawide government will result in increased responsiveness and efficiency. Instead, they see consolidation leading to a deterioration in public services, reduced efficiency, decreasing responsibility among officials, and decreasing confidence among citizens about their capacity to articulate their preferences and have them responded to.

It is not surprising that the community control movement grew within large heterogeneous central cities and not suburban areas; after all, it is in suburban areas where small homogeneous groups control small political structures which appear to respond to the preferences of their citizens. In many respects advocates of community control in large cities are asking for nothing more than a governmental structure like that enjoyed by suburbanites—instead of being subject to the monopoly authority of large, unmanageable, bureaucratic organizations run by professionals who claim to know what is best for the citizens.

There has been little experience with community governments in large cities; hence there is even less evidence to draw on regarding community governments than there is for consolidated structures. Most of the arguments proposed by community control advocates, however, are consistent with our own analysis of urban government for services which are labor intensive or involve face-to-face service delivery.

Reconciling Diverse Approaches: Two-Tier Solutions

The challenge of the new reformers demanding community control has had a substantial appeal. One response was to propose a two-tier solution. The traditional reform approach is used to propose consolidation of all major units of local government into one general jurisdiction that has authority over all areawide functions in a metropolitan region. The new reform approach is used to propose small local units to deal with community or neighborhood problems within the larger consolidated unit.

While differences between the traditional reformers proposing consolidation and the new reformers advocating community control are striking at first glance, there are conditions that have facilitated the formulation of the two-tier solution.[30] One important factor facilitating this is recognition of the differences in the nature of many public goods and services. The most avid advocates of community control recognize that there is a role for larger governmental units in controlling air pollution, providing large regional water supply and sewer systems,

---

[30]For example, compare Altshuler, ibid., pp. 50–51; and Committee for Economic Development, *Reshaping Government in Metropolitan Areas* (New York: Committee for Economic Development, 1970), p. 19.

creating mass transportation facilities, and redistributing income to improve the fiscal capabilities of lower-income communities. There is less agreement on which specific functions are appropriate subjects for local community control, but it appears that traditional reformers are modifying their position. They now recognize that different groups of people may prefer different mixes and levels of public goods and services and that bureaucracies organized on an areawide basis for all public functions may not be the most efficient way to respond to the diversity within each metropolitan area. The most likely functions for community control would appear to be functions where face-to-face service delivery by a labor-intensive bureaucracy is characteristic and where economies of scale are exhausted at a relatively small size. Services such as police patrol, education, garbage removal, fire protection, and street maintenance would fit these criteria.

Discussion of a single unit of metropolitan government to perform areawide functions appears very reasonable until one confronts the practical problem of specifying boundaries for specific metropolitan regions. Just how inclusive is the overall tier to be? Are Washington and Baltimore, Philadelphia, Camden, and Trenton, Newark and New York, and New Haven, Providence, and Boston to be grouped in single or several metropolitan governments? Appropriate boundaries for the urban agglomerations of the Atlantic Seaboard, the Great Lakes, California, or the Puget-Willamette Trough of the Pacific Northwest are simply not very clear.

On the other hand, what size government is appropriate to deal with community problems as the lower tier of an urban government? The communities of interest and the scope of problems vary in size; therefore a single lower tier of governments for a large megalopolis may be insufficient to deal with them appropriately.

Many questions remain unanswered in a two-tier solution. For example, how do we deal with the local aspects of areawide functions, the areawide aspects of local functions, or functions such as planning and zoning which have direct impacts at both the community and areawide levels? Should functional assignments be rigid, creating quasimonopolies for each function, or flexible to promote rivalry and competition? Are one large and one small political unit, defined by the geographic scope of their functions, more efficient for demand articulation and production than political units organized on a functional basis—units that undertake activities over a variety of geographic areas? The two-tier solution represents greater cognizance of the complexity of urban government than demonstrated in traditional metropolitan reform literature, but it still does not come to grips with the complexity of the urban public sector.

A Closer Look[31]

The urban public sectors of our metropolitan areas are extremely complex. They are not without organizational problems, but the most severe problem may be the lack of responsiveness of the simplified big-city governmental structures to the preferences of their hetero- geneous citizens, not the traditionally condemned fragmentation and overlapping jurisdictions of suburban areas. Public goods and serv- ices are sufficiently diverse so that there is nothing irrational or illogical about having different functions performed by different juris- dictions. Suburban jurisdictions with their functional specialization and the extensive use of special districts in urban areas may well be a necessary response to meeting the demands of citizens for goods and services with diverse characteristics. Areawide special districts may be created for functions such as rapid transit and air pollution control and to facilitate the extensive intergovernmental contracting that exists in water supply and sewage disposal. This arrangement appears to provide an efficient scale for these functions while permitting smaller jurisdictions to supply goods and services where economies of scale are exhausted at a smaller size or where preferences of different juris- dictions differ from one another.

With so many governmental units serving any given urban area, both cooperation and rivalry among governmental units would occur.

We have already examined some elements of intergovernmental cooperation when, in Chapter 6, we observed that functional grant programs were used to account for spillovers from small-government provision of goods and services in education and highways and to fi- nance income redistribution programs. We also observed that there was both competition and cooperation in taxation and tax administra- tion. While most economists have focused on the fiscal aspects of intergovernmental relations, other aspects of these relations are equally important to understanding how the public economy functions.

Service Contracting Intergovernmental service contracts are a means for one governmental unit to purchase public goods and services from another governmental unit. Contracts are also let to private firms for the production of public goods and services, as was seen with Scottsdale's purchase of fire services from the Rural-Metropolitan

[31]Parts of this section are from Bish and Ostrom, op. cit., chap. 5.

Fire Protection Company. Contracts are most common among local governments, although state and federal agencies sometimes participate in buying and selling public services.

Service contracts are used mainly when a relatively small unit purchases a public good or service from a larger unit because the larger unit can supply it more cheaply than the smaller unit could produce it for itself. At the same time, the smaller unit is able to specify the quantity or quality of the service to be provided; thus citizen preferences are met more closely than they would if the small unit were simply merged with the larger unit.

A common type of contracting is the purchase of police services by a small community, which would rather not operate its own police force, from a larger city or county. Even medium-sized cities with their own police forces enter into contractual arrangements to secure communication services, crime lab services, jail facilities, and police training services from larger units. The diversity in the nature of public goods and services means that different kinds of services are produced efficiently by different-sized jurisdictions. Contracting permits relatively small jurisdictions through which citizens can indicate their preferences more precisely. They can also, in this way, obtain the advantages of lower-cost production when economies of scale or reduced costs through specialization accrue in the production of some types of public goods or services. If a single unit of government must serve both to articulate preferences and produce a full range of municipal public goods and services, it will be either too large to perform some services efficiently or too small to produce other goods and services at low cost. With adjustments through the use of contracts, many different goods and services can be provided more efficiently and more responsively at the same time.

An extreme form of contracting, called the Lakewood Plan, is used by many California cities. Lakewood (approximately 80,000 population) was incorporated in 1953 to avoid annexation by Long Beach. Lakewood's citizens felt that they would be better able to get the public services they desired through their own city rather than by being annexed to a larger city. The city began with only ten employees and relied upon special districts and contracts, primarily with Los Angeles County, for most of its municipal services. Police services, animal control, engineering services, street maintenance, and other functions were provided under contract with the county. Following Lakewood's incorporation, twenty-five other cities incorporated in Los Angeles County between 1954 and 1961—all relying primarily on contract services rather than becoming independent producers of local municipal services. Since that time contract cities have been organized in other urban areas of California.[32] Contracting for services among municipalities is also commonplace among different metropolitan areas in many parts of the United States.

We have already observed how the contracting for fire protection services in Scottsdale led to greater responsiveness, lower cost, and increased provision of information on costs and benefits for different levels and kinds of fire protection services. Some of these consequences have been observed from intergovernmental contracting as well. A major observed consequence of the Lakewood Plan is that the county as the producer is forced to measure and cost out all services provided—a rather unusual procedure for governments—and then offer a price lower than that at which a city could produce a service for itself. Cities have also encouraged private producers and adjacent municipalities to bid for contract services. Such efforts have brought lower prices and consequently forced cost-saving innovations among public producers.[33] Contract producers are exposed to potential competition and run the risk of losing customers. At the same time, small cities receive benefits from lower-cost production. They are also able to adjust service levels to meet the needs of their citizens. It appears that contract systems contain within them incentives for responsiveness to diverse preferences, incentives to keep costs of production down, and an ability to adjust production economies to produce diverse public goods and services more efficiently.

Service contracting also represents a way in which neighborhood governments within big cities could operate. The neighborhood units could contract with the big-city government for functions where the big city government could offer lower costs, and they could also encourage improved efficiency in big-city bureaucracies by seeking competitive bids from private vendors or other governmental units. There is no reason, for example, why a neighborhood government could not manage its own police patrol force while contracting with a larger department for laboratory services, police academy training, major case investigation, and detention facilities. The result would be both

---

[32]For an analysis of the Lakewood Plan development see Robert Warren, *Government in Metropolitan Regions*. For an analysis of information and market-type incentives see Robert Warren, "A Municipal Services Market Model of Metropolitan Organization," *Journal of the American Institute of Planners*, 30 (August 1964), pp. 193–204.

[33]The county of Los Angeles, which provides police services for many cities, probably does not produce at as low a cost as many cities could produce for themselves. The county, however, has developed a pricing system whereby it is selling services below cost to maintain its customers. Donald C. Shoup and Arthur Rosett, "Fiscal Exploitation by Overlapping Governments," in Werner Z. Hirsch, Phillip E. Vincent, Henry S. Terrell, Donald C. Shoup, and Arthur Rossett, *Fiscal Pressures on the Central City* (New York: Praeger, 1971), pp. 241–301.

higher levels of citizen satisfaction and more efficient provision of police services. While decentralization of big-city governments may appear politically unfeasible, there may come a time when big-city governments will be willing to undertake radical experimentation to improve service delivery and to help slow the suburban exodus that is exacerbated by the high costs and relatively low levels of citizen satisfaction with services provided. Service contracting also represents one way to bring public employee unions under some market control, because if producers cannot keep costs of production down to competitive levels, they face the potential for losing their contracts.

Service contracts are not going to solve all urban public sector problems and their greatest potential may be for new cities not encumbered with existing bureaucracies. They do, however, have the potential for permitting adjustments of demand articulation and production separetely, in response to the tremendous diversity in the nature of public goods and services, while at the same time providing incentives to encourage responsive and efficient production.

Rivalry and Cooperation   Rivalry or competition among governmental units is often viewed as a problem to be avoided. However, competition and a potential for conflict always exist when individuals share a common environment and a limited supply of resources. To attempt to eliminate rivalry among governmental units by consolidating them into a single hierarchy does not eliminate different interests, it merely submerges the ability of small communities to articulate their preferences and cloaks bureaucratically dictated solutions in secrecy.

Rather than view competition among governmental units as undesirable, it would appear more fruitful to concentrate on how the energy it generates can be channeled to achieve beneficial results. The existence of forums where different preferences can be articulated and debated, for example, can lead to the design of new, previously unrecognized, mutually beneficial solutions to joint problems. We should also recognize that unresolved disagreements may represent situations that are simply not amenable to the provision of net gains to all participants; and even the most knowledgeable should hesitate to recommend policies that would inevitably cause one party to gain at the expense of the other.[34]

Metropolitan areas, in fact, do have a rich structure of formal and informal arrangements for considering interjurisdictional problems

[34]Voluntary agreements substitute decision-making costs for political-externality costs, in contrast to hierarchical directives, which substitute political-externality costs for decision-making cost savings.

and for working out cooperation among the many governmental units. Informal negotiations are organized through general associations such as councils of government and associations of cities and public officials; furthermore, nearly every functional area such as police, fire services, education, and so on has its own organization. At the same time, where stalemates among local jurisdictions would result in damages, as with failure to agree on the regulation of pollution, the remedy lies in the fact that local governments themselves are part of an overlapping system of governments in which disputes can be carried forward to state legislatures, the courts, and the federal government.

Understanding the Urban Public Sector Preoccupation with eliminating the multiplicity of governmental units in urban areas has led to many prescriptions for reform but very little analysis of how the public sector operates. Understanding and predicting the consequences of different organizational arrangements is made still more difficult if one approaches the study of government as the study of political decision making where one group dominates another. Instead, the urban public sector is composed of a multiplicity of independent political units which, in terms of their relationships with one another, may be better characterized as firms in public service industries than as sovereign governments. Different political units, like different firms in private markets, serve different clienteles. Some will be small and serve small neighborhoods and communities. Others will be larger, taking into account a wider range of interests. Some will be specialized, like school districts, while others will be multipurpose like cities or counties. Some will serve primarily for citizens to articulate preferences, like Lakewood Plan cities; others may be primarily producing organizations, like the Rural-Metropolitan Fire Protection Company and the large water supply districts which wholesale water to small water districts and municipalities—which, in turn, retail it to households and businesses.

Such an approach to understanding diverse overlapping jurisdictions leads one to contemplate orderly relationships among the numerous agencies within different functional areas characterized as public service industries.[35] Many firms in an industry—including public service industries such as the police, education, water, health services, and transportation industries—need not mean chaos. Also, an industry perspective facilitates the inclusion of private firms—such as the Rural-Metropolitan Fire Protection Company, private developers

---

[35]Vincent Ostrom and Elinor Ostrom, "A Behavior Approach to Intergovernmental Relations," *Annals of the American Academy of Political and Social Science*, 359 (May 1965), pp. 137–146.

and manufacturers of equipment purchased by governmental units, and voluntary associations such as leagues of cities or councils of government—as important agencies in the public economy of metropolitan areas.[36] The view of government as a simple hierarchical organization run by a few elected officials is simply inadequate for understanding the urban public sector.

We believe that the illusion of the crazy-quilt pattern of urban government stems from the free associations of map gazers; and a way of thinking that equates simple political systems and hierarchical symmetry with efficiency. In short, this view is not based on an empirical analysis of the operation of urban governments. Economists should be the first to recognize that ordered relationships may result from multiplicity and diversity.

When we begin to look at the public sector as a series of industries integrated with voluntary associations and private firms, evaluation of public sector performance becomes considerably more difficult. We must consider not only the efficiency with which a single firm transforms inputs into products but also the overall dynamic performance of the industry in developing new technologies and encouraging innovation to respond to new conditions. In short, can public service industries be organized so that they are not like public fire departments and more like Rural-Metropolitan in Scottsdale? We believe that a decentralized public services industry characterized by overlapping and rivalry, not one composed of a series of monopolists, is the most likely to demonstrate improved performance in the long run. This means that a reform of the urban public economy will require much more careful analysis of its operation than has been common in the past.

SUMMARY

In Chapter 5 we indicated that economic theory is extremely rich with implications for understanding the urban public sector. Most empirical work, however, has focused on benefit-cost analysis, determinants of public expenditures, and economies of scale. There has been very little economic analysis of issues of demand articulation and

---

[36]Some studies consistent with this conceptualization include those in a Haynes Foundation Monograph Series entitled *Metropolitan Los Angeles: A Study in Integration.* This series includes the following: Winston W. Crouch, Wendell MacCoby, Margaret G. Morder, and Richard Bigger, *Sanitation and Health,* 1952; James K. Trump, Morton Kroll, and James R. Donoghue, *Fire Protection,* 1952; Vincent Ostrom, *Water Supply,* 1953; and Helen L. Jones, *Libraries,* 1953. The reader is also referred to Joe S. Bain, Richard E. Caves, and Julius Margolis, *Northern California's Water Industry, the Comparative Efficiency of Public Enterprise in Developing a Scarce Natural Resource* (Baltimore: Johns Hopkins, 1966).

heterogeneity of tastes and almost no analysis of incentives generated under alternative institutional structures, such as the study of contracted fire provision. We believe that the studies of economies of scale and benefit-cost analyses of urban public functions themselves provide the rationale and emphasize the importance of a public sector composed of many relatively small demand-articulating and producing units. Such studies should also provide the rationale for applying economic analysis more closely to understanding the operation of urban governments. What evidence there is indicates that economic theory may be very useful. It does provide a rationale for the complex system of public enterprises that exists in urban areas; it does fit well the studies of police services—a face-to-face activity where small organizations may easily out perform larger ones, and it fits extremely well with the study of contracted fire service provision. Even this limited empirical base does permit one to infer that critics of big governments may be correct in that the governments are too big to be responsive or efficient. Neither empirical evidence nor theory lends any support to the position that improved performance can be expected by consolidating existing governments into supersized areawide governments. It may well be that economists, who specialize in the study of incentives and market systems, may be much better prepared to understand the functioning of the urban public economy than are political scientists and administrators, who describe complex systems as chaotic and equate order and efficiency only with hierarchical arrangements.

This chapter does not conclude our analysis of the urban public sector. In the following chapters, elements of location theory and the theory of public goods and collective action are used together to analyze a series of important urban problems. In each of these problem analyses, it is important to remember the complexity of the public policy system with which one must deal in analyzing and proposing solutions to urban problems. We do not take the position that if only the policy-making system were simpler, *our* solution would be imposed.

SELECTED READINGS

Ahlbrandt, Roger S., Jr.: *Municipal Fire Protection Services: Comparison of Alternative Organizational Forms* (Beverly Hills, Calif.: Sage Professional Papers in Adminstrative and Policy Studies 03–002, 1973).

Altshuler, Alan A.: *Community Control: The Black Demand for Participation in Large American Cities* (New York: Pegasus, 1970).

Bish, Robert L., and Vincent Ostrom: *Understanding Urban Government: Metropolitan Reform Reconsidered* (Washington, D.C.: American Enterprise Institute for Public Policy Research, 1973).

McKean, Roland N.: "Property Rights within Government and Devices to Increase Governmental Efficiency," *Southern Economic Journal*, 39 (October 1972), pp. 177–186.

Ostrom, Elinor, et al.: *Community Organization and the Provision of Police Services* (Beverly Hills, Calif.: Sage Professional Papers in Administrative and Policy Studies 03–001, 1973).

Prest, A. R., and R. Turvey: "Cost-Benefit Analysis: A Survey," *Economic Journal*, 75 (December 1965), pp. 683–785 (Bobbs-Merrill Reprint, Econ.–316).

Warren, Robert: *Government in Metropolitan Regions: A Reappraisal of Fractionated Political Organization* (Davis, Calif.: Institute of Governmental Affairs, University of California, 1966).

CHAPTER **8**

HOUSING SEGREGATION: POVERTY AND RACE

Neither poverty nor racial discrimination are peculiarly urban problems, and yet they often appear as special urban problems in the literature on social questions. The reason is, once again, that things urban are related to population density. Scattered, poor families do need help, but in densely populated urban communities the poor and the black are isolated by housing segregation. The massiveness of their poverty is more observable, and its concentration creates further problems, such as crime and morbidity. In this chapter we continue to carry forward the theme that urban questions are a mixture of locational and public goods problems. The problem of urban poverty and racial discrimination will be presented by exploring a model of housing segregation. We will then describe the variety of public responses to poverty and racial segregation and show their impact on the spatial structure of the city and on the well-being of those to whom the public responses are supposedly directed.

HOUSING SEGREGATION—AN ARBITRAGE MODEL

The model that we will describe is an adaptation and modification of the one, previously described in Chapter 4, that was developed by Martin Bailey.[1]

---

[1]Martin J. Bailey, "Note on the Economics of Residential Zoning and Urban Renewal," *Land Economics*, 35 (August 1959), pp. 288–292.

The Static Model

Consider a community or neighborhood with housing units of the same size and physical quality. There are five parallel streets of the same length. The streets are A, B, C, D, and E. There are neither vacant houses nor families without houses. There are as many houses as families.

The first problem is to assign the families to houses. Half the families have sufficient income to buy new housing; half do not. We want to show the impact preferences by high- and low-income families for adjacent housing—that is, housing grouped by income level. For this purpose, we initially divide the households into those that can afford to buy new housing and those that cannot. Later we will expand on why a household can or cannot afford a new house. This is not, however, a purely economic division because building codes and zoning regulations can so change the cost that many people cannot afford to buy new housing. Nevertheless, let us assume this as a beginning. We will later change the building code and zoning requirements and show the impact of those changes on housing and the well-being of the households.

From the previous discussion of housing and land use in Chapter 4, we know that the high-income families prefer to live together and probably on the side away from the downtown center of the city and away from any boundary between the two groups. They will pay a premium for living within a neighborhood surrounded by others with the same high income. They will pay less, however, for housing on the boundary between the high-income and low-income neighborhoods. Initially, we are avoiding problems of expectations, so the discount only appears in the immediate vicinity of the boundary. The poor pay a premium for houses adjacent to the boundary with the high-income families and a discount for houses within the low-income area completely surrounded by others of the same income level. This preference may be based on the potential for amenities on the boundary.

You may wonder how a poor family could be buying a house when we have defined these families as having incomes so low that they could not afford to buy new housing. Part of the answer is that they are buying older housing, but part of the answer is also, that we can always convert an annual or monthly rent to a present value with the appropriate interest rate. Thus although we will discuss the market in terms of buying and selling houses, the arguments apply to rent payments also.

Of course, it would not always be true that high-income families would live on the side away from downtown. In a particular sequence of blocks, they would tend to live on the side away from nuisances, such as railroads and polluting industries. In most cities these nuisances would be associated with downtown and its immediate surroundings. But with the spread of industry, such nuisances may be located anywhere in the city. If there were a particular amenity in some area, such as a good view, the higher-income families would be attracted to that area.

For one or the other of these reasons, the high-income families live on streets A, B, and one side of C, while the low-income families live on streets D, E, and the other side of C. Prices for housing on streets A and B would be internal to the high-income neighborhood and would be the highest, P_h. Houses on C street occupied by high-income families would be priced at a discount, $P_h - d$, to get the high-income families to occupy the places. Houses on streets D and E would sell at the lowest price, P_l, since they are completely surrounded by the houses of other families with low incomes. Houses on the low-income side of street C would be priced at a premium, $P_l + p$, because of their nearness to high-income families.

As we learned in Chapter 4, equilibrium occurs when the prices for high- and low-income families on the boundary are equal, or more realistically that the price for occupancy by high-income families is less than the price for low-income occupancy by the cost of converting to low-income occupancy. It may be worth repeating that the higher price for low-income occupancy is not obtained by having the poor pay more out of income but by having more families occupy the same space.

This is an equilibrium determined during a short-run period when the number of houses is fixed. The analysis is modified somewhat if the long run is considered. In the long run, new housing can be built, but only high-income families can afford it. Furthermore, the number of families in each income group is changing through births, deaths, and migration.

Consider the situation with the five streets to be in equilibrium, so that $(P_h - d) = (P_l + p)$, ignoring conversion costs. P_h is greater than P_l. If P_h is greater than the cost of constructing new houses, then there will be an increase in the number of houses in the long run. The number of houses will increase until P_h is reduced to the price of new construction. This automatically implies that the price of housing on the boundary is less by the discount. Furthermore, the price within the low-income area is still lower by the difference between P_l and $P_l + p$. The controlling price becomes the cost of building new. With no population growth or expectation of change, a stable boundary would be attained. Houses priced below P_h, however, could not be maintained at the same quality as the best houses. They would deteriorate until the maintenance cost was such that it would be covered by the lowered rent that lower-income families could afford.[2] In equilibrium, prices would be such that all houses would be held. So far we are not including any restrictions on the quality of the older housing. We will do that in a later section analyzing the impact of a building code.

The Model with Population Growth Included

If population growth is assumed, the model will show a changing boundary, but it will depend upon which population group is increasing in size. If population growth occurs only in the high-income group, P_h would rise, doubling up would occur temporarily, and perhaps the boundary between low- and high-income groups would be pushed toward the low-income group. In the long run, however, new housing would be built to accommodate the high-income families since, by definition, they could afford to buy new. If population growth occurs among the low-income families. P_l would rise and arbitrage would occur at the boundary. Since $P_l + p$ would be greater than $P_h - d$, houses would be shifted from use by the rich to use by the poor. The reduction in the number of houses available to high-income families would cause an increase in P_h. The increase in P_h would give incentive for new construction. New housing would be built, while housing for low-income families would expand by shifting houses along the boundary and moving the boundary until the boundary prices in the two uses were equal again. The difficulty may be that the price could rise for the poor, causing doubling up, and we do not know the lag in time before the price increase would be transmitted to high-income families and new construction undertaken.

One more step toward realism would be to allow continuous increases in the population of both the high- and low-income groups. As long as there is any absolute increase in the number of low-income households, P_l would have to increase. Simultaneously the boundary would move toward the high-income families by arbitrage of housing resources from use by the high-income group to use by the low-income families. Continuous population change, however, adds an element that is difficult to handle—expectations. The boundary would have to move continuously if low-income population were increasing continuously. Expectations by high-income families would anticipate the direction in which the boundary would move, and would, most likely, discount prices ahead of the actual change in the boundary. This would,

[2]Ira S. Lowry, "Filtering and Housing Standards: A Conceptual Analysis," *Land Economics*, 36 (November 1960), pp. 362–370.

in effect, cause a deterioration in quality ahead of the anticipated conversion to low-income use or even ahead of immediate propinquity
to low-income families. Expectations, then, would cause an increase
in the demand for new housing over what it would have been to just
keep pace with the changing size of the two income groups.

The Model with Racial Prejudice Included

So far we have not discussed racial prejudice, but its impact is very
similar to the hypothesized preference for living in all high-income
neighborhoods. Racial prejudice could result in all-black neighborhoods that were not necessarily poor. There could also continue to
exist areas of low-income whites separate from those areas occupied
by blacks. Nevertheless, many blacks are poor and start in the low-
income areas of cities. Since there is racial prejudice against blacks,
they find it difficult to find housing outside the low-income areas. The
next best place is the boundary. With rising incomes they can afford
better housing and can thus afford the premium for boundary-street
housing. The middle-income blacks would also pay a discount for living
adjacent to poorer families, since they are trying to escape the inner
ghetto. Therefore two boundaries develop. One is the leading edge
of black middle class. White prejudice results in a discount at the
boundary of the areas. The blacks in the middle class, in turn, pay a
premium for living adjacent to the high-income neighborhood, but they
pay a discount for those streets adjacent to poor families. This middle
class has insufficient income to buy new housing but high enough income to get out of the center of poverty. The numbers of middle-
income blacks, however, are insufficient to maintain the prices in the
black middle-class area, so that prices fall and low-income families
can afford to live in the integrated area. As income and prices decline,
the middle-income blacks are once again forced to move the boundary
to find better neighborhoods.

Since there are insufficient numbers of middle-class blacks to
stabilize the boundary, it has an accelerated movement beyond that
necessary to accommodate increases in the population of blacks and
low-income families. Furthermore, the entrance of blacks, if this
scenario is true, is also the first harbinger of change to a low-income
neighborhood, even though the blacks do not have low incomes
themselves. High-income whites would then discount prices in anticipation of change wherever they expect blacks to move next.

With these changes, one can immediately see the implications for
the market if the growth of low-income and black families should
decline by a reduction in migration in the urban area. People would

continue to expect the same rate of change in use of housing from high-income families to low-income families. It would take a while before they realized that their expectations were unrealized. Nevertheless, the expectation of change is sufficient to bring about changes in the boundary between low- and high-income families. Since the increased space for low-income families is not needed after lower migration rates, the number of vacancies would rise on the low-income side of the boundary, rents and prices would fall, and houses would become vacant and abandoned.

One can easily see, however, that a wide variety of market responses are possible whenever the racial composition of a particular neighborhood changes. Prices on the black side of the boundary could easily be higher than on the white side if social institutions were expected to continue to prevent further change and if there were a continuing increase in the population of blacks relative to the number of whites. On the other hand, isolated suburbs whose inhabitants might be considered upper middle class might not consider integration to be a reason for leaving as long as they expected only a few blacks with incomes comparable to their own. Expectations of price decreases may occur most strongly in areas with definite racial boundaries that change in a more massive way. Thus there is not necessarily any specific price response to the entrance of blacks into a particular neighborhood. It depends on the circumstances.[3] It depends on expectations, incomes of whites and blacks, and the relative growth in size of the two populations. This ambiguity has made the interpretation of statistics comparing house prices and racial changes difficult. A number of studies have shown that racial change in a given neighborhood may result in relative increases, decreases, or no change in property values.[4]

[3]Luigi Laurenti, *Property Values and Race* (Berkeley, Calif.: University of California Press, 1960), pp. 8–27; David McEntire, *Residence and Race* (Berkeley, Calif.: University of California Press, 1960), pp. 157–171.

[4]Laurenti, op. cit., pp. 28–239; McEntire, loc. cit.; Chester L. Hunt, *Research Report on Integrated Housing in Kalamazoo* (Kalamazoo, Mich.: Upjohn Institute for Community Research, 1959); William M. Ladd, "Effect of Integration on Property Values," *American Economic Review*, 52 (September 1962), pp. 801–808; Donald Phares, "Racial Change and Housing Values: Transition in an Inner Suburb," *Social Science Quarterly*, 51 (December 1971), pp. 560–573; Joseph P. McKenna and Herbert Werner, "The Housing Market in Integrating Areas," *The Annals of Regional Science*, 4 (December 1970), pp. 127–133; Martin J. Bailey, "Effects of Race and of Other Demographic Factors on the Values of Single-Family Homes," *Land Economics*, 42 (May 1966), pp. 215–220; and Hugh O. Nourse, Donald Phares, and John Stevens, "The Effect of Aging and Income Transition on Neighborhood House Values," in Hugh Nourse, *The Effect of Public Policy on Housing Markets* (Lexington, Mass.: Heath, 1973), pp. 107–119.

Some Implications and Modifications

As we have noted previously in our discussion of the property tax, the income elasticity of demand for housing has been estimated to be around unity. Therefore, since there are more than two levels of income among families, the above model is unrealistic in the sense that it only reveals two basic price levels, P_h and P_l. In reality, within each of those groups of structures, we would find many gradations determined by the levels of income of their occupants. Nevertheless, we should not assume that everyone living on the low-income side of the boundary between neighborhoods has an income that would not allow him to buy better housing.[5] Some proportion of households in slum areas could afford better housing. From our previous discussion, it is obvious that racial segregation may be partly responsible for the fact that some families who could afford to live elsewhere nevertheless do live in slum areas.[6]

A further implication of the variation of P_l within the low-income sector is that the quality of housing may be even lower than indicated by the levels of property value first described. The lowest value of P_l may be very low indeed, assuming no controls on building standards.

As we noted in Chapter 4, on land use, if properties are held by individuals competitively rather than by one monopolist, the boundary between the high- and low-income families would tend to move too far in converting houses to low-income use. That conclusion was a result of investigating a static model with no population growth and no anticipations of change. Inclusion of these two factors, as was done above, suggests that the boundary will tend to convert houses to low-income families much faster than required by the growth of low-income families.

One implication of the segregation model is that we would observe neighborhood changes in income and socioeconomic class having more influence on property values than age of housing. Furthermore, we would expect changes to be transmitted from one area to adjacent neighborhoods. In recent work by Nourse, it was found that changing income class had far more impact on prices of houses in a neighborhood than aging of housing structures.[7]

Comparisons were made in the income and price trends of sever-

[5]Robert Moore Fisher, *Twenty Years of Public Housing* (New York: Harper, 1959), p. 40.

[6]Karl E. and Alma F. Taeuber, *Negroes in Cities* (Chicago: Aldine, 1965), pp. 78-95.

[7]Hugh O. Nourse, *The Effect of Public Policy on Housing Markets* (Lexington, Mass.: Heath, 1973), pp. 107-119.

al neighborhoods and communities in St. Louis with different ages of development. Income trends were estimated by determining the occupations of a sample of heads of households in the West End, Wellston, University City, Normandy, and Webster Groves from 1930 to 1970. Median income ranks were estimated by determining the decile in the income distribution that each occupation held. The ranks went from 1 for the lowest decile to 10 for the highest. Price and rent data were taken from the decennial census of 1940, 1950, 1960, and 1970. Webster Groves was developed prior to University City but was not adjacent to other areas of declining income, as was University City. In 1950 prices and rents were higher in University City than in Webster Groves. By 1970, however, income ranks in University City had begun to drop, while in Webster Groves they remained the same and even increased. The income rank of occupations in both areas had been nine (includes such occupations as artists, draftsmen, pharmacists, insurance agents, electricians, foremen, linemen, and printing craftsmen) prior to 1965. After that those of University City fell to six (which includes welfare workers, salesmen, bricklayers, and managers of eating and drinking places), while those in Webster Groves rose to 10 (college professors, authors, engineers, managers, professionals, and locomotive engineers). The pattern was similar for prices and rents. Relative prices and rents in Webster Groves declined from 1950 to 1970, as one would expect from older housing, but those of University City fell far more. By 1970 prices and rents were higher in Webster Groves than in University City. Although relative prices fell, absolute prices rose in both places.

Finally, we must modify our analysis by considering the impact of the special treatment of housing under the federal income tax laws. Owner-occupied housing receives special treatment because most interest, most property taxes, and some casualty losses are deductible from other income as if they were business expenses or costs of earning income. At the same time, the imputed rental value of the house (the amount the owner could earn by renting it to someone else), is not taxed. Renters pay property tax and mortgage interest in their rent but cannot deduct them for income tax purposes. This difference in tax burden between renters and owners leads to a price differential of 20 to 25 percent in favor of home ownership.[8]

Thus, the differential tax treatment of ownership encourages homeownership and increased housing consumption. The advantage, however, accrues to middle- and upper-income families. The higher one's marginal tax rate, the more one benefits from the special tax

[8]Henry Aaron, *Shelter and Subsidies* (Washington, D.C.: Brookings, 1972), pp. 53–55; Richard F. Muth, *Cities and Housing* (Chicago: University of Chicago Press, 1969), pp. 100–105.

treatment. Low-income homeowners receive very little benefit because their incomes are too low to incur a tax liability from which expenses can be deducted. The increased expenditure by middle-and upper-income families, then, would increase the demand for new construction and reduce the demand by these families to own older housing on the boundary between higher- and lower-income families. Therefore, the tax treatment increases the volume of housing available to lower-income families and shifts the boundary between upper- and lower-income families toward the higher-income areas.

SLUMS

Housing segregation thus leads to concentration of poor families in specific neighborhoods within urban areas. Many of these areas, but not all, would be described as slums. Neighborhood areas segregated by race obviously may not be slums. The dictionary describes a slum as "a thickly populated, squalid part of a city, inhabited by the poorest people."[9] The quality of housing would deteriorate within the poverty areas. Associated with the areas of poor-quality housing would be increased juvenile delinquency, incidence of tuberculosis and other diseases, immorality, increased death rates, and incidence of unemployment and fire hazards.[10]

In the twenties and thirties the social environmentalists saw the correlation between areas of the city with poor-quality housing and social disorders; they concluded that the cause of the social problems was the environment, especially the squalid housing in which families were living. Although some analysts were careful to say that merely putting the poverty families in better housing would not be the only thing you had to do to reduce crime, incidence of disease, and immorality, others were not so careful.[11]

Another view that has always prevailed but has been best expressed by Banfield in recent years is that the cause of the social problems of the slums is poverty, and that poverty is a result of poor

[9]*The Random House Dictionary of the English Language* (New York: Random House, 1968).

[10]Edith Elmer Wood, *Slums and Blighted Areas in the United States,* U.S. Federal Emergency Administration of Public Works, Housing Division, bulletin no. 1 (Washington, D.C.: U.S. Government Printing Office, 1935). See also John P. Dean, "The Myths of Housing Reform," *American Sociological Review* (April 1949), p. 283; and Robert Moore Fisher, *Twenty Years of Public Housing* (New York: Harper, 1959), pp. 24–72.

[11]Ibid. See also President's Conference on Home Building and Home Ownership, *Housing and the Community—Home Repair and Remodeling* (Washington, D.C.: National Capital Press, Inc., 1932).

planning and shortsightedness on the part of some people.[12] Others hold that while the social problems of the slum are caused by poverty, poverty itself results from some dysfunction of the labor market, segregation of the labor market, or exploitation.[13]

Low-income jobs and unemployment are direct causes of poverty, but these may result from lack of good-paying jobs in areas where workers live, workers' lack of necessary skills to hold better-paying jobs, lack of information about better employment, or lack of transportation to get to the better job. These are problems with the demand, supply, and efficiency of the labor market. We have shown how racial discrimination affects the housing market. There may also be a dual labor market in which the market for minority and ghetto workers may be separate from all other labor markets, so that even if a person has better skills, discrimination or segregation prevents him from being hired. A more radical view is that poverty results from the exploitation of these segments of the labor market through segregation.

The view expressed and implied in the above model of housing segregation is that some people are poor. Until all incomes are equal, there will always be someone at the bottom end of the income scale. Higher-income families prefer not to live near poor families, but the reverse is not true. If the incomes of the poor are insufficient to buy new housing, then the poor will be concentrated in slum areas. The social disorders associated with these areas are all indicators of poverty. Additional areas will be converted to slums as they are needed, where need is determined by the number of poor households relative to the supply of housing available to them. The areas to be converted are not necessarily the oldest houses but those nearest to the current boundary between high- and low-income families.[14]

The poverty level implied by the model is much too high. The cutoff between high- and low-income neighborhoods is useful for understanding the housing market, since it distinguishes between those who can and cannot buy new housing. That income level, however, is in the neighborhood of $6,000 to $9,000. To buy a new house takes an income equal to nearly half of the value of a new house plus assets for a down payment and closing costs. The level of income necessary for a minimum standard of living depends upon the number of persons in a family and whether they are living in a high-cost urban area, a low-cost rural area, in the warmer southern areas of the country, or

[12]Edward C. Banfield, *The Unheavenly City* (Boston: Little, Brown, 1968), pp. 45 –66.

[13]David M. Gordon, *Theories of Poverty and Underemployment* (Lexington, Mass.: Heath, 1972).

[14]Hugh O. Nourse, *The Effect of Public Policy on Housing Markets* (Lexington, Mass.: Heath, 1973), pp. 107 –119.

in the colder northern areas of the country. In any case, there is the implication that another boundary probably exists between those with low income who cannot buy new housing and those with income below a level that would generate an acceptable standard of living. One estimate of this level is the minimum standard estimated by the Bureau of Labor Statistics for a family of four living in a metropolitan area. In 1972 this was estimated to be $7,386.[15]

Although the cause of poverty is not explicitly outlined in our model of housing segregation, the model certainly implies that racial segregation contributes to it. Poverty has its roots in bad luck, lack of skills, low income, unemployment, and discrimination. The fact of poor-quality housing, however, is a symptom of the general problem and a contributing cause to the environment of poverty of the slums.

Market structures derived from housing segregation further exacerbate the situation. Because of prejudice, it is possible for speculators to operate along the boundary between black and white neighborhoods and between low- and higher-income neighborhoods and make money by shifting housing to blacks and low-income families. In some circumstances it may be the only way more housing could be made available to blacks in segregated areas. That some people profit from the misery of others is difficult to accept, but the speculator is providing a service to a population against which society is discriminating. The speculator could not exist without the prejudice reflected in prices along the boundaries.

As we noted before, in a dynamic setting people anticipate changes in the spatial extent of low-income areas. Mortgage lenders, too, can anticipate these changes. Bankers, savings and loan associations, and insurance companies provide the bulk of home financing. They must try to lend on relatively safe investments. Houses that in the near future may fall in value because of absorption into the segregated, low-income areas would not be good risks. If loans were to be made in such areas, they would require higher interest terms and higher down payments than other, less risky loans. Because of the poor credit risk of the low-income families and because of the conditions of housing in the low-income neighborhoods, institutional investors begin to withdraw from lending in such areas. In their place come individual lenders who require higher interest rates and more stringent terms.[16]

It is often argued that the financial institutions and speculators cause the boundaries to exist and cause the decline in prices in low-income areas because of their withdrawal of financing from such

---

[15]Jean Brackett, "Urban Family Budgets Updated to 1972," *Monthly Labor Review* (August 1973), p. 70.

[16]Leo Grebler, *Housing Market Behavior in a Declining Area* (New York: Columbia, 1953).

markets. Certainly they do effect change faster, but they could not operate in the way that they do if the underlying market situation were not as described in the model of housing segregation.

PUBLIC POLICY TOWARD SLUMS

Improvement of Housing Quality

In the thirties the reformers finally persuaded Congress that housing conditions were bad and that improvement of these conditions would reduce crime, immorality, incidence of disease, and unemployment. At that time and to this day the improvement in the quality of housing was and is thought of as the removal of an external diseconomy. If that were true, legislation to improve public housing would be undertaken at the local level. In fact, it is a redistribution of income in kind from upper-income families to lower-income families who cannot afford good-quality housing. As we have noted, redistribution cannot be undertaken at the local level of government, since upper-income families could always move away. Thus the federal government established the Public Housing Act of 1937 to improve housing for the poor.

The point that improvement of housing quality is really income redistribution rather than removal of a factor causing external social costs can perhaps best be seen by trying to determine what is a good-quality house or, as it is described in the literature, a standard-quality house. It would appear easy to list the attributes of an adequate or standard-quality house. Nevertheless, when the International Labor Office discussed the question, no specific attributes could be universally included:

A housing standard is defined—usually in terms of numbers of families per dwelling, standard of facilities per dwelling, and number and size of rooms needed for different families. These standards are largely arbitrary. They are based finally on what a particular investigator considers the needs of a family to be . . .

There are no absolute and universal standards of housing, and it is impossible to develop such standards. For one thing, the specific requirements which need to be met in order to safeguard health and to assure a given standard of comfort vary greatly in different climates and locations; and, more important, what is regarded as an adequate standard of comfort will be determined according to local customs and local levels of income, and in response to long-term increases in real income and changes in taste and social conscience. It is easy to list the considerations that should be taken into account in determining housing standards . . . To translate such a list of principles into terms of living space and facilities is a different matter. In fact, there are nearly as many housing standards as there are investigations into housing requirements.[17]

Thus the standard depends upon the charity of the upper-income families being taxed to support the improved housing of the poor. In the Housing Act of 1937 a limited reform was undertaken.

Public Housing   In general the Federal Public Housing operation can be described in the following way.[18] For federally subsidized public housing to be built in any community, a local housing authority must be established. The local authority, with the advice and consent of the local government, then decides on a plan and location for the public housing development. In the traditional procedure, the federal government would have to approve the plans and location and would grant development loans. Once the housing had been constructed, all the development and construction costs would be transferred into a long-term debt financed by public housing bonds sold by the local housing authority. These were, of course, tax-free municipal-type bonds.

The local authority would determine the rents and income eligibility for tenants in the project. These, however, would have to be approved by the federal government. The rents would be low so that low-income families could afford to live in the housing. As a rule, rents represented around 20 percent of gross family income. These rents, of course, would be insufficient to cover the cost of operating and developing the public housing project. The federal government subsidized the units by paying the local housing authority an annual contribution for the difference between rents and costs up to the actual interest payments and amortization of the bonded indebtedness. In recent years they have been given authority by Congress (Brooke Amendment) to grant subsidies greater than this amount.

Since the housing is owned by a local government agency, it is not subject to the property tax. At the time of the discussion and enactment of the 1937 law, it was thought that the city would lose by having private property off the tax rolls for the construction of public housing. Therefore the local authority was asked to pay the local government a sum in lieu of taxes equal to 10 percent of receipts from tenants. The evidence is clear that this payment in lieu of taxes results

[17]International Labour Office, *Housing and Employment* (Geneva: 1948), pp. 4 and 9, cited in Robert Moore Fisher, *Twenty Years of Public Housing* (New York: Harper, 1959), p. 29.
[18]Robert Moore Fisher, ibid.

in greater payments to local government than could have been generated in property taxes from the same low-income family occupancy of private housing.[19]

An economic evaluation of the public housing program could compare the costs of the program against the benefits achieved. There has been a difference of opinion about the total subsidy transferred to the poor through the construction of public housing. Some would say that it includes only the direct outlays subsidized by the federal government, but others indicate that it should represent the market value of resources transferred to the public housing program.[20] There are at least two reasons why the subsidy should be calculated as the market value of resources. First, the rules of construction encourage local housing authorities to substitute capital for maintenance expenditures. In the beginning, capital costs were the only subsidy allowed, so that it paid to reduce maintenance costs and build much longer-lasting buildings requiring little or no maintenance. This was true, even if a private decision maker would not have made the trade-off, because the subsidy was established as the interest and amortization of the capital indebtedness. Second, the mortgages were municipal bonds. These types of bonds have less interest because their income is not taxable. Thus there was incentive to shift more capital from the private sector to public housing that would have been done without the subsidy, and the return was less than would have been received for a private development.

Nourse has estimated the difference between what would have been necessary rent to pay off the project if it were privately financed and the rent actually paid by public housing tenants in 1956 to be $115 per unit per month plus the value of utilities provided.[21] More recently Muth estimated it to be $130 per unit per month.[22]

The benefits received for this subsidy are better housing for those occupying the public housing units and possible reduction of social disorders within the project area as well as in the surrounding areas. The poor, given a choice of slum housing for 20 percent of their income or public housing for 20 percent of their income, choose in large numbers to opt for public housing. With the exception of some problem projects, there are waiting lists and few vacancies in public hous-

[19]Hugh O. Nourse, "Redistribution of Income from Public Housing," *National Tax Journal*, 19 (March 1966), reprinted in Hugh O. Nourse, *The Effect of Public Policy on Housing Markets* (Lexington, Mass.: Heath, 1973), pp. 29-42.

[20]Richard F. Muth, *Public Housing: An Economic Evaluation* (Washington, D.C.: American Enterprise Institute for Public Policy Research, 1973), pp. 7-20; and Hugh O. Nourse, "The Effect of Public Housing on Property Values in St. Louis," *Land Economics*, 39 (November 1963), reprinted in Nourse, *The Effect of Public Policy on Housing Markets*, op. cit., p. 3.

[21]Nourse, ibid.

[22]Muth, op. cit., pp. 24-25.

ing. The actual number of units available has been small relative to the number of families eligible. Estimates of the percent of all eligible families housed in public housing have ranged from less than 4 percent to 10 or 15 percent.[23] With the amount of space determined by rules about family size per unit, the actual amount spent per square foot would entice many of the tenants to buy more space if they could. For this reason many spend less than they would have spent in the private market at that price per square foot.[24]

In the past public housing advocates have undertaken before-and-after studies showing the improvement in family and social life because of occupancy in public housing projects. Dean pointed out, however, that these early studies were biased because the authorities were selective in the families that they would allow into projects.[25] Only one recent study in Baltimore carefully determines the environmental impact of better housing with appropriate controls.[26] Groups of poor families from slum areas, some of whom stayed in slum housing and some of whom moved into public housing, were compared for differing rates of morbidity. Better housing improved the health and school performance of children because they had fewer accidents and days of illness. The differences were not found among persons over thirty-five years of age. A weakness of the study, however, was that no statistical test of significance was used to determine how different the test and control sample means really were.

The additional benefits that have often been ascribed to public housing have been the benefits to those in the neighborhood immediately surrounding the public housing project. Two studies have tested whether there were social benefits or costs to neighboring families by comparing whether there was any effect on neighboring property values.[27]

Changes in site value express the changes in the relative value of one neighborhood environment over others. Site value itself is difficult to measure, but changes in property value can be used as a measure of these changes as long as care is taken with respect to changes in improvements occurring on each site. The technique requires comparing

[23]Muth, op. cit., p. 23; Robert L. Bish, "Public Housing: The Magnitude and Distribution of Direct Benefits and Effects on Housing Consumption," *Journal of Regional Science*, 9 (1969), pp. 432.

[24]Bish, ibid., pp. 434–436.

[25]John P. Dean, "The Myths of Housing Reform," *American Sociological Review* (April 1949), pp. 281–288.

[26]Daniel M. Wilner, Rosabelle Price Walkley, Thomas C. Pinkerton, and Matthew Taybeck, *The Housing Environment and Family Life* (Baltimore: John Hopkins, 1962).

[27]Nourse, op. cit., pp. 3–13; Salvatore V. Ferrera, "The Effect of Urban Renewal and Public Housing on Neighborhood Property Values and Rents in Chicago," unpublished Ph.D. dissertation, Department of Economics, University of Chicago, 1969.

the changes in property values in blocks surrounding a given project with changes in property values in other neighborhoods that were of comparable quality and accessibility prior to the introduction of public housing.

The first study by Nourse compared the trends in prices of property located in a ring two to three blocks wide surrounding three public housing project areas in St. Louis with three control neighborhoods for the period 1937–1959. A statistical test of significance was used to compare whether the price indexes in each public housing and control area were significantly different. It was found that there was no significant difference in the indexes with the exception of one comparison in one year, and that showed a control neighborhood index to be significantly greater than the index for the comparable public housing neighborhood.

The second study by Ferrera compared the trends in contract rents of tenants in housing units in two rings around the Lake Meadows–Prairie Shores public housing projects in Chicago. He regressed relative changes in average contract rent per census block from 1950 to 1960 and from 1940 to 1960 against several explanatory variables, such as percent substandard, percent crowded, percent occupied by nonwhite households, and vacancy rates. Included in the independent variables was a dummy variable indicating whether the block was in the first or second ring around a public housing project. He found that the relative change in rents in the first ring around public housing units was significantly higher than general changes in the neighborhood from 1950 to 1960. However, he did not find any significant impact in the second ring, nor did he find a significant impact for the period 1940 to 1960.

Ferrera concluded that this rise in rents resulted from the demand for property for commercial uses and from the desire by families to put their children in the schools in the public housing area. Significantly, the boundary for the new school in the public housing complex rarely extended more than a block or two outside of public housing. Other attractive amenities included playgrounds, community recreation facilities, social welfare, and health facilities.

These results might well be expected if the housing segregation model is a good hypothesis of the market. Local governments must approve projects and their location. Projects have usually been located within the previous low-income neighborhoods. The representatives in government reflected the will of the voters.[28] Therefore, since no socioeconomic change in neighborhood resulted from the construc-

---

[28]For the Chicago experience see Edward C. Banfield and Martin Meyerson, *Politics, Planning, and the Public Interest* (Chicago: Free Press, 1955).

tion of any of the projects, it is unlikely that property values would change unless there was an increase or decrease in the number of housing units available to the poor. In practice, projects have sometimes increased density and on other sites decreased density over that existing prior to public housing.[29] Thus, it is unclear in total whether there was pressure to expand or contract the boundary between high-and low-income families on net as a result of public housing construction.

Thus the attempt to improve the quality of housing for the poor has not rectified the social disorders. It has improved the housing of some poor, but at a higher cost than expected. There has been a limit on the willingness of the electorate to support public housing beyond small projects. Furthermore, they have never shown a willingness for these projects to be located on the upper-income side of the boundary between low-and high-income families.

Rent and Interest Subsidies   There have been other types of subsidies by the federal government to encourage the construction of good housing for families who might not otherwise afford it. They have included limited experience with rent subsidies. In this case families find a standard-quality house and the government pays the difference between what they can afford (say 20 to 25 percent of their income) and what they have to pay. The idea was that families could then live wherever they could find such housing. In practice, however, Congress has not allowed many funds for this type of subsidy. Often these subsidies have been tied to the below market interest rate (BMIR) subsidies that were developed to reduce the construction cost of apartments for middle-income families and to cover the mortgages of older standard-quality housing bought by low-income families in older neighborhoods.

The BMIR subsidies have been subsidies that make up the difference between actual interest costs on mortgages on property and a rate of 1 to 3 percent. This reduction in cost has allowed rents to be lower than on other new apartments and houses, but the rents have only been cut to levels that middle-income families could afford. The poor, accommodated by public housing, were not eligible until the rent subsidy was added. Still, the number of units in any apartment complex allotted for rent subsidy use were restricted.

Nonetheless, the segregation of housing markets operated so as to keep most BMIR projects out of neighborhoods with a higher income or a different race. Thus these types of subsidies, once again,

[29]Nourse, op. cit., p. 40.

probably increase the available quality of housing to the poor but do not alleviate other problems of poverty. To the extent that these houses are net additions to the housing stock on the low-income side of the boundary, they do relieve the pressure for expansion of the spatial territory of the poor.

Building Code Regulation   Building codes use the regulatory power of the city to improve housing to a standard quality. In the early history of such cities as Boston, New York, Chicago, and St. Louis, repeated, costly fires caused local communities to require regulations so that buildings would not be as flammable and so that there would be adequate water for controlling fires. In the same way the spread of communicable diseases, because of inadequate sewer systems, caused the collective community to require the development of sewer systems for the disposal of household waste.[30]

These are instances of the external social costs of actions by a single individual or of transactions between a household and a builder. The community could direct behavior in the appropriate way by means other than direct regulation. They could have charged the households the cost of increased fire hazards for building with flammable materials, or they could have subsidized the construction of appropriate buildings by taxing in order to provide a subsidy. If the appropriate charges or subsidies could be established, each individual would adjust his actions so as to avoid as much of the charge as possible or to use as much of the subsidy as possible. Regulation, however, does not allow for alternative individual responses. Regulations require specific materials to be used, even though by performance standards other materials might have reduced the external social costs just as much.

As the social environmentalists pointed out the hazards to society of social disorders alleged to be caused by substandard housing, new, tighter building codes were created. Today there are detailed conflicts over such minutiae as whether plumbing can be built with plastic pipe, whether 2 × 3 studs can be used in non-load-bearing interior partitions, or whether preassembled plumbing cores can be used. Such controversies, however, constitute labor disputes rather than discussions as to whether a particular feature will increase fire hazards, damage health, or cause walls to fall down on neighbors.[31] The discussion itself would appear to be evidence that the codes in use are

---

[30]Carl Bridenbaugh, *Cities in Revolt* (New York: Knopf, 1955), pp. 292–333.

[31]Allen D. Manvel, *Local Land and Building Regulation*, Research Report No. 6 (Washington, D.C.: The National Commission on Urban Problems, 1968), pp. 11–19.

more detailed than they need to be in order to prevent external social costs.

A building code may be written in such a way that any materials may be used as long as they meet certain performance requirements, such as not burning except after a certain heat intensity is reached. Such a requirement is called a performance standard. Performance standards would be better than very restrictive specifications, as, for example, calling for a specific kind of material with a particular thickness. The reason is that performance standards enable new technologies to develop new and less expensive ways of meeting the needed performance. One current debate is over the use of plastic pipe. The question is whether it is durable and as good as current materials being used. Of more importance, however, is the debate over whether a performance standard is necessary to prevent an external social cost. Would other nearby households be damaged in some way if plastic pipe were used? That would be the relevant question to ask.

If we refer to the chapter on land use, we will find the principles guiding the construction or rehabilitation of buildings. There we noted that new additions to a building or original construction would occur as long as the present value of expected future earnings would cover the present value of the costs of construction or of the new additions. Applying this principle to the building code regulations, we would expect building codes to be complied with as long as the expected returns from renting or selling a house or building would cover the construction or rehabilitation costs. There is a ceiling, however, on what many families can pay for housing—a ceiling determined by their income. More stringent building code requirements that increase the cost of new construction put more and more people into the group unable to buy new housing. Furthermore, without enforcement of any code, the buildings on the low-income side of the boundary would deteriorate to very low quality because families at the low end of the income scale would be unable to afford the rents necessary to justify maintenance and repairs to keep the buildings up to their original standards. Enforcement of tight regulations would work as long as increases in rents for the increased costs would be forthcoming. But we have already indicated that low incomes of the families occupying these houses would prevent this. Therefore owners would tend to abandon any structures for which increased rents would not cover the costs of maintenance in compliance with the code.

In the early postwar period, after years without any new housing construction, there was a shortage of housing. Cities did not enforce their codes stringently because it would have reduced the housing supply for the poor. In the sixties, codes were enforced more rigorously. As would be expected, many houses and buildings on the low-income side of the boundary have been abandoned. The reduction in the supply of houses for low-income families caused increased pressure for the expansion of housing for low-income families. Unfortunately, many do not have the income to keep them up, so that these houses either waste away or are abandoned. The increases in building code requirements may also remove more families from the new housing market if they significantly raise new housing costs faster than the rate of inflation. One other response to increased costs of housing caused by codes would be increased density, but occupancy regulations today also regulate the number of persons allowed per unit.

Since poverty is the central cause of low-quality housing, it is difficult to see how a community can enforce higher building standards unless it is also willing to subsidize families so that they can afford the better housing. The enforceable standard, as indicated at the beginning of this section, is the standard that the community is willing to subsidize for its poorest citizens. Once again, however, these transfers would have to take place throughout a wide geographic district to prevent migration for the sake of avoiding such progressive taxes. Strict enforcement without subsidy to the poor will probably result in endless chewing up of housing resources through arbitrage.

Urban Renewal

In 1949 Congress enacted a housing act whose purpose was as follows:

> The general welfare and security of the nation and health and living standards of its people require housing production and related community development sufficient to remedy the serious housing shortage, the elimination of substandard and other inadequate housing through the clearance of slums and blighted areas, and the realization, as soon as possible, of the goal of a decent home and suitable living environment for every American family, thus contributing to the development and redevelopment of communities and to the advancement of the growth, wealth, and security of the nation . . . .[32]

To implement this policy, Congress encouraged the establishment of local urban renewal agencies. A local agency could declare an area to be an urban renewal area with the advice and consent of the local and federal governments. The agency would be responsible for initiating action, buying the property, clearing it, and selling it to private interests. Two-thirds of the project costs of federally approved projects would be subsidized by the federal government through direct grants-in-aid.

Two new kinds of assistance from the federal government were

[32]Public Law 171, 81st Congress, S. 1070, Housing Act of 1949.

established by the Housing Act of 1954, which made federal grants available to help finance public improvements in urban renewal areas: (1) two-thirds of the cost of such projects as landscaping, expanded recreational and educational facilities, and limited replanning of streets were to be subsidized by the federal government and (2) Federal Housing Administration insurance was to be provided for mortgages secured by rehabilitated or newly constructed properties in urban renewal areas. Still later, the law incorporated grants for rehabilitation.

Although the purposes stated in the urban renewal legislation and the tools developed seemed to be aimed at the removal of slums and the development of decent and safe housing for the poor, there were several other purposes in the minds and actions of those undertaking urban renewal in many cities. The additional purposes included renovation of downtown business districts, rolling back slums around hospitals and universities while providing land for their expansion, increasing the proportion of middle-income families in the city, and attracting clean industry to the city, which would help increase the sagging tax base of the central city.[33]

The impact of urban renewal on poverty, slums, and housing segregation depended upon where the renewal areas were located, the demolition of slum housing, and the construction of housing for low-income families now living in the renewal areas. If the projects demolished housing on the low-income side of the boundary and rehoused the families in better housing through public housing construction or rent subsidies, the poor were obviously better off. If the new density was greater than before, then the boundary between high and low income would tend to move back toward low-income areas. If the density in the new projects was less than before renewal, there would be additional pressure to expand housing for low-income families, since part of the housing stock available to them would have been destroyed. If no housing were made available for the previous tenants of the renewal area, the pressure on the boundary between segregated housing areas would be intense and blockbusting would surely occur.

In the early history of urban renewal, the evidence shows that more housing for the poor was demolished than was replaced. As of June 30, 1963, the 106 completed urban renewal projects had demolished almost twice as many units as were being considered to replace them. Furthermore, the replacement units were out of reach of the poor tenants who were moved. Only 8 percent of the replacement units were in public housing.[34] Congress was considerably dissatis-

[33]Jerome Rothenberg, *Economic Evaluation of Urban Renewal* (Washington, D.C.: Brookings, 1967), pp. 33-34.
[34]Rothenberg, ibid., p. 65.

fied with the progress toward housing the poor. The later modifications of the law were intended to improve the replacement of housing for low- and moderate-income families in renewal areas. As of June 30, 1971, however, some 538,000 units had been demolished (beginning in 1967), while only 201,000 units had been replaced. Of the replacement units, about half were for low- and moderate-income families.[35]

It is clear that if the housing segregation model has any validity, the urban renewal activity of local government may have caused far more high-income families to leave their borders than were replaced in projects because of the massive pressures on the housing segregation boundaries caused by the demolition of housing for blacks and and poor. Certainly some poor were helped, but more were moved. Furthermore, these actions were taken in the immediate post-World War II period, when housing was in short supply because of the lack of construction through the war years. Ironically, as we have pointed out, there is a tendency for the boundary to move and absorb more middle- and high-income housing than is required for expansion in the population of low-income families. The result has been the large vacancy rates within central cities of metropolitan areas and the number of abandoned housing units. Some have noted that good- as well as bad-quality housing has been abandoned, but this would be expected if the socioeconomic class of the neighborhood was a more important determinant of housing value than physical quality.

Since the supply of land in a metropolitan area is limited, it would be expected that as housing was abandoned or was declining in value, there would be a point at which the value of sites in new uses would be sufficient to buy the older sites and put them to new uses. The problem, however, is that the sites are surrounded by housing occupied by low-income families. Given the preferences of many higher-income families, new construction of housing and apartments in such areas would not generate sufficient income for the developer to undertake the project. Davis and Whinston argue that the real justification for renewal lies in this interdependency of demand for real property.[36] The logic is the same as for many other public goods. No one individual property owner could redevelop a site to a potential new use because of incompatible uses in the surrounding and adjacent sites. If, however, coordination of decisions of all of the property owners could be accomplished to redevelop a particular area and if the benefits from re-

[35]John C. Weicher, *Urban Renewal, National Program for Local Problems* (Washington, D.C.: American Enterprise Institute for Public Policy Research, 1972), p. 6.
    [36]Otto A. Davis and Andrew B. Whinston, "The Economics of Urban Renewal," *Law and Contemporary Problems*, 26 (Winter 1961), pp. 105–118.

newal would exceed costs, then public action might be required.[37] This logic, however, tends to channel analysis away from the real problem of poverty and to an allocation question. If the cost-benefit analysis is confined to a small geographic area, benefits could be construed when, in fact, all that has been accomplished is the exchange of geographical location by two income groups.

Still, a private developer attempting to assemble lots for redevelopment could have his development profits bargained away by a few owners holding out property from him in the area. Nevertheless, if this were the justification for urban renewal, then the subsidy for buying and developing the sites would not be required. Local communities could undertake urban renewal without the subsidy because the sale of land after demolition would more than pay for the cost of the old sites plus demolition. The shortage of housing in the early years of urban renewal may have caused the need for subsidy. That is, the sites were needed for low-income housing. As the number of units becoming abandoned increase, the opportunities for urban renewal to develop vacated sites may become important.

Nonetheless, we must reiterate our principle that the purchase or rent of a housing unit is really a purchase of a bundle of rights including schools, neighborhoods, access, and other public services. Unless the total package can be made attractive, renewal for residential purposes will be difficult. One possible solution would be to let such urban renewal areas become fragmented local governments in the way that the suburbs have developed. Self-determination of the local communities' demand for the mix and level of public services desired would likely increase the demand for the renewal sites. The large central-city governments, we have noted, are less likely to serve the demands of local citizens because of their size and heterogeneity. Such policy alternatives, however, would not mitigate the problems of

---

[37]Davis and Whinston carefully indicate owner A would be best off if owner B renewed B's property and A received positive spillovers. Similarly, owner B would be best off if A renewed A's property and B received positive spillovers. Both would be better off than with a no-renewal situation if both agreed to renew simultaneously, and this agreement could be a political agreement such as urban renewal. We propose that a more reasonable interpretation of urban renewal in the Davis and Whinston framework is that one owner, say A, who has good access to city political decision makers, gets the city to sponsor urban renewal of B's property so A can gain through positive spillovers. The location of many urban renewal projects adjacent to business areas of central cities, to universities, to hospitals, to museums, etc., fits very well into this framework. At the same time the original occupants of B are renewed out of the area and may or may not have received net gains. The use of urban renewal to generate gains for some, while possibly injuring others, is a classic example of reducing decision-making costs at the risk of higher political-externality costs being imposed on some members of the group.

poverty. They are merely reactions to the flow and movement of the poverty population.

Income Maintenance and the Negative Income Tax

Policy measures aimed at the quality of housing are, as we have seen, very indirect ways of alleviating poverty. Other subsidies in kind that also imply that direct transfers of money would be improperly spent by the poor include such distributions as food stamps. Economists argue that it is better to grant the poor direct transfers of cash rather than goods or services. The reason is that family preferences differ and each family would choose a different mix of goods for a given level of income. They would feel better off with their own chosen mix of goods rather than the particular mix imposed on them by the community. In the technical jargon of economics, the consumer would be on a higher indifference curve if he would move along his budget line to a preferred mix of goods rather than being forced to a particular point on the budget line by the mix of goods given to him, which he is not allowed to resell.

Direct payments to the poor in the United States include aid to families with dependent children, unemployment and disability compensation, social security, and general assistance. Some of these payments such as social security go to the poor and to many others. Nevertheless, there is some mitigation of poverty through these transfers. Obviously, a tour of our cities would show that poverty has not been eradicated nor slums eliminated by these measures. Surprisingly, there have not even been any studies to evaluate the impact of these programs on slums.

We have already noted that the income elasticity of demand for housing is around 1. Thus, any increase in income should cause a proportional increase in the amount families would be willing to spend on housing. In principle, we can determine whether any particular increase in income would so increase rents that the quality of housing would be improved to the building code standard. At any time an investor will convert, merge, or improve real property if the cost is equal to or less than the increase in value caused by the change. If expected annual rents for the life of the investment were equal over time, the decision rule could be written as follows:[38]

$$\text{Invest if } C \leq \left[\frac{(1 + r)^n - 1}{r(1 + r)^n} \right] a' - \left[\frac{(1 + r)^m - 1}{r(1 + r)^m} \right] a$$

---

[38]Nourse, op. cit., pp. 76–78, reprinted from Hugh O. Nourse, "The Effect of a Negative Income Tax on the Number of Substandard Housing Units," *Land Economics*, 46 (November 1970).

or if the lives of the investments are the same $(m = n)$,

$$C \leq \left[\frac{(1 + r)^n - 1}{r(1 + r)^n} \right] (a' - a)$$

where C = the cost of conversion, merger, or improvement
a' = the expected annual rent after change
a = the expected annual rent before change
r = the sum of the tax rate, rate for maintenance and repair, a vacancy rate, and the opportunity cost of capital
m = the economic life of the structure before change
n = the economic life of the structure after change or the period of time during which the investor wants to recapture his investment

$$\left[\frac{(1 + r)^n - 1}{r(1 + r)^n} \right] = \text{gross rent multiplier, a number by which}$$
gross rent may be multiplied to approximately estimate property value

Similarly, the increase in value that would just equal the construction cost could be written in the following way:

$$C = \left[\frac{(1 + r)^n - 1}{r(1 + r)^n} \right] (c' - a)$$

where c' is the increased rent that would just make the change in present value equal to cost. Therefore the decision rule may be rewritten:

$$\left[\frac{(1 + r)^n - 1}{r(1 + r)^n} \right] (c' - a) \leq \left[\frac{(1 + r)^n - 1}{r(1 + r)^n} \right] (a' - a)$$

or, $c' - a \leq a' - a$.
Dividing both sides by a,

$$\frac{c' - a}{a} \leq \frac{a' - a}{a}$$

Under the assumption that the gross rent multiplier is equal before and after the change, an investor will undertake a given change as long as the percentage increase in rent required to make the change in value equal to cost is equal to or less than the expected percentage increase in rents. The assumption that gross rent multipliers are equal before and after a change in use would be inappropriate for most types of changes in real property because the multiplier is a function of the economic life of the structure, the tax rate, rate for maintenance and repair, vacancy rate, and the opportunity cost of capital. Nevertheless, the equality of the multipliers may be a reasonable approximation for the rehabilitation of housing.

If we make the reasonable assumptions that the income elasticity of demand for housing is equal to unity and that the price elasticity of supply of housing construction is infinity, the above decision rule is reduced to determining whether the percentage increase in income is equal to or greater than the percentage increase in rent necessary to pay off the construction costs.

If the percentage increase in income is great enough, families will be demanding the better housing at the boundary between low- and high-income groups. To prevent vacancies, houses in the interior adjacent to the border housing would be improved, since the rents people would be willing to pay would cover the costs of improvement. We would have to know the exact percentage increases in income and the exact percentages required to cover construction costs in order to determine whether any explicit income maintenance program would bring houses up to a code standard.

Since slums and poverty still exist, current policies of the income maintenance type are obviously not eliminating poverty or poor quality housing. One proposal that has received wide notice in recent years has been Milton Friedman's negative income tax.[39] This proposal would substitute direct transfers of money for all current welfare measures: social security, subsidies in kind such as public housing, and aid to dependent children. The supplements proposed in Friedman's plan, however, fall below the assistance payments now made to families with dependent children in two-fifths to two-thirds of the states.[40] Nonetheless, it is a plan worth considering because the level could be raised.

The negative income tax would work in the following way. When a family's income falls below its tax deductions and exemptions, they would receive a benefit equal to 50 percent of the difference between their allowed deduction and exemptions and their income. For example, if the basic deduction was $200 for each family plus $100 for each person in the family and the standard exemption was $750 for each member of the family, the allowable deduction and exemptions for a single person would be $1,050 and for a family of four $3,600. For the family of four, if income fell below $3,600 to $2,000, the family would receive benefits equal to half the difference between $3,600 and $2,000. They would receive $800. If their income increased by $800, they would still receive benefits, but the benefits would be reduced to $400. For each dollar earned, benefits would be reduced 50 cents.

All such income maintenance programs have disincentive effects

[39]Milton Friedman, *Capitalism and Freedom* (Chicago: The University of Chicago Press, 1962), pp. 190–195.

[40]Clair Wilcox, *Toward Social Welfare* (Homewood, Ill.: Irwin, 1969), p. 258.

on work. Why work if an adequate income will be given to you by society? The negative income tax, however, does not take away all incentive for work. The worker still receives increases in income if he works rather than quits. The incentive effects of such plans, even the conservative 50 percent plan, are still contested. The first experimental research in economics, however, was to study the impact of a negative income tax on work incentives. For three years a sample of families were given payments each month as if they were participants in one of several alternative plans. The results indicated a slight reduction in hours worked by prime-aged married males in families receiving benefits. While there was no significant decrease in numbers of this group working, there was an increase in individual earnings. Although the percentage reduction in hours worked by prime-aged married women in families receiving benefits was more than for males, the difference from control group families was not statistically significant. These results indicate only slight work disincentive effects from the negative income tax plans, and they are consistent with other studies of disincentive effects.[41]

Nourse has made one study of the impact of a 50 percent negative income tax on reducing the level of nonfarm substandard housing.[42] Benefits were calculated for families who lived in substandard housing and whose income in 1960 was generated from wages, salaries, and self-employment income. Those already on welfare were excluded. From these estimates, a frequency distribution showing the percentage of families that would have received alternative percentage increases in income from the negative income tax plan was calculated. Estimates of the percentage of families for which different percentage increases in income would be required to bring their houses to code standard were taken from a study by Schaaf, in which these calculations were made for a slum area in Oakland, California.[43]

Assuming the percentage increases in income would cause the same percentage increase in rent families would pay for housing, all that was needed was a comparison of the percentage increase in income against the percentage increase in rent required to bring houses to code compliance. There was, however, no direct evidence on the association between family income, family size, and the cost of code compliance. In the absence of such evidence, it was assumed that these

[41]Irwin Garfinkel, "Income Transfer Programs and Work Effort: A Review," in Joint Economic Committee, *Studies in Public Welfare*, paper no. 13, "How Income Supplements Can Affect Work Behavior" (Washington, D.C.: U.S. Government Printing Office, February 18, 1974), pp. 1–32.

[42]Nourse, op. cit., pp. 75–89.

[43]A. H. Schaaf, *Economic Analysis of Urban Renewal: Theory, Policy and Area Analysis*, Research Report no. 14 (Berkeley, Calif.: Real Estate Research Program, Institute of Business and Economic Research, University of California), 1960.

two events were independent, random events. The relative frequency distribution of each represents its probability distribution. The joint probability of any pair of possible increases in rents families would pay and required rent increases can be calculated. It is simply the product of (1) the probability that any family in substandard housing without welfare payments will receive a given percentage increase in income from negative income tax benefits and (2) the probability of a substandard housing unit requiring a given percentage increase in rent to pay off the rehabilitation cost.

Using this procedure, it was found that 24 percent of the tenant families and 43 percent of the owner families in substandard housing in 1960 would have improved their housing to code standard. Translated into numbers of units, it represented 857,000 housing units. In 1960, however, 11 million units were considered substandard.[44]

Thus a conservative negative income tax would probably have a small impact on slums and would not alleviate poverty inasmuch as its benefits would be less for many poor than they currently receive. To improve the plan, many have suggested raising the income limits at which families would begin paying taxes. The higher the income limit, the fewer people are left on the tax rolls, so that tax rates would have to be higher. This, of course, would cause some disincentive for work. Furthermore, the amount of money needed for the transfers would be much higher the higher the income limit. Notice also that many families with low incomes would not be considered poor. They could be temporarily poor, like college and graduate students, or self-employed persons having a bad year, or part of their income might be nontaxable income—elderly homeowners, for example, are not taxed on the value of the flow of utility from their homes. Thus, the higher the limit, the larger the number of nonpoor families who would receive benefits. So far, Congress has been little disposed toward such large transfers. Although an adequate negative income tax would eliminate slums and poverty, we have yet to learn its impact on work incentives, and it would not affect housing segregation based on race or other social distinctions.

Labor Market Policies

As Norton Long has noted, all the previous policy approaches treat the low-income and ethnic areas of the city as if they were reservations requiring higher-income families to do something for others.[45] They

---

[44]United States Bureau of the Census, *Statistical Abstract of the United States: 1968*, 89th ed. (Washington, D.C., 1968), p. 706.
[45]Norton Long, *The Unwalled City* (New York: Basic Books, 1972).

treat the symptoms of poverty and segregation but not the causes. Alternative approaches that deal more directly with the causes of poverty—unemployment, low-wage employment, lack of skills, lack of education, shortsightedness, and discrimination—might be termed labor market or economic development policies. These can be categorized into (1) those that affect the demand for labor within slums or black ghettos by encouraging investment in job-creating activity within these areas, (2) those that affect the supply of labor by training and retraining poorly skilled workers, or (3) those that affect the efficiency of the market by providing funds to workers to migrate or by providing transportation to suburban jobs for ghetto workers.

In general, unemployment in the low-income areas of cities is twice as high as the national average. When unemployment declines with the tightening of the labor market in general, employment is easier to find for workers in low-income neighborhoods.[46] Nevertheless, Edward Kalachek and John Goering, in a study of St. Louis ghetto labor markets, found that workers in these areas were not unemployed for especially long periods of time. Instead, the basic problem was the low-wage jobs available to these workers.[47] With high aspirations to achieve betterment through education and job opportunities, the workers held jobs that were low-paying and without prospects for future improvement. The jobs held did not provide for improvements in skills that would lead to advancement. Therefore, for young blacks under thirty years of age, the unemployment rate was especially high, but it was caused by a very high quitting rate. Job turnover was high, but it was not difficult to find another dead-end job. Older workers, more fatalistic about their place in life or responsible for dependents, tended to have more stable job experiences.

Black Capitalism   Under the slogan "Black Capitalism," the argument has been made that investment in slum areas should be subsidized in order to provide jobs for residents. The argument is somewhat parallel to the arguments made years ago that poor southern towns or rural areas should receive subsidies to encourage creation of jobs because of low incomes and high unemployment. Since these are low-wage areas, it might be thought that it would be attractive for firms to locate in these slum areas. The evidence is not very strong that they do consider these sites profitable. First, low wages must be considered along with productivity. The figure that is important to the firm is the wage

---

[46]Edward Kalachek and John Goering, *Transportation and Central City Unemployment* (St. Louis: Institute for Urban and Regional Studies, Washington University, March 1970), pp. 1-2.
[47]Ibid., pp. 8-9.

cost per unit of output. Low-wage, unskilled workers could mean higher wage costs per unit than a few high-paid, skilled workers would. Second, the social disorders and violence of the slum location would be unattractive to the other workers the firm would want to employ. Therefore a subsidy would be required to attract firms to such locations. It might indeed have to be a large subsidy.

John Moes argued that small southern towns should provide subsidies to attract firms to their locations and generate employment.[48] However, since there were better income opportunities in other locations and the residents stayed for reasons of personal preference, he thought the appropriate tax scheme was a wage tax on those communities wanting the jobs. The main difficulty with this approach would hinge on the question of whether the resultant real wages would really alleviate poverty. In the case of slums, the residents do not have any real choice about migrating to other parts of metropolitan areas. If the subsidy is to be a transfer from high-income families to low-income families, it cannot be done by local government, as we have so often mentioned. Such subsidies would have to come from the federal government. Indeed, the Small Business Administration has been making grants and special loans for such businesses to be established in slum areas. The first question about these subsidies is whether they do attract establishments that would offer good jobs—not dead-end jobs paying low wages and offering no opportunity for skill improvement and advancement. Unless the employment opportunities do provide for skill improvement, the subsidy is unlikely to improve the income of the employees. Furthermore, it perpetuates the segregation of housing and the type of thinking that promotes racial prejudice.

Nevertheless, there is a strong feeling among blacks that if they could only own their own businesses, they would have more control of their own environment. The segregation in housing that we have described has been shown to permeate enterprise development and labor markets too. The whites preference not to conduct business in ghetto areas means that only above-average profits can lure white entrepreneurs to stay in business in the slums. Marginal profits are earned by the black businesses crowding into the slum area. Capital market imperfections are said to prevent black business from competing effectively with the white entrepreneurs and taking a fair share of the profits. They are unable to reach the same scale. There is evidence of a dual labor market in which blacks, in spite of increased education and training, are not able to find the career tracks to higher incomes that similarly educated whites find. The impact of all these

[48]J. E. Moes, *Local Subsidies for Industry* (Chapel Hill, N.C.: The University of North Carolina Press, 1962).

setbacks to integration have led many to see the slum or ghetto as a colony within the developed United States. The economic and political institutions controlling the life of people in such areas are not controlled by them but by people who live outside the segregated areas. Thus, the blacks' drive for black economic development is really their attempt to obtain economic power to control their own situation.[49]

It is unclear whether the types of businesses that would have to be subsidized for many years would lead to the kind of independence desired.[50] The Minority Enterprise Small Business Investment Company was established within the Department of Commerce to supply venture capital to small businessmen. It has been criticized for requiring high minimum amounts of capital, for funding only small black businesses, and for not supporting cooperatives. The criticisms seem contradictory, since they are aimed at both small business finance and overly high capital requirements. The Small Business Administration helps increase funding, but it also participates in finding markets for these businesses by acting as a prime contractor for goods and services delivered to other government agencies. Minority firms are then subcontracted to deliver the goods. Cooperatives are excluded from this provision. The effort, however, has increased capital flows to minority business. Government grants, loans, and guarantees for black business rose from $200 million in 1969 to over $430 million in fiscal 1971. The government procurement contracts for minority business rose from $8.8 million in 1969 to $66 million in 1971.[51] Small firms, however, do not have high survival rates, and no one has studied the survival of these firms.

Since 1966 there has been an effort by large corporations to establish branch plants in ghetto areas. Studies of these efforts show that they are operating with substantial excess capacity and that many have closed down. Furthermore, the corporations have been able to set lower wage scales than prevail elsewhere without union objections. Thus the jobs have not been necessarily better, nor has the ghetto community had control of these corporate branch plant investments.[52]

An alternative is the development of enterprise by community development corporations. Their goals are not just the establishment of enterprise employing minority people but also the development of public services and other facilities that would smooth the develop-

[49]William F. Haddad and G. Douglas Pugh (eds.), *Black Economic Development* (Englewood Cliffs, N.J.: Prentice Hall, 1969); and Bennet Harrison, "Ghetto Economic Development: A Survey," *Journal of Economic Literature*, 12 (March 1974), pp. 1–37.
[50]Bernard H. Booms and James E. Ward, Jr., "The Cons of Black Capitalism," *Business Horizons*, 7 (October 1969), pp. 17–26.
[51]Harrison, op. cit., pp. 14–15.
[52]Ibid. pp. 16–17.

ment of further enterprise in ghetto areas. With such multiple goals, these corporations have had to find projects that would provide sufficient revenues to cover the cost of operations plus these other efforts. Shopping centers, manufacturing plants, and an office building are some of the investments made by several community development corporations in Harlem, East Boston, Denver, and Seattle. The Model Cities Program of the Department of Housing and Urban Development and the Office of Economic Opportunity have provided grants for developing these corporations. Although some economists are optimistic about the success of these development cooperatives, their reliance on outside subsidy and political support for at least the next ten to twenty years makes them vulnerable to criticism from the outside community, especially if they should become successful.[53]

Kain and Persky have made the point that such efforts would gild the ghetto.[54] It would make the ghettos even more attractive for southern poor. Furthermore, as we have described housing segregation, it can be easily understood that it is a fundamental part of today's urban problems. Therefore Kain and Persky argue that federal policy would be better directed to providing development or labor market type aid for the southern poor in the South, so that migration would be slowed down and would not intensify the current problems of ghettos in metropolitan areas.

Manpower Development and Training Programs   A second group of labor market policies to alleviate poverty are those providing vocational training and retraining to workers in order that they may help themselves to improve and escape poverty. The purpose, of course, is to invest in human resources so that the present value of the future earnings of these workers will increase by more than the cost of the investment.

The federal government made a major thrust in this direction in 1962 with the Manpower Development and Training Act. A wide variety of institutional training, on-the-job training, counseling, and other efforts to upgrade ghetto and depressed area labor markets have been instituted.[55] Studies evaluating the impact of these programs have shown resulting increases in the present value of future earnings

[53]Ibid. pp. 18–23.
[54]John F. Kain and Joseph J. Persky, "Alternatives to the Gilded Ghetto," *The Public Interest*, 14 (Winter 1969), pp. 74–87.
[55]David M. Gordon, *Theories of Poverty and Underemployment* (Lexington, Mass.: Heath, 1972), pp. 6–7.

several times the costs of the training.[56] There is some question, however, whether the increased earnings attributable to the programs have been correctly evaluated. Several studies showed that the difference in earnings between those workers who had participated in manpower programs and those not so trained were large in the first year after the program but then narrowed rapidly. By the fourth year, differences were insignificant. In spite of this, benefit calculations were made showing large differences for ten years subsequent to the training programs. Thus the benefits could have been less than or equal to costs rather than several times cost.

Furthermore, there is some doubt as to whether the benefits, if estimated correctly, could be attributed to the training program. The better jobs may have been a result of the placement counseling associated with the programs or they may have resulted from the credentialing of certain workers. The latter point is the same point made for all evaluations of education. Business uses the credentials of a particular degree or certificate as a device for screening for the best applicants. Furthermore, some studies have found that neither grades nor earnings are associated with cognitive achievement.[57] Education seems to affect earnings through its impact on strength of character and self-discipline rather than through its impact on cognitive achievement.

No one has attempted to evaluate the indirect impact of these manpower programs on the social problems associated with poverty. As might be inferred, however, the direct benefits have been difficult enough to pin down.

Banfield makes a strong case that the very personality traits that the culture of poverty develops in workers make them unreachable through training programs. Furthermore, it is impossible to give such a worker the kind of job that would provide for improvement and advancement because his life-style makes it impossible to give him such a job.[58] Nevertheless, Kalachek and Goering found ghetto workers to have aspirations similar to those of middle-class workers. True enough, more ghetto workers were fatalistic and present-oriented, but the differences in the two populations were very small.[59]

Radicals would argue that improvements in education and skills will not result in improvements of earnings because the labor market is segmented so that certain groups, including ghetto workers, will

[56]The Joint Economic Committee, Congress, *The Effectiveness of Manpower Training Programs: A Review of Research on the Impact on the Poor*, Studies in Public Welfare, paper no. 3, Washington, D.C., November 20, 1972.
[57]Gordon, op. cit., pp. 120–121.
[58]Edward C. Banfield, op. cit., p. 242.
[59]Kalachek and Goering, op. cit., F32–F37.

not be able to find jobs. A related general argument against the ability of the education policy to improve skills is that the job definitions are unrelated to that of training but are related to technology. Partial evidence is the fact that increases in education among blacks have not led to improvements in earnings. In fact, improvement in the proportion of all workers with more education has not led to more equalization of earnings.[60] For whatever reason, the evidence indicates that attempts to alleviate poverty by improving productivity have not been outstandingly successful.

Labor Market Efficiency Programs A third group of policies have been developed in attempting to improve the efficiency with which the labor market operates. For example, we pointed out in Chapter 3 that even if he were offered a new job with projected earnings high enough to pay for moving and retraining, a worker might not make the switch because he lacked the funds to finance the change. Furthermore, the usual job-search technique of ghetto workers depends on word-of-mouth leads from friends. Thus most of the manpower training programs include counseling services to help inform workers about job opportunities. Another experimental program has involved the subsidizing of public transportation from low-income minority areas to employment centers in the suburbs. Since the suburbanization of population and the improvement in transportation networks has made possible the shifting of industry and commerce to the suburbs and since the low-income families are caught on the inner city side of the segregated boundary between housing markets, it has been argued that workers from the ghetto would find it increasingly difficult to search for jobs and hold them without public transportation from the slum areas to the outer work centers.[61]

One cost-benefit study, however, found that suburban plants were relatively scattered and that their shifts were so staggered—to avoid auto traffic jams—that bus service from the ghetto to employment areas was only minimally helpful. A mere enumeration of the number of people who had obtained jobs was a misleading gauge of success because of the high turnover following hirings. Job instability was the problem, not the finding of a job. And low paying, dead-end jobs without chances for skill development and opportunities for ad-

[60]Gordon, op. cit., pp. 119–121; and Lester C. Thurow and Robert E. B. Lucas, *The American Distribution of Income: A Structural Problem*, Joint Economic Committee, Congress, Washington, D.C., March 17, 1972.

[61]John F. Kain, "Housing Segregation, Negro Employment and Metropolitan Decentralization," *Quarterly Journal of Economics*, 82 (May 1968), pp. 175–197.

vancement were the problems causing job turnover.[62] Nevertheless, personnel officers in suburban manufacturing plants did reveal that if two candidates for a job were equally qualified except that one had a car, the one with the car would get the job because this would mean less absenteeism and greater job stability. The suburban areas are badly served by public transportation, so that it is difficult to get to work on time unless a car is available. Then too, if a worker has a car, he is probably making payments on it, so he has an incentive to keep his job rather than quit.[63]

In summary, there is a need for transportation help for workers in the inner city, but the spatial structure of employment centers and their staggering of work shifts make public transportation with large buses not practical and not particularly successful. Job counseling has provided additional information, and retraining has been subsidized through innumerable programs. The latter, however, have usually been associated with manpower retraining programs.

SUMMARY

Neither poverty nor racial segregation are peculiarly urban problems. Nevertheless, the density of population in urban areas creates special problems because attitudes toward these groups at such close quarters cause them to be isolated by housing segregation. The concentration of poverty and ethnic groups in particular areas exacerbates the social problems generated by poverty and the feelings of alienation induced by discrimination.

One model of housing markets explains the creation of slums through segregation. The families in a community can be divided into those able to afford a new house and those unable to do so. The upper-income families are willing to pay a premium to avoid lower-income family neighborhoods. They pay a discount for living in neighborhoods that adjoin lower-income housing. On the other hand, the lower-income families are willing to pay a premium for neighborhoods adjacent to upper-income families while paying a discount for houses in neighborhoods entirely surrounded by other poor. This creates the potential for arbitrage on the boundary between the two groups. In a dynamic setting, increases in the number of low-income families can only be accommodated by expansion of the boundary between the two groups and a shift of housing resources from high-income families to low-income families. Nevertheless, the decrease in rents that people within

[62]Kalachek and Goering, op. cit.
[63]Ibid.

low-income neighborhoods can afford causes a deterioration in the condition of their housing.

Racial segregation results in another boundary between neighborhoods occupied by middle-income white families and middle-income black families. The small number of middle-income black families is insufficient to support integrated middle-income neighborhoods if whites refuse to buy into such neighborhoods. Therefore prices in such neighborhoods decline and the housing is shifted to low-income users.

The concentration of poverty creates the "thickly populated, squalid part of a city, inhabited by the poorest people"—the slums. Associated with the areas of poor-quality housing are increased juvenile delinquency, crime, tuberculosis, immorality, increased death rates, unemployment, and increased fire hazards. Early social environmentalists associated the social problems with the quality of housing, but today we associate these problems with poverty. The segregated housing model sets a high income for poverty, but we can think of many housing markets in a gradation by income group from highest to lowest. Although poverty is not explicitly a part of the model, the model does imply that racial segregation and isolation of poverty families is part of the problem. The causes of poverty include lack of skills, unemployment, insufficient capital for migration to better jobs, insufficient capital for transportation to better jobs within the metropolitan area, bad luck, discrimination, and segregation of labor markets. Radicals would include exploitation.

Whatever the cause of poverty and slums, the segregated housing market causes institutional reactions that exacerbate the problems. Speculation is created at the boundary, and financial institutions are justifiably reluctant to invest in areas that they anticipate may decline in value because of change in use from higher-income to lower-income families.

Social reformers in the twenties and thirties argued that improved housing would ameliorate poverty and reduce fire hazards and the incidence of tuberculosis, delinquency, crime, etc. As a result, the public housing administration was created at the federal level to subsidize good housing for poor people. The difficulty with the policy from the very beginning is that the so-called standard-quality house that would do all the good things represents no more than the standard that the electorate is willing to subsidize. None of the empirical studies of the benefits from public housing have found very large social benefits to families moving in, although no one would deny that better housing has been provided. Furthermore, no one has found external benefits or costs to families living in houses surrounding such projects. Part of the reason may be that practically no community has allowed public housing to be constructed in neighborhoods on the high-income side of the segregated housing market boundary.

Similar problems have dogged rent subsidy and interest subsidy policies to provide housing to low- and moderate-income families.

Building codes have been established to maintain housing above some standard, but these standards usually have more to do with labor disputes than performance standards that might cause external costs to surrounding buildings. Furthermore, attempts to force all housing to be maintained at standards the poor cannot afford without subsidies will result in the continual movement of slum areas, abandonment of housing, and chewing up of housing resources.

In 1949 Congress passed a Housing Act creating urban renewal subsidies for communities to eliminate slums and provide better housing. In fact, slums were eliminated by destruction, but the number of new housing units made available to the poor represented only a small proportion of the housing that had been available to them and had been destroyed. The result was pressure on the boundary of the segregated housing market and an increased transfer of houses from high-income to low-income use. With lower-income residents, however, these houses could not be maintained at the quality previously established.

Policy measures aimed at the quality of housing are indirect ways of alleviating poverty. Public housing, interest rate subsidies, and rent subsidies are all considered to be subsidies in kind. Economists argue that it is better to grant the poor direct transfers of cash rather than goods or services. The reason is that family preferences differ and each family would choose a different mix of goods for a given level of income. They would feel better off with their own chosen mix of goods than with the particular mix imposed on them by the community.

Direct payments to the poor in the United States include aid to families with dependent children, unemployment and disability compensation, social security, and general assistance. These payments, however, have not stopped the creation of slums. One proposal has been to substitute a negative income tax for all welfare programs. One specific suggestion, the 50 percent negative income tax, however, would not provide as much income as is currently provided under such programs as social security and aid to dependent children. One analysis has also indicated that it would have a small impact on improving substandard housing in the United States to standard quality. Any negative income tax that would pay more would include many people who were not poor, would increase disincentive for work, and would increase taxes while taking more off the tax rolls.

All the previous policies have been directed at alleviating the symptoms of poverty rather than the causes. Alternative approaches that deal more directly with the causes of poverty—unemployment,

low-wage employment, lack of skills, lack of education, shortsightedness, and discrimination—might be termed labor market or economic
development policies. These policies can be categorized into those that
affect the demand for labor within slums or black ghettos by encouraging investment in job-creating activity within those areas, those that
affect the supply of labor by training and retraining poorly skilled workers, or those that affect the efficiency of the market by providing funds
to workers to migrate or by providing transportation for ghetto
workers to suburban jobs.

Development within slum areas would require continuous subsidy, tend to gild the ghetto, and not necessarily attract jobs improving skills. Moreover, because of the subsidy, it would not build
power for the ghetto entrepreneurs. In 1962 the federal government
established the Manpower Development and Training Act to provide
training and job counseling for ghetto and depressed-area labor
markets. The evaluations of these efforts have shown increased
earnings for short periods after retraining for participating workers as
opposed to those not so trained, but the increases dwindled to insignifi-
cance after three or four years. Even the efforts to improve the efficiency of the labor market by providing public transportation from
slum areas to suburban employment centers have been unsuccessful.

From the New Deal programs of social security and public
housing in the 1930s to the War on Poverty programs of manpower
development and black capitalism in the 1960s, policy efforts to alleviate poverty have appeared to have but a marginal impact on the
growth of slums and indeed in some cases have made problems worse.
The problem is still fundamentally poverty and discrimination. The
conservative response to this record is that poor people are inherently
present-minded and will be brought up from poverty only gradually,
over a generation or so. Furthermore, the process is cultural, and policy directed to help will not do much good. The radicals, on the other
hand, would contend that segregation or discrimination is the root
cause and that only a restructuring of jobs will turn the situation
around. In all, one has the impression of a society willing to consider
marginal efforts to eliminate slums and alleviate poverty but not as yet
willing to consider any really fundamental change in its economic
organization.

SELECTED READING

Gordon, David M.: *Theories of Poverty and Underemployment* (Lexington, Mass.: Heath, 1972).

Kalachek, Edward, and John Goering: *Transportation and Central City Unemployment* (St. Louis: Institute for Urban and Regional Studies, Washington University, March 1970).

Lowry, Ira S.: "Filtering and Housing Standards: A Conceptual Analysis," *Land Economics* (November 1960), pp. 362–370.

Nourse, Hugh O.: *The Effect of Public Policy on Housing Markets* (Lexington, Mass.: Heath, 1973).

CHAPTER 9

ZONING AND LAND-USE CONTROL

Property values are expected values. They depend upon people's expectations about the future trend of rents on a property. That expectation is not just for the physical property but for the bundle of private rights and public goods associated with the ownership of the property. If uncertainty about changes in the bundle of rights associated with a property could be reduced, property values should be enhanced. This would be especially true if it were possible to exclude undesirable uses of land on adjacent sites. A major purpose of zoning is to exclude from a neighborhood such uses of land as would tend to cause values to decline.

RATIONALE FOR ZONING[1]

Consider only two adjacent properties at a time. Part of the bundle of rights purchased by each owner is the external economy, external diseconomy, or neutral effect of the adjacent property. Since rights purchased go into the future, the bundle of rights purchased includes

[1]Otto A. Davis, "Economic Elements in Municipal Zoning Decisions," *Land Economics*, 39 (November 1963), pp. 375–376.

not only any externalities present now but also expectations of externalities that may exist at some future time. With only two properties to consider, there are six possible ways in which these two could interact with each other. These are as follows:

1 If two land uses on adjacent sites should create external economies for each other, the property value of each would be enhanced because the expected earnings for each use would be higher on these adjacent sites than on alternative locations. No regulation is required to bring about adjacent location by such uses. Private owners seeking the highest rent for their land would take advantage of mutual externalities. Examples of such mutual externalities are abundant in retail location. Those stores selling goods that are expensive and for which consumers find comparison shopping worthwhile tend to locate adjacent or near to other stores selling the same good. We observe "automobile row" or "furniture row" in cities for this reason. Those stores selling goods or services that consumers might want to purchase on the same shopping trip would tend to locate on adjacent sites also. Thus, a shopping center is a cluster of stores that often includes a department store, drugstore, supermarket, dry cleaner, bank, and variety store. The size of the cluster and the types of business represented depends, of course, on the size of the market accessible to the site. The department store itself is the ultimate in mutual attraction. In such a store the sites of different types of retail selling are not only adjacent but also under one ownership.

2 If two land uses on adjacent sites should create external diseconomies for each other, the property value of each would be reduced because the expected earnings for each would be lower on these adjacent sites than on alternative locations. Private owners seeking the highest rents for their land would avoid placing such uses on adjacent sites. Examples of mutual external diseconomies do not come readily to mind. However, churches or synagogues and taverns or brothels might be mutually repelling.

3 If two land uses on adjacent sites should create neither external economies nor diseconomies for each other, property values would be unaffected by adjacent locations. There would be no need for interference in the market in these circumstances either.

4 If land use A would create an external economy for use B on an adjacent site but B would be neutral in its effect on A, property values of use B would be enhanced if located adjacent to A. Property values of use A, however, would be unaffected by location near B. Once a site is used for use A, private owners would want to establish use B on adjacent sites. Location decisions for use B would not affect those for use A. An example might be the location of a department store (A) and specialty shoe or dress shop (B); another, the location of a university (A) and restaurants (B). A department store or a university would generate traffic that would enhance revenues for specialty shops in the case of the department store and for restaurants in the case of the university. But the single specialty store would not generate traffic to enhance the earnings of a department store, nor would the traffic generated by a restaurant enhance the academic quality or size of a university. In these circumstances private ownership would take advantage of the possibilities for external economies. For example, a department store is often given a rental advantage to entice it into a particular shopping center.

5 If land use A would create an external economy for land use B but land use B creates an external diseconomy for use A, property values for use B would be enhanced if located adjacent to use A but property values of A would be reduced if located adjacent to B. Private owners would attempt to locate B on sites adjacent to A in order to take advantage of the enhanced value, but this would reduce the values of sites in use A. On the other hand, private owners would not attempt to place use A near sites in use B. A prime example of this is the boundary between housing for low- and higher-income families that we described in the arbitrage model in Chapter 8. In the past, private owners in a market have used restrictive covenants to protect against such diseconomies. Such convenants were agreements between owners on adjacent sites that the property would not be used for certain purposes, including occupancy by certain races. The latter covenants have been declared unenforceable because they are against public policy.

6 If land use A is neutral in its impact on use B but use B creates an external diseconomy for use A, property values for use A would be reduced by locations adjacent to sites in use B while property values for use B would be unaffected by location adjacent to site A. Private owners would try to locate uses A on sites away from uses B, but those owners developing use B would be indifferent about locating use B adjacent to use A. This is probably the most common example of external diseconomies used to support zoning regulations. The situation would include using land for stockyards, soap factories, cement plants, and gasoline service stations in residential areas. Even in common law there was a remedy against invasion by such nuisance uses that could damage adjacent property.[2] Today in Houston, a city without zoning, restrictive covenants between owners on adjacent sites are used to prevent these damages from occurring.[3]

[2]Ronald H. Coase, "The Problem of Social Cost," *Journal of Law and Economics*, 3 (1960), pp. 1–44.
[3]Bernard H. Siegan, *Land Use without Zoning* (Lexington, Mass.: Heath, 1972).

The purpose of zoning ordinances has been to prevent the kind of externalities described in items 5 and 6 above from occurring. These diseconomies are supposed to abound in the urban property market; therefore the original ordinances developed classes of land uses, or zones, into which the city would be divided. In one of the first ordinances, in New York in 1916, there were three categories: residential, commercial, and industrial. The highest use would be residential zones in which nuisance uses would be excluded. Commercial zones would be next. Although residences could be located in such zones, industrial uses could not. The last zone was industrial. The main feature was that industry could locate only in such zones, but all other uses would also be permitted. Later, more highly developed categories of land use were drawn up. Residential zones would be divided into exclusive single-family areas with a variety of height and density restrictions. Single-family houses with 1-acre lots might be in one zone, and single-family houses with smaller lots in another zone. Other residential zones would include areas in which row houses, two-family dwellings, and apartment houses could be located. Detailed height and density requirements would also define varying grades of commercial and industrial land-use zones.

Ordinances usually also provide procedures that make variances in the code possible.

Although external diseconomies in the tradition of common-law decisions with respect to nuisances are always seen as the dominant reason for zoning, it has also always been known that the insulation of the single-family, detached dwelling was the primary objective.[4] Even before the model zoning ordinance of New York in 1916, residents of Modesto, California, had managed, after several attempts at direct legal exclusion, to design a zoning ordinance to exclude Chinese by zoning laundries into special areas.[5] This type of exclusion is consistent with external damages in which B damages A but A provides benefits for B, as we noted above.

ZONING CRITERIA

As in most situations in which some public action is required, there is no simple criterion that a city planner or other administrator could use to determine the ideal allocation of land to alternative uses. The private market operates on the principle that each site should be occupied by

[4]Richard F. Babcock, *The Zoning Game* (Madison, Wis.: The University of Wisconsin Press, 1966), p. 3.
[5]Sam Bass Warner, Jr., *The Urban Wilderness* (New York: Harper & Row, 1972), pp. 28–29.

that use that would pay the highest site value. If the demand for sites were independent between demanders and if there were no external diseconomies, as in cases 5 and 6 above, each site would then be allocated to its most productive use. The rule, however, may not lead to the ideal when externalities exist, as we have seen, because it does not account for potential diseconomies to adjacent sites.

An alternative rule would seem appealing. The city planner should attempt to maximize total land value.[6] The rule would suggest that if a gas station would increase site value on one corner by more than any decreases it causes in surrounding residential property, it should be allowed; otherwise it should not be allowed. Two problems immediately arise. In the first place, the authority must estimate the value that residents place on the external diseconomy. As in the case of all other public goods, there is real difficulty in estimating this value. The individuals incurring the damages have no reason to reveal their true preferences. Since they incur no costs in obtaining their wishes, they have every reason to exaggerate their claims on damages.

In the second place, the rule would lead to greater or lesser amounts of land in each use than would be desired for efficiency. For example, in the case of the housing segregation model, such a rule would suggest that the amount of land devoted to high- and low-income use should be that distribution which maximized total land value. However, this might be achieved differently depending upon the elasticities of demand by each group for space. If the price elasticities of demand should be unity, then the total value of all space would not change as land was shifted from high- to low-income use or vice versa. Or if high-income families had a lower price elasticity of demand than low-income families, land could be taken from high-income users and given to lower-income families. The increase in site value for crowding high-income families on a few sites would be greater than the decrease in value for allowing the low-income users to spread out. Or if the low-income users had the lower price elasticity of demand, land would be taken from them and given to high-income families in order to maximize land values. The discriminating monopolist (the planner) would increase the land available to those users with elastic demands and decrease the land available to those users with inelastic demands (apartments and gas stations?). No, maximizing the sum of all land values in a metropolitan area could easily lead to distortions in efficient allocation of land.[7] The rule would work for small areas in large cities or for other areas that have no spatial monopoly.

---

[6]Alan W. Evans, "Two Economic Rules for Town Planning: A Critical Note," *Urban Studies*, 6 (June 1969), p. 227; W. Lean, "Town Planning and Economics," *The Journal of the Town Planning Institute*, 52 (February 1966).

[7]Evans, op. cit., pp. 228–229.

Robert Murray Haig long ago suggested a different criterion for zoning.[8] He suggested that competitive firms choose sites so as to minimize the costs of friction—transportation costs. From previous analysis you should know that this would be true only if all other costs and revenues were the same in all locations in the city—a result likely for manufacturing firms but for few other activities. Residents would maximize utility rather than minimize only these costs of friction. Thus since firms and households take other costs and benefits into account, the total land values or overall arrangement of land use would not necessarily be best by these other criteria if the cost of friction were minimized. The absurdity of the rule may be seen if one imagines the city in which all costs of friction were minimized. All uses would be on one site.[9]

The usual rule given in economic analysis for the most efficient use of resources is that each unit of the resource should be allocated so that it yields the same return as every other unit. This rule does not apply in the case of land for several reasons. First, the existence of externalities means that the return considered for each unit of land must take into account its potential negative impact on adjacent sites. We have already indicated the difficulty in measuring such costs. Secondly, land for the same use will not be equal in price because price differentials must exist to compensate for the differing advantages of each site. Thus in the case of residential-use land, prices decline with distance from the center of employment and shopping in order to partially compensate for increased transport costs. Business firms in the same industry at different sites may pay different land prices because of the relative advantages of particular sites. After price differentials are established, households with the same income and firms in the same industry—other things being equal—would be equally well off. Thirdly, each site is unique, and it is not possible to shift infinitesimal units of land from one spot to another, so that indivisibilities will occur in the use of land. Thus, ceiling prices by different uses for the same site may differ by large amounts rather than smaller, continuous amounts.

The only rule that would work is the one that would consider the total welfare of a community under alternative land-use arrangements and would select that arrangement which maximized benefits. Such a rule, however, would require ability to indicate the marginal utility to each individual of a dollar change in wealth or income. We have no such ability in theoretical economics and must therefore rely on political processes to resolve the issues.

[8]Robert M. Haig, "Toward an Understanding of the Metropolis," *Quarterly Journal of Economics*, 40 (May 1926), p. 421.

[9]William Alonso, *Location and Land Use* (Cambridge, Mass.: Harvard, 1964), pp. 101–105.

ECONOMICS OF REGULATORY CHOICE[10]

Zoning ordinances are determined by the legislative body of local government. We will assume that a majority vote could determine approval of any particular ordinance. Since few towns would meet in a town meeting to vote on legislative matters and most would vote for a few representatives for the city or county council or board of aldermen who would vote on these matters, it is necessary to explain the legislative representatives' behavior in order to see how they would vote on zoning regulations. If politicians have a goal of maximizing the number of votes they get for reelection and if individual voters know their own self-interest and vote on the basis of their own interests rather than some nebulous public interest, the politicians will vote for regulations that the majority of voters would desire.

The next step is to look at parts of the city and determine for which kinds of regulations voters in any particular district would vote. After the analysis of districts, we will see whether a vote of the whole municipality on regulations in a particular district would be different. Three kinds of districts have been analyzed by Davis within the rules outlined. The first is a new subdivision in which there is a single owner—the developer. The second is a partially developed district in which there are now many homeowners and renters but there is also still vacant land available for development. Perhaps as much as half the land could be developed. The third is an older transition district in which there is little or no land available for new development. In fact, the problem is whether sites should be changed from current uses to new and different uses. Let us see how the voting mechanism would cause restrictions to be developed in each of these types of districts in turn.

First, the new subdivision. If the district is relatively isolated or if there are no problems along the boundary of the district, the developer would suggest variances from any proposed zoning code as long as it would increase the total value of all property to him. He would indeed suggest a gas station if the increase in land value for use on that site would be greater in this use than in residential use. If all land were zoned residential, he would ask for the variance as long as the increase in value on the gas station site would be greater than any potential losses to adjacent residential sites. The politician would go along with the single owner, since he is the only voter in the district, and, at this stage of the argument, we are maximizing the vote in the district. As long as the subdivision were only a small part of the metropolitan area,

[10]Davis, op. cit., pp. 378–385.

he would not have the power to discriminate among uses with different elasticities of demand for land.

Second, let us consider the partially developed subdivision. This is a more difficult case because we must look at alternative outcomes depending on the proportion of renters and how we treat their voting patterns. First we shall assume that all the residential developed land is single-family housing owned by its occupants. The undeveloped land is owned by a single developer. The homeowners would not want to allow uses on the vacant sites that would be likely to cause decreases in value to adjacent sites. In fact, as zoning regulations prohibit particular uses, they would prohibit all uses that might cause decreases, whether the net effect on all property values in the district would be positive or not. Thus regulations would result in a less efficient solution than would single ownership. An additional problem arises, however, because the homeowners would prefer that the undeveloped sites enhance their own property values rather than be neutral in impact. Thus, they would vote zoning prohibitions that would disallow housing of equal or less value than their own. They might require larger yards and setbacks. The politician would decide with the majority so that, as long as the homeowners outnumbered the owners of developable land, zoning regulations would tend to be more prohibitive. If the sites to be developed were not especially desirable for the directed zoning classification, the developers could find their sites decreasing in value. It could pay them to bribe the politicians. Since the politician is representing the owners on many issues, it could be that he would vote against their wishes on some votes. Nonetheless, the general tendency would be for zoning regulations to be changed to upgrade property in the district.

Consider the same situation if some of the residences are occupied by renters rather than owners. The renter should expect his annual rents to rise if the prohibitions of the zoning regulations upgrade the neighborhood and enhance property values. On the other hand, if the prohibitions in the regulations were relaxed, then the renters might expect lower-income families to occupy the remaining area and rents for them might decline. Keeping the current regulations would maintain the same neighborhood, and rents would remain the same. Since renters are fairly mobile, we must assume that they are located in the type of neighborhood with the preferred bundle of rights at the current rent level. If they wanted a nicer neighborhood, they could have moved to one for the appropriate higher rent level. Furthermore, most zoning plans tend to exclude multifamily units, so renters would oppose such "upgrading." Thus renters might be expected to vote for the current level of zoning rather than under- or overzoning. Therefore if the renters and developers outnumber the homeowners, zoning regulations would be passed to maintain the status quo. If the homeowners outnumber the renters and developers, the district would tend to be zoned for upgrading.

Renters, however, may be transient residents who are uninterested in voting at all. In such a circumstance, of course, they would be disregarded altogether. On the other hand, if annual rents should tend to be inflexible and not adjust readily to changes in the environment, the renter would find it advantageous to vote with the homeowner for upgrading the area.

Third, there is the older transition district. Consider a district completely built up with owner-occupied single-family houses. Some of the owners now think that they could sell their properties for new uses which are greater in value than the current use (single-family homes for the income group in the area). The new use could be a shopping center, a gas station, or even a changeover of the present buildings to rooming houses or apartments. If the property owners desiring the rezoning for the change of use are all in the same contiguous part of the district, then the district boundaries could be changed, allowing rezoning in the area desiring it. The rest of the district would fear the nuisance effect of these uses and would not allow the zoning change in other parts of the district. If the property owners desiring the rezoning for the change in use are scattered throughout the district, then the zoning change would occur only if the majority of owners in the district anticipated that values would rise in the new use. Once again, if some of the property owners expect values to rise in the new use, there may be sufficient incentive to bribe politicians. The politicians can allow the variances because it is only one of many issues that will affect the vote for them—provided that it is not a critical issue that would turn the majority of voters against them. Here is where the renters may be more important. They represent part of the voters of any district, but other issues may be more important to them than the zoning issue, which is of major importance to the owners. If, however, the renters have an important interest in zoning, it is to keep the district the way it is and to avoid change. They would in this case be on the side of the owners not anticipating an increase in value. Zoning changes would depend on which group was in the majority.

Now that we have explored the possible vote outcomes within districts in the urban area, it is time to consider the outcome of votes if they were taken for zoning regulations for the entire area.[11] The main difference between the voting outcomes for small, homogeneous districts and the larger, heterogeneous one is the exclusive nature of

[11]At this point in the discussion we depart from Davis's conclusion. He argues that the vote of the sum of the districts would be no different than the district-by-district vote.

most zoning regulation. If the principal reason for zoning is to provide exclusive residential neighborhoods for families with sufficient income to live in such districts, if other districts were zoned to allow both housing and other uses, and if, in fact, the income distribution of the community is such that there are more who would be excluded from exclusive districts than would be included, the vote would not be for upgrading these districts but for eliminating zoning.

It is clear that not every district in the community being developed can be zoned in such a way that newer houses must be better than those that were built earlier. There are, on the average, an insufficient proportion of people with these above-average incomes to make it work. The vote for zoning, then, would depend upon the income distribution of families living in the municipality. In a large metropolitan area with an income distribution similar to that of the nation, zoning, if seen as developing exclusive residential districts for upper-income families, would not be approved. The lower-income families do not want to be excluded from the potential external benefits of living adjacent to such neighborhoods. Only in a small, homogeneous subdivision with its own zoning and municipal regulations would exclusive zoning regulations easily be passed.

If zoning is interpreted as only a problem of external diseconomies, the votes in metropolitan-area decisions would depend on the proportions of homeowners, renters, and property owners in transition areas wanting changes in land use. The homeowners would vote for upgrading, the renters would vote for the status quo, and the property owners in transition areas would vote for changing land uses depending upon their expectations about their impact on property values. If decisions on zoning reflected these voting patterns, the outcome would be difficult to predict.

It turns out that there have actually been few referendum votes on zoning regulations. They are usually voted only by the council or board of aldermen. In those cases in which they have been submitted to the voters, the record shows that zoning has usually lost. The only major city to allow a referendum vote has been Houston. A vote in 1948 restricted to property owners and another in 1962, when no such restriction was made, defeated zoning by votes of 14,142 to 6,555 and by 70,957 to 54, 279. An analysis of the vote shows that the districts voting for zoning by a majority were middle-middle- to upper-middle-income homeowners having the newest homes. Older areas voted against zoning.[12] Thus, it is easy to see why small suburban municipalities with homogeneous residents voted for such regulations. Large cities would install zoning because there is a diversity of interests that

[12]Siegan, op. cit., pp. 25–26 and 28–29.

make it difficult, when voting for one representative who will vote on many issues, to ensure that he will vote any of the voting patterns of his constituency. Furthermore, there is the added incentive of the attractiveness of bribes once this system is installed, as we have indicated at several points in the discussion.[13]

From our discussion of the political economy of zoning regulation, we find that zoning may not increase the economic welfare of a community (broadly defined) for the following reasons: In the first place, zoning is exclusionary. If a use might cause an external diseconomy, it is excluded under zoning regulations, when in fact it might result in a greater net increase in total property values in a district. Second, one of the reasons for zoning is exclusion of families with lower incomes and of a different race, which has been rejected as contrary to public policy when explicit in restrictive covenants and when voted in referendum in many areas of the United States. Third, restrictive zoning will tend to occur in partially developed districts. Fourth and last, resistance to potential change in transition neighborhoods, even if it raised property values, would be probable.

ECONOMIC IMPACT OF ZONING

Zoning has probably had some very unexpected effects on urban economic structure and development. If zoning is effective, it tends to prohibit multifamily land uses, low- and moderate-income housing (including mobile homes), and gas stations from partially developed districts. Such restrictions would probably raise the cost of sites for these uses over what they would have been without zoning, since the relative amounts of land available would have been restricted.

Nevertheless the political economy of zoning suggests that homogeneous suburbs have a better chance of passing such regulations than do the larger, central cities with larger, heterogeneous populations and with less control of the voting behavior of the puliticians, which creates conditions favoring bribery. Therefore the suburban areas around the central city are the areas in which the restrictions on land for these uses are likely to occur. Indeed, Siegan does indicate several areas in which land for multifamily use carries a special premium because of the difficulty of obtaining zoning for such use.[14]

These two tendencies have a startling impact on the grouping of higher- and lower-income families in the metropolitan area. Since zoning can be rigorously installed in homogeneous suburbs and not

[13]Siegan, op. cit., p. 196. Notes the prevalence of graft in zoning practice.
[14]Siegan, op. cit., pp. 88-92 and 112-121.

within the larger central city, higher-income families would consider the suburban sites more desirable than inner-city sites. That would have a tendency to cause an increase in vacancies on the higher-income side of the boundary between higher- and lower-income families in the inner city. At the same time, the exclusion of multifamily housing and housing for lower- and moderate-income families would tend to increase the pressure for expanding the area available for such groups in the inner city. Thus one would expect rapid transition within the large central city from high-income groups to lower- and moderate-income groups. The suburbs would tend to become upper-middle and middle-middle class areas. Further increases in the absolute size of the lower-income groups, however, would increase the price on the lower-income side of the boundary between the two groups when that boundary reached the first ring of suburban municipalities. If the arbitrage model is correct, prices in the upper-income suburb would tend to fall in the blocks adjacent to change. The expectation of further change would cause the occupancy within the whole suburb to change, since it no longer would be able to maintain exclusive higher-income occupancy. Housing in the community would become vacant unless occupied by lower-income families.

In addition to these effects on location and relative values, zoning may increase the cost of development. In particular the cost of obtaining rezoning of a particular area for commercial or apartment development may be increased because the developer must signal his intentions before purchasing property, thus making it possible for individual property owners to raise their prices and absorb part of the development profit. This may indeed make the project unprofitable. Furthermore, the time delay in obtaining approvals and the cost of bribing officials will also increase the costs of development without increasing the potential return from any project. The new procedure for Planned Unit Development, in which the zoning for a whole subdivision is approved at once through bargaining with appropriate local authority, can increase costs and lower the potential profit for the whole project because of requested changes. Uses that might cause negative effects but be more than compensated by the increase in overall value of the project may be excluded. The time delay in negotiations, of course, always means an increase in project cost.

While we have focused on the effects of zoning in housing markets, a kind of restrictive zoning is also often promoted by local merchants, especially retailers. Existing retailers often encourage zoning which excludes potential competition, essentially discouraging rezones to permit new retailers as population density of developing areas increases. For example, in a suburban New Jersey municipality the central business district was declining while business was starting up in outlying areas within the municipality. The CBD businessmen prevailed on the city council to use zoning to prevent any further business growth in outlying areas, thus preserving the local spatial monopoly for established firms.[15] Thus residents of the developing areas could expect to travel further to shop and pay higher prices when they got there.

Finally, the usual prohibition of commercial, industrial, and often multifamily uses in many suburban municipalities raises the property tax above what it could be and causes the burden of governmental expenses to fall on the single-family houses in the district.

The costs and effects that we have described could be justified if zoning restrictions prevented external diseconomies of the sort described in the first section of this chapter. However, several statistical studies that have attempted to determine or estimate the external economies or diseconomies from potential uses have not found any of significant size.[16] The one significant impact on property values that we have been able to show has been the case of the boundary between high- and low-income families and between races.

Are these results surprising? Not if one recognizes that the assumption that particular uses generate external diseconomies for other uses is valid only if all potential purchasers of the affected use feel the same way about the effects of the "undesired" use. Thus, if some or many individuals feel that no negative effects are generated by proximity to apartments, these persons will be the ones who tend to bid the the most for single-family homes in neighborhoods mixed with apartments. This self-selection of residents will remove differences in property values.

The standard, postulated external effect of one land use upon another in the zoning literature will be observed only if all citizens have similar preferences. It is important, however, to recognize that in economics it is the behavior of individuals at the margin, not the average behavior, which determines market results. It is only in political decision making that "average" preferences are more likely to predominate. Thus, if citizens' tastes differ, postulated relationships based on average or planner tastes are not likely to be validated by the observation of market results. This appears to be one of the most likely explanations of the studies indicating that postulated negative effects of apartments on single-family dwellings cannot be identified empirically. The other reason may be that the census-block data used

[15]Daniel R. Mandelker, *The Zoning Dilemma* (Indianapolis: Bobbs-Merrill, 1971), p. 40.

[16]John P. Crecine, Otto A. Davis, and John E. Jackson, "Urban Property Markets: Some Empirical Results and Their Implications for Municipal Zoning," *Journal of Law and Economics*, 10 (1967), pp. 79–99. Frederick H. Reuter, "Externalities in Urban Property Markets: An Empirical Test of the Zoning Ordinance of Pittsburgh," *Journal of Law and Economics*, 16 (1973), pp. 313–349; and indirectly the studies mentioned in Chap. 8 on the impact of various projects on house values.

is too large an area to observe results because the effects of apartments or other "nuisance" uses may be limited to one or two adjacent single-family dwellings. If this latter reason is the dominant one, then these external diseconomies could probably be handled by injunctions against nuisances rather than by zoning.

In spite of the nebulous benefits to accrue from prohibiting particular uses from specific sites, such prohibition may cause direct losses in property value without compensation to owners. If the land had all been under single ownership, the so-called "nuisance" use might have more than compensated for slight losses to adjacent property. Zoning procedures, however, do not allow for such bargaining but require complete prohibition of the "nuisance" use.

Babcock cites several cases that clearly indicate the problems.[17] He cites the case of an intersection of two heavily traveled two-lane roads near Chicago located about 2 miles from a suburb. The surrounding area has developed in single-family houses on large lots. The lots on three corners of the intersection have remained vacant under zoning regulations that require single-family houses with a minimum lot of 1 acre. The fourth corner is occupied by a horse stable. The community will not allow the zoning to be changed to commercial because if one corner is changed, all the corners will become commercial, and that would tend to erode house values in the surrounding community. The property owners on the corners, however, could argue that the community is forcing them to provide green, open space without compensation because a busy intersection with traffic signals is not thought to be a good housing location. If bargaining were allowed, the property owners might be able to compensate surrounding residential owners for any losses from commercial use.

LEGAL PERSPECTIVE

At the time of its introduction in 1916, zoning, or the designation of specific land uses for a property without compensation if the permitted uses were of lower value than alternatives, was of questionable constitutional status. Article V of the U.S. Constitution clearly states, "nor shall private property be taken for public use, without just compensation." And the U.S. Supreme Court had previously ruled that "there can be no conception of property aside from its control and use, and upon its use depends its value," (*Cleveland, etc. Ry. Co. v. Backus*, 154 U.S. 439 (1894), 455 inter alia).

On the other hand, under police power interpretations of the Constitution, governments do have the authority to undertake action

---

[17]Babcock, op. cit., pp. 169–171.

to enhance the public welfare. It was inevitable that property owners who were not able to use their property for its most remunerative use would challenge zoning in the courts.

The first case to reach the U.S. Supreme Court was the *Village of Euclid v. Ambler Realty Co.* (1926).[18] Prior to the adoption of zoning, Ambler Realty Company had accumulated 68 acres between a rail line and Euclid Avenue in anticipation of industrialization spreading out from Cleveland along the rail line. When Euclid introduced its zoning ordinance, it designated that the land fronting on Euclid Avenue could be used for single-family residences only, a strip behind the single-family residences could be used for apartments, and the rest could be used for industrial purposes. Ambler Realty Company sought to have the zoning held unconstitutional as a taking of their property without compensation. They argued that the zoning reduced the value of their land from $10,000 to $2,500 per acre and that the land along Euclid Avenue was reduced in value from $150 to $50 per front foot.

In the trial court Judge Westenhaver upheld Ambler's position and ruled the zoning invalid. Of special interest, in light of contemporary problems of zoning and of our previous analysis, are his observations on zoning in general:

> The plain truth is that the object of the ordinance in question is to place all property in an undeveloped area of 16 square miles in a strait-jacket. The purpose to be accomplished is really to regulate the mode of living of persons who may hereafter inhabit it. In the last analysis, the result to be accomplished is to classify the population and segregate them according to their income or situation in life.[19]

The judge also observed that "If police power meant as claimed, all private property is now held subject to temporary and passing phases of public opinion, dominant for a day, in legislative or municipal assemblies."[20]

The trial court decision of *Euclid v. Ambler* was overturned by the U.S. Supreme Court.[21] The Supreme Court ruled that as long as the zoning bore some resemblance to the use of government police power, asserted for the public welfare, zoning was valid. The court indicated that the separation of legitimate and illegitimate use of police power was not subject to specific delimitation and would vary with circumstances.

Another case provides insight into the scope of potential police powers. Justice Douglas wrote in *Berman v. Parker*, "Public safety, public health, morality, peace and quiet, law and order—these are

---

[18]Siegan, op. cit., p. 203.
[19]Cited in Siegan, op. cit., p. 205.
[20]Cited in Siegan, op. cit., p. 204.
[21]*Village of Euclid v. Ambler Realty Co.*, 272 U.S. 365, 47 Sup. Ct. 114, 71 L. Ed. 303 (1926).

some of the more conspicuous examples of the traditional application of the police power to municipal affairs. Yet they merely illustrate the scope of the power and do not delimit it. . . ."[22]

The concept of public welfare is broad and inclusive. In the *Euclid* case itself the Court did not attempt to answer the trial court interpretation that zoning would be used for class segregation purposes.

Other important zoning cases are *Zahn* in 1927, where the Supreme Court ruled that the municipal legislature had to be the interpreter of the proper scope of police power, thus emphasizing a court practice of not interfering with legislative affairs and interpretations, and *Nectow*, where the Court slightly reduced legislative discretion by ruling that there had to be some "substantial relationship" between zoning and public welfare.[23]

In 1974 the Supreme Court upheld the right of a community to ban communes by restricting occupancy of each house to one family. The court indicated that zoning ordinances that single out or discriminate against some residents are consistent with police power as long as such laws are "reasonable" and bear a "rational relationship" to a permissible local goal. The court held that the goals to preserve the traditional family organization of the town, to halt unwanted growth, to restrict population density, and to regulate parking and traffic were permissible.[24]

These are the only zoning cases to reach the U.S. Supreme Court, although there have been hundreds of lower court and state supreme court decisions on zoning matters. One cannot easily generalize about zoning authority in the fifty states. However, as long as some element of police power to protect the general welfare can be argued, there is a good chance zoning will be upheld.[25] Only if direct taking for

---

[22]Siegan, op. cit., p. 206.

[23]Charles M. Haar, *Land Use Planning* (Boston: Little, Brown, 1959), pp. 169–170.

[24]"High Court Makes Rare Zoning Ruling," *Los Angeles Times*, April 2, 1974, p. 1.

[25]For example, there is a piece of beachfront in Redondo Beach, California, that is zoned for "beach recreation use only," which means the owner can install a fence and charge admission to sunbathers if he wishes. The land was originally zoned single-family and had a tax bill of $9,000 per year. When the owner requested a re-zone for commercial use, the city council instead zoned the area for beach recreation and effectively took the owners property rights without any compensation. See Donald G. Hagman, *Urban Planning and Land Development Control Law* (St. Paul: West, 1971), pp. 214–215. An alternative to the city would have been to buy the property for a park but a rezone was cheaper; because the city did not take the property for public use, its zoning was legal. Other examples of zoning which appear to an economist to take property without compensation include zoning scenic easements along shorelines— where the owner can continue to own the land but not do anything with it—or where zoning in some categories is so excessive that land values fall way below what free market prices would have been—as when vast areas are zoned for industrial use only by a small city hoping someday to find users for the land.

public purpose occurs would the ordinance fall under constitutional provisions against taking and require eminent domain procedures and compensation.

One interesting facet of the issue of taking property without compensation is that it may be the zoning itself that causes property to have a much higher value in a forbidden use than in a permitted one. If there is an underallocation of land for some uses, especially uses with inelastic demands, prices for property where that use is permitted will be very high. Thus landowners not permitted to use their land for that use will claim that their property has been taken because they cannot use their land where prices would be highest. However, if the zoning were changed to permit more land in the underallocated category, the price of land for that use would fall.

ZONING PROBLEMS[26]

One of the main problems with zoning as we have discussed it so far is that the ordinances require prohibition of the use considered to cause an external diseconomy without room for consideration as to whether the gains might more than offset these diseconomies. The economists have argued that this is a nonoptimal procedure.[27] Lawyers with a different perspective have come to a similar conclusion, in which they find that prohibition of sites for particular uses amounts to taking property value without compensation.

A second major problem has been the tendency toward restrictive zoning in partially developed districts, particularly homogeneous sub-

[26]It turns out that the zoning ordinance of 1916 that was originally the model for most zoning ordinances in American cities was modeled after a hierarchical scheme used by German cities. There, the highest-use zones were most restrictive and each lower-use zone permitted higher-use activities within it. The city-planning supporters were strongly in favor of the German model and emphasized that once zones were established, they were to be maintained to preserve stability and predictability. In their view, once zoning was established, it should be relatively permanent, more like a constitution within which future decisions would be made.

While a German model of zoning was recommended for the United States, there are at least three significant differences in the environment into which zoning was introduced in the United States. First, land use in German cities had patterns which were primarily stable, with growth and renewal taking place within zones. In American cities, on the other hand, rapid population growth expanded city limits and caused successions of land uses in different areas. Secondly and more importantly, in most German cities the municipal government owned 50 to 60 percent of the land, greatly reducing the pressure for rezoning contrary to the plan. American municipalities owned very little land. Third, German municipal government was strong, honest, and very well developed. American city government was noted for its relative weakness, high levels of corruption, and constant adjustment to pressures and popular opinion. One would have to raise serious questions about the ability of American municipal governments to undertake zoning on the German model.

[27]Davis, op. cit., p. 386.

urban municipalities. We have already noted the theoretical roots of it in the voting mechanism and self-interest of homeowners. We have also noted its impact on urban structure and the location of low-and moderate-income families. Furthermore, it is an exacerbating influence on the arbitrage process, causing further concentration of poor in ghettos and the development of abandoned housing.

Such restrictive zoning has recently come under attack as "snob zoning."[28] The common type of exclusion that fits this definition occurs when a municipality specifies very large lot sizes and large minimum square-footage requirements which raises the price of housing above what can be afforded by all but a very small percentage of persons. Building code ordinances that increase construction costs could also serve the same purpose. The effect is to exclude all but the highest-income residents desiring single-family housing from the area. For example, within 50 miles of Times Square in New York City, 50 percent of the vacant land is zoned with minimum lot sizes of 1 acre (compared to normal subdivision lot sizes of 1/5 to 1/3 acre); in New Jersey 60 percent of potential residential land is so zoned.[29]

There are also zoning ordinances drawn to achieve other kinds of exclusion, as when apartments with more than one bedroom are not permitted in order to exclude families with school-age children who would add to the cost of schooling in the district.

A third major problem that we have noted is a tendency for zoning to hinder development in districts ripe for changes in land use. We noted the difficulty both in the problems of voting on changes in zoning in a fully developed district and in the increased costs of development caused by zoning regulations in a developed district.

The fourth problem that many find with zoning as it is practiced is that the planning commissions that make decisions on land use are often made up of laymen who are not knowledgeable about land-use development.[30] Laymen on these commissions are prone to be guided by the latest popular whim rather than by any facts about external economies or diseconomies that might exist.

The fifth problem is that current procedures for deciding zoning decisions and appealing them are inequitable and inadequate. On this point Babcock has written:

> The running, ugly sore of zoning is the total failure of this system of law to develop a code of administrative ethics. Stripped of all planning jargon, zoning administration is exposed as a process under which multitudes of isolated social and political units engage in highly emotional altercations over the use of land, most of

[28]Siegan, op. cit., p. 174.
[29]Seymour Toll, *Zoned American* (New York: Grossman Publishers, 1969), p. 295.
[30]Babcock, op. cit., pp. 41–61.

which are settled by crude tribal adaptations of medieval trial by fire, and a few of which are concluded by confused *ad hoc* injunctions of bewildered courts.[31]

In fact, two problems are distinguished here. One is that the procedures by which zoning decisions are made are not orderly, not recorded adequately, and do not provide the same rights to those pleading change that would be accorded them in a court of law. The other is that the criteria used for making a decision are too often local (say suburban) when they should be broader in scope, including the whole metropolitan area. The external diseconomies may be local, but the economies justifying a variance may be metropolitan rather than local. Thus narrowing the criteria to the net benefits to the local community may be incorrect.

POLICY ALTERNATIVES

In response to the above problems, lawyers, planners, and economists have suggested a variety of ways to improve the system. Many of the suggestions would fall into the following groups:[32]

1 Abandon the concept of fixed land-use zones. The old fixed land-use zones are regarded as too crude for the complex urban environment.

2 Replace the concept of fixed zones with a grant of additional discretion of authority to planners. Planners must, however, be professionals. Untrained citizens serving on planning boards are not well enough prepared to make decisions on land use.

3 Accompany the grant of increased authority and flexibility to planners with a grant of power to use tax money to compensate property owners whose property values are reduced through zoning. The ability to compensate would provide the planners with more flexibility.

4 Take areawide consequences into account in zoning decisions. This is necessary to prevent the exclusion of particular uses or residents from the entire metropolitan area.

These recommendations are strikingly close to the recommendations by political reformers, discussed in Chapter 7, for reorganizing urban governments. Essentially, the solution is to delegate extensive

---

[31]Richard F. Babcock, "The Chaos of Zoning Administration," 12, *Zoning Digest* 1 (1960), cited in Babcock, *The Zoning Game*, op. cit., p. 154.

[32]Babcock, loc. cit.; Presidents Commission on National Urban Problems, *Building the American City* (Washington, D.C.: Government Printing Office, 1968); Daniel Mandelker, *The Zoning Dilemma* (Indianapolis: Bobbs-Merrill, 1971).

public authority to good professionals under the expectation that they will then act benevolently in the areawide public interest. The recommendation for increased discretion for planners to do more zoning and undertake more land-use control is based on an analysis that concludes that zoning in the past has failed to achieve its objectives. Is there any evidence that an areawide planning and zoning agency run by professional planners would in fact lead to more efficient land-use patterns; higher levels of predictability, stability, and security for property owners; less taking of property without compensation, and less manipulation of property values for the gain of a few individuals? Public goods theory would suggest that the greater heterogeneity of larger jurisdictions would increase total political decision-making costs. In this light suburbanization is an attempt at more efficient local government. The recommended reforms in the institutional framework would simply provide increased discretion to planners—not delimit their behavior in any particular way. It would increase political-externality costs— by restricting decisions to a few appointees—while reducing decision-making costs.

It is somewhat ironic that zoning was originally proposed to bring more stability and predictability to urban property markets and that proposed reforms would result in just the opposite. Reliance on landowner-requested rezones—as with planned unit development, floating zones, or contract zones introduces a particular instability and unpredictability because a landowner or potential purchaser never knows for sure for what purpose his or adjacent land can be used; permission for use is at the discretion of the planning board or city council. This uncertainty has predictable effects on the structure of the land development industry and provides incentive for corruption. Where uncertainty is high, small developers are precluded from participating. Small developers seldom have the capital and support to undertake the long bargaining process when there is no assurance that they will in fact be able to use land in a profitable way. Large builders, on the other hand, can operate on the insurance principle—win some and lose some—in developing contacts, both professional and corrupt, with planning and zoning officials. Since few actual developers would be involved, the task of hiding payoffs and corruption would be facilitated.[33]

Davis, after considering the economics of the politics of zoning, made suggestions for making zoning more efficient.[34] His first suggestion was to try to prevent restrictive zoning in partially developed areas. For this he suggested that the subdivider or developer should

[33]Mandelker, op. cit., pp. 45–55.
[34]Davis, op. cit., pp. 385–386.

make up the zoning ordinance, subject to some constraints at the boundaries, and that no change be allowed in the ordinance for ten years. By the end of ten years the land should be developed. It would naturally be required that the developer notify prospective buyers of the land-use zones so that the buyer would not be unexpectedly confronted with a gas station next door. A person buying knowingly next to the gas station, would, of course, pay the appropriate discount for the location.

The only person to suffer from improper zoning would be the developer, since each person buying would pay only what he deemed appropriate given the land-use plan and known external diseconomies. This would be an advantage of the plan. Furthermore, one would avoid current incentive for restrictive zoning that is typical in a partially developed district.

For other areas, both partially developed and transition areas, a new scheme for allowing variances from the zoning plan is suggested. Current procedures for allowing variances would be eliminated and substituted by the following procedure. Variances would be granted only by a vote of the property owners in the district. All owners on adjacent property would have to approve the variance, and, maybe, 90 percent of the rest of the owners in the zoning district would have to approve the variance to make it effective. Bribes would be allowed. Thus a prospective gas station could obtain permission to use a site if the adjacent owners and 90 percent of the other owners in the given residential district approved the site. To get the approval he could compensate (bribe) adjacent owners and others. In this way adjacent owners and others would receive compensation for any external diseconomies that they might incur. The gas station would obtain the site as long as the compensation paid did not eliminate a reasonable return from locating on the particular site.

Since renters would not be voting, new development in transition neighborhoods would probably not be prevented except where it would not cover potential external diseconomies. Restrictive zoning in partially developed districts might be hard to prevent, so a rule preventing upgrading of zoning might be necessary.

It should be emphasized that Davis considered these reforms as suggestions based on his untested model. They are not a panacea, but they are certainly moves toward more efficient zoning.

The most radical reform is to eliminate zoning altogether. Siegan has suggested that zoning be eliminated and replaced with the use of restrictive covenants.[35] The only significant external diseconomies that we have found evidence for are those along the boundary between

[35]Siegan, op. cit., pp. 231–245.

low- and high-income families and between blacks and whites. The greatest incentive for zoning has been by upper-income groups to create isolated residential areas. Studies attempting to find external diseconomies from apartments on single-family housing or from commercial uses on these areas have been inconclusive. Siegan has gone one step further by investigating the impact of no zoning on the city of Houston. We have already incorporated many of his results in our analysis of the economic impact of zoning. For example, Siegan found that Houston with no zoning probably had more multifamily dwellings with lower rents than nonzoned cities. Single-family houses financed with mortgages insured by the Federal Housing Administration showed the same appreciation in values as those in zoned cities. Furthermore, the cost of redevelopment was less than in zoned cities.

Restrictive covenants actually could work in the same way as Davis's suggestion that the subdivider determine the zoning for ten years. A covenant is usually drawn up by the developer to restrict the use of land for a number of years or into perpetuity. All the property in the subdivision is subject to the covenant, and as owners buy in they sign the agreement. The covenant can restrict the type of building, the building's size, and the type of architecture. In the past covenants were used to prohibit persons of specific races from occupying housing in an area. This last restriction has been unsupported in courts as contrary to public policy.

The buyer agrees to comply with the restrictions of the covenant. The agreement is usually for a number of years, say fifteen years, or may be rescinded by a vote of 51 percent of the owners under the covenant. Or, if breaches to the covenant are not fought, the courts may consider the covenant rescinded. In Houston the city has taken over enforcement of restrictive covenants, so that notice to the city by one owner of a breach of a covenant would bring the case to court.

It is fascinating that restrictive covenants again exemplify developments in common law that handle problems of external economies and diseconomies in a way that moves people toward efficient allocation of resources.[36] Covenants would do what Davis thought would lead to more efficient allocation of uses. The subdivider would deter-

---

[36]A similar case is that of beekeeping and alfalfa or orchards in which there are mutual gains from the two activities being located together. Economists have argued that under separate ownership, production would not take place optimally because the orchard grower would not take account of the beekeepers' needs. However, the law of beekeeping has developed over many years, and solutions have been worked out so that contracts between beekeepers and orchards do take account of joint needs in honey production. See Steven N. S. Cheung, "The Fable of the Bees: An Economic Investigation," *Journal of Law and Economics*, 16 (April 1973), pp. 11–33; and David B. Johnson, "Meade, Bees, and Externalities," *Journal of Law and Economics*, 16 (April 1973), pp. 35–52.

mine the land-use pattern in the district. If he is wrong, he is the only one to suffer, since the buyers can read the covenant on restrictions of each site and know the potential diseconomies or economies and pay what they consider sites to be worth. Since the covenant is usually established for fifteen years or more, the land will probably be developed before the covenant runs out, so that when the land is partially developed the restrictions will not be upgraded. Finally, once the district has become much older, the restrictions may be rescinded by a vote of 51 percent of the owners under the covenant. Therefore transitions to new uses could be handled more optimally. In fact the covenant may be broken if changes occur and no owner takes the case to court. Change in transition areas would not be put to a vote that would include renters, who would be the most likely residents to vote against change.

Nonetheless, the restrictions under such covenants may be more exclusionary than those that would occur under zoning, since even architectural details may be specified. Shifting from zoning to the use of covenants would not prevent snob zoning. It would not change the scenario that we described earlier as to the shift of higher-income families from the city to suburban municipalities. Thus the problems created by separation of the housing market into submarkets by income, class, or race would not be resolved.

In Chapter 5 we observed that because many public goods had to be provided at similar levels over some geographic area, higher levels of welfare in public goods consumption would be achieved by groups of people with similar tastes for public goods than would be achieved by heterogeneous groups. We also noted that costs of political decision making would be lower in homogeneous groups than in heterogeneous groups. If this is the case, we would predict that groups of similar people residing together would incorporate themselves into political organizations to provide their own public goods and services and simultaneously would take action to maintain the homogeneity of their municipality. For example, people with children and high preferences for above-average schools might well attempt to exclude individuals without school-age children because they might fear that childless voters would reject higher-than-average school expenditures. We might also find groups of childless families who preferred limited school expenditures trying to exclude families with children in order to avoid higher school expenditures.

The use of zoning to encourage homogeneity within a political jurisdiction to facilitate the achievement of preferred levels of public goods is generally neglected in analyses of zoning and its effects. Many analysts, for example, still perceive the ideal municipality as one with a balanced mix of income groups and business and industrial uses—not one responding more efficiently to a specialized set of demands than a heterogeneous political unit is likely to be able to do. There is a basic incompatibility between the predicted behavior of individuals acting to achieve preferred public goods and services for themselves and an ideal of heterogeneous mixing of residents and different land uses within the boundaries of a single political unit. A recognition of this incompatibility is essential to an understanding of the complexities and difficulties of zoning.

On the one hand, one may recognize the potential desirability of permitting groups of individuals to reside together and provide public goods at preferred levels. But this goal conflicts directly with the ideal that everyone should be permitted to reside where he wishes or to use his property as he wishes. This dilemma may be as difficult to resolve as any other problem associated with zoning and land-use control.

SUMMARY

Property values are expected values, and they are expected values of the rights to use of the whole bundle of characteristics surrounding a site, including the building, the external effects of surrounding property, and the public goods provided for occupancy of the site. If uncertainty about changes in the bundle of rights associated with a property could be reduced, property values should be enhanced.

An analysis of the potential external economies and diseconomies disclosed that most would be handled by private owners in their own interest. Two situations, however, might not be resolved in the private market and could cause future uncertainty about values to particular sites. In the one case, a land use A could create an external economy for land use B, but land use B creates an external diseconomy for use A. A prime example of this is the boundary between housing for low- and higher-income families and between occupancy by whites and blacks. In the other case a land use A is neutral in its impact on use B, but use B creates an external diseconomy for use A. The situation would include using land for stockyards, soap factories, cement plants, and gasoline stations in residential areas. Although the latter situation has been cited as the dominant reason for zoning, in practice the insulation of the single-family detached dwelling was the primary objective.

Since zoning requires legislative decisions, it was necessary to explore the economics of the political choices. It was found that districts that are partially developed are likely to be restrictively zoned because the residents would hope that better housing in the area would enhance their own property values. In transition districts, however, renters and owners that do not anticipate increased values would block changes of land use. In general, zoning excludes uses entirely and does not allow for variances in which the nuisance might be able to compensate those properties damaged and still increase the net value of all properties. If the primary aim of zoning is the establishment of exclusive, higher-income residential areas, zoning is not likely to be approved in large heterogeneous central cities but would occur in small homogeneous suburban municipalities.

In the light of the last conclusion, it is likely that the major impact of zoning is to reinforce the tendency for higher-income families to live in the suburbs on the periphery of the metropolitan area and to concentrate those families who cannot afford to buy new houses in the inner-city areas. Thus zoning is likely to exacerbate the problems associated with the arbitrage model of segregated housing markets. Furthermore, land for uses that tend to be excluded, such as land for multifamily units, will tend to increase in price. Zoning will also increase the cost of development by causing construction to take a longer time and meet more regulations. These effects would have to be compared to the benefits of preventing the creation of external diseconomies. Statistical studies testing for such externalities, however, have not been very conclusive. But perhaps we might expect these results if we remember that in the marketplace the people who buy property near nuisances are those who will pay the most for such sites and consider the problems of the site to be less of a problem than other people would.

Not only may land be caused to increase in price because little land for that use is made available, but in some cases land may be caused to fall in value because the best use of the land is excluded by zoning. The first case testing zoning was taken to the Supreme Court for just this reason. The Court has ruled, however, that as long as the zoning restrictions are linked to the public welfare, they are justified.

Thus far, then, zoning has led to the following problems. First, zoning requires prohibition of a use considered to cause an external diseconomy without room for consideration as to whether the gains might more than offset these diseconomies. Second, partially developed districts tend to be restrictively zoned. Third, zoning tends to hinder development in districts ripe for changes in land use. Fourth, planning commissions are often made up of laymen who do not understand real property questions. Fifth, the administrative procedures for handling zoning cases are inequitable and inadequate.

Suggestions for resolving these questions have ranged from granting more discretion to professional planners to removing the zoning ordinance altogether. Granting more discretion to professional planners may or may not work, but it does not delimit their actions in any way. Both lawyers and economists have proposed a variety of schemes to compensate people who might suffer a loss in property value. Lawyers see it as just compensation for loss of value incurred without taking of property by government, while economists see it as an opportunity to allow variances that can more than pay for any diseconomies caused. Surprisingly, the recommendation that zoning be eliminated and that restrictive covenants be substituted, an old practice, is nearly the same as the recommendation made by Davis. To avoid restrictive zoning in partially developed districts, Davis suggested that zoning be established by the developer and maintained for ten years. Restrictive covenants amount to nearly the same proposal. None of these reform suggestions, however, come to grips with the fundamental dilemma. Zoning ordinances enhance the community's opportunity to maintain a homogeneous district for better articulation of the demand for public goods, but they directly conflict with the ideal that everyone should be permitted to reside where he wishes or to use his property as he wishes. This dilemma may be as difficult to resolve as any other problem associated with zoning and land-use control.

SELECTED READINGS

Babcock, Richard F.: *The Zoning Game* (Madison, Wis.: The University of Wisconsin Press, 1966).

Davis, Otto A.: "Economic Elements in Municipal Zoning Decisions," *Land Economics*, 39 (November 1963), pp. 375–386.

Siegan, Bernard H.: *Land Use Without Zoning* (Lexington, Mass.: Heath, 1972).

CHAPTER **10**

EDUCATION

Public education is an extremely important part of the urban public economy. It is not only the largest single responsibility of state and local government—accounting for over 6 percent of the gross national product and involving nearly one-third of the population as either a producer or consumer[1]—but important issues in the provision and consumption of education are related to urban spatial patterns and local government organization. The provision of different kinds or qualities of education in different locations influences residential choice. In turn, residential spatial patterns resulting from housing market operation, often consciously modified by local government zoning, affect the grouping of students from families with different incomes or of different races. The responsiveness of local school systems to diverse needs of different populations, especially in big cities, is also important to the role of education in providing equal opportunity and upward mobility for students from low-income families. Finally, the different land-use development patterns in an urban area result in different wealth levels among different school districts, which in turn complicates the issues of equal opportunity and education financing. The

[1]Estimated from appropriate tables, U.S. Bureau of the Census, *The Statistical Abstract of the United States* (Washington, D.C.: Government Printing Office, 1972).

issues surrounding residential choice, poverty, unemployment, exclusionary zoning, racial segregation, governmental responsiveness, managing large service bureaucracies, and unequal fiscal capacity are all part of the problem of education in urban areas. Given education's crucial relationship to these problems and its importance in the urban public sector, the organization and provision of education require serious attention in any application of location and public goods economics to an understanding of urban problems and policies.

In this chapter we begin with discussions of benefits from education, how demands are articulated, how education is produced, and how it is financed. In these discussions we will pay special attention to the relationship between education and urban problems. In the discussion of educational finance, we will go on to explore implications for urban spatial patterns and public sector operation of proposed changes in educational financing. Following this we will proceed to examine other approaches to resolving education problems identified in the description of demand articulation, production, and financing. Among the approaches to be considered are school district consolidations, performance contracting, decentralization or breaking up large systems, and voucher systems.

BENEFITS FROM EDUCATION

Education is provided directly to students. Students can be identified, and there are no administrative reasons why students and their parents could not be charged for the educational services provided. Education is not like many public goods where consumers are not easy to identify or where consumers can benefit from the provision of a public good even when they have not paid for it. Education is, however, generally provided publicly and without charge to students throughout the United States.

Two rationales underlie the public provision of elementary and secondary education in the United States. First, benefits from education accrue to others in society as well as the student educated; second, the provision of equal opportunity in a democratic society requires that education be available to everyone, regardless of ability to pay for its provision. Analysts stressing the external benefits from education argue that education would be underconsumed if parents of children had to bear all the costs. The underconsumption would occur because parents would demand education up to the quantity where marginal private benefits equaled marginal private costs, neglecting the benefits accruing to others. The underconsumption problem would be complicated by the lack of a good capital market for developing human resources. It is difficult to borrow money to invest in education because those families who needed loans the most would lack financial assets to serve as security for borrowing.

There are many classifications of benefits from education. Benefits accruing to students and their families include increased productivity and income, benefits to the family because of school custody of children during the day, and intangible benefits associated with being educated or enjoying school and learning. Benefits identified as accruing to others include monetary benefits of reduced taxes (for a constant quality of public goods) because other citizens have higher earnings and hence pay higher taxes, reduced taxes for welfare expenditure, and increases in income and consumption due to higher levels of economic development associated with a society of highly educated individuals. It is also alleged that intangible benefits accrue from the interaction of people with others of higher educational and cultural levels.[2]

It is sometimes difficult to separate the second rationale for the public provision of education—equal opportunity—from arguments based on externalities; but there are substantial differences in the inferences derived from the different rationales. For example, a focus on externalities generally implies that more education is good per se. However, some supporters of the equal opportunity rationale have argued for the promulgation of policies through which family and socioeconomic differences in children's capacities are reduced or eliminated, so that every one has a truly equal opportunity for social and economic advancement in American society.[3] Some advocates of equal opportunity have gone so far as to argue that wealthier families should be penalized if they wish to provide higher-than-average levels of education for their children because this reduces the ability of the educational system to provide equal opportunity for all children. The implications of different rationales for the provision of public education will become apparent in subsequent analyses, especially our analysis of educational financing problems.

DEMAND ARTICULATION

Education is provided primarily through independent school districts. School districts boundaries are not necessarily coterminous with those

---

[2]A good discussion of benefits within an economic framework is contained in Werner Z. Hirsch, Elbert W. Segelhorst, and Morton J. Marcus, *Spillover of Public Education Costs and Benefits* (Los Angeles: University of California, Institute of Government and Public Affairs, 1964).

[3]James S. Coleman, "The Concept of Equality of Educational Opportunity," in Harvard Educational Review, *Equal Educational Opportunity* (Cambridge, Mass.: Harvard, 1969), pp. 9–24.

of any other political unit, although it is common in the Southeast to have countywide districts and, in many areas, for cities and school districts to share common boundaries. School districts may be either larger or smaller than cities. For example, the Los Angeles school district contains not only the city of Los Angeles but also twenty-three additional suburban communities, while Kansas City is served by seventeen and San Antonio by fifteen independent school districts.[4]

There appear to be at least two reasons for the separation of school districts from other local governments. First, education is of large enough magnitude that both demand articulation and production may be undertaken more efficiently by having independent units for its provision. Second, the creation of separate school districts was supposed to keep "politics" out of educational policy. Within school districts, however, demands are articulated in political ways, just as in other political units. Preferences are indicated by voting directly on some issues, voting for representatives who in turn make policy, and by directly confronting elected officials, administrators, or teachers either individually or through groups such as PTAs and community councils. Demands are also articulated through state and federal political mechanisms; all states and the federal government have policies for and provide financial aid to education. In addition, the court system has provided an access point for individuals and groups dissatisfied with state and local policies, and court orders have been important in areas of integration and educational finance. Thus, as in other areas of the public sector, there is more than one way in which and more than one place where preferences can be indicated.

The demands for education vary in the same way as do demands for other public goods. Within a single school district, especially one containing a heterogeneous population, individuals' preferences for different kinds or levels of education differ, and not everyone is satisfied with the programs provided. If the political process is working reasonably well, however, and no single group is able to dominate, we would expect the level of service which is provided to reflect majority or median voter preferences, with a heavier weighing of the preferences of organized groups such as teachers and PTA members and a lesser response to preferences of unorganized citizens. Individuals preferring educational services other than those provided have the options, as with all local public goods, of (1) trying to exercise greater influence on local policy through either the local school board, state or federal agencies, or the courts; (2) moving to another school district; or (3) purchasing education from a private school. However,

[4]Seymour Sacks, *City Schools/Suburban Schools* (Syracuse, N.Y.: Syracuse University Press, 1972), p. 10.

because of income limits and segregation, these options are not equally available to all citizens.

Low-income individuals dissatisfied with the provision of education in their area may have limited options. Their political influence may be low, their residential mobility restricted, and their incomes insufficient to allow for private schooling. Children of low-income families may really have two choices—to attend school even though it is less than satisfactory or simply to drop out. The high drop-out rates in many school systems, especially big-city systems populated by low-income families, would indicate that many school districts are not providing a mix of services that meet the demands of large proportions of their potential clientele.[5] Dropping out per se may not be undesirable if there are sufficient employment and earnings opportunities for dropouts. The apparent lack of these opportunities and high costs of reentry into the school system may indicate, however, that students leave school because of dissatisfaction with it, not because of better opportunities for advancement elsewhere.[6]

The fact that high-income individuals who feel their demands are inadequately met within a school district are better able to take advantage of options may also enhance the responsiveness of school districts to the well-to-do. This contrasts with their lack of responsiveness to low-income families, who are subject to the monopoly power of a single district. For example, within large systems it is common to find that higher levels of educational services are provided in high-income neighborhoods, as teachers with seniority gravitate toward the "more desirable" schools in the system—usually defined as schools

---

[5]A report by the National Commission on the Reform of Secondary Education, sponsored by the Kettering Foundation, indicated that in many inner-city schools attendance averaged less than 50 percent of enrolled students. (Jack McCurdy, "National Commission Urges Lowering of School Age to 14," *Los Angeles Times*, December 9, 1973, Part 1, pp. 1, 26–27.) In New York City over 50 percent of black and Puerto Rican students drop out before graduating from high school, and in Bedford-Stuyvesant, an area of 450,000 people in New York City served by a single high school, over 80 percent of the students drop out prior to high school graduation. Marilyn Gittell et al., *School Decentralization and School Policy in New York City* (A Report to the State Commission on the Quality, Cost and Financing of Elementary and Secondary Education, 1971), p. 80; and Adam Walinsky, "Review of Maximum Feasible Misunderstanding," *The New York Times Book Review*, February 2, 1969, section 7.

[6]The dropping out of less interested and potentially more disruptive students may be encouraged to improve the environment for teaching and learning by more motivated students. One commission has emphasized this aspect of the drop-out problem by recommending that compulsory attendance laws be lowered at least to age 14 instead of the 16, 17, or 18 common in most states. Along with a lowering of the compulsory attendance age, the commission recommends that a wide variety of different kinds of learning environments from apprenticeships, on-the-job training, and occupational education be added to provide greater choice for students to engage in learning and enhance their earning capacity. McCurdy, op. cit.

with student populations having socioeconomic characteristics similar to those of the teachers. Low-income-area schools, on the other hand, are likely to have high teacher turnover and to be neglected in other ways by the educational administrative bureaucracy.[7] Even with these adjustments, however, most large-city school systems are continually losing their higher-income clientele to either private schools or suburban school systems.

The combination of high drop-out rates among low-income students and the outmigration or transfer to private schools of higher-income students has served to focus considerable attention, during the past decade, on the school systems of large cities. Analysts of demand articulation into big systems have consistently concluded that the systems are sufficiently large that several breakdowns have occurred simultaneously.[8] First, the systems are large enough and diverse enough that it is impossible to tell what a vote for different school board members, or a mayor who appoints school board members, means. This relegates demand articulation to lobbying and bargaining rather than electoral politics. Second, the bureaucracies providing education are so large that they are unmanageable. For example, it is common for principals and teachers to simply ignore directives from the superintendent's office, and there is little the district superintendent can do to check up to see whether directives are carried out. The combination of weakened electoral control and bureaucratic unmanageability has left most educational policy making up to professional administrators and teachers. And while they can easily ignore directives for change, they cannot introduce new programs or processes either, because of the extensive bureaucratic approvals that are required.[9] The result is a system of public education in big cities in which neither citizens nor elected officials have much say in educational policy. This is precisely the kind of political situation in which one would predict opting out of the system (by moving, the use of private schools, or dropping out) by individuals who can afford alternatives rather than ex-

[7]A useful summary of these problems in education and other municipal services is contained in Gershon M. Ratner, "Inter-Neighborhood Denials of Equal Protection in the Provision of Municipal Services," *Harvard Civil Rights and Civil Liberties Law Review*, vol. 4, 1968–69, pp. 1–63.

As we will see when we look at the relationship between inputs and student performance in education, however, there is no reason to expect students to perform better with more experienced teachers.

[8]A survey and analysis of case studies reaching this general conclusion is contained in Harvey A. Averch et al., *How Effective is Schooling? A Critical Review and Synthesis of Research Findings*, Prepared for the President's Commission on School Finance (Santa Monica, Calif.: The Rand Corporation, 1972), pp. 93–99. Good case studies include David Rogers, *110 Livingston Street: Politics and Bureaucracy in the New York Schools* (New York: Random House, 1968), and Melvin Zimet, *Decentralization and School Effectiveness* (New York: Teachers College, 1973).

[9]Averch, op. cit., p. 156.

pending effort for reform, because reform efforts have little chance of success. On the other hand, citizens without any other option but to use public schools if they are to receive education may become very frustrated at the system's lack of responsiveness. Their frustration may often be manifested in vandalism of school buildings, low attendance rates, high drop-out rates, and voting down taxes to finance education when given the opportunity.

The situation appears to be different in smaller suburban districts. The suburban districts are more homogeneous and there is apparently a higher level of agreement on educational programs and policies.[10] The citizen preferences are probably also closer to the preferences of teachers and educational professionals. Because of the difference in socioeconomic characteristics, it is difficult to attribute higher achievement levels in smaller suburban districts to district size alone. However, both theory and evidence indicates that smaller, more homogeneous districts are likely to provide more satisfactory service levels to their students than larger, heterogeneous districts.

THE PRODUCTION OF EDUCATION

Public education is provided primarily by the school districts through which demands are articulated and educational policy decisions made. This makes each public school district essentially a monopolist for the provision of public education within its area. The development of a system of monopoly provision is a consequence of historical conditions. Initially, in all except a few cities, the population densities were so low that the provision of education was a natural monopoly, that is, the lowest costs of production were achieved when a single school served the geographic area surrounding it. Often in rural areas, population densities were so low that one or two classrooms with one or two teachers were the most efficient way to provide education for all grades. As population densities increased and travel times decreased, it became possible to have larger schools and to consolidate schools in rural areas. Within big cities, increasing enrollments were met by both larger schools and new schools. When new schools are provided, however, new attendance areas are designated, so that each school retains its monopolistic position as the only provider of public education for children within its area. There are only a few exceptions to this generalization, usually with specialized programs or vocational education where students may come from anywhere within an entire school

---

[10]Basil G. Zimmer and Amos H. Hawley, *Metropolitan Area Schools: Resistance to District Reorganization* (Beverly Hills, Calif.: Sage Publications, 1968), p. 87. Zimmer and Hawley also found that the gap in citizen satisfaction on a variety of indicators was larger between the larger cities and adjacent suburban districts.

district. There are also many illegal exceptions where parents residing in one attendance area or district send their children into other attendance areas or districts by using false addresses for enrollment. This problem is so serious in some school districts surrounding Los Angeles that the school districts have retained private investigators to identify students who are attending their schools illegally.

During the past several decades, considerable attention has been devoted to consolidating low-attendance rural districts in hopes of providing higher levels of or more diversity in education than could be provided by extremely small schools.[11] At the same time, however, very little attention has been paid to the growth of large school districts and the problems associated with demand articulation and production of education by a large, labor-intensive bureaucracy to diverse populations. Because our concern is with urban issues and problems, we will take a closer look at large rather than small school systems.

Several kinds of studies have been undertaken of middle-sized and large school systems, which are the sizes commonly found in urban and suburban areas. These studies focus primarily on relating inputs to outputs or identifying determinants of educational achievement, studies of bureaucratic operation, and studies of compensatory education. The major difficulty with studies of education is defining outputs. Learning is generally classified as cognitive and noncognitive. Cognitive skills are measurable through tests of various kinds and are what we generally associate with analytical reasoning and academic aptitude. Noncognitive learning, on the other hand, concerns the ability to deal with social situations, motivation, attitudes, self-awareness, learning styles, and the social functions of education in general. Virtually all studies of educational output utilize only simple measures of cognitive skill and thus do not measure all aspects of educational outcomes. And, more important for some purposes, it is not cognitive skills as measured by educational testing that are associated with higher incomes. Instead, noncognitive characteristics such as reliability, motivation, and social skills are the those that appear to be necessary for enhanced earning capacity.[12]

---

[11]Between 1942 and 1972, the number of school districts was reduced from 108,579 to 15,781. U.S. Bureau of the Census, *Census of Governments*, 1967, vol. 1 *Governmental Organization* (Washington, D.C.: Government Printing Office, 1973), p. 23.

[12]David M. Gordon, *Theories of Poverty and Unemployment* (Lexington, Mass.: Heath, 1972), pp. 120–121. Other studies also indicate that the kind or quality of schooling is not related to earnings, although an additional year of elementary or secondary school boosts future income less than 4 percent, college about 7 percent, and a year of graduate school about 4 percent when differences in initial ability and family background are taken into account. Christopher Jencks et al., *Inequality: A Reassessment of the Effect of Family and Schooling in America* (New York: Basic Books, 1972), p. 223.

Economists are accustomed to identifying production functions, that is, the relationships between different inputs and outputs at different scales of operation. Knowledge of production function relationships would permit one to know what increments to outcome would occur with additions of different inputs; thus an optimum production strategy could be identified. Unfortunately, in educational research, we have not yet reached the production function stage with any degree of certainty. To summarize the conclusions of a RAND study for the President's Commission on School Finance: "Research has not identified a variant of the existing system that is consistently related to students' educational outcomes."[13] The study does not conclude that educational inputs have *no* relationship to educational outcomes; it says only that in spite of extensive research on education, researchers have not been able to identify such relationships with consistency. The state of this research makes it difficult to say much about education. We do not know what the relationships between inputs and outputs are. The commission report goes on to indicate that "increasing expenditures on traditional educational practices is not likely to improve educational outcomes substantially"[14] and that "there seem to be opportunities for significant reduction or redirection of educational expenditures without deterioration in educational outcomes."[15]

Other economists undertaking or reviewing educational research have focused more directly on the question of economies of scale, or whether or not there are lower average costs for similar achievement levels by different-sized school districts or schools.[16] This research indicates that, within the size ranges of suburban school systems, there are no economies of scale from growing larger, and there may be diseconomies of scale for larger jurisdictions. However, the difficulty of evaluating large, diverse jurisdictions has resulted in very few analyses of school systems over 75,000 to 100,000 pupils except to note that the large systems usually have higher expenditures and lower performance levels than smaller systems.

A second kind of research has focused on the organizations which produce education. The focus of these studies has been on administrative efficiency, responsiveness to change, ability to innovate, and the general functioning of the producing organization. These kinds of studies are more difficult to evaluate because they are often case studies with limited potential for replication by other analysts. The conclusions of these studies, however, are remarkably consistent, so

[13]Averch, op. cit., p. 154.
[14]Ibid., p. 155.
[15]Ibid.
[16]Henry M. Levin, "The Effect of Different Levels of Expenditure on Educational Output," in Roe L. Johns et al. (eds.), *Economic Factors Affecting the Financing of Education*, (Gainsville, Fla.: National Educational Finance Project, 1970), pp. 173–206.

that one can feel reasonably confident about their conclusions. The major conclusions are that (1) the larger the system, the greater the expenditure devoted to central administration and control; (2) the larger the system, the more centralized its policy and decision making, and (3) innovation, responsiveness, and adaptation in school systems decrease with size and depend upon exogenous shocks to the system.[17]

While evidence from input-output and bureaucratic studies is not as "hard" as economists prefer, it is consistent with the theory of public goods and services developed in Chapter 5 and with our observations on urban government in Chapter 7. In those chapters we indicated that one should expect difficulty in articulating demands for publicly provided services in large heterogeneous political units and that labor-intensive services are extremely difficult to manage. Furthermore, we noted that these problems are both more severe when outputs from the service provision are difficult to measure. One should not be surprised that New York City's school system—with over one million students, 58,000 teachers, and 900 public schools—is sufficiently large to be unmanageable and much too large for citizens to indicate their preferences effectively.

In spite of researchers' inability to relate educational inputs to outputs consistently, the determinants of educational achievement— or at least some of the variables that are significantly associated with educational achievement as measured by cognitive skill tests—have been identified. The major determinants of educational achievement appear to be the socioeconomic characteristics of the student's family.[18] That is, students whose parents have high incomes and are highly educated do well on exams and students whose parents have lower incomes and are less well educated do relatively less well. Thus, given the lack of identified association between educational achievement and educational inputs, one may conclude that the superior reputations of many suburban school systems are not due to any unique provision of education but rather to the higher socioeconomic characteristics of the children's parents. If this is in fact the case and educational strategies cannot be designed to give educational services per se a greater impact on student achievement, there may be little big-city schools can do to increase the achievement levels of their students.

There is an alternative interpretation of the same evidence, however, that leads to a much more optimistic conclusion. First, existing educational delivery systems are designed primarily by professional educators who come from middle- and upper-middle-income classes.

[17]Averch, op. cit., p. 156.
[18]This is the single most important conclusion of Jencks, op. cit.

It is likely that the design of the provision is highly suitable for students from similar backgrounds, but it may well not be suitable for children from significantly different backgrounds. Some support for this interpretation is indicated by the favorable attitude of poor city dwellers toward education per se but their negative attitudes toward education as provided in their local public schools. This dissatisfaction is most directly reflected in their low attendance rates, high drop-out rates, and high levels of school vandalism. If this is the case, then extensive innovation to develop alternative kinds of educational services would appear warranted. It is precisely in the largest school systems, however, that resistance to innovation and lack of adaptation to changing conditions is strongest. Thus it is precisely where the environment requires the most innovation and adaptation to meet demands for education by heterogeneous constituencies that the production systems are the least well suited for the purpose. It appears that those who demand decentralization within big-city school systems are very well aware of those problems to which the large systems are incapable of responding. The smaller suburban systems, on the other hand, not only have an easier educational task but are small enough to be innovative and adaptive. If our analysis is correct, then education as it is currently provided in urban areas may actually diminish rather than equalize opportunity for differently situated citizens.

There is some other evidence that may indicate a solution to the dilemma of producing appropriate educational services. This evidence indicates that different students respond differently to different educational inputs. Thus, when an innovation or new technique is tried, some students improve, others remain the same, and still others do relatively less well. Thus the innovation produces ambiguous results. This interpretation of the difficulty that educational researchers have had is quite consistent with the theory of public goods when we recognize that within a single classroom (and throughout a school system), the educational program provided is virtually the same for all students. The educational service level provided may meet the preferences of some students but miss the mark for others. Recognition of different skill levels among students has resulted in a variety of class selection techniques, including tracking, honors sections, and remedial sessions. But it is possible that individual students also differ in the ways they react to teachers' personalities and the ways in which materials are presented, not only in terms of skill levels as measured on cognitive ability tests. If these other differences exist, it would appear that students may require relatively more variety and some choice, so that students and teachers can be matched and the highest levels of achievement obtained. This would imply considerably more variety of offerings within single subject matters than present schools generally offer, but there is really no reason why, for example, all eighth grade English classes or any other classes in a school system must use the same readings and format. It may be much more desirable to permit teachers to select and use the materials and techniques that they feel to be most effective, and to combine this freedom with a student-teacher mutual selection process.[19]

GROUPING VERSUS SEGREGATION

The fact that the education provided within a classroom must be consumed by all the students in that classroom—combined with the observation that different students have different preferences, different skills, and learn in different ways—leads one to the conclusion that some kind of grouping of students to match subject matter, method of instruction, and even teachers' personalities may lead to greater learning than random assignment of students to classes. However, once grouping begins, it has the potential for segregating students not only by preferences, skills, and method of instruction but also by race and socioeconomic class. And grouping by race or social class may itself be undesirable and illegal. For example, in *Hobson v. Hansen*, the U.S. District Court in Washington, D.C., ruled that any grouping or tracking that leads to racial segregation was illegal.[20] In addition, some educators argue that students with lesser skills will make greater learning progress if they are placed in classooms where a majority of students have superior skills. This argument has been extended to conclude that blacks and other minority students will do better if they are a minority among higher-skilled whites than if grouped with equally unskilled peers.[21] There is some systematic evidence to indicate that blacks attending school with whites where the blacks are a minority do better on cognitive skill tests than blacks with comparable socioeconomic characteristics attending predominantly black schools.[22] This evidence is weak, however, because while the blacks attending majority white schools have similar socioeconomic characteristics as other blacks, most of them do live in predominantly white neighborhoods and their families may have decided on that residential location choice specifically because they placed a relatively high value on edu-

---

[19]Some interesting experiments and attempts to group students are discussed in H. A. Thelen, *Classroom Grouping for Teachability* (New York: Wiley, 1967).
[20]269 F. Supp. 401 (D.D.C. 1967).
[21]Department of Health, Education and Welfare, *Equality of Educational Opportunity*, also called the Coleman Report, (Washington, D.C.: Government Printing Office, 1969), summary, p. 22.
[22]Ibid.

cation in "better" schools for their children. There is no evidence, however, to indicate whether or not blacks transferred from predominantly black schools to predominantly white schools can be expected to improve their skills. Rulings on integration have been based on racial segregation per se, not on evidence of any potential for better education.[23] It is certainly hoped, however, that integrated education will be better.

Providing integrated education under existing residential patterns is not an easy task. Not only are neighborhoods often segregated but a majority of students in many big-city school systems are blacks or other minorities. To provide integration, busing of students to suburban jurisdictions would be required in addition to transferring students within the big-city school system. The introduction of students of lower socioeconomic characteristics and lower skill levels into suburban systems, where parents may have specifically chosen to come to avoid big-city schools and their students, is not popular. Even less popular would be busing children of suburban families back into schools in the city, from which the closer-in suburbanites—residing in older suburban housing—may have just fled.

While most of the discussions of busing and integration have been in terms of costs of busing, the desirability of neighborhood schools, and racism, there are implications for urban housing patterns and the political relationship between parents and schools. One reason neighborhoods are relatively homogeneous may be that parents like to reside where their children will attend school and interact with other children with similar values.[24] If schools were not tied to residential choice, families might select much more diverse residential environments than at present. Or, if they had no control over which public school their children would attend, they might adjust their residential location to the availability of private schools, simply opting out of the public school system. Residential patterns, in either case, might turn out to be more diverse and more mixed than those which occur when a specific school is associated with a specific residential location.

The relationship between parents and school systems under a system of busing to achieve integration could pose several problems. First, it is not clear what access parents of children bussed to other

---

[23]Henry S. Deyer, "School Factors and Equal Educational Opportunity," in Harvard Educational Review, *Equal Educational Opportunity* (Cambridge, Mass.: Harvard, 1969), p. 56. Deyer is just one of several analysts who have reanalyzed data upon which the Coleman Report conclusions were drawn and concluded they were not in fact supported by Coleman Report data.

[24]Cultural reinforcement as a motivation for suburban clustering of white middle-class residents is explored and its implications are further examined in Anthony Downs, *Opening Up the Suburbs* (New Haven, Conn.: Yale, 1973).

school districts have for influencing policy in that district. They would not be voting citizens of that district, and it is unlikely that poorly educated black parents with low incomes would have the resources and take the time to journey to PTA or school board meetings in the suburbs, where they would be a distinct and, most likely, unpopular minority. While considering integration, one should keep in mind that preferences for education do differ among different socioeconomic groups. At least one case study indicated that middle-class whites, blue-collar workers, and blacks tend to favor instruction which emphasizes three-R skills and disciplined learning, while upper-middle-class whites favored instruction that emphasized flexibility, creativity, and innovation—under the assumption that the three-Rs themselves were not of any special difficulty.[25] If school boards do try to provide education of the kind desired by a majority of their citizens, it may well be that the kinds of programs provided will not be those desired by students coming in from other areas. There is sufficient nonresponsiveness in present big-city systems to indicate that one cannot just assume that the teachers and educators will design appropriate programs to meet student needs. Many blacks and other minority leaders are rightly skeptical of the potential responsiveness of educators to their needs if the blacks and other minorities comprise a minority of every school district rather than a majority of some districts, where they can force programs to be designed specifically for their own needs.[26]

There is no good evidence on the advantages of integration relative to the advantages of grouping students for efficient consumption of preferred public goods. These problems of analysis and policy are difficult ones, made still more difficult by problems of educational finance. In the next section we will analyze issues of educational finance before returning to an examination of potential solutions to other problems of education.

FINANCING EDUCATION

Expenditures on public education have more than tripled during the last fifteen years. Of the increase, about one-fourth was related to increasing enrollments and the other three-fourths to rising costs of

[25]The difference in preferences regarding education among diverse communities in a consolidated district is brought out in Lillian B. Rubin, *Busing and Backlash: White against White in a California School District* (Berkeley, Calif.: University of California Press, 1972), especially chaps. 2 and 3.

[26]Perceptive questioning of integration as a desirable strategy is presented in Charles V. Hamilton, "Race and Education: A Search for Legitimacy," and Noel A. Day, "The Case for All-Black Schools," both in Harvard Educational Review, *Equal Educational Opportunity* (Cambridge, Mass.: Harvard, 1969), pp. 187–202, 206–212.

educational inputs.[27] These cost increases appear to have led to a taxpayers revolt as increasing numbers of school bond and tax levy elections have been defeated. For example, prior to the middle 1960s, it was common for over 70 percent of all school tax elections to result in favorable votes; by 1971, the passage rate was only 47 percent, and on a declining trend.[28] In addition to taxpayer resistance to rising costs of education, a second issue in education finance has become predominant with the *Serrano v. Priest* decision.[29] This decision by the California Supreme Court ruled that if extreme wealth differences among school districts resulted in greatly different expenditures for education, the equal protection clauses of the U.S. Constitution (Fourteenth Amendment) and California state constitution were being violated. The court did not rule on what remedies would be appropriate. The decision, however, has led to considerable reexamination of local public school finance in California and the rest of the United States.

Current Financing

During the 1971–1972 school year, 55 percent of all revenues spent on public education were raised by local governments, 39 percent were raised by state governments, and the federal government provided a little over 6 percent. Of the local government share, 82 percent was raised from property taxation; only two states permit income taxation for education. These figures are aggregate figures for the entire United States. The financing of education, like other locally provided services, however, is determined independently within each state and the funds raised by local governments varied from 85.3 percent in New Hampshire to 2.9 percent in Hawaii. Conversely, state funding ranged from 89.4 percent in Hawaii to 9.9 percent in New Hampshire, and the federal contribution varied from 3.5 percent in Wisconsin to 28.1 percent in Mississippi.[30] Because of the different formulas used to distribute state aid within states, the percentage contributions of state government for education also varies considerably within each state.

Along with different sources of funding within and among different states, the actual expenditures per student also varied over a wide

---

[27]Robert D. Reischauer and Robert W. Hartman, *Reforming School Finance* (Washington, D.C.: Brookings, 1973), pp. 18–19.

[28]Ibid., p. 23.

[29]487 P. 2d 1241, 96 Cal. Rptr. 601 (1971). A good analysis of this and other decisions is contained in Ferdinand P. Schoettle, "Judicial Requirements for School Finance and Property Tax Redesign: The Rapidly Evolving Case Law," *National Tax Journal* 25 (September 1972), pp. 455–472.

[30]Reischauer, *Reforming School Finance*, pp. 4–12.

range. The average amount spent per pupil was $929, but the range among states was from $213 in the lowest-spending district of Missouri to $14,554 in the highest-spending district of Wyoming. The median expenditures within states ranged from $407 in Alabama and Arkansas to $1,077 in New York. All but eleven states had at least some districts spending over $1,000 per pupil.[31] These differences within and among states should be kept in mind as we continue the analysis of educational finance.

All states provide financial support for locally provided education. State aid is basically of three kinds: First, there are functional grant programs such as aid for vocational education or aid for educating children with special problems such as the deaf or blind; second, there are equalizing grants which provide greater amounts of money to poorer jurisdictions; and third, there are flat minimum grants which guarantee each district some level of state aid. Some states only provide one of the kinds of aid, but most have some kind of equalizing grant program. Along with state aid go state regulations, which generally set standards for teacher certification, specify a minimum age through which students must attend school, and specify a minimum school-year term. Some states also specify approved text materials and designate specific required classes for different grade levels or as diploma requirements. While local governments traditionally provide education, state regulations play an important role in determining just what programs are provided and, in most states, the state government is constitutionally responsible for assuring that education is available to every potential student. Within state guidelines, however, local school districts provide considerable variety in educational programs because state requirements are generally minimums which any district may exceed if it can raise sufficient funds to do so. Only where states must approve all textual materials are there really constraints on school district operations which exceed minimum requirements.

All federal aid to elementary and secondary education is through functional grant programs. Traditional aid has been available for vocational education, the handicapped, research, and areas where the federal government owned large amounts of untaxed property such as military bases. Beginning in 1965 with Title I of the Elementary and Secondary Education Act, the amount of federal aid for education doubled.[32] This new functional grant program is for compensatory education for children from low-income families. The aid can make a

---

[31] Ibid.
[32] The history and development of Title I is described in John F. Hughes and Anne O. Hughes, *Equal Education* (Bloomington, Ind.: Indiana University Press, 1972).

difference in resources available to a school district of as much as $150 to $200 per low-income student.

Results from the Title I compensatory aid programs have been mixed. Tremendous enforcement effort has been required to assure that school districts actually spent their funds for programs aimed at low-income populations instead of just using the federal aid for general school expenditure. Noncompliance problems of these kinds were especially severe in big-city school systems of the North and East.[33] In addition, evaluations of the outcomes of programs actually targeted on low-income students have indicated relatively few major successes. Most programs were for "more of the same" in terms of regular classroom experiences and did not generate significant student improvement. Sufficient successful experimental programs have been identified, especially in southern and smaller, less bureaucratized school districts, to indicate that the aid levels are sufficient to provide higher achievement levels for disadvantaged students. Congressional funding for Title I programs has never been sufficient to provide compensatory education for *all* eligible students, so the program is like many other federal subsidy programs—those who benefit receive relatively large benefits while other equally eligible children receive nothing at all from the program.[34] It was in this educational finance environment that, in 1972, the Supreme Court of California ruled that present methods financing education violated equal protection clauses of the United States and state of California constitutions.

Equal Opportunity in Education

The *Serrano v. Priest* decision by the California Supreme Court was only the first of a series of court decisions which have ruled that if the level of wealth within a school district determines expenditures on education, then equal opportunity for education by all children within a state does not exist. While the *Serrano* decision was the first major school finance decision based on equal protection grounds, a Texas case, *Rodriguez, et. al., v. San Antonio Independent School District, et. al.*,[35], was the first to reach the U. S. Supreme Court. The Supreme Court ruled that poor people did not necessarily live in poor districts

[33]Ibid., pp. 68–69.

[34]In this respect Title I programs are like Public Housing as discussed in Chap. 8. A small percentage of the eligible people receive large benefits and the others receive nothing.

[35]337 F. Supp. 280 (W.D. Tex. 1972). Brought before the U.S. Supreme Court as *San Antonio Independent School District v. Rodriguez*, 411 U.S. 1, 93 S. Ct. 1278, 36 L. Ed.2nd 16 (1972).

so poor people as a class were not disadvantaged by the Texas school finance system, and that equal provision of education, in contrast to a minimum foundation program, was not required under equal protection clauses of either the U. S. or Texas constitutions. The Court also ruled that the Texas system, which is like most other state systems, was not irrational and did fulfill a legitimate purpose. Even with the reversal of *Rodriguez*, however, present systems of school financing are coming under increasing scrutiny by state courts and state legislatures.

The basic argument put forth in *Serrano* and the major writings advocating that decision is that (1) the wealth per student of school districts is widely different within states, (2) the wealth differences permit richer districts to provide higher levels of education at lower tax rates, (3) the level of education provided is dependent on the level of wealth, and (4) equal educational opportunity should be available to all children regardless of the wealth of the school district within which they reside.[36]

One should note that in *Serrano* and in most of the major writings supporting *Serrano*, no direct inference is made that low-income families reside in low-wealth districts or that high-income families reside in high-wealth districts. For strategic purposes in presenting the *Serrano* case, the lawyers selected for comparative purposes two extreme cases, Baldwin Park and Beverly Hills. The former contains only residential property of low-income families; the latter contains residential property of high-income families plus highly valued commercial business property.[37] Many interpreters of the *Serrano* decision have also implied that low-wealth districts are populated by low-income families and high-wealth districts are populated by high-income families, but this is not in fact the case. When we look at all school districts, it is common for lower-income families to reside in areas where there is business and industrial property offsetting their low-valued residential property, and many high-income residential enclaves lack business or industry, resulting in relatively low property values. Rural districts, inhabited primarily by relatively low-income families, also often have extremely high assessed valuations per student because of high-valued agricultural and forest lands. In California, for

---

[36]The logic of this position is best developed in John E. Coons, William H. Clune III, and Stephen D. Sugarman, *Private Wealth and Public Education* (Cambridge, Mass.: Harvard, 1970).

[37]Baldwin Park had an assessed value per student of $4,169, a tax rate of 3.340 percent, and expenditures per student of $708. Beverly Hills had an assessed value per student of $49,501, a tax rate of 2.552, and expenditure per student of $1,535. The tax rate times assessed value per student is less than expenditure per student because state and federal aid was $569 per student in Baldwin Park and $272 per student in Beverly Hills.

and assessed value per student is only 0.02 for all school districts, 0.03 for all elementary districts, and 0.004 for all high school districts. When family income instead of average family income within a school district is correlated with assessed value per student, the coefficients of correlation are even lower. Thus in California at least, there is essentially no relationship between family income and school district wealth per student.[38] The lack of a relationship between family income and school district wealth, when combined with the fact that district wealth itself is partially determined by education taxes and benefits, makes the determination of fiscal capacity and the design of educational finance programs to achieve equal opportunity a difficult task.

Financial Reform

How can we approach equal opportunity? Does equal opportunity mean equal expenditures on education for every child? Or does it mean equal educational achievement for each child, which would require greatly different expenditures? How do these criteria relate to efficiency in the sense of investing in education where the greatest increases in productivity will result, or to equity in the sense of permitting parents who earn high incomes (because they are more productive in the economy and society) to spend more on their children's education?

Rather than use the undefined or ambiguous term "equal opportunity," let us explore proposed changes in educational finance in terms of whether they would facilitate or restrict equal expenditures, provide compensatory expenditures to move toward equal achievement, and provide freedom of choice for parents to spend as much as they desired for their children's education. It is not possible to maximize all these values simultaneously because they are contradictory and each has some value. The problem is to design a system in which marginal benefits per dollar spent to achieve each criterion are equal. While we could define such a situation as optimal and use the marginal principle as a guide, the actual evaluation of alternatives emerges from political processes.

[38]Millicent Cox, "Analysis of the Characteristics of School Districts, California, 1970," mimeographed paper prepared with funds from the Ford Foundation, grant no. 740-0088, March 1974. These results and other analyses of school finance alternatives are forthcoming in Millicent Cox, "Equality in Educational Finance: An Analysis of the Distribution of Taxes and Educational Benefits by District," Ph.D. dissertation, Center for Urban Affairs, University of Southern California, 1975. For another analysis reaching similar conclusions see Note, "A Statistical Analysis of the School Financing Decisions: On Winning Battles and Losing Wars," *Yale Law Journal*, 81 (1972), p. 1303.

While ultimate decisions are political, it is important, however, that analysts be able to predict the consequences of alternatives in educational finance so that when policies are adopted outcomes will be those predicted.

Power Equalizing   Power equalizing is proposed to make the tax price of education the same for everyone.[39] This means that any given tax rate will raise the same amount of money per student in any district regardless of the district wealth level. For example, if the average wealth per student statewide is $50,000, all school districts would receive revenues equal to their tax rate times $50,000 per student. The deficits for school districts with wealth levels below $50,000 would be financed by state collection of surpluses collected by all districts with above-average wealth levels. Thus no matter how rich or poor a district, the same number of dollars per student would be available for expenditure for each percentage of tax rate throughout the state.

Power equalization is the financial reform recommended to achieve equal educational opportunity by supporters of the *Serrano* decision. From their perspective, if the same tax rate raises the same amount of money per student anywhere in the state, fiscal capacity has been equalized with regard to educational finance.

We have already noted that there is no direct relation between school district wealth and family wealth, and it is easy to become concerned as to whether power equalization will lead to net redistribution of income from higher-income families to lower-income families. Some analysts have begun to explore this question. However, we believe that there are more fundamental issues in any significant change in property tax financing of education that have not been given significant recognition. These issues revolve around the evidence of property tax and public service benefits capitalization into property values. In other words, what are the consequences of power equalization if property taxes are in fact capitalized into land values instead of being analyzed as if they were simply excise taxes paid by occupants of residential units within a school district? As we indicated in Chapter 6, economic theory and the strongest evidence indicate that capitalization should be expected.

Let us examine a simple example of two equal-sized school districts. District A is a rich district, containing high-income families, business, and commercial property. It has high expenditures on education with a low tax rate. District B is a poor district, containing low-income families and no business or commercial property. It has low

[39]Coons, Clune, and Sugarman, op. cit., pp. 201–242.

TABLE 10-1   School Taxes and Expenditures

	District A	District B
Wealth per student	$100,000	$8,000
Average residential wealth	50,000	10,000
Tax rate	1.5%	6.0%
Average residential tax bill	$750	$600
Expenditures on education per student	$1,500	$480

Note that we are assuming that each district raises all funds for educational expenditures, so that the tax rate times wealth per student equals expenditure per student.

expenditures on education with a high tax rate. The total property per student, average residential property value, per student educational expenditures, tax rates, and residential tax bills are presented in Table 10-1.

Now let us assume that we introduce an equalization program so that each district may set its own tax rate and determine its own educational expenditure level—but that the state government shares or supplements revenues collected from school property taxes so that the same tax rate yields the same dollar revenue per student for all districts.

Assume in this case that the state government has decided that for each 1 percent tax the local school district will be entitled to $400 per student. Districts where a 1 percent rate would result in higher revenue would turn the surplus over to the state government, and the state government would supplement district revenues to achieve the $400 per 1 percent rate where local property taxes would not raise that amount. Let us also assume that both districts in this example initially wish to retain the same expenditure per student—$1,500 for district A and $480 in district B. Under power equalizing, district A would have to have a tax rate of 3.75 percent to raise $1,500. This is because for each 1 percent rate it would receive the state-adjusted $400. Residents of district A would find their tax rate increasing from 1.5 percent to 3.75 percent to maintain their $1,500 expenditures per student. This would mean that the average residential tax bill would increase from $750 to $1,875. At the same time residents of district B would be able to achieve their desired expenditure of $480 with a tax rate of 1.2 percent instead of their former rate of 6 percent. The average residential tax bill would fall from $600 to $120. The figures for the power equalized situation are presented in Table 10-2.

With these changes in tax burdens, could we anticipate any other changes? We must remember that the market value of property is partially determined by the associated tax liabilities and public

TABLE 10-2 School Taxes and Expenditures with Power
Equalization

	District A	District B
Expenditure per student	$1,500	$480
Tax rate required at $400 per 1 percent	3.75%	1.2%
Actual revenue collected per student	$3,750	$96
State government share or supplement	−$2,250	+$384
Average residential tax bill	$1,875	$120
Average residential tax bill before power equalization	$750	$600
Change in residential tax bill due to power equalizing	+$1,125	−$480

service benefits. If there is a change in tax burden without a change
in public service benefits, we anticipate a change in the market value of
the property. This change is called capitalization of taxes into property
values.

You may remember that, in Chapter 3, we presented the reasons
why the present value of property is determined by expectations of
future benefits and costs which accrue as a consequence of its ownership. The formula for calculating present value is

$$PV = \frac{\text{net benefits}}{(1 + r)} + \frac{\text{net benefits}_2}{(1 + r)^2} + \ldots + \frac{\text{net benefits}_n}{(1 + r)^n}$$

where PV is present value, net benefits are the difference between
revenues and costs, and r is the discount rate. The sum of the discounted value of net benefits for all years 1 through n equals the total
present value. To calculate capitalization or the *change* in present
value, one uses only the change in net benefits. In the above example,
the change in the annual tax burden for an average residence in district A was $1,125. If we assume that this change will be in effect
indefinitely, we can calculate the change in present value by the formula.

$$\text{Change in } PV = \frac{\text{change in net benefits}}{r}$$

or in this case, $(-\$1,125/0.10) = -\$11,250$. This means that if the
change is fully capitalized at 10 percent, we can expect the market
value of the average residence in district A to fall $11,250, from
$50,000 to $38,750. At the 10 percent discount rate, the decrease in

present value of $11,250 is exactly equal to the amount that would have to be invested at a 10 percent return to pay the increase in taxes. While property values are falling in response to the tax increase in district A, property values would be rising in response to the fall in taxes in district B. In Table 10-2 we observe that the average residential tax decrease was $480. If residents in district B also have a 10 percent discount rate, we can estimate that the value of the average residence would increase by $4,800 [($480/0.10) = $4,800] to $14,800.[40]

The new market values calculated from the initial tax changes, however, would not be equilibrium values. This is because at the lower market value the tax bill on property in district A would decrease and the tax bill in district B would increase in response to the increase in market values there. After several rounds of tax changes and market value adjustments, we would anticipate a new equilibrium for average residential value in district A of $41,700, with a tax payment of $1,564. In district B, the new residential value would approach $14,285 with a tax payment of $171. Power equalizing has resulted in a reduction in market values and increase in taxes for residents in district A and an increase in market values and decrease in taxes for residents in district B. Has this "power equalized" the districts? What about new residents?[41]

New residents moving into district A would view the reduction in housing prices ($50,000 to $41,700) as being exactly offset by the higher tax liability they face ($750 to $1,564)—for them there is no change between their status before and after power equalization. The change was borne totally by property owners at the time of the tax change. What about new residents in district B? Are they better able to purchase education with the new lower tax rates? New residents buying into district B would expect to pay an average of $14,285 for their house, accompanied by a future tax liability of $171 per year. While new residents have lower taxes than old residents did before power equalizing, for the new residents the lower taxes are exactly offset by the increase in the price they had to pay for their house. Thus,

---

[40]These calculations have been simplified for the purpose of clarifying the capitalization process. In analyzing an actual change, one would have to take into account the net cost to a taxpayer of a change in taxes and housing prices after taking income tax deductibility of taxes and interest into account. The effects of an increase in property taxes, when these factors are taken into account, would be slightly less than indicated in the numerical example, because all property taxes are deductible but only the mortgage interest payments on the reduced housing price are deductible. On the other hand, the numerical example slightly understates the amount of capitalization when property taxes are decreased and housing prices increase.

[41]These examples have been presented under the assumption of full capitalization of property tax changes into real estate values. We believe the current evidence on tax capitalization as presented in Chap. 6 supports an expectation of full or a very high level of capitalization on both owner-occupied and rental housing.

new residents in district B are no better off than old residents were before power equalizing. The property owners at the time of the equalization may have made nice capital gains, however. Just what has power equalizing accomplished? Nothing more than to generate one-time capital benefits for property owners in districts where tax rates can be lowered and one-time capital losses on property owners in districts where property tax rates must be raised.

Can we say that power equalizing has raised the fiscal capacity of the low-income district? As new owners move into district B, their ability to spend on education will be limited by the fact that their housing payments are higher. New residents in district A will face higher taxes but be able to spend more because their housing payments are lower. Fiscal capacity has not changed because costs of residing in the district have not changed.

It is likely that in the short run the income effects on existing homeowners of capital gains and losses will lead the residents in district A to spend less on education. They paid $50,000 for their houses, expecting taxes to be $750; if taxes suddenly rise to $1,564, they may decide to tax and spend less. On the other hand, homeowners in district B who paid $10,000 for their houses, expecting to pay $600 annually in taxes, may find that they want to expand financing for education when their new taxes come in at $171.

Much more important than wealth effects for influencing changed expenditures on education are price effects. Originally in district A, each $1 per pupil spent on education cost each homeowner 50 cents, because residential valuation represented only half of the wealth of the district. Under the new situation each $1 of educational expenditure costs each homeowner $1.39, which is a price increase of 178%. In district B each $1 per pupil of expenditure originally cost $1.25 per homeowner. Now with equalizing, we can expect each $1 of expenditure to cost only 33 cents, a price decrease of 92 cents or 74 percent. With these relative price changes, we would anticipate reduced spending on education in district A and increased spending in district B. The changes in the level of education provided, however, are a consequence of relative price changes of education, not relative wealth changes or equalization of fiscal capacity.

The data selected to illustrate power equalizing and capitalization in the above example represent an extreme case where the rich district contains both rich people and highly valued business property and the poor district contains low-income families with low-valued residential property. Thus in the example, the changes in capital values were progressive; that is, the rich lost and the poor gained. When we recognize that there is almost zero correlation between high district property values and high-income residents, capital gains and losses from a switch to a power-equalization formula would simply generate windfall gains and losses randomly. The consequent price effects may encourage increased spending among formerly low-wealth districts (which may well contain middle- or high-income residents) and decreased spending among wealthier districts (including central cities). Other than these price effects, there is nothing equalizing about power-equalizing formulas when capitalization of tax changes into property values occurs.

Virtually all writing on equal opportunity in education has used equal wealth per student as its criterion. However, equal wealth per student as achieved through power equalizing tells us nothing about fiscal capacity when we recognize that property or wealth values are themselves determined by public services and taxes. This poses a real dilemma for advocates of equal fiscal capacity who wish to achieve equal opportunity, however that is defined. It would be a sad commentary if power equalizing were introduced in hopes of equalizing fiscal capacities among districts with different levels of wealth only to discover that fiscal capacity was related to income, not wealth, leaving the distribution of both income and educational programs (except for random windfall capital gains or losses) essentially unchanged.

There is one other aspect of power equalizing that is important. It is that as one changes the tax price of education so that a dollar collected locally does not result in a dollar spent locally, the tax price of education is changed relative to the tax price of other goods and services. Thus, while a 1 percent tax may yield $1 million for education in a wealthy district, a 1 percent tax may yield $1.5 million for other goods and services. The rational procedure for any group of citizens who desire higher levels of education is to utilize another unit of local government, perhaps a municipality or a park and recreation district to provide school-related services. Then such activities as music programs, athletics, and arts and crafts could be undertaken by the other unit of local government, using a lower tax rate than would be necessary to raise the same amount of funds for the same activities if they were undertaken by the school district. In the extreme, one could end up with a park and recreation district providing every aspect of education not specifically required by state government of school systems.

One should also expect that school districts in low-wealth areas would find it rational to provide extensive extracurricular activities—perhaps absorbing all the functions of a city park department or park and recreation department—because for each tax dollar the school district raised, additional funds would be supplied by the state. This would lower the price of any activity undertaken by the school district relative to having the function undertaken by another unit of local government.

While it looks very simple to adjust relative prices to get the same tax price per student for educational finance no matter what a district's wealth level, the issue is more complex. One must recognize that this change in relative tax prices also alters relative tax prices for different units of local government, and citizens may defeat the purpose of equalization by adjusting the division of responsibilities between local school districts and other local government units.

Percentage Equalizing Percentage equalizing is a process by which the state government guarantees that all school districts can spend a specified minimum, even if at a specified tax rate their own wealth level is insufficient to raise that amount of revenue. The state, for example, may determine that an appropriate tax rate is 2 percent and that all districts should be able to spend $600 per student if they utilize a 2 percent tax rate. Then any district with a wealth level below $30,000 per student would receive state supplements equal to an amount that would bring total revenues to $600 per student if the district levies a 2 percent tax rate. For example, a district with per student wealth of only $25,000 would raise only $500 per student with a 2 percent tax rate. The state government would then grant the local district an additional $100 per student to bring its total expenditures to $600.[42] This permits all low-wealth districts to maintain some minimum level of expenditure without excessive tax effort no matter how poor they are.

The crucial aspect of percentage equalizing is the level and percentage rate selected relative to the wealth levels within school districts and the tax rates necessary to provide a high level of education. In most states, either the wealth level or tax rates are set so low that the foundation level is too low to satisfy most districts. This means that while low-income districts are given some help, they also tax above the minimum level and face a higher tax price for additional educational expenditures than do wealthier districts. At the same time, the lower the established wealth level, the fewer districts that are affected at all, because districts with above-foundation wealth levels do not receive any state aid. At the other extreme, if the foundation level is set high, most districts will face the same tax price; in an extreme situation, where the foundation wealth level was set as high as the wealth level of the wealthiest district, all districts would face the same tax price. This would certainly stimulate higher educational ex-

---

[42] The mechanics of percentage equalizing are presented in Coon, Clunes and Sugarman, op. cit., pp. 163-172.

penditure and would equalize potential tax bases. It would also be very expensive, raising total educational expenditures 60 to 100 percent in most states. It is the higher costs of guaranteeing higher minimum foundation levels that keep state governments from doing so.

Percentage equalizing is specifically criticized by advocates of the *Serrano* decision because most states have relatively low foundation levels and thus tax rates to finance a given expenditure per student above the foundation still relate to the wealth of the district, with wealthier districts facing lower rates than poorer districts. Percentage equalizing is designed to assist low-wealth districts, not to provide equalization among districts at all expenditure levels, as would power equalizing. Property tax changes brought about with percentage equalizing are subject to the same reservations on property tax capitalization as power equalizing. The difference is that while property owners in low-wealth districts would receive the same capital gain, no capital losses would occur in high-wealth districts because percentage equalizing does not raise the tax cost of providing education in those districts, as would power equalizing. The revenue to finance percentage equalizing would come, instead, from statewide taxation.

Separation of Residential and Commercial Tax Bases Another method proposed for providing some equalization in educational finance is to collect and redistribute all property tax revenue from nonresidential property on a statewide basis while individual school districts continue to set their own tax rates on residential property. The flexibility of allowing a school district to set its own tax rate on residential property would permit internal flexibility and local citizen control, while the greatest element of wealth differential, nonresidential property, would be collected statewide and passed back on a per student basis.

The changes in tax burdens occurring due to the separation of residential and nonresidential property would result in capitalization of changes, just as with power equalizing. The major difference would be that for the most part capital gains and losses would be smaller, and wealthy districts would not face the situation of raising tax rates only to have part of the revenues flow into the state treasury, so that their tax price would remain equal to that of lower-wealth districts. A problem would still remain, however, if residents of the area were permitted to utilize a park and recreation district for school-related activities when the park and recreation district could levy property taxes on all property in the district instead of just residential property, like the school district. Thus a tendency would still exist for high-wealth areas to utilize nonschool districts to take over school functions and thus retain their wealth edge in the provision of educational services.

School District Reorganization The suggestion has been made that equal opportunity could be achieved by readjusting school district boundaries so that each district contained an equal amount of wealth per student within its boundaries. In general, such reorganizations would have to move toward larger districts because of the uneven distributions of wealth within small areas. The major difficulty with designing boundaries to equalize wealth internally is that it would specifically require grouping diverse land uses and individuals with diverse preferences into single political units. The evidence indicates that large and heterogeneous school districts have had considerable difficulty in responding to the diverse preferences of their citizens, and we are afraid that an effect of district reorganization to equalize wealth would lose more than it would gain in terms of making it more difficult for citizens to have their preferences responded to.

Statewide School Financing One response to different wealth levels within districts has been to propose that state governments assume all school financing. This would equalize wealth bases, and formulas could be built in to cover extraordinary costs in high-cost areas or for districts with special problems. The major difficulties we perceive here involve the questions of (1) whether or not a single basic statewide spending level would increase the satisfaction of different groups within the state and (2) what political control local citizens would exercise if they were dissatisfied with programs provided by their school district. At present considerable diversity exists in the level of educational spending, and much of that diversity is due to differences in preferences among different citizens. It is hard to determine whether the losses in responding to different preferences would be greater than the gains by assuring more equal expenditures statewide.

We still believe the fact that local school administrators have to go to the electorate for approval of bond and expenditure levies provides a straightforward mechanism whereby citizens can indicate satisfaction or dissatisfaction with school district performance. If all taxing and expenditure decisions were made in state legislatures, one might expect considerable dominance by organized groups, primarily the teachers and professional educator lobbies, and the neglect of individual citizen interests.

Conclusions on Educational Finance Reform We believe that recognition of the potential for capitalization of property taxes into real estate values leads to the conclusion that educational finance reforms such as power equalizing or separating the residential and non-residential tax basis will not provide for equalization of fiscal capacity or equal educational financing among school districts.

Manipulation of the property tax alone is not likely to affect fiscal capacity in the long run. Provision of equal opportunity depends on equal incomes much more than equal property; thus equal school finance programs must rely on general taxation to enhance the fiscal capacity of districts with low-income residents. Solutions to educational finance problems—if equalization is desired—based on the assumption that the property tax is a simple excise tax will not produce results expected by advocates of programs like power equalizing.

We expect that educational finance reforms are likely to be much less drastic than the introduction of power equalizing. Percentage equalizing, with the funds for equalization purposes raised from general tax sources, does provide a method for equalizing the tax prices of education for lower-wealth districts, and compensatory education grants such as Title I of the federal government's aid to education can supplement educational expenditures of children from low-income families. Neither of these approaches prevents higher-income families from spending more on the education of their children than lower-income families. The costs of actually preventing higher-income families from providing higher levels of education than others would appear to be very high, and it may be much more useful to try to provide higher levels of resources for the disadvantaged than to attempt to prevent high-income families from using their incomes as they desire.

It is now time for one final observation on educational finance reform. We must repeat the conclusion of the report to the President's Commission on School Finance: "increasing expenditures on traditional educational practices is not likely to improve educational outcomes substantially."[43] Throughout this discussion of finance reform, and throughout virtually all the education finance literature, is an unstated assumption that increased expenditures on education will lead to higher performance levels by children. At present this conclusion is not warranted. There are examples of successful compensatory education and an even larger number of examples of its failure. When this reservation is added to the debates over school finance reform, we believe that there is little evidence to indicate that "equal

[43]Averch, op. cit., p. 155.

opportunity" will be a consequence arising from power equalizing, other manipulations of the property tax base or rates, or even simple increased spending in low-income or low-wealth districts. We believe problems of equal opportunity are much more likely to be resolved by creating schools which meet the needs and preferences of many diverse groups of children in our society. For these changes we must look more closely at other aspects of educational reform.

RESOLVING MULTIPLE DILEMMAS

Several problems have been identified in this analysis of urban education. These problems include citizen dissatisfaction with many large-city school systems, involuntary segregation, a need to slow cost increases or get more performance from educational expenditures, and the need to assure every child an opportunity for education not restricted by fiscal inadequacy in his school district. While we were identifying problems in previous sections, we reviewed some findings of research on educational performance. The most important conclusions were that student performance does not appear directly related to expenditure levels or particular programs, but that different students react differently to different programs and that big-city school systems are unresponsive and unmanageable as well as costly. Finally, we found that there do not appear to be economies of scale in educational provision beyond the size of smaller suburban districts, especially when small districts cooperate on the provision of audiovisual material, the purchasing of supplies, and vocational training. We may conclude from current educational research that a successful educational system is likely to be characterized by variety and choice as well as be small enough to be manageable.

Not all proposals for educational reform deal with all the problems at once, yet each problem is an important one. We will review major proposals for resolving educational problems, indicating which changes we feel are more likely to lead to resolution of the problems.

School District Consolidations School district consolidations have been proposed in metropolitan areas to achieve better racial balances and thus reduce involuntary segregation and to spread fiscal resources over a broader base. It is difficult to weigh the benefits from reducing segregation against the difficulties of articulating demand and obtaining responsive programs in larger districts composed of more heterogeneous populations. We certainly do not want to create more big-city school systems, with their excessively high costs for administration and their poor responsiveness to the changing preferences and needs of their student populations. Of all the issues, the greatest conflict occurs between integrating heterogeneous populations and the ability to provide public services to meet the preferences of citizens more effectively. There has been no real solution to the problem of segregation and public goods provision in other areas of the public economy, and we see no easy answer through the consolidation of school districts. As with other public goods and services, it may actually be more difficult for a minority group to get responsiveness from a large system than from a smaller system in which it is a majority. It may well be that if minority students continue to be offered the sorts of educational programs that have traditionally been oriented toward the middle class, even in an integrated environment, minority preferences will not be met nor will their educational achievement be enhanced.

The consolidation of school districts would average their wealth out over larger areas.[44] An important question is whether we should attempt to achieve income redistribution within a few consolidated school districts or use the fiscal base of the entire state for equalizing purposes. We believe that it is more equitable and more efficient to tax higher-income individuals and businesses and provide subsidization of educational programs on a statewide basis, using statewide taxes and intergovernmental grants, than to try to achieve equalization by manipulating local government boundaries. Statewide programs can achieve equalization while still permitting relatively small groups of citizens to adjust educational provision in their district to meet their preferences. This is desirable because it becomes more difficult to adjust the provision of public goods to citizen preferences as the size of the jurisdictions increases.

Performance Contracting One of the major difficulties in larger educational bureaucracies is that teachers and administrators are reluctant to make the effort required to develop more effective programs. Incentives are needed to encourage such efforts, especially since the lack of incentives for adaptation to change appears to be one reason for the poor performance of big-city systems.

Performance contracting has been suggested to introduce direct

[44]Some analysts argue that state governments support consolidation at least partially because the merger of poor districts with wealthier ones usually leads to reduced total state aid for local school education. For example, when four elementary districts were merged in Richmond, California, total state aid declined and spreading expenditures out from the wealthiest district to the poorer three to replace state aid contributed to a district fiscal crisis while voters had been promised "economy and efficiency" due to consolidation. Rubin, *Busing and Backlash*, pp. 31–32.

incentives into the provision of education. Performance contracting is the letting of a contract whereby payment to the contractor is based on the achievement levels of students. The payment schedules rise with the levels of student achievement, and thus direct profit incentives for innovation and adaptation are introduced to the production of education.

There have been several experiments with performance contracting. There has also been a confused situation with regard to the objectives of the experiments, the performance being tested, and the results. One highly popularized contract was that of Gary, Indiana, with Behavioral Research Laboratory (BRL) of Palo Alto, California. Payment to BRL was based on the number of students exceeding median national norms after a three-year time period. The results of the experiment are very mixed and indicate little change in average performance levels within the school. At least one analyst has concluded that BRL did adopt a profit-maximizing strategy: they devoted little effort to high achievers who would exceed national average norms without additional instruction, and they devoted little effort to low achievers who simply could not be brought up to national norms in three years. Instead, they concentrated their efforts on the middle group, where students could be brought above national norms with additional effort. The results were predictable. The averages of high achievers fell, the averages of low achievers also fell, and the averages of the middle group rose. The increases in the middle group were sufficient to offset the losses by the other groups; hence the average, overall school scores remained the same. Other analysts have concluded that even evidence on the results of the profit-maximizing strategy is weak. In either case, it is clear that such contracts should be more carefully drafted.[45]

The Office of Economic Opportunity sponsored a series of performance contracting experiments across the United States. The results of the experiments are described as mixed, with some contractors providing higher achievement and others lower achievement than control groups over a one-year period. One has to be careful in interpreting the results of the OEO experiment as well as those of the Gary experiment, but for a different reason. Under the OEO experiments, contractors had to specify in advance a particular program of instruction to be followed. They then were to maintain that program through the school year. If program consistency had been maintained, the experiment would have been a test of educational techniques, not a test of performance contracting where the educators have a direct incentive

---

[45]George E. Peterson, "The Distributional Impact of Performance Contracting in Schools," Urban Institute Working Paper 1200-22, March 1972.

to modify their programs to improve their results. However, OEO did permit some program modification during the year. Thus the results are a mix of contractor response to direct incentives and of tests of different educational techniques. Hence these results are extremely difficult to interpret. At present we really have very little evidence on the introduction of performance contracting or other incentives to promote student achievement in school systems. Before we can really understand the potential for contracting or other incentive systems, more experimentation is needed.[46]

Performance contracting does not alter school system boundaries or financing. It is designed to assist with the improvement in performance and control of costs in existing situations. It also has no relationship per se to segregation or integration. Our best estimate of the potential for performance contracting is as a device to promote innovation and change within existing systems, with the more successful approaches being adopted by regular educators.

Decentralization, or Breaking Up Large Systems Most large cities have had proposals for either decentralization or breaking up of their large school systems. For example, the Bundy report recommended that New York City's system should be broken up into at least thirty smaller systems, and a legislative act to break up the Los Angeles City School System has been introduced into the California State Legislature twice.[47] The benefits expected from decentralization, or breaking up large systems, are increased responsiveness to citizen preferences and more effective cost control because of better manageability of the smaller bureaucracy. It is much easier to discuss the decentralization of large school systems than it is to achieve it. For example, in New York City, it is estimated that the United Federation of Teachers union spent between $250,000 to $500,000 campaigning against the New York decentralization proposal.[48] Teachers groups and professional educators realize that they have much more control over large systems than they could over smaller, more politically responsive systems. One should not anticipate that any organized group that benefits from holding a monopoly position is going to give

---

[46]Dennis R. Young, "Evaluating Organizational Change in Public Services," in Willis D. Hawley and David Rogers (eds.), *Improving the Quality of Urban Management* (Beverly Hills, Calif.: Sage Urban Affairs Annual Reviews, 1974), pp. 93–126.

[47]Zimet, *Decentralization and School Effectiveness*, p. 3. William Niskanen and Mickey Levy, "Suggested Changes in the California Code to Promote Responsive and Efficient Local Government," A Report to the Local Government Reform Task Force (Berkeley, Calif.: Graduate School of Public Policy, University of California, 1973), p. 69–70.

[48]Zimit, op. cit., p. 26.

up that position without a struggle. While a partial decentralization was implemented in the New York system, control over both budget and personnel were not decentralized. In fact, it appears that by creating an ambiguous line of authority between the community and the city board of education, the professional educators, especially the teachers, have been able to exercise even more authority to maintain their own preferred positions.[49]

When one examines local public education in big cities, he must ask why big city school systems should be decentralized rather than simply broken up. State governments already regulate teacher certification, provide curriculum requirements, and specify other aspects of local school system performance, and there is no evidence that the nonteaching administrators in big systems are better at designing curricula than are teachers or lower-level administrators in smaller districts. It would appear much more reasonable simply to break up large school systems instead of decentralizing them. The initial fiscal hardships for some districts could be dealt with by the state as it deals with other low-income or low-wealth districts in the state. Given no identification of economies of scale in large systems, one can only assume that a dual-decentralized administration is going to be more costly than independent smaller administrations, and there is considerable evidence to indicate that the smaller independent districts would certainly be more responsive and adaptive to the needs of their citizens than are present big-city school systems. It may be that only by providing education in big cities by a variety of smaller districts, as is done in the suburbs, can big city education be improved.

Unless all programs in all districts were uniform, one problem that would have to be dealt with in a system of smaller districts within big cities would be segregation and student choice. One way of promoting both integration and flexibility with regard to program selection would be to permit interdistrict transfers with only the consent of the district and school the student wants to go to. At the same time the state would direct state aid associated with that student to the district he actually attends, and the district a student leaves could be required to provide a payment equal to its average local tax collections for one student. This kind of flexibility would expand the range of choices for students and could even permit small districts to provide specialized programs that would attract students from other districts as well as from their own.[50]

---

[49]Ibid., pp. 146–162.
[50]This is a major recommendation of the Niskanen-Levy proposal for the California Local Government Reform Task Force. Niskanen and Levy, op. cit., pp. 87–92.

Voucher Systems   Voucher systems are systems where each student is issued a voucher that can be used to "pay" his tuition at any school of his choice, public or private.[51] Vouchers would be paid for by taxation of local and state funds and could either be for a fixed amount for all students, or they might provide for higher amounts for students with special educational problems or requiring compensatory education. The key feature of the voucher system is that it permits students and parents free choice of schools based on whatever criteria they prefer to use as the basis for their choice. This free choice eliminates the monopoly position of local public schools, and schools have to provide attractive programs if they are to obtain sufficient student enrollment to remain in operation.

The expectation with voucher systems is (1) that public schools would have to decentralize much of their decision making to the individual school level to be responsive to student preferences and (2) that new private schools would probably spring up to compete with public schools. The need to attract students should also generate many more different and innovative programs and perhaps, through student-parent selection of a program which they feel meets the student's needs, higher levels of achievement will be reached. The schools would also be subject to cost control competition in that the more efficient the program, the more it can offer students for the fixed amount of the voucher. Schools where costs increased more rapidly would face the potential of losing students and going out of business.

Voucher systems have a potential for relating financing to student needs more closely than functional grants can be related to school districts. The local school district could determine the amount it wished to raise locally—an amount to be divided equally among all students. State government could make equalizing contributions on a district basis or move to a specific compensatory aid program for disadvantaged students. The federal government could also adjust compensatory aid programs such as Title I to go directly to disadvantaged students, who in turn could pick schools with programs to meet their special needs. These would be funded by the higher-valued low-income-student vouchers.

Voucher experiments, like performance contracting, have been

[51]Vouchers were first proposed by Milton Friedman in "The Role of Government in Education," in Robert A. Solow (ed.), *Economics and the Public Interest* (New Brunswick, N.J.: Rutgers, 1955). A comprehensive analysis is contained in *Educational Vouchers: A Report on Financing Elementary Education by Grants to Parents* (Cambridge, Mass.: Center for the Study of Public Policy, 1970), The U.S. Supreme Court appears to have ruled that vouchers cannot be used for religious schools in *Committee for Public Education and Religious Liberty v. Nyquist*, 37 L. Ed. 2d (1973).

resisted strongly by school professionals, especially teachers.[52] The Office of Economic Opportunity funded six preliminary proposals for voucher experiments, but only one survived the political environment to implementation. The voucher experiment that is in progress is in Alum Rock School District, near San Jose, California. The Alum Rock experiment began in 1971–1972 and will not be formally evaluated until after the 1974–1975 school year. Some results of the experiment thus far have been made available, and it looks very interesting.[53]

During the first year, six elementary schools, all public, participated in the program. Within the six schools, twenty-two separate minischool programs were developed, ranging from traditional to teaching all subjects in the context of space exploration, the future, or ecology. Parental response the first year was cautious. While 50 percent of the parents selected a special program for their children, only 3 percent sent their children to a school outside their neighborhood. Early indications of satisfaction with the program are that absenteeism and school vandalism declined.

Beginning in 1973–1974, seven new schools with an additional twenty-three minischool programs were added to the experiment. Parental interest was much higher than during the first year. Over 70 percent of the parents registered their children before the summer deadline and 40 percent of the parents with two or more children picked different programs for them. Twenty-five percent of the children are also attending schools outside their neighborhood. While we must wait for a formal evaluation of the results, interest on the part of public school administrators and teachers in the Alum Rock system has been very high. They have demonstrated that teachers can be creative in designing programs if incentives and decentralized decision making on curriculum and program design are permitted by school administrators. Their attitudes have certainly differed from those of teachers and administrators in the larger city systems, who have resisted experiments in both decentralization and vouchers.

Voucher systems do not deal directly with integration, but designers of voucher experiments have recommended that participating schools be required to accept minority students, at least in proportion to the students of each race applying for that school. This would permit some flexibility on the part of schools but also prevent them from discriminating on the basis of race. By breaking the local school monopoly

[52]Ed Willingham, "Education Report/OEO Goes Ahead with Voucher Plans Despite Opposition from Teachers Groups," *National Journal* (May 1, 1971), pp. 939–946.
[53]Jack McCurdy, "School Voucher: Disputed Idea Proves Itself," *Los Angeles Times*, July 5, 1972, part 1, p. 1.

position, it would be possible to get integrated schools in segregated neighborhoods or segregated schools in integrated neighborhoods. It would not be surprising if many blacks, for example, preferred schools which stressed black history and culture and if Chicanos preferred schools which offered bilingual instruction programs instead of placing students from Spanish-speaking homes in remedial programs because of their initial difficulty with English. Vouchers permit choice while reducing involuntary barriers to segregation. Their use cannot assure integration, but they can offer opportunities for integration for those minority students who prefer it.

SUMMARY

It is very likely that the poor performance of big-city schools has contributed to suburbanization, especially for families who can afford to move if they are not satisfied with city services but who are not wealthy enough to afford private schools. The implication of this observation is that central-city school systems may have to be improved if the cities are to become desirable residential locations for such families.

The major problem in big-city systems does not appear to be a lack of funds. Big cities have higher-than-average wealth levels, and even though their wealth levels may not increase rapidly enough to keep up with their increasing costs, there is little evidence that higher expenditures would result in higher student performance. The solution to big-city educational problems appears to be more closely related to their large size, which results in both nonresponsiveness to demands by citizens for educational programs to meet heterogeneous preferences and unmanageability of large bureaucracies. Decentralization may help resolve some problems, but simply breaking up large systems may be a superior alternative.

Even more important, however, may be relatively easy transfer policies among schools and districts or even free-choice voucher systems. The dense areas of many large cities contain heterogeneous populations within small geographic areas; to really meet diverse preferences, it may be necessary to break the traditional monopoly provision of public education by a single school for each designated area. It may be only by providing a relatively wide range of choices that higher-income families can be attracted back to the central city. If students and parents are given a chance to make choices, schools should also be encouraged to innovate and to adapt to the needs of different students. That is, they will be much more responsive than schools with legal monopolies over their attendance areas have been.

With regard to school finance, we must remain skeptical of the potential impact of equalization through the manipulation of property tax rates. When it was first announced, the *Serrano* decision sounded as if it would make a major difference in the provision of education and perhaps in spatial patterns within urban areas because differences in educational provision in different areas might be reduced. After examining the implications of proposals for equalization more closely, however, we must conclude that the major impacts are likely to be short-run capital gains and losses for property owners at the time the change is implemented and that long-run consequences will be nil. If equalization or compensatory education is to be achieved, it must be related to the incomes of citizens, not the wealth of school districts, and taxes for redistribution will have to be raised from broad-based sources such as income or sales taxes rather than the property tax, which is so easily capitalized into property values.

There are not many reasons to be optimistic about the future of big-city school systems. Educators appear to be concentrating on programs such as property tax manipulation, which are unlikely to make any difference in the education that children get, while at the same time they oppose experiments which have the potential for introducing wider student choice and reducing the monopoly position of educators in the system. If improvements are made in public education in the near future, the stimulus will have to come from outside the educational system. Education is much too important to be left to educators. They, like others, are looking out for their own self-interest, and it is necessary to organize school districts so that the interests of teachers and administrators coincide with the preferences of citizens, students, and taxpayers much more closely than they presently do.

SELECTED READINGS

Averch, Harvey A., et al.: *How Effective Is Schooling? A Critical Review and Synthesis of Research Findings*, Prepared for the President's Commission on School Finance (Santa Monica, Calif.: The Rand Corporation, 1972).

Harvard Educational Review: *Equal Educational Opportunity* (Cambridge, Mass.: Harvard, 1969).

Reischauer, Robert D., and Robert W. Hartman: *Reforming School Finance* (Washington, D.C.: Brookings, 1973).

Schoettle, Ferdinand P.: "Judicial Requirements for School Finance and Property Tax Redesign: The Rapidly Evolving Case Law," *National Tax Journal*, 25 (September 1972), pp. 455–472.

U.S. Department of Health, Education and Welfare: *Equality of Educational Opportunity* (Washington, D.C.: Government Printing Office, 1969), also called the Coleman report.

Zimet, Melvin: *Decentralization and School Effectiveness* (New York: Teachers College, 1973).

CHAPTER

THE URBAN ENVIRONMENT

In this chapter we will develop more fully than we did in Chapter 5 the way that pollution of the environment is a neighborhood effect or external diseconomy caused by the increased density of population in urban areas. Disposal of wastes will cause people to incur costs in cities either through pollution or through increases in costs as alternative waste disposal methods are discovered. Previously we showed that as long as there were clear property rights and bargaining costs were low, private bargains would solve questions of neighborhood effects. But air and water rights are unclear. They are really common pool resources in which no one has clear rights, so that they are overused. Furthermore, the external diseconomies of air and water pollution are a function of the number of people affected and so are an aspect of congestion. Thus the worst problems are in large cities, but this also means that the costs of bargaining and of gaining the necessary information are high. Therefore public solutions have to be found to resolve the conflicts. In this chapter we will explore some alternative public policies to reduce pollution of the urban environment.

POLLUTION AS AN URBAN PROBLEM

Newspaper discussions of current affairs often lack historical perspective, and their discussions of the current problems of air and water pollution are no exception. Although it is true that there are current global problems in the way our environment is being changed by economic progress, cities have always had problems with water and air pollution. Global problems, such as the balance of carbon dioxide, the particulate content of the stratosphere, the level of carbon monoxide, spillage of oil on the high seas, the changing chemical content of products that are difficult to recycle, and the use of pesticides will not be analyzed in this chapter.[1] We will concentrate on pollution within urban areas, a problem resulting from the density of land use.

In the early colonial cities of the United States there were major problems with the location of slaughtering operations, tanneries, and the disposal of waste which were all related to the quality of the air and water for the citizens of these communities. During those times, however, citizens were more concerned about water supply to fight fires than for drinking. Breweries were developed early. Brewery beverages may have been preferred to water, or people may have so distrusted the quality of water that they demanded these beverages. Nonetheless, people did show concern for drainage problems related to health and the quality of the air. In Boston and New York City in the 1600s, laws were passed to regulate the location and activities of tanneries and butchers because of the stench of their operations. Regulations also had to be promulgated to keep butchers from throwing entrails from animals into the streets. Streets were dirty and garbage was thrown from houses into the street. Regulations had to be established to have garbage buried. People had to be prohibited from building privies on the street, to improve the air and walking conditions on public streets. Obviously, urban environmental problems are not new in the United States.[2]

Other cities, such as London, had similar problems. Spanish explorers also noted the way smoke from Indian fires was trapped in

[1]On these issues see Clifford S. Russell and Hans H. Landsberg, "International Environmental Problems—A Taxonomy," *Science* (June 25, 1971), pp. 1307–1314; and Barry Commoner, "The Environmental Costs of Economic Growth," paper presented to Resources for the Future Forum, Washington, D.C., April 20, 1971; both reprinted in Robert Dorfman and Nancy S. Dorfman, *Economics of the Environment* (New York: Norton, 1972).

[2]Carl Bridenbaugh, *Cities in the Wilderness* (New York: Knopf, 1960), pp. 61–63, 85–86, 238–239, and 373–374; and Carl Bridenbaugh, *Cities in Revolt* (New York: Knopf, 1955), p. 128.

the Los Angeles basin; drinking water in Rome was becoming polluted before the first century B.C.[3]

EXTERNAL DISECONOMIES—NEIGHBORHOOD EFFECTS[4]

Economic goods are goods that have value because of their scarcity. To contrast economic goods with free goods, economists often describe the air we breathe as a free good because it is, under normal circumstances, very abundant. The demand for it does not exceed the supply. It is usually so abundant that rationing a restricted supply among demanders is not required. Nonetheless, air is a resource to every user of an automobile, to factories, or to other waste disposers as well as to humans, animals, and plants. If there is only one factory in a community or if there are only a few automobiles, carbon monoxide and other matter can be diffused into the air and only persons nearby will be affected.

In the same way water has been used by economists to show that the price of an economic good is not dependent on its intrinsic worth to life but on the supply relative to demand at the margin. In usual circumstances, water is so abundant that an additional gallon of clean drinking water is low in price. Indeed in some rural areas drinking water may be a free good.

People and jobs, however, tend to concentrate in large central places. As they do, each person's use of the air and land as a resource for waste disposal begins to interfere with their use by others. This interference is an external diseconomy, a neighborhood effect. The effluent of autos and factories causes increased costs of operations to many people and to other factories because it increases the cost of building and housecleaning and maintenance and because it causes illness, which means that workers are absent from work temporarily or permanently. Sewage enters streams and lakes, causing increased costs of treating water for drinking, causing fish kills, and possibly making the water unusable for recreation, swimming, and boating. Some of these costs of waste disposal may also be incurred by the waste disposer, but the cost the disposer incurs is small relative to the costs to others. Otherwise, the waste disposer would find ways to avoid polluting the air or water.

---

[3]Larry Ruff, "The Economic Common Sense of Pollution," *The Public Interest* (Spring 1970), p. 70.
[4]At this point the reader would benefit from rereading the sections on neighborhood effects and common pool resources in Chap. 5.

If the disposer incurred the external costs that his effluent imposed on others, he would attempt to avoid that cost. He might utilize a device that would remove obnoxious materials from his waste. He might reduce his production. On the other hand, if the actual group of people and businesses incurring the costs caused by the disposer were localized or were small, they could go to court and obtain redress by causing the waste disposer to pay damages and perhaps by obtaining injunctions against further damages. As noted in Chapter 5, optimal levels of activity could be achieved by causing the disposer to internalize these external social costs. Optimal levels of activity could also be obtained if the damaged parties paid a bribe to the polluter in an amount not exceeding the damages incurred. Redress through the courts or in private by either of these methods is often impossible because the cost of determining the damages to many persons and firms or of organizing the injured parties, or both, is excessive. Thus the courts and the private market economy have been unable to prevent these external social costs.

Economists have argued that the way to control pollution appropriately is to have the government do what the private market would have done if it could. This would mean taxing or bribing the polluters an amount equal to the value of damages that they cause. The revenues of the tax should be directed to the damaged parties, or a nonoptimal allocation may occur.[5] By making the benefit-cost framework of the economic analysis more explicit, we can see why the economist might argue that this would be an optimal way to handle the problem.[6]

In Figure 11-1, levels of pollution from one particular source are measured along the horizontal axis. It is better to measure the level of effluent rather than the level of production associated with it because they may not necessarily be directly related. There may be ways of achieving the same level of output with reduced pollution by undertaking different actions. For example, increasing the height of a smokestack, scrubbing air, or treating any effluent before discharge may reduce damage costs without reducing output. For the same reason, the charge should be on the effluent, not on the level of the associated pro-

---

[5]The nonoptimality can be seen by referring to Fig. 5-2. If the charge was ONA in order to achieve output OA but this tax was not returned to the damaged parties, it would be a reduction from the net marginal benefit curve and cause it to shift as a straight line from MB to MA. If the parties are still allowed to negotiate, a new optimum intersection of the external MC curve with the new net marginal benefit curve MA will intersect at an output less than OA. If the parties could negotiate, a less than optimum output would be achieved, but we are assuming that the costs of information and bargaining are so high that such negotiations could not take place.

[6]The analysis of the following graph is from Ronald Ridker, *Economic Costs of Air Pollution* (New York: Praeger, 1967), pp. 1–11.

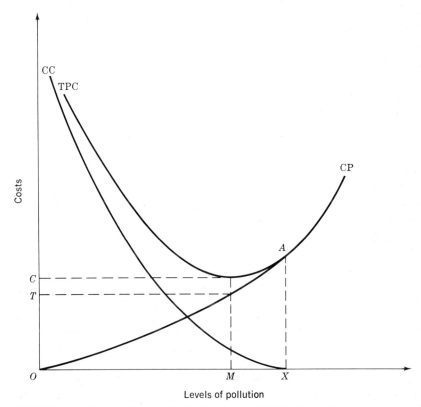

FIGURE 11-1   Control Costs, Pollution Costs, and Total Pollution Costs

duction. As we shall see, one of the costs of controlling pollution may be reducing production, but it may not be the only way.

There are many measures of the level of contaminants in the air or water: dustfall, sulfur dioxide per square milimeter, dissolved oxygen, floating solids, coliform bacteria, water temperature, etc. Assume for the moment that we could measure some levels of pollution on a cardinal scale. As the levels of pollution increased, we would expect the external diseconomies (social costs) to increase also. In the case of air pollution, these would include increased maintenance costs, absenteeism from work, shorter working lives, moves to new locations, installation of air conditioning to avoid illness, and psychic costs. The level and combination of costs, of course, would depend on the particular pollutant. The line CP in Figure 11-1 depicts a possible graph of these costs of pollution. If the current level of pollution were X without any attempts at control, XA would be the social costs to the economy.

If individuals and businesses would install devices to reduce the levels of pollution, if they would spend money in other ways so that levels of pollution would be reduced, or if they reduced production if no other alternatives were available, we would have a schedule of the opportunity costs of controlling pollution. In Figure 11-1, the line CC graphs such a schedule. The assumption underlying the line CC is that small changes in pollution levels may cost small amounts, but that these incremental costs will rise.

The sum of the costs of control and the costs of pollution are the total pollution costs, or we might think of them as the total waste-disposal costs of the effluent. TPC in Figure 11-1 depicts this total pollution cost. From the point of view of the community, the optimal level of pollution is that level at which total pollution and control costs are a minimum. In our particular illustration, this is OM. It is important to note that in one way or another the cost of waste disposal must be paid. It may be paid as an external social cost or as an explicit cost of production to control the waste. In the latter case, the cost would be passed on to the consumer in the prices of goods.

For this level of pollution to be an optimum both today and for the future, all costs should be estimated as the present value of expected costs into the future. One of the toughest problems, which economists often neglect, is that continuous low levels of pollution for many years may eventually cause a serious change in the environment with much higher costs each year than would at first appear. If we knew these effects, they would have to be included in the costs through present value estimates.

As indicated, the minimum level of total pollution and control costs is the economic optimum. As long as the cost curves behave in a smooth and regular fashion, the optimum can also be described as that level of pollution at which the change in control costs to reduce pollution levels an increment are just equal to the damage costs saved by that reduction. Thus it pays to reduce the levels of pollution as long as the increment of damage costs saved (marginal social benefits) are greater than the increment of control costs (marginal costs of control).

If a government were to try to achieve the optimum, that is, if it were to know that it had achieved such a level, a good deal of information would be required, no matter how it went about achieving the goal. For example, each auto dumps a certain amount of carbon monoxide into the air. This causes a certain incremental change in air quality, which would then need to be linked to damages throughout the surrounding area. It would then be necessary to identify the increased incidence of disease and death, increased cleaning and maintenance costs, increased use of air conditioning, and other costs caused by the specific source of pollution.

INFORMATION AND MEASUREMENT PROBLEMS

Economists often suggest market solutions to problems because the information costs are less. Decentralized decision making only requires each firm or household to know the data that it requires for its own decision rather than the myriad of demands and costs that a central planning agency would need to achieve the appropriate price and quantity in each market. The problem of pollution is difficult because we cannot use such decentralized decision making. Individuals suffering damages from water or air pollution do not know who caused the damage. Nonetheless, if the sum of all such damages were known, it would be apparent whether damages involved greater costs than the costs of control. The individuals and firms know the costs of control but do not know the sum of damage costs and do not have any incentive to learn. The purpose of this section is to indicate the difficulties of actually measuring the costs described in Figure 11-1.

Direct Measure of Damages

There is strong evidence that the increased incidence of respiratory and cardiovascular diseases is linked to greater air pollution.[7] The incidence of these diseases also depends upon weather conditions, smoking habits, socioeconomic class, and occupation, but the evidence is clear that the quality of air is a significant factor. The cost of the increased incidence of disease and premature death can be estimated by calculating the cost of medicine and doctors as well as the present value of the foregone earnings from days of work lost. Lave and Seskind estimate in this way that "4.5 percent of all economic costs associated with morbidity and mortality would be saved by a 50 percent reduction in air pollution in major urban areas."

This is only a measure of the health costs of air pollution in cities, but it does indicate that we can make some estimates. Another economic cost of air pollution would be increased maintenance costs from soiling and wear and tear on exposed equipment and buildings. One attempt to estimate costs associated with these aspects of pollution, however, showed that most buildings were on a regular maintenance schedule, such as having all windows washed once a month, so that soiling in areas with different levels of pollution had no impact on fre-

---

[7]Ibid., 30–34; and Lester B. Lave and Eugene P. Seskin, "Air Pollution and Human Health," *Science* (August 21, 1970), pp. 723–733, reprinted in Dorfman and Dorfman, op. cit., pp. 356–383.

quency of cleaning or on cleaning costs. Buildings just became dirtier.[8]
These estimates would measure only part of the costs of pollution. There is still the psychic cost of living in a polluted environment. An alternative way to directly measure the damages would be to ask people through personal interviews what they would be willing to pay to avoid living in an environment with polluted air. They would indicate not only the expenses from increased sickness but would perhaps also put a value on the psychic damages. The main difficulty with such an approach is that there may be biases to consumers' responses. It is the same difficulty as that which obtains with all public goods that are collectively consumed. If the air would be cleaned up because other people were willing to pay to have it done, then the consumer could be a free rider, enjoy the clean air, and perhaps not have to pay for it. Thus each consumer has an incentive not to reveal to public authorities how much the clean air is worth to him for fear that he might have to pay that amount. His strategy is to get others to pay for it. Interview data would then tend to be an underestimate if the person thought he would be charged his value. On the other hand, it could be an overestimate if it were clear that the cost of the cleaner air would be borne by someone else, for then the consumer would have an incentive to prove how much more cleaner air he ought to have. Thus interview data showing how much people would be willing to pay for an improved environment must be used cautiously.

Water pollution damages can be estimated more directly if we are considering downstream pollution. Lake pollution would be more like air pollution, since the polluters would be hurting themselves as well as others, and it might be as difficult to identify the source of some of the pollutants as they interact in complex ways depending on the temperature. The loss of fish for commercial use could be valued at the market price of the fish less opportunity costs to indicate the loss of production caused by pollution. The increased cost of purifying water for drinking could also be attributed to the pollution. The value of the recreational benefits of water areas, however, would be more difficult to estimate. How do you measure the value of the loss of fish for recreational fishing, the value of swimming or boating pleasure as a leisure activity? One way, of course, would be to return to the questionnaire method and ask people what it would be worth to them to clean up some particular recreational area. Such a questionnaire, however, would run into the same potential biases as we have indicated could occur in judging the impact of cleaner air.

Interview methods have been used in several situations. Ridker estimated soiling damages in this way without very good results, since

[8]Ridker, op. cit., pp. 57–89.

the data did not reveal much about soiling costs from air pollution.[9] Davis, however, used the method to estimate the recreation value of the Maine woods.[10] He was apparently able to make reliable estimates of value. This can be said because he checked the information by making an alternative estimate of the value of the recreation area. The use of an alternative estimate is a technique commonly used to measure such benefits. He obtained data on the number of trips to the area people made from different distances. The value of the recreation would be reflected in the travel costs that people would be willing to pay to make the trips. The farther away people live, the fewer trips they would make because of the increased travel costs. By putting a dollar value on each mile distance from the recreation area, a demand curve could be developed showing how many trips would be made at various prices. By valuing the actual trips made by families and individuals, a valuation could be made of the benefits of the recreation area. A similar method could be used for valuing swimming, boating, and fishing areas along waterways.

Thus one can see that information on damage costs from air and water pollution could be estimated directly, but it does cost money to obtain these estimates. Information is not costless. One way to get around this has been to see if land values might reflect pollution damages.

Property Value as a Measure of Damages

As we pointed out in Chapter 4, most land is built upon, especially in urban areas in which we would be trying to measure the impact of damages. Thus we would have to look at differences in property values. We have already shown that property values reflect the merits expected of a particular site given the amenities, size of building, and particular public goods associated with it. Thus, we would expect, given two properties with similar characteristics except that one was situated downwind from a particular type of pollution, that the property values would reflect differences in the quality of the environment. Nevertheless, we might expect from our discussion on interdependence of demand and on zoning that overall land values would be a poor estimate of damages.

The theory can be outlined best by adapting a model developed

[9]Ibid.
[10]Jack L. Knetsch and Robert K. Davis, "Comparisons of Methods for Recreation Evaluation," in Allen V. Kneese and Stephen C. Smith, *Water Research* (Baltimore: Johns Hopkins, 1966); reprinted in Dorfman and Dorfman op. cit., pp. 384–402.

TABLE 11-1 Housing Demand Matrix

Household Income	House Quality					
	A	B	C	C'	D	E
1	L	+5	+10	+5	+15	+20
2	+10	**+16**	+22	+16	+28	+34
3	+20	+27	**+34**	+27	+41	+48
4	+30	+38	+46	+38	**+54**	+62
5	+40	+49	+58	+49	+67	**+76**

by Wallace F. Smith for another purpose.[11] Assume for the sake of isolating the relevant variables that all houses in a community are alike and that the only difference in amenities and public goods is the quality of the air. Array the houses of a community from A through E in Table 11-1 from the worst in quality to the best in quality, where quality represents degrees of fresh air. For the moment ignore column C'. These are the only five houses in the community. There are also five families or households of the same size that are to live in these houses. They earn different incomes. The households are numbered from 1 through 5. (One can also consider these five families as five homogeneous groups of families and the five houses as five homogeneous groups of houses, the groups being equal in size to each other.) The first family earns the lowest income, the second family earns more, and the fifth family earns the highest income. The lowest amount in rent that any family is willing to pay is L by household 1 for the lowest-quality house. For better-quality housing, household 1 will pay more. According to the hypothetical example, the household will be willing to pay $5 more for each increase in quality. The rent offer is a monthly rent figure that can be converted into a property-value figure by capitalizing the rent income at the market rate of interest.

Furthermore, as household income increases, the family is willing to pay more for the same quality house. This is illustrated by the column of offers for quality A house. Each increase in income brings out an offer of $10 more. To fill in the rest of the table with only the data in row 1 and column 1 would imply that household 2, with more income than household 1, would pay L + 16 for house B and would

[11]Wallace F. Smith, *Filtering and Neighborhood Change*, Research Report 24 of the Center for Real Estate and Urban Economics of the Institute of Urban and Regional Development at the University of California, Berkeley, Calif., 1964, pp. 17–33. This material is taken directly from Hugh O. Nourse, "The Effect of Air Pollution on House Values," *Land Economics* (May 1966), which has been reprinted in Hugh O. Nourse, *The Effect of Public Policy on Housing Markets* (Lexington, Mass.: Heath, 1973), pp. 63–74.

pay no more for the increase in quality than family 1. It would seem more realistic that quality would have some income elasticity and that family 2 would pay more for the increase in quality than family 1. Additional amounts that might be offered for increased quality at each level of family income are used to establish the offers that each family will make for each quality of house in Table 11-1.

The market solution to the allocation of the five houses among the five families is that family 5 is the highest bidder for the best house. Family 4 is the highest bidder for the next best house, etc. Thus the diagonal of the matrix in Table 11-1 shows the market value for each house. The market solution yields the highest total rent.[12]

When we observe the market, we see five houses, each with a property value as indicated by the diagonal of the above matrix. The observed differences in property value are directly related both to differences in the income of households and the differences in the quality of the air. For example, the difference in value between houses B and C is $L + 34$ less $L + 16$, or 18. Controlling for income, however, the improvement in air quality would be worth only 6 for income level 2 and 7 for income level 3. The difference of 18 also includes the $12 more that household 3 is willing to pay for house C because that household has a higher income. Thus the difference in property value between B and C overestimates the value of better-quality air for either family. Statistical analysis may not be able to separate these different relations unless there are many observations with similar income but different levels of pollution. Nevertheless, the households with high incomes live in neighborhoods devoid of pollution and their rents reflect it.

Another way to attack the problem would be to find a specific instance in which the air quality of a place within a city changed and then to observe the impact on property values. In the following illustration we will apply the matrix demand approach to a case in which the quality of one house changes.

Once again, assume that there are five families, 1 through 5, with increasing levels of income, and five houses, A through E, with increasing levels of fresh air quality. Furthermore, assume that the offers for houses are as shown in Table 11-1. For some reason, perhaps the location of a paint plant, the air quality of house C falls to that of house B. The demand matrix would then change so that the offers for house C were the same as those for house B, as indicated in column

---

[12]One might argue that the diagonal yields the maximum possible rents. In this example there is room for bargaining. The best house could be valued from $L + 63$ to $L + 76$ and still be occupied by household 5. If we think of the 661,000 families in the St. Louis metropolitan area arrayed by income, the differences between offers would be smaller.

C'. By comparing column C, the situation before the change in pollution, to column C', we find that house C would fall in value from $L + 34$ to $L + 27$ as a result of the reduction in its quality from the air pollution. This difference is a measure of the value attached to the air pollution.

Nevertheless, consider a case in which the change in pollution occurs simultaneously with an increase in households and houses. Add a house of the same quality as D—call it D'—and then add a family with income 2, calling it 2'. From the relationships previously postulated, we can once again construct a new demand matrix, Table 11-2.

The income distribution of the population has changed so that family 3 could move up and out of the polluted house, C, to a better house, D'. Family 4 stays in house D by offering $L + 54$; family 3 moves up to house D' by offering $L + 41$; and the two families at income level 2 offer the same for houses B and C since they have been reduced to the same quality by air pollution. The final result, comparing Table 11-2 to Table 11-1, is that the value of C falls from $L + 34$ to $L + 16$. This difference in the value of house C cannot be attributed entirely to the change in quality. Part of the reduction in value is a result of new housing that made it possible for the previous higher-income occupants of house C to move to better-quality housing. Thus one has to take account of the incomes of families in a neighborhood affected by air pollution before attributing the whole decline in price, if there is one, to air pollution.

The implication of this analysis for empirical studies of the economic impact of air pollution on house values is that only estimates of the price effect holding income constant catch the psychic and increased maintenance costs of air pollution. When income effects are introduced, statistical estimates of the impact of air pollution on property value may reflect changes in income distribution as well as in increased air pollution.

TABLE 11-2 Housing Demand Matrix with Migration and Construction—Rent Bids

| Household Income | House Quality | | | | | |
	A	B	C	D	D'	E
1	L	+5	+5	+15	+15	+20
2	+10	+16	+16	+28	+28	+34
2'	+10	+16	+16	+28	+28	+34
3	+20	+27	+27	+41	+41	+48
4	+30	+38	+38	+54	+54	+62
5	+40	+49	+49	+67	+67	+76

Finally, consider a case in which the air quality for each house is improved, so that pollution is no longer a differential between houses. Return to Table 11-1 for the demand matrix for houses in the community. Our initial reaction to considering the new situation with no air pollution is to reconstruct the demand matrix so that the bids on each house depend only on income. If air quality were that of house E after the change, then the matrix would be five columns identical to column E. The diagonal would be the same as each column and would represent the market prices. All houses except house E would increase in value. The increase would represent the improvement in air quality.

These increases would not necessarily occur, however, in the case of an entire metropolitan area. The reason is that the level of the prices would depend on population growth in the area. The differentials for income groups would continue to exist, but the price might not rise as much as indicated. The price would be just high enough to ensure new construction for increases in the number of households (should such growth exist). Once pollution is eliminated, the highest price, $L + 76$, might not be required to achieve that air quality and house. A lower price might be all that was necessary to build the house. Thus, although the relation between income and prices might remain the same, the whole set of prices might decline. In particular, if new construction were not required, there would be no need to have a price equivalent to the cost of new construction.

There is, however, an additional important problem. We have dealt with the problem as if the change in pollution came like manna from heaven. In the previous sections we have pointed out the costs of pollution control. The bids for better-quality air space in Table 11-1 indicate the maximum that individuals and families would pay for the improved quality. If they were required to pay that sum to prevent pollution, there would, in fact, be no change in property prices after pollution control—the reason being that if you were in property A you would be required to make higher bribes than if you were in house E. If payments to prevent pollution were less than the maximum that families were willing to pay, property prices might rise, but that increase would be subject to the constraint of building costs and growth as suggested in the previous paragraph. Thus aggregate property values are a poor indirect measure of the damages caused by pollution.

There have been several studies of the impact of pollution on property values. In one, Ridker made a cross-sectional study of property values and air pollution levels in the St. Louis metropolitan area in 1960.[13] He attempted to explain the difference between neighborhoods in the average property values of single-family dwellings by

[13]Ridker, op. cit., pp. 115–140.

using twelve independent variables. Since neighborhoods tend to be homogeneous with respect to income and other socioeconomic variables, idiosyncrasies of households and structures would tend to wash out using the neighborhood data. Neighborhoods were defined as census tracts because they were the most convenient to use and because it was assumed that they were sufficiently homogeneous with respect to the variables relevant for the study.

Controlling for such influences on property value as household income and accessibility, the study found that average values in each area were $245 less for every increase of 0.5 milligrams sulfur trioxide per 100 square centimeters per day. This estimate is a weighted average of the price difference offered for cleaner air by all families. For low income levels, the differential for cleaner air would be expected to be less; for high income levels, the differential for cleaner air would be expected to be higher. This dollar difference would therefore change with changes in income distribution, whether air pollution changed or not.

All in all, land or property values do not appear to be an easier way to indirectly estimate damages from air pollution than to make direct estimates.

COLLECTIVE ACTION

As we have noted in the last section, the costs of information about pollution costs are not zero. They must be added to the other direct costs of control. We have also indicated that market solutions to pollution questions were not possible because bargaining costs were too high. At this time it is convenient to spell this out in more detail and to develop the problems of collective action to achieve the optimal level of pollution.

Under what circumstances will such a group actually organize in their common interest and actually provide the public good? Figure 11-2, a slightly different version of the situation in Figure 11-1, will help to clarify the points under discussion. In Figure 11-2, the vertical axis is measured in dollars and measures the costs of controlling pollution and the damages from pollution. The horizontal axis measures the levels of pollution with all the qualifications that were previously stated. As we reduce pollution levels, we move to the left until we reach zero. OX is the level of pollution without controls.

The curve ACC is the cost of controlling pollution. We are making an additional assumption about the specification of the cost curve over those previously made. There is probably a discontinuity in the controlling of pollution so that the total costs of controlling pollution

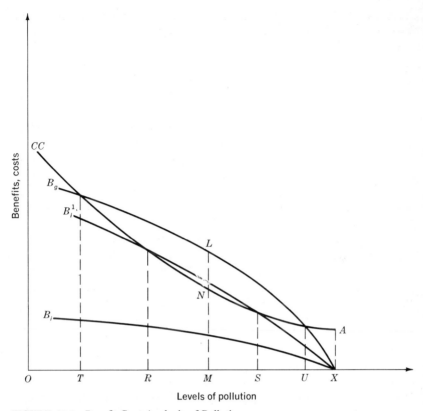

FIGURE 11-2   Benefit-Cost Analysis of Pollution

probably begin with some large costs no matter how little attempt is
made to reduce pollution levels. This may be attributable to the information search costs discussed in the last section. Thus ACC begins
with a fixed cost XA and rises continuously.

The curve XB_g needs more explanation. It represents the benefits of pollution control: the reduction in actual pollution damages as
pollution levels are reduced. It is derived from the CP line in Figure
11-1. Thus it measures the reduction of maintenance costs, air conditioning costs, psychic costs, etc., associated with lower levels of pollution. These are the valuable benefits to the group affected by pollution.

In terms of our previous discussion, the optimum level of pollution can be presented as the minimum total pollution and control costs.
In this diagram, it is represented as the level of pollution at which
benefits less costs are maximized. The two would result in the same

level of pollution. In Figure 11-1, the minimum occurs where the marginal increase in costs of pollution is just equal to the marginal decrease in costs of control. In Figure 11-2, the optimum occurs at that level of pollution at which the marginal benefit from control is just equal to the marginal costs of control at the last level of pollution, level OM.

Now, if at least one of the damaged members of the group were to obtain benefits from reduced pollution that were greater than the total costs of control from some level of pollution, action would be taken. For example, if XB_i^1 represented the benefits to one person in the affected group, it would pay him to bribe the polluter to reduce pollution to a level between R and S. This outcome is most likely to occur when the group is small, so that one person might suffer the most damages from pollution. An alternative open to the one individual, of course, would be to go to court and seek damages. The damages being greater than the costs of control, the polluter would seek to avoid damage payments in the future by controlling pollution. In any event, since one person gains enough to cover the costs of control from reducing pollution, action will voluntarily be taken. Such groups are called privileged groups. The name is appropriate because the other beneficiaries of reduced pollution get a free ride. They receive benefits without paying any of the costs.

If the group should be such that instead of one person receiving large benefits from pollution reduction, two or three persons receive benefits summing to XB_i^1, pollution control may or may not occur. The outcome is indeterminate. If the few could cooperate and agree on sharing the costs of a bribe or of court action, pollution would once again be reduced to the benefit of a number of free riders. This is an intermediate group. In neither the case of the privileged group nor the case of the intermediate group will the level of pollution achieved likely be the optimum.

The last case is that of the latent group. If the group should be very large so that the individual benefits that would be received, XB_i, would be a small proportion of the aggregate benefits to the whole group and so that neither one individual nor several would receive benefits large enough to be greater than total costs over any range of action, then the group is unlikely to get together and act. To each individual the costs of acting are greater than the benefits he would receive. If the group could organize in order to act together and could agree on the share of the costs for each, their benefits, XB_g, would be greater than costs over the levels of pollution, TU. Two factors would usually keep them from voluntarily cooperating for their common good. First, the costs would shift upward because of the costs of organizing into a formal group. Second, each person in the group would have an incentive to stay out of the formal organization. If they formally join the group, they must share in the costs of reducing the pollution, including the costs of organization. If they do not join the group, they will receive the benefits of the action of the group and will not have to share in any of the costs. Therefore it is unlikely that the group can get together voluntarily.

In the case of latent groups affected by pollution damages from specific and identifiable sources, several organizational responses have occurred. First, small homogeneous suburbs have been established in which all the members of the community have similar values toward such pollution sources and have agreed to zone such industrial land uses from their territory. The pros and cons of zoning have already been covered in Chapter 9. Nonetheless, families with income to afford these suburban communities and who have strong preferences against pollution would move to areas zoned exclusively residential.

Second, politicians in the community in which pollution occurred, in competing for leadership, may find the pollution issue of the latent group and be elected on the basis that they would do something about pollution. In a moment we will investigate the kinds of action that such politicians have undertaken.

Third, there is a serious boundary problem in many instances of pollution. In the case of water pollution, the downstream city suffering increased water purification costs may be in a different state from the city dumping the wastes that cause these costs. One of the important sources of urban air pollution has been carbon monoxide from automobile exhausts. Control of these emissions from mobile sources made for a national market requires jurisdiction over manufacturing and over cars that may enter a particular place. The air shed downwind from a particularly important air pollution source may be in a different jurisdiction than the source, so that even if a politician wanted to do something, action would be required at a higher level of government. In particular, since the group affected is likely to be a latent group, it is unlikely that a logical new jurisdiction for pollution control would be established by the affected group. Thus, politicians seeking to make issues of pollution activity that they can affect have been primarily those being elected at the federal level.

As we noted at the beginning of the chapter, very localized problems of pollution have been solved by local government since earliest times by the use of police power. Local governments have regulated emissions by some kind of smoke control ordinance, by determining the kind of coal that could be used for generating heat or power, and by other direct regulations of emissions. They have excluded some activities from any site within the city, as they did with tanneries. They have used zoning ordinances to control the sites where sources of pollution could locate. In the 1950s, California had some control of automobile emissions, which was tightened in 1960.[14]

Although the first federal legislation to control pollution was the Refuse Act of 1899, it was really only recently rediscovered. That act prohibits the dumping of "any refuse matter of any kind or description whatever" into any waters without a permit from the U.S. Corps of Engineers. The courts and the Department of Justice, however, became so busy with cases that they had to find a way to reduce the workload. The Justice Department decided not to bring charges against firms holding a permit issued by a state or local government. This has led to a backlog of permit applications and selective nonenforcement of the 1899 Refuse Act.[15]

The Water Pollution Control Act of 1956 authorized the federal government to provide technical and financial assistance for communities to construct waste treatment plants. There were also provisions for data collection, analysis, planning, and research. The most important provision, however, was that the federal government was empowered to regulate such discharges into water resources as would lead to interstate pollution. A revision of the act in 1965 urged states to establish water quality standards for water resources within their jurisdictions. If states did not set standards acceptable to the federal government, then the federal government was empowered to do so. These standards allow government to pursue the pollution dischargers in court without having to prove that damages have been caused thereby.[16]

One evaluation of the subsidy for municipal sewage treatment plants found that in spite of $5.4 billion spent on such plants over a twelve-year period, the rivers were more polluted than before. Part of the problem was that the subsidy was for construction and not for operation of the plants. A review of the facilities found that over half of the plants were treating sewage inadequately because of efforts to economize on operating costs. Furthermore, the states did not

[14]Harold W. Kennedy and Martin E. Weekes, "Control of Automobile Emissions —California Experience and the Federal Legislation," *Law and Contemporary Problems*, 33 (Spring 1968), pp. 297–314. Lawrence W. Pollack, "Legal Boundaries of Air Pollution Control—State and Local Legislative Purpose and Techniques," *Law and Contemporary Problems*, 33 (Spring 1968), pp. 331–357.

[15]A. Myrick Freeman III, Robert H. Haveman, and Allen V. Kneese, *The Economics of Environmental Policy* (New York: Wiley, 1973), pp. 120–121.

[16]This summary is taken from that of Edwin S. Mills, *Urban Economics* (Glenview, Ill.: Scott, Foresman, 1972), pp. 260–262; and Freeman et al., op. cit., pp. 115–118.

target assistance for those places with the most harmful discharges.[17]

Legislation at the federal level for air pollution control was patterned after the water pollution control act. Federal support for research, data collection, and technical assistance to improve air quality was passed in 1955. In 1963 Congress passed the Clean Air Act. As amended in 1965 and 1967, the act authorized the federal government to collect data, conduct analysis and research, and provide grants and technical assistance to state and local governments, which were encouraged to establish air quality standards. But enforcement by the federal government was limited and reliance was placed primarily on voluntary cooperation. Federal intervention was authorized if there should be imminent danger to public health. Emission standards for motor vehicles, however, are established by the federal government. Some states, such as California, maintain higher standards.[18]

The 1970 Clean Air Amendments have set deadlines for the delineation of air quality regions, for setting air quality standards by the states, and for preparing implementation plans for achieving these standards. Enforcement of the new standards is to be stiffened over the previous state-by-state enforcement by the establishment of national emission standards to be applied to new stationary sources of air pollution. National standards for automobile emissions were also established. Furthermore, in case of emergency, all polluting activities may be banned. More recently, the federal government has ordered states to submit plans for regulating construction or modifying traffic-generating projects such as shopping centers, sports complexes, recreation areas, and other developments in order to support the national air quality standards. Here is the beginning of national control of land use.[19]

The resulting mix of state, local, and federal pollution standards has not been established by the careful estimating of damage and control costs but by pressures from business and consumers for particular standards. Public health damages, since they have a long tradition, have been the most important source of emission or discharge stand-

[17]Comptroller General of the United States, *Examination into the Effectiveness of the Construction Program for Abating, Controlling, and Preventing Pollution* (Washington, D.C.: Government Printing Office, November 3, 1969); and Comptroller General of the United States, *Need for Improved Operation and Maintenance of Municipal Waste Treatment Plants* (Washington, D.C.: Government Printing Office, 1970). Both cited and the analysis extended in Freeman et al., op. cit., pp. 118–120.

[18]Mills, loc. cit., Freeman et al., op. cit., pp. 130–131; and Robert Martin and Lloyd Symington, "A Guide to the Air Quality Act of 1967," *Law and Contemporary Problems*, 33 (Spring 1968), pp. 239–274.

[19]Freeman et al., op. cit., pp. 130–132; and Heinz Kohler, *Economics and Urban Problems* (Lexington, Mass.: Heath, 1973), pp. 358–360.

ards. There have been no studies as far as we know to evaluate whether these standards are too strict or too lenient. The development of this legislation is strikingly parallel to that for regulating building code standards and zoning. Regulations to establish standards in all these cases have been set up, but there has been no attempt to determine the appropriate standards through cost calculations. Furthermore, there has been little research testing and evaluating whether the standards, once established, were appropriate. It is surely true that the costs of becoming appropriately informed are extremely high. But there are not even many partial studies that attempt to evaluate alternative standards.

The standards, just like those for zoning and building codes, are not voted directly by popular vote but are written by vote of representative legislatures. The legislator represents his district on many issues. Specific pollution controls of some kind may keep votes, but other issues in a particular election may be more important. The voter must choose the best mix of votes by a legislator. Thus the voter may give up his own view on pollution standards in order to achieve something else. As was pointed out in Chapter 5, we are willing to do this to avoid high political decision costs.

Since regulation does not require the voter to pay any direct cost other than the administration cost (he is not required to bribe the polluter), he is more likely to vote for stricter regulations and standards than he would be if he had to pay a bribe. And, the costs of controlling pollution by treating emissions into the air or discharges into the water will become part of the cost of goods and services requiring these emissions in production. For example, the emission control devices on cars that have been required by federal regulation have increased the cost of automobiles. They have also reduced the fuel efficiency of modern cars, so that newer cars achieve fewer miles per gallon than older cars without emission control equipment. This means that waste disposal costs are being brought directly into the market price. That is a good thing, since consumers can evaluate costs of alternative goods and services on the basis of their true resource costs. Nonetheless, these costs could be higher than necessary if standards are set too high.

Besides the problems already stated, the setting of uniform standards has another drawback. By requiring each waste disposer to meet the same emission or discharge standard, the regulator is not controlling for the different costs of achieving these standards. Some producers may be able to achieve these standards with very low costs, while for others it may require very high costs. If costs were compared to damages, it might be possible to achieve the same overall air quality at lower cost by setting different regulations for each producer. The polluters who can achieve high standards easily would have more strict controls than those polluters for whom the control of emissions would cost more.

Impact of Regulation on the Poor

The poor probably do not set as high a value on freedom from pollution as do higher-income families. Therefore poor consumers might prefer to suffer waste disposal problems through damages rather than enjoy freedom from pollution at the price of more expensive goods. Some goods might be priced beyond the reach of poorer consumers, as in the case of strict building code standards.

To enforce emission standards on every car may be impossible, just as in the case of housing. If the community wants stiff emission standards, it may be required to subsidize the poor so that they can afford the appropriate equipment. If it does not, the poor may avoid these standards by using older cars, but in so doing, the standards that the community establishes will be undermined, since these cars will not have the appropriate equipment. An alternative would be to subsidize mass transit systems, so that everyone would not have to have a car to obtain a job or shop in the city. We will return to this problem in the next chapter. Thus, it is likely that any direct referendum on pollution standards would be split among income classes in the same way as it was for zoning.

POLICY ALTERNATIVES

The usual response by economists to federal pollution policies has been that standards do not represent the right approach to resolving pollution problems. If information is to be gathered properly, its cost would make control by regulation much more expensive than other alternatives, especially effluent charges. When regulation is not properly established, that is, when standards are not established so that the marginal damage costs are equal to the marginal costs of control, they are inefficient. The almost uniform recommendation is to establish charges for polluting that are equal to the damages incurred by the groups affected.[20]

It is important to realize that the effluent charge should be equal to the damages caused at the optimum level of pollution. Then, if

---

[20]Allen V. Kneese and Blair T. Bower, *Managing Water Quality: Economics, Technology, Institutions* (Baltimore: Johns Hopkins, 1968); Larry E. Ruff, "The Economic Common Sense of Pollution," *The Public Interest* (Spring 1970), pp. 69–85.

the costs of controlling pollution were greater than damage costs incurred, the firm or polluter could pay the fine. If the damage costs, however, were greater than the costs of controlling pollution, the polluter would avoid pollution by treating his wastes. Decisions would be decentralized. Each waste disposer would make the appropriate decision on the basis of his own costs of control compared to the damages that he would cause if he should pollute. If the effluent charge were set at the appropriate rate, the optimum air quality would be achieved.

Unfortunately, the damage costs of pollution are the hardest costs to determine. It is easier to determine the costs of control. So many of the costs of environmental pollution are intangible, such as the psychic cost of living in a smoggy city or boating in polluted water. Even the tangible costs, such as the costs of sickness, soiling, and fish kills would take time and many man-hours to calculate. Furthermore, we do not need the *current* damage costs from pollution, we need the damage costs at that level of air quality which is an *optimum*. Therefore we must know both the costs-of-control curve and the damage curve to set the appropriate charge.

Some economists have begun to argue that the model of damage and control costs presented in this chapter is a useful way of understanding the problems of the environment, but that we will never be able to know what the optimum level of pollution is. Therefore, they say, standards should be determined through the political process.[21]

Nonetheless, these economists argue that the uniform standard of emissions allowed to each polluter is inefficient. Although the standard of air quality that the polity decides for a goal must be politically determined, the means of achieving that goal does not have to be regulation. As we noted earlier, if a uniform emissions or discharge standard is set for every waste disposer, some will find it easy to meet the standard with low costs while others may incur very high costs to dispose of their waste in alternative ways. The least-cost way to achieve the goal is to charge for emissions or discharges. The charge should be set so that the total water or air quality in the area under study is the level that is desired. It could take some experimentation to find the appropriate charge. However, those polluters who could reduce emissions a great deal at the same cost as another would incur to reduce pollution only a little would do so. As long as the appropriate charge were set,

[21]J. H. Dales, *Pollution, Property, and Prices* (Toronto: University of Toronto Press, 1968); Hugh O. Nourse, "Is There an Economic Solution to the Air Pollution Problem?" Bureau of Community Planning, University of Illinois *Newsletter*, Fall 1969; and William J. Baumol and Wallace E. Oates, "The Use of Standards and Prices for Protection of the Environment," *The Swedish Journal of Economics* (March 1971), pp. 42–54.

each disposer could adjust his waste disposition until it would cost more to reduce pollution than to pay the charge.[22]

Dales suggests that there is a way to use markets to determine the appropriate waste charge once the polity has decided on the standard of water or air quality it desires.[23] He suggests that once the total amount of a particular effluent that is to be allowed into an air shed or watershed is agreed upon, stock certificates for that volume of effluent should be issued. These stocks should then be auctioned to the highest bidders. The people who obtained the stocks would value the opportunity to dump waste into the water or air more than others. These would include firms for whom alternative disposal costs would be higher. Firms that could treat their wastes in alternative ways for less would not be able to obtain rights to pollute. Conservation groups, if so minded, could pay for rights to pollute in order not to exercise those rights and improve the environment still more. If it were decided to reduce pollution further in the future, the pollution control agency would simply reduce the number of stock certificates for rights to pollute for succeeding years. The costs of regulating and policing the pollution should be paid out of the fees from selling the stocks for the right to pollute.

It is easy to see how such a system might work in the case of water pollution, but it is harder to see how it might work for many types of air pollution, especially the case of emissions from motor vehicles. Who would pay for the right to pollute? The car owner or the manufacturer? It would probably have to depend on the emission tests of different brands of cars. Thus the consumer would have to pay the charge depending upon which car he bought. Nonetheless, the number of people who had this right and could buy it would probably depend more on the income distribution than any other factor. But these are all problems associated with setting charges for the right to pollute rather than with the specific plan suggested by Dales. Dales himself suggests that multisource pollution, such as auto emissions, domestic heating plants, and general runoff of insecticides, herbicides, and detergents could not be controlled by his plan.

Dales makes a further point about setting standards of emission into the air or of discharges into the water. He points out that uniform standards could result in uniform pollution. We should keep in mind that some areas should require stricter standards than others. He suggests that recreation areas should have much stricter standards than industrial areas; otherwise the enforcement of the same standards

[22] Ibid.
[23] Dales, ibid.

could lead plants to move from industrial areas where they can no longer pollute to recreation areas where they can because overall pollution is less. The impact would be to pollute the entire country uniformly. This notion is suggested by our designation of some areas for no smoking and others for smoking. Mishan first coined the term "separate facilities" for the establishment of different standards in different locations.[24]

Not many people have suggested that instead of effluent charges or regulation we should subsidize effluent control equipment. We should pay the polluters not to pollute by paying for their equipment. Theoretically, the provision of a subsidy or bribe should lead to the same allocation of resources as a charge imposed on the polluter would produce. Nonetheless, the equity of the situation has caused many people to prefer not to consider the subsidy as a viable alternative to current policy. Furthermore, a subsidy plan could cause some companies to threaten to move into an area and pollute it unless they were subsidized. The possibility for blackmail is quite apparent. Therefore, on equity grounds, the subsidy solution is usually rejected. Nonetheless, the construction of waste treatment plants for cities has been subsidized, and pollution control equipment has received favorable tax treatment from state, local, and national governments.

We have previously mentioned that the federal government has begun to try to tackle pollution problems by getting states and local governments to undertake appropriate land-use controls. Since watersheds and air sheds are usually larger than a municipality or metropolitan area, it is not surprising that states have undertaken control of some environmental problems where those affected are located within one state. For example, Hawaii passed its Land Use Law in 1961. The objective was to restrict urban development in order to preserve prime agricultural land and to conserve the natural landscape that has been a tourist attraction and one of the state's largest industries. The state Land Use Commission divides the state into four use districts: urban, rural, conservation, and agricultural. Concentrated development can take place only in the urban districts. As one might expect, the resultant shortage in developable land for urban use has increased the cost of housing in Hawaii to double the average price in the rest of the United States.[25]

Many of the state land-use regulations that have been passed since Hawaii's (1961) have been attempts to restrict or control development in areas that want to maintain or conserve a particular natural

[24]E. J. Mishan, *Technology and Growth, The Price We Pay* (New York: Praeger, 1970).

[25]Fred Bosselman and David Callies, *The Quiet Revolution in Land Use Control* (Washington, D.C.: Government Printing Office, December 1971), pp. 5–53.

environment. Vermont established regulations to control the boom in second homes and ski resorts resulting from increased access because of new highways. The San Francisco Bay Conservation and Development Commission was established to preserve the development on the edges of the bay for water-oriented uses. Massachusetts has created regulations for use of the coastal and inland wetlands as well as some regulation to prevent the complete exclusion of low- and moderate-income families from suburbs.[26] As we have emphasized throughout this book, increased density of development distinguishes urban from rural development. Thus, these regulations all affect the density of development and the future directions of urban development within the respective states. The problems with zoning and land-use regulation were amply outlined in Chapter 9. The dilemma between a better environment for higher-income families and better housing and other goods for lower-income families merits special notice.

ECOLOGY AND THE ECONOMY

The presumption in our analysis so far has been that problems of pollution will not be handled automatically within a free market economy and that government intervention of some kind is required. We have found that the theoretical optimum level of allowable pollution depends upon a knowledge of marginal damage costs and the marginal costs of control. Since information costs are high and perhaps because some information is unknowable, we can only seek the appropriate standards without knowing whether we have in fact achieved them.

Ecologists such as Barry Commoner and economists such as Allen V. Kneese who have studied the problem of pollution for some time argue that the approach described so far is too piecemeal and does not underscore the interdependence of the ecological system within which we live.[27] These scientists begin with the proposition that all materials used in producing goods and services must return to the ecological system in one form or another. When population and industry are dispersed, residuals return to the ecological system and are recycled. Sewage discharged into water may, by aerobic degradation, be assimilated. But if the discharge exceeds that which can be assimilated by the stream, the ecology of the stream changes; fish and other animal and plant life will die out. Another interdependency between the economy and our ecological system is that residuals can be

---

[26]Ibid. for these examples as well as several others.

[27]Barry Commoner, *The Closing Circle* (New York: Knopf, 1971); and Allen V. Kneese, "Background for the Economic Analysis of Environmental Pollution," *The Swedish Journal of Economics* (March 1971), pp. 1–24.

treated, but they must return to the ecological system in some form. Thus we might be able to avoid some types of air pollution by treatments that produce either liquid or solid residuals that must then also be assimilated.

Thus, even though we attack levels of emissions with charge systems, we must consider the other residuals that will result as well as their possible impact on the environment. Charge systems and regulations are a part of any control system, but there should be coordination between controls on water pollution, air pollution, and solid waste disposal.

Some residuals, however, are not degradable or have a tendency to persist without being either assimilated by the environment or recycled. Mercury, for example, is nondegradable. Persistent pollutants include synthetic organic chemicals such as DDT and phenols. It turns out that much of the shift in consumption since 1946 has been toward goods and services causing more of these types of residuals.[28] This has caused Commoner to suggest that we should use only processes that produce recycleable residuals. This leads to his most provocative question. Are the incentive effects in our current economic system compatible with our existence in the natural ecological system? The answer generated by economists as surveyed in this chapter is "maybe." The fundamental difficulty, however, stems from the fact that we simply have no reliable way of determining when or whether we have reduced pollution enough.

Both ecologists and economists agree upon the interdependency of actions and changes. Nevertheless, the very complexity of such systems indicates that the information on which action must depend is bound to be costly—that is, at least in those instances where such information can be obtained at all. Thus, as we have suggested in the previous two sections, it is unlikely that an overall systems approach will be possible. Most likely, action will take the form of a piecemeal approach involving small incremental steps. In fact, this may be the only way in which agreement on collective action can be reached. As we have indicated, there are changes in policy—the use of charges—that can make public action more efficient. Nonetheless, to reject this approach in favor of some bureaucratic control of the environment by experts would lead to the same kinds of monopoly by government and unresponsiveness to the demand for public goods that we have vividly described in Chapter 7 and in Chapter 10 on education. In the last analysis, subjective values are required. In voting by feet or by ballot box, citizens can articulate demand for public goods. Political external-

[28]Commoner, ibid.

ity costs are incurred in the voting process, but they would be higher if decisions were made by only a few in a bureaucracy.

SUMMARY

Urban pollution problems have existed as long as there have been cities. The sort of waste disposal that may not create problems in a rural area becomes costly to residents in a densely populated urban environment. In the market economy, costs to parties not involved in the production process or transaction will not be considered by the relevant decision makers. Thus, some kind of legal or government action is necessary to force those causing the pollution damage costs to take account of them. Nonetheless, it may be that we should not attempt to eliminate pollution completely. The costs from pollution damage at some point may be less than the costs incurred in trying to prevent the damage. In one way or another, society is going to have to pay for the disposal of waste. It must incur either the external social costs resulting from pollution or the costs of controlling pollution emissions and discharges. The problem is to find the optimum level of pollution or the minimum total waste disposal costs to the community.

One of the major problems, however, is information. It is difficult and costly to determine the damage costs from pollution. In some cases we may not know the problems until years after low pollution emissions have persisted and finally cumulated into a problem. Attempts have been made to calculate the health effect of air pollution as well as damages to materials and buildings. The results indicate that pollution does indeed increase morbidity and premature death. Furthermore, these costs can be measured by calculating the costs of medicine, doctors, and foregone earnings. Other effects of pollution, such as fish kills and the destruction of recreation areas, are less directly measurable since they require some kind of response from the citizen as to how much he values certain activities. To try to solve the measurement problem indirectly through measuring the impact of pollution on land values runs into a host of similar problems.

Since the private market is unlikely to account for these pollution damages, especially when the affected group is a latent group, politicians have found the environmental issue a good one in seeking votes. Although there is insufficient information to determine the optimum level of air or water quality, reductions in emissions and discharges have been achieved by establishing levels of acceptable emissions. Discharges or emissions above these acceptable levels are illegal. Because we have no information and are operating under uncertainty, we do not know whether these standards are too strict or too lenient. Nonetheless, we do know that regulating pollution in this fashion may be inefficient. Furthermore, the burden of the cost of control may be shifted to the poor.

Economists have long suggested that the best means of control would be to tax polluters the amount equivalent to the social damages they cause. Actually the charge should be equivalent to the pollution that would be allowed at the optimum level of pollution. Unfortunately we do not know the optimum level of pollution, so we must resort to standards.

Nevertheless, it would be more efficient, when controlling single source pollution, to use charges. The polluters should be made to pay a uniform charge such that the entire air shed or watershed under consideration achieved the quality levels desired by the polity. The charge is better than the regulation because it allows each firm to respond in the most efficient way. Furthermore, some firms may be able to reduce pollution emissions more than other firms for the same cost. Thus, those firms for whom pollution control is cheaper than paying the damages will do so. Those firms for whom pollution control costs are greater than the charge would continue to pollute. The total emissions or discharges, however, would be reduced to the desired level without the setting of a specific emission standard for each plant.

One possible way to determine what the charge ought to be would be to establish markets in the rights to pollute. The total certificates sold would represent the total level of pollution to be allowed. The certificates would be sold at auction. Competition would force the price for these certificates to reach the charge sought.

Ecologists and knowledgeable economists have been critical of the piecemeal approach taken by traditional economics. All materials going into the production of goods and services must eventually return to the ecological system in some form. Some residuals may be easily assimilated, but others may not. Furthermore, controls on one form of pollution such as air pollution may lead to the production of residuals that will become pollutants in water or take the form of equally problematic solid wastes. Therefore, knowledgable critics stress the importance of taking a more complete, systematic view of the environment in considering pollution and its control.

Commoner in particular finds that modern technology has resulted in the consumption of goods requiring more of the nondegradable or persistent pollutants than previous technology. He is forced to wonder whether the incentive effects in the modern economy are consistent with survival in our ecological system.

One is left with real uncertainty in studying the problem of environment. Risk is based on a measurable knowledge of the impact of future events. We can, for example, measure the probability of death for groups of people. Uncertainty, however, involves such vague knowledge of the future that it is impossible to insure against loss because there is no way to measure probabilities. Our knowledge of the future impact of current pollution levels on our environment and on each other is such that we must consider the outcome uncertain.

SELECTED READINGS

Dales, J. H.: *Pollution, Property, and Prices* (Toronto: University of Toronto Press, 1968).

Dorfman, Robert, and Nancy S. Dorfman (eds.): *Economics of the Environment* (New York: Norton, 1972).

Kneese, Allen V., and Blair T. Bower: *Managing Water Quality: Economics, Technology, Institutions* (Baltimore: Johns Hopkins, 1968).

Ridker, Ronald: *Economic Costs of Air Pollution* (New York: Praeger, 1967).

12

URBAN
TRANSPORTATION

Transportation is an important element in both the location of cities and their internal development patterns. Prior to the development of railroads and automobiles, nearly all large cities were located at the water's edge, where water transportation provided access abroad and along rivers to hinterlands. Even today most major cities are port cities, but the development of rail and highways has also permitted large cities to locate away from water access. While we could expand on the relationship between transportation, city location, and urban and regional growth, our major focus in this chapter will be on how transportation is related to the land-use pattern within cities and with what are commonly called issues of urban transportation.

HISTORICAL PERSPECTIVE

Prior to the nineteenth century, most of the world's cities were small compared to late-nineteenth and twentieth-century developments. One reason for the smallness was that the movement of people and goods within urban areas was difficult, being limited to walking or transportation by horse and wagon. It is not easy to haul heavy loads, such as coal or other raw materials or even finished products, by horse and wagon on unpaved streets. Thus pre-nineteenth-century cities tended to be clustered very closely around seaports, where manufacturing and retailing took place in a central location, while workers walked to work from high-density dwellings nearby.[1]

Early in the nineteenth century the railway was developed. The steam railroad facilitated the hauling of goods and people long distances, and the horse-drawn street railway facilitated the movement of goods and people within urban areas. While the horse-drawn street railway was more efficient than the horse and wagon, it had been introduced in only fifty-one cities by 1890. It was only with the development of the electric street railway that urban people-moving transportation began to expand. By 1895, the number of cities with street railways had expanded to 850; by 1902, 97 percent of the route miles were electrically powered.[2]

The introduction of the electric street railway greatly reduced the difficulty people had in moving about within urban areas. The major impact was to permit the spread of residential areas beyond the already built-up areas, with workers and shoppers then using the street railway to get downtown to work or shop. Some retailers also utilized street railways for moving goods and moved their stores away from downtown locations to be closer to the new residential markets. The street railways were an important innovation which permitted cities to expand because people could travel further within an urban area at low cost and in a reasonable amount of time.

The next major transportation innovation was the truck. The truck greatly reduced the costs of moving heavy goods about within metropolitan areas. This facilitated even more rapid decentralization of retailing and also permitted manufacturing plants to locate away from dockside or railside.[3] Following the introduction and impact of the truck came the automobile, which also had an important effect on urban form. Automobiles introduced a very high level of flexibility and mobility for citizens who could afford them, and, thanks to Henry Ford's introduction of assembly line production methods, the automobile provided America with greater mobility than any society had ever possessed. For the first time it became possible to live away from existing public transit lines and still have access to a wide range of job locations. The automobile also greatly expanded shopping areas and permitted stores to serve very large market areas—in competition with

[1]General information on the history of urban transportation in American cities is presented in Charles N. Glaab and A. Theodore Brown, *A History of Urban America* (New York: Macmillan, 1967), pp. 136–166.

[2]Ibid., pp. 151–152.

[3]Leon Moses and Harold F. Williamson, Jr., "The Location of Economic Activity in Cities," *American Economic Review*, 57 (May 1967), pp. 211–215.

other stores that were not located nearby. Following the introduction of the truck and widespread ownership of the automobile, a cyclical pattern of land use emerged in urban areas. The automobile permitted city workers to live further away from the city on low-cost, formerly unused or agricultural land. Retailers, some wholesalers, and service businesses such as banks, barbershops, and cleaners followed the people. The new retailers and other businesses provided employment in the distant suburbs, and people could move still further out onto still cheaper land because jobs were located closer to the fringe development area. The land-use patterns resulting from such processes were spread-out low-density uses, with small nodes of commercial or industrial activity distributed throughout the region. This replaced the older pattern of a concentration of business, employment, and retailers in the downtown area of a central city with residents surrounding the downtown area.

While transportation technology has influenced our land-use patterns, transportation is also closely related to other urban problems which we have considered in earlier chapters. We have noted that lack of mobility to seek employment outside the ghetto contributes to the difficulties ghetto dwellers have in finding good employment. We have also observed that improvements in transportation facilitated the consolidation of rural school districts and could permit overlapping competitive service areas among schools in urban areas. Finally, we have noted that it is our major mode of transportation, the automobile, that is the largest single contributor to air pollution. In our analysis of urban transportation, we will see how each of these issues is affected by modes of urban transport and proposed transportation systems.

The public sector has always been heavily involved in urban transportation. Streets have the characteristic of a public good; once they are constructed, many people can use them simultaneously with only minimal effects of one person's use upon another's. Streets may also become congested, however, and resemble a common pool where each person's use directly reduces the usefulness of the street to others. Both public goods and common pool congestion problems in transportation can be facilitated by governmental provision and management. Because it has long been recognized that improved transportation usually results in increased land values for the property with improved accessibility, the local property tax has long been the primary source of financing for city streets.[4] There is also considerable financing of state, United States, and interstate highway system high-

---

[4]This conclusion follows only from partial equilibrium analysis. Property values are related to *relative* accessibility; thus if accessibility to all property within a land market area were increased simultaneously, little change in values may be observed.

ways through automobile-related user charges such as gasoline taxes and excise taxes on automobiles and their accessories. All levels of government are involved in the provision of highway facilities over different areas.

In addition to provision of highways, the public sector has been heavily involved in the regulation and provision of transit, including railroads, street railways, bus systems, and taxicabs. Governments have not always been involved in regulating and providing urban public transit. After the development of electric street railways, automobiles, and trucks, public transit was provided by many independent business-men and car or truck owners who set their own routes and fares, often simply using a newly purchased automobile to earn a little extra money when not employed at a regular job. The electric street railway, how-ever, had a characteristic that made it superior to auto and truck trans-portation—that of economies of scale in operation, stemming from the integration of an entire system of electric power provision to rail vehicles. It was in response to the integration of electrified street railway systems that nearly all local governments began granting fran-chises for operation and also began regulating fares charged by pro-viders of private transit.[5]

Throughout the early twentieth century, typical urban transpor-tation consisted of an electric street railway, often a system of com-muter trains which connected outlying nodes of residences and busi-nesses to the central city, and a melange of owner-operated small buses and taxicabs. There was considerable competition among modes within the city, especially between the fixed-route street railways and the more flexible buses and taxis. As with many regulated systems, the street railways tended to have a single fare per ride, usually 5 cents. This meant that riders making very short trips were subsidizing riders who made very long trips. The small bus and taxi owners would run along fixed-route transit lines and offer waiting passengers a ride di-rectly to a destination close to the route line for 5 cents. For the low fare they could provide better service than the fixed-route system for very short routes, and for slightly higher fares they could also provide better service for longer trips.

The competition between the regulated operators of the fixed-route systems and independent bus and taxi owners was often intense, and it was carried on in city council chambers as well as in the market-place. By the end of the 1920's, the better-organized operators of fixed-route systems were able to have laws passed to prevent small, inde-pendent bus operators from offering their services. At the same time, extensive regulation of taxis was introduced, usually to limit the num-

---

[5]Ross D. Eckert and George W. Hilton, "The Jitneys," *Journal of Law and Eco-nomics*, 15 (October 1972), p. 294.

ber of taxis permitted within a city and often granting specific area-monopoly franchises to single taxi companies.[6] The resulting public transit structure for nearly all major cities was a single citywide fixed-route transit system complemented by a heavily regulated taxi industry. Larger cities also usually had a few independent suburban or commuter rail systems which made longer trips from suburban areas to downtown.

There is no question that the natural monopoly characteristics of some urban transit systems makes collective regulation important to maximize their efficiency, and thus we find that public regulation has contributed to some improvement in the provision of public transportation. We may also observe, however, that public regulation has been utilized to maintain monopolies and prevent competition from more efficient transit modes and thus also contributes to public transportation problems. In this respect, as in housing, zoning, education, and environmental management, governmental authority to resolve important public goods and natural monopoly regulation problems has also led to the use of governmental authority to make problems worse rather than better.

URBAN TRIP PATTERNS

When we think of urban transportation, we still generally think of journeys to and from work as the major purpose for trips. While up to the 1950s a majority of all trips were for work purposes, by the later 1960s the proportion of all trips for work purposes had fallen to between 25 and 30 percent in most areas. Other major travel purposes include shopping (around 20 percent) and social or recreational activities (around 20 percent). A variety of other purposes account for the remainder of urban travel.

The mode of travel in urban areas is primarily the automobile. Table 12-1 provides information on the modes used for urban travel in 1960 and 1970 and the relative changes between the two years.

While only 25 to 30 percent of all trips in most urban areas are for work purposes, about half of all public transit trips are for work purposes. The second most important purpose of transit trips is for school travel. Together, work and school trips account for 65 to 70 percent of all public transit usage.[7]

---

[6]Ibid.; and Richard N. Farmer, "Whatever Happened to the Jitney?" *Traffic Quarterly*, 19 (April 1965), pp. 263–279.

[7]U.S. Department of Transportation, *1972 National Transportation Report* (Washington, D.C.: Government Printing Office, 1972), p. 189.

TABLE 12-1 Urban Passenger Miles by Mode: 1960-1970

| | 1960 | | 1970 | | |
Mode	Passenger Miles (millions)	Percent of Total	Passenger Miles (millions)	Percent of Total	Percent Change: 1960-70
Automobile	423,300	88.4	736,689	93.9	74.0
Bus	28,328	5.9	20,864	2.7	−26.3
Rail transit	18,504	3.9	16,928	2.2	−8.5
Commuter rail	4,600	1.0	4,600	0.6	0.0
Taxicabs	3,900	0.8	5,100	0.6	30.8

Source: U.S. Department of Transportation, *1972 National Transportation Report* (Washington, D.C.: Government Printing Office, 1972), p. 189.

The data in Table 12-1 are aggregate data for all urban places. It is important to recognize that only six United States cities have major rail transit systems (New York, Boston, Philadelphia, Chicago, Cleveland, and Oakland-San Francisco), with two more under construction (Atlanta and Washington, D.C.). Of all the rail trips indicated in Table 12-1, over 75 percent were undertaken in the New York region. Thus, the common mode in all but a few large cities is the automobile, supplemented by bus and taxi.[8]

Along with the decline in the relative importance of the journey to work relative to other urban travel has come a shift in work trip patterns. It used to be common for employment to be centralized in the downtown, port, and railside industrial areas of larger cities. Thus the journey to work involved many people traveling from their homes throughout the urban area through a few heavily traveled corridors to the central work location. This pattern was well served by the commuter railroads and rail transit systems because of their capacity to carry many people through a single corridor in a short period of time. With the decentralization of employment, journey-to-work patterns have changed. For example, in New York City, only 28 percent of employment remains downtown; in many other cities, the percentage of the work force employed downtown is even less (Chicago, 14 percent; San Francisco, 17 percent; Washington, D.C., 24 percent). Furthermore, a majority of persons working downtown also live within the central city itself. Thus only 5 to 10 percent of all journeys to work are of a suburban-downtown pattern.[9] The spread of employment has tended to increase the relative attractiveness of automobiles, which do

[8]Ibid., p. 53.
[9]Martin Wohl, "Urban Transport We Could Really Use," *Technology Review*, 72 (June 1970), p. 5.

not follow fixed routes but are utilizable for any kind of trip pattern. The spread of trip patterns also reduces the necessity of moving many thousands of people per hour along a single route.

The current land-use and trip patterns in urban areas are the consequence of the availability of relatively low-cost individualized transportation—the automobile combined with governmental provision of streets and highways. The dispersed trip patterns and heavy reliance on automobiles has enabled urban areas to grow to enormous size and still permit families to reside in low-density single-family environments not formerly available to urban dwellers. Without flexible transportation in order to obtain urban amenities and the advantages of agglomeration economies, we would all have to be crowded into high-density multistory dwellings adjacent to workplaces. Without low-cost transportation to create large market areas, it would not be possible to obtain the advantages of economies of scale and specialization associated with our life-style.

PREFERENCES, PRICES, AND TRANSPORTATION CHOICES

Many analysts have considered the shift of commuters from public transit to the automobile as a consequence of a "love affair with the automobile" rather than a rational choice by consumers for a particular transit mode which best meets their preferences. As economists we cannot say why people make the choices they do, but the shift from public transit to automobiles can be understood in terms of travel time, price changes, and comfort—without recourse to speculation on a love relationship. In fact, there are many reasons to believe that the choice of the journey-to-work mode and route are among a consumer's more calculating decisions.

We generally expect consumers to be more calculating in their choices the more important the choice is to them and the more often it is repeated. The cost of any single journey to work does not represent a large proportion of individual income, but over a year the cost of ten trips a week for fifty weeks may easily total from $300 to over $1,000. More important, however, is the fact that commuters repeat their choice over and over, so that an improved choice results in a continued stream of benefits in the future. We all know individuals who know exactly how long trips take from point to point along a route, who have alternative routes in case of even slight congestion on the regular route, and who know the precise timing of stop lights so that they can avoid frequent trip-lengthening stops and starts. We really have no sure way of knowing precisely what motivates consumer choice in travel, but the theoretical and empirical evidence based on analysis of travel time, price, and comfort seems to be pretty much what one would expect to determine the choice of travel modes and routes by individuals.

Two methods are commonly used for estimating demands for travel from one place to another. The simplest methods involve forecasting total trips between different zones. The more difficult methods call for predicting the modal choice of travelers, with specific emphasis on predicting changes in mode used in response to changes in either the travel time or price of one of the alternatives. The simpler aggregative trip-forecasting models are usually not based on assumptions of economics but are related to "gravity" models of the physical sciences, because it has been observed that the number of individuals traveling from one place to another is related to the concentration of individuals in each place and the distance in between, much as gravity models in the physical sciences are related to mass and distance. Recently abstract formulations of gravity models have been related to economic theory. It appears that the models derived could be developed to enable one to predict responses to changes in travel time or the price of travel, even though empirical use of these more recent theoretical formulations has not been attempted.[10]

Modal choice models are based on economic theory and attempt to answer such questions as "how many bus riders will switch to automobiles if fares are raised 25 cents" or "if automobile trips are lengthened by twenty minutes and bus trips shortened by thirty minutes by assigning one lane of a heavily traveled freeway to exclusive bus usage, how many automobile riders will switch to buses?" These are the kinds of questions commonly asked when new fare structures are being considered for public transit, new public transit systems are proposed, or changes in existing transit facilities are contemplated.

A major focus of modal split models is the attempt to identify the cross elasticities of demand among modes with respect to changes in price and travel time. That is, what percentage of riders can be anticipated to change modes in response to a percentage change in either the price or travel time of any of the present travel modes? For example, in four different studies, estimates of the percentage of bus riders shifting to automobiles in response to a 30 percent increase in bus travel time range from 6.4 to 9.0 percent.[11] Three of the same four studies

[10]A. G. Wilson, "A Statistical Theory of Spatial Distribution Models," in Richard E. Quandt (ed.), *The Demand for Travel: Theory and Measurement* (Lexington, Mass.: Heath, 1970), pp. 55–82. For the economic derivation of gravity models see J. H. Niedercorn and B. V. Bechdolt, Jr., "An Economic Derivation of the 'Gravity Law' of Spatial Interaction," *Journal of Regional Science*, 9 (1969), pp. 273–282.

[11]Robert G. McGillivray, "Demand and Choice Models of Modal Split," *Journal of Transport Economics and Policy*, 4 (May 1970), p. 198.

conclude that a 30 percent increase in bus fares would lead 1.6 to 6.4 percent of bus riders to switch to automobiles.[12] Similarly, decreases in bus travel time or price would not yield large increases in riders. The conclusions from these recent efforts are consistent with the classic Moses and Williamson study in which they concluded that to attract 50 percent of the automobile riders in Chicago to public transit, a 50 cent payment to each rider for each trip was necessary.[13]

Consistent conclusions from attempts to identify cross elasticities of demand among modes with respect to price and travel time are that (1) both are very inelastic, that is, large percentage changes in prices or travel times are necessary to get small percentages of passengers to switch modes; and (2) the effect of changes in travel time is always stronger than effects from changes in price, that is, smaller percentage changes in travel time generate larger percentage changes in ridership than percentage changes in price do. The importance of these two conclusions will become apparent as we examine proposals for changes in public transit to reduce reliance on automobiles.

Identification of the changes in ridership in response to time and price changes are not the only information obtained from empirical studies of consumer choice among alternative transport modes. Considerable effort, for example, has been spent on identifying the value of travel time to consumers so that time savings can be compared with price changes. Knowledge of the value of time saved is also important because the largest single benefit from transportation investments are savings in travel time. Two of the better empirical estimates of the amount consumers are willing to spend to save travel time are Lave's estimate that consumers value time saved at 42 percent of their wage rate[14] and Beesley's estimate that middle-income commuters value time saved at approximately 33 percent of their wage rate and high-income commuters value time saved at approximately 50 percent of their wage rate.[15] These estimates are consistent, even though one was based on San Francisco and the other on London data.

In addition to estimates of the average value of time savings to commuters, several studies have concluded that commuters value time spent waiting, walking, or looking for a parking place as much as three times more than time spent in movement; that is, commuters will pay

[12]Ibid.

[13]Leon N. Moses and Harold F. Williamson, Jr., "Value of Time, Choice of Mode, and the Subsidy Issue in Urban Transportation," *Journal of Political Economy*, 61 (June 1963), p. 262.

[14]Charles A. Lave, "The Demand for Urban Mass Transportation," *Review of Economics and Statistics*, 52 (August 1970), p. 323.

[15]M. E. Beesley, "The Value of Time Spent in Travelling: Some New Evidence," in Richard E. Quandt (ed.), *The Demand for Travel: Theory and Measurement* (Lexington, Mass.: Heath, 1970), p. 232.

more to avoid waiting, walking, or looking for a parking place than they will to save time spent en route.[16] This observation is especially important when one realizes that in automobile travel, virtually all time is spent moving, while many public transit routes involve waiting for the public transit vehicle, time spent transferring from one vehicle to another, and time spent walking from the station to and from home or work. This implies that even if travel time and comfort of an automobile and public transit were identical, consumers would be willing to pay more to travel in their automobile if traveling by public transit required waiting, walking, and transfer time exceeding the time it takes the auto driver to find a good parking place.

The least explored aspect of modal choice in transit is that of comfort. In transit studies, comfort, along with time and price, appears continually as one of the three crucial variables. However, while most observers agree that riding in an automobile on uncongested streets is more comfortable than hanging on a strap in a crowded subway, and that riding in an air-conditioned rail car while reading the morning paper is more comfortable than driving in stop-and-go traffic during a winter storm, little in the way of quantifiable data on comfort preferences has been collected to enable predictions of responses to changes in comfort to supplement predictions of responses to changes in price or travel time. What has been concluded in most studies is that comfort is important, but apparently no more important than price or time. This implies that large changes in comfort levels, like large changes in price or time, will result in relatively small changes in the number of riders changing modes.

Studies of consumer choice of transportation modes reinforce our conclusion that consumers are rational choosers of their travel mode. Consumers respond to price changes for transport modes as they do to price changes for other goods and services, and responses to changes in travel time appear equally rational. The shift from the use of fixed-route public transit to automobiles and the increasing usage of taxicabs, both appear to be predictable responses to changing patterns of origins and destinations, improved highways, and a preference for uninterrupted point-to-point transportation. The decline in the use of fixed-route public transit—especially where waiting and transferring are required—appears to be a predictable response to the spread of urban activity, which has left fewer and fewer people traveling from home to work in close proximity to single-mode public transit routes.

Rational consumer choice in private markets for purely private

[16]Gerald Kraft and Thomas A. Domencich, "Free Transit," in Matthew Edel and Jerome Rothenberg (eds.), *Readings in Urban Economics* (New York: Macmillan, 1972), p. 466.

goods and services will result in economic efficiency. However, if the prices consumers face do not really reflect the value of the resources used or if external effects are generated by particular actions, rational consumer choice may well produce inefficient results. There is considerable evidence to indicate that urban transportation systems fall in the latter category, especially with regard to problems of peak-hour traffic congestion and pollution. In the next section we will turn to an analysis of urban transportation problems.

URBAN TRANSPORTATION PROBLEMS

Along with the advantages and benefits of relatively low-cost, individual, flexible transportation come several problems, the most important of which are traffic congestion, air pollution from the internal combustion engine, financial problems of public transit systems, and the lack of access to transportation, especially in urban ghettos and for persons unable to drive or afford automobiles. After we analyze these problems, we will examine alternative transport modes in relation to their suitability for meeting transportation demands while resolving present problems. We will then turn to an examination of current governmental policy toward urban transportation and evaluate the prospects of its success.

Congestion

Traffic congestion is considered by many to be a major urban transportation problem. Congestion occurs when too many people try to use highway facilities at the same time and they get in each other's way. In extreme conditions excessive usage leads to traffic stoppage, and automobiles traveling on congested highways generally have higher accident rates and produce more pollution than automobiles moving at steady speeds. A congested highway is analogous to an overused common pool resource where any single user would not be able to realize benefits by reducing his use, but if all users together would curtail their use, everyone could obtain net benefits. For example, a freeway lane can accommodate up to 1,500 cars per hour at a steady speed of 40 miles per hour, but if more than 1,500 cars per hour per lane enter the freeway, congestion will occur, speed will decline, and the actual flow of automobiles will fall much below the maximum rate. All drivers would benefit if they all agreed to wait in line off the freeway and enter the lane at a rate of 1,500 cars per hour. However, it is not in any single driver's interest to wait unless a restrictive system applies to all.

Systems to improve the flow of freeway traffic are in use, but the more common approach to reducing congestion is to construct additional highway facilities. Just how much highway investment would be required to eliminate all highway congestion? If one looks at forecasts of highway usage, one is continually amazed at the lowness of peak-hour forecasts relative to realized travel. Far in advance of the time predicted, the new freeway has traffic exceeding its capacity and is congested. This phenomenon appears over and over again.

There are two reasons why highway congestion is so difficult to eliminate.[17] First, highway users generally find more than one route to work that takes about the same amount of time. This is true because, if any single route were much quicker than alternatives, drivers would switch from the slower to the faster route until it became congested and travel time equalized. The same phenomenon will occur when a new highway is opened. Drivers will switch from many old routes to the new route until travel time on the new route is the same as travel time on alternative routes. If the former routes were city streets, travel time will not be equalized until travel on the new route becomes slow and congested. However, travel time will be lower on both the new and old routes than it was prior to construction of the new highway.

The second reason new routes congest prior to the time forecast is that drivers who formerly avoided the congestion by going to work either earlier or later than their preferred time will begin to travel closer to their preferred time because the new highway or its alternatives will be faster than they formerly were. The result of drivers shifting from many old routes to the new route and more drivers traveling directly at the peak-hour time will lead to a shortening of the rush hour but very little reduction in congestion during the new shorter rush. In order to eliminate congestion through construction one would have to construct sufficient highway capacity in all directions from employment locations that all drivers could travel at their most preferred time in an uncongested manner. This would entail very costly investment in new highways, 90 percent of which would be used only two hours a day during very short rush hours.

The implications of what it would take to really remove highway congestion also need to be seen in the context of just what has been happening to automobile travel times in urban areas. When one examines journey-to-work data, he observes that travel times have been remaining about constant while the average length of journeys has

---

[17]This analysis follows that of Anthony Downs, "The Law of Peak-Hour Expressway Congestion," *Traffic Quarterly* 16 (July 1962), pp. 393–409.

been increasing.[18] Thus the actual miles-per-hour speed of the journey to work, in spite of highway congestion, has been increasing. This may indicate that concern with congestion may be generated by a failure to meet expectations rather than by a failure to decrease travel times. The failure to meet expectations may occur because, as highways have been expanded to meet journey-to-work traffic, an individual's ability to move about in an urban area during the rest of the day has been greatly expanded, and he would like to make his journey to work at a comparable speed. The failure to meet this expectation may not be an economic efficiency problem, because it is very doubtful that drivers would be willing to pay the price necessary for sufficient highway capacity to travel all the time at speeds now possible during non-rush-hour times.

The fact that congestion cannot be eliminated by highway construction except at costs that would exceed benefits has not stopped highway engineers from trying to build sufficient highways so that everyone can travel at an uncongested "design speed" of 50 to 60 miles per hour at any time during the day. While the engineers have been accused of using too much land for automobile transportation, it does not appear excessive if one looks at the amount of land used for highway transport. An examination of land requirements in five automobile-oriented urban areas in California (Los Angeles, San Diego, Sacramento, Fresno, and Santa Rosa) indicates that 50 to 60 percent of the automobile miles traveled are on freeways using 1.6 to 2.0 miles of the land area. The other 40 to 50 percent of the miles traveled are on city streets using 22 percent of the land area. This means that 24 percent of the urban land area is devoted to streets and roads. To judge just how much 24 percent is, it is useful to examine some historical data. When John Sutter laid out Sacramento in 1850 he allocated 38 percent of the city area for streets and sidewalks. This amount was necessary because heavy pedestrian traffic requires short blocks with many cross streets, so that to go around a block does not require a mile walk. The part of Sacramento laid out between 1900 and 1930 had 21 percent of the area in streets, and the parts developed since World War II have about 15 percent in streets. The resulting overall city average is 22 percent. Current projections for servicing urbanizing areas in California with freeways indicate that 1.6 percent of the land area will be needed for those freeways. Even when parking requirements are added,[19] it would appear that less land is needed for trans-

---

[18]J. R. Meyer, J. F. Kain, and M. Wohl, *The Urban Transportation Problem* (Cambridge, Mass.: Harvard, 1965), pp. 74–81.

[19]It is estimated that it would take 2.4 percent of Los Angeles's land to park all cars on a single level. Because not all cars are away from home at once and multilevel parking is used in downtown areas, from 0.4 to 1 percent of the land for parking is plenty.

port in an automobile age than in a horse-and-buggy era unless we try
to eliminate all traffic congestion from our cities.[20]

Pollution

Over half of the air pollution in the United States results from transportation uses, with approximately 45 percent resulting from automobiles, trucks, and buses.[21] As indicated in Chapter 11, air pollution is
a classic externality case where the generator of the cost does not see
the costs he imposes on others; even if he cleaned up his own automobile engine, he would not see any difference in air quality because
of the large number of individuals involved.

Air pollution from automobiles, trucks, and buses can be reduced
in several ways, but all appear to require governmental restrictions
or regulation. One strategy is to require emission control devices to
be installed and maintained on all internal combustion engines. A
second strategy would be to regulate traffic flows so that steady
40-mile-per-hour speeds are maintained. Emissions at a steady 40
miles per hour are approximately half of the emissions at 20 miles per
hour, and stop-and-start congested driving produces the highest level of
air pollution.[22] A third strategy would be to move toward a new technology such as electrically powered vehicles; but while electric automobiles would reduce air pollution in urban areas, the production of
electricity necessary to recharge batteries from nuclear or coal- or
oil-burning generating plants might also cause environmental problems.
Still another strategy would be to encourage car pooling or the use of
mass transit systems. And finally, an important long-run strategy may
be to channel urban development so that the average journey to work
is shortened. This is occurring as places of employment as well as
residential areas continue to spread out away from cities. Along with
this latter strategy would go measures to reduce the cost of buying and
selling houses, so that the adjustment of residence to work place
would be easier and less costly. These strategies for reducing air pollution will be treated further in the next section on alternative transport modes.

[20]Karl Moskowitz, "Living and Travel Patterns in Automobile-Oriented Cities,"
in George M. Smerk (ed.), *Readings in Urban Transportation* (Bloomington, Ind.:
Indiana University Press, 1968), pp. 155–160.
[21]John T. Middleton and Wayne Ott, "Air Pollution and Transportation,"
Traffic Quarterly 22 (April 1968), pp. 175–189.
[22]Ibid.

Financial Problems of Public Transit

Between 1959 and 1970, 235 public transit systems went into bankruptcy. Governments purchased 89, and these continued in operation; 146 simply went out of business, leaving their areas, mostly smaller towns, without any public transportation. If we look at all profits and losses of public transit systems together, the industry as a whole first ran a deficit in 1963. By 1965, losses exceeded profits by $11 million; by 1972, losses exceeded profits by $513 million. The greatest losses were incurred on the rail systems.[23]

Public transit systems face financial difficulties. Ridership has maintained a steady decline since the 1920s (with a slight upward rise during World War II), and costs of labor and equipment have continued to rise. The construction of highways, increasing automobile ownership, and flexibility of automobile travel have all combined to make public transit less attractive than alternatives, and even taxicabs took in higher revenues than all other forms of public transit combined in 1970.[24]

The typical demand-cost situation that public transit systems appear to face is illustrated in Figure 12-1. It should be noted that at no place does the demand curve (D) cut the average cost curve (AC); hence there is no price and output level that would permit the company to cover its production costs unless it can develop a system of price discrimination (charging higher fares to those with higher demands). The gross revenue-maximizing output would be output B and price P_B, where marginal revenue (MR) equals zero. The loss-minimizing output would be output C at price P_C, where marginal revenue equals marginal cost (MC). At either of these outputs the price would be less than average cost (AC_B and AC_C). The optimal output for the transit system in terms of maximizing net benefits would be output A and price P_A, where the demand curve intersects the marginal cost curve. Up to that output, net benefits are increased by expanding output. For most transit systems, the major issue is not one of optimum production levels; it is simply to avoid bankruptcy.

Several rationales are advanced for subsidizing public transit systems. First, there are benefits to nonriders. They include the value of time saving to highway users because highways will be less con-

---

[23]George W. Hilton, *Federal Transit Subsidies: The Urban Mass Transportation Assistance Program* (Washington, D.C.: American Enterprise Institute, 1974), p. 98; and U.S. Department of Transportation, *1972 National Transportation Report*, p. ix.

[24]Ibid.

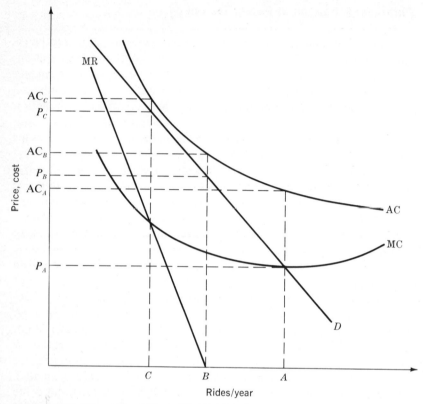

FIGURE 12-1 Demand and Cost of Public Transit

gested (since some people who would otherwise drive use public transit instead), reduced air pollution, and the availability of a transit option in case it is needed. One may also place a special value on assuring that public transit is available for the young, the elderly, and the poor, even though their effective demands are not sufficient to cover the cost of the system.

One must remember that the demands for public transit are, like any demands, directly related to substitutes and complementary goods. Among substitutes for public transit use are the availability of vast highway networks, especially freeway systems that are financed largely from revenues collected by the Federal government. One would expect that any decrease in spending on the provision of highways or increase in the cost of goods complementary to highway use, such as automobiles or gasoline, would cause the demand for public transit to shift to the right, perhaps even far enough so that public transit systems were financially viable without subsidization. We must remember, however, that the low cross-elasticity estimate for a shift in mode in response to a price or time change indicates that a large increase in price or time for auto users would be necessary for many of them to shift to transit.

The issues of highway finance have been controversial. It would seem to be safe to conclude that (1) highway users as a whole pay taxes about equal to the costs of all highways except local streets, which are financed primarily through property taxation; (2) rural highway users receive net subsidies while urban users generate more revenues than is spent on urban highways; and (3) at the margin, rush-hour highway users whose demands lead to extra highway capacity do not generate sufficient revenues to cover the costs of additional investments to meet peak-load requirements.[25] Thus freeway users at rush hour are subsidized, and if they had to bear full costs of extra highway capacity to meet peak-hour demands, many rush-hour drivers might shift to public transit. Finally, it should be recognized that these financing estimates do not include any estimate for costs generated by air pollution, costs which, if borne by motorists (in addition to current emission control devices for which motorists do pay), might lead to still further public transit usage. Many analysts have concluded that unless costs of automobile usage increase significantly, public transit systems will require continued subsidization.

Providing Transportation for Youth, the Elderly, and the Poor

In this automobile age it is easy to lose sight of the fact that many families and individuals do not have access to automobiles and may have insufficient incomes to afford taxicabs. For example, in 1970, 20.4 percent of all American families and 57.5 percent of all families with incomes under $3,000 did not own an automobile. While families and individuals without automobiles tend to be located where there are public transit systems (for example, 41.2 percent of the families in New York City but only 17.2 percent of the families in Los Angeles do not own automobiles), there are severe mobility problems for many who do not own cars.[26]

In Chapter 8 it was indicated that lack of transportation in the ghetto areas of many cities makes efficient shopping and easy access to employment opportunities difficult. Several analysts have concluded that the lack of transportation from ghetto areas to employment leads to higher unemployment levels in the ghetto than would otherwise be

[25]Meyer, Kain, and Wohl, op. cit., pp. 60–74.
[26]U.S. Department of Transportation, op. cit., pp. 45–48.

the case.[27] Most public transit systems including bus routes were designed very early in the twentieth century, and many have undergone little change. They still tend to be oriented to carry workers from residential neighborhoods, often in the suburbs, to the downtown area of the central city. Central-city residents have quite different needs. Their need is for transit which runs from city residential neighborhoods to employment centers, which may be in suburban areas. Most outbound lines from central cities run to suburban residential neighborhoods, not suburban employment centers.

Ghetto dwellers are not the only persons without automobiles who are not well served by public transit. Most transit routes are designed for journey-to-work trips. One reason why routes are not designed for other uses such as shopping or recreational trips is that persons who do own automobiles very seldom use public transit for nonwork purposes—especially for shopping, where heavy packages or bags of goods would have to be carried. This means that the actual number of persons needing transit service for shopping, to get to recreation centers, or to get to medical facilities or other nonwork locations from any residential area is very small—virtually always too small to generate sufficient demand for paying the costs of running buses on fixed routes to service these needs. At present the accessibility needs of these groups are met by the use of taxicabs which, while more costly than public transit, are available to those without automobiles for purposes not well served by public transit. In many areas the income groups with the highest incidence of taxi usage are not the wealthy, but low-income, non-automobile-owning families and the elderly.

URBAN TRANSIT ALTERNATIVES

Rail Transit Systems

Rail transit systems hold considerable fascination as a potential solution to urban transit problems. There are only six areas served by rail mass transit in the United States, and 75 percent of all rail passenger miles are within the New York City area.[28] The major advantage of rail systems is their high capacity, even though they are not especially fast. For example, maximum average speed with 1-mile station spacing is about 35 miles per hour; with 2-mile station spacing it is about 45 miles per hour.[29] The major problem with rail systems is that they are

[27]Meyer, Kain, and Wohl, op. cit., pp. 144–170.
[28]U.S. Department of Transportation, op. cit., p. 53.
[29]John B. Rae, "The Mythology of Urban Transportation," *Traffic Quarterly*, 26 (January 1972), p. 87.

very expensive and their capacity is meaningless unless a lot of people actually want to go from one point to another within an urban area at the same time, an occurrence of decreasing likelihood as urban areas decentralize journey-to-work patterns.

The older rail systems are divided into two kinds, commuter rail and mass rail. Commuter rail are the longer lines with few stations which run from suburban communities into downtown areas. Mass rail systems are those with many stations serving the densest areas of large cities. Most new systems (BART in San Francisco; Metro in Washington, D.C.) are neither strictly commuter rail or mass rail. They are designed to serve large areas, including distant suburbs, but have stations throughout their service area like a mass rail system. In order to maintain relatively high speeds for long-distance commuters, stations are spaced far apart relative to station spacing in older systems. For example, in New York City, station spacing is 1/2 mile and in Chicago it is 2/3 mile. In the Washington, D.C., system, station spacing will be 1.5 miles; in San Francisco, it will be 2 miles. The new systems are not designed to provide dense nearby service for city residents. In San Francisco, for example, only 8 of BART's 75 miles of track are within the city and there are no stations in either of the two highest-density residential areas in spite of the fact that 72 percent of the persons employed in the city live in the city.[30]

How will rail systems currently being designed affect problems of congestion, pollution, financial deficits, and access problems of people who do not own automobiles and of ghetto dwellers? Actually the only items affected in a significant way are financial deficits, as it is estimated that new systems will have to have full construction-cost subsidization plus continual operating-cost subsidization. For example, BART in San Francisco is financed through property taxation, sales taxation, and federal grants—and in addition BART management, as of October 1973, was forecasting a $27 million annual operating deficit by 1978, for which it is now seeking tax authorization.[31] When both the annual value of capital costs and operating expenses are considered, rides on the BART system are estimated to cost $1.97 each. Of the $1.97, 64 cents will come from fares and the other $1.33 from public subsidies, of which 85 cents will be from local property taxes, 16 cents from local sales taxes, 13 cents from federal sources, and 19 cents from tolls on motorists using cross-bay bridges.[32] This indicates

[30]Martin Wohl, "Urban Transport We Could Really Use," *Technology Review*, 72 (June 1970), pp. 3–9.

[31]"BART Officials Plead for New Tax Support," *Los Angeles Times*, October 10, 1973, part 1, p. 12.

[32]Leonard Merewitz, "Public Transportation: Wish Fulfillment and Reality in the San Francisco Bay Area," *American Economic Review*, 62 (May 1972), p. 83.

that a regular commuter utilizing the system twice a day for fifty weeks during the year would receive a net subsidy of $1,330 annually. There are certainly many low-income auto and cab users who would appreciate such a subsidy for their own journeys to work.

Effects on congestion and pollution are more difficult to estimate precisely. In San Francisco, for example, it is estimated that there has been sufficient BART-related construction near stations to increase rather than decrease automobile congestion in those areas.[33] At the same time the increased transit capacity to distant areas is expected to contribute to longer average journeys to work, many of which will be by automobile, and it is quite possible that the net effect will be an increased rather than decreased number of miles traveled by automobile in the region.

Rail mass transit is not designed to serve nonwork trips of nondrivers or ghetto dwellers. In fact, mass rail is designed to serve quite a different population: the higher-income, employed suburbanites who work in central cities. For example, the incomes of riders on comparable lines in existing systems are considerably above the average income in their SMSA (standard metropolitan statistical area). On the Skokie Swift line in Chicago, for example, the average rider has a median income 75 percent higher than the SMSA median; and on the heavily subsidized Boston Highlands run, median incomes are 40 percent higher than the Boston SMSA median.[34]

Analysis of the chances of resolving transportation problems in urban areas with rail systems indicates that the major way 95 percent of the area's citizens can expect to be affected is through taxation to cover subsidies to support a system which may carry a small number of high-income commuters from the suburbs to a downtown area. It is not even anticipated that rail systems will result in many shifts from alternative modes of travel for suburban-downtown commuters. This is because, with dispersed residential patterns, suburban residents must still utilize another transit mode to get to the rail station, and they must spend additional time waiting for the transfer. Thus, while the line-haul portion of the rail commuter's journey may be faster than the automobile commuter's trip on the freeway, overall door-to-door trip time is unlikely to be much less by rail. Furthermore, even if the rail trip is quicker, the evidence is that consumers dislike waiting more than they dislike time spent in movement. Therefore a longer automobile trip may still be preferred to a shorter trip involving walking and waiting for transfers. Finally, even if rail services are provided

---

[33]Werner Z. Hirsch, *Urban Economic Analysis* (New York: McGraw-Hill, 1973), pp. 122–123; and Hilton, op. cit., p. 101.

[34]Wohl, op. cit., p. 5; and Wohl, "Users of Urban Transportation Services and Their Income Circumstances," *Traffic Quarterly*, 24 (January 1970), pp. 21–43.

at lower cost (through subsidization) the low price elasticity indicates that only small numbers of automobile commuters will transfer to it. Instead, riders on the new system are likely to be persons who formerly used other, now slower public transit.[35] Our prognosis for the future of mass rail systems is that they will not have a major impact on urban transit problems unless focus on them takes attention away from other modes of transit which may have greater positive impact. In this case the fascination with fixed rail systems may result in negative rather than positive results.

Express Bus Systems

An innovation in mass transit that appeared after the development of the freeway is the freeway flyer or express bus operating on exclusive reserved freeway lanes.[36] Freeway flyers combine residential collection, the line haul, and downtown distribution in a single vehicle. The bus makes residential pickups, goes to a freeway, and enters immediately, proceeding to the downtown area on an uncongested exclusive lane. When it reaches downtown it exits, often on an exclusive ramp, for downtown distribution of riders. Some cities also provide reserved lanes in city streets so that the downtown distribution can be undertaken more quickly than if the bus had to move in mixed city traffic. Some cities are also experimenting with radio-controlled stop lights where the bus driver, upon approaching an intersection, can signal the traffic light to turn green so the bus can move through without the usual downtown stop-and-start for intersections in addition to passenger stops.

Freeway flyers have several advantages over fixed rail systems. They may actually be faster in terms of total travel time because riders are not required to change modes. Also, because buses are relatively small, they are filled fairly quickly and can then move directly downtown at 60 to 65 miles per hour rather than the average 45 miles per hour attainable by a rail train with 2-mile station spacing. Finally, routes can easily be adjusted and smaller centers as well as downtown can be served. Universities, hospital complexes, airports and other areas of concentrated employment appear to possess sufficient demand to warrant express bus service. Given our decentralized development patterns in urban areas, point-to-point bus service may be the only

[35]Hilton, op. cit., p. 100.
[36]Vergil G. Stover and John C. Glennon, "A System for Bus Rapid Transit on Urban Freeways," *Traffic Quarterly* 22 (October 1969), pp. 465–484.

competitive alternative to the automobile for the most congested routes.

At present, the most heavily traveled exclusive bus lane is from northern New Jersey into New York City, where 485 buses move 21,000 passengers during the peak hour. These buses replace 14,900 automobiles, which substitutes one freeway lane for the ten that would be required to move the automobiles at maximum flows.[37] That single lane also carries more persons during the peak hour than maximum peak-hour single-corridor flows in all except the largest seven cities in the United States. ·

Freeway flyers generally cost less per ride than rail transit for traffic flows below 10,000 per hour. The costs per ride of the two modes are about the same for flows between 10,000 and 35,000 per hour. Because only New York and Chicago have corridor flows in excess of 30,000 per hour and most urban areas already have well-developed freeway systems, the freeway flyer mode of mass transit may be a solution to many commuting problems.

Freeway flyers, like rail transit, however, have thus far been primarily oriented to suburban–central city commuting. It appears that they have an advantage over rail systems in being able to attract a higher proportion of riders who would otherwise use automobiles, and they are less costly than rail systems. Their impact on congestion and pollution is uncertain, because if a freeway lane is allocated exclusively for buses, the remaining automobiles must travel in fewer lanes and hence be more congested and perhaps generate greater pollution through stop-and-start driving. Of course, the increased congestion and longer travel time by automobile may also encourage more drivers to switch to the freeway flyer because it can maintain its speed while everyone else is tied up in traffic.

Metered Freeways[38]

As indicated earlier in the chapter, the response to highway congestion is to recommend additional highways or other additional transportation investment. However, it is also possible to improve the carrying capacity of existing freeways by regulating traffic inputs to maintain steady rates of 1,500 cars per lane per hour, thus reducing congested stop-and-start driving while maintaining maximum traffic flow. Freeway metering requires large on-ramps, with computerized traffic-flow sensors imbedded into roadways. Cars waiting to enter the freeway line

[37]U.S. Department of Transportation, op. cit., p. 198.
[38]Meyer, Kain, and Wohl, op. cit., chaps. 8–11.

up on the on-ramp, and one car at a time enters as the light turns green. While part of a commuter's travel time is spent sitting on the on-ramp and part is spent driving, total trip time is reduced. Along with the reduction in total trip times comes reduced wear on automobiles, fewer accidents, and reduced air pollution—all of which result from being able to maintain steady 35 to 40-mile-per-hour speeds instead of having to stop and start in heavily congested traffic.

Where freeways are metered, it is also possible to mix express buses with traffic, the bus's only advantage being priority access to the freeway. Automobiles plus 200 buses in three lanes of mixed traffic metered to maintain 40 miles per hour, for example, could move 15,510 persons per hour.[39] This would be sufficient to handle peak corridor movements in all but the largest seven cities in the United States. Running express buses in traffic on metered freeways also represents an efficient way to move people in corridors where sufficient traffic to warrant an exclusive bus lane does not exist.

At present, most freeways in the Los Angeles system are metered.[40] While the results of metering have not been analyzed, it does appear that metering has led to smoother traffic flows and higher traffic movement. This in spite of the fact that the highway department has not been able to restrict entry as much as would be desirable because of the lack of large-capacity on-ramps for waiting cars. At present, to restrict entry to optimal levels would cause too great a backup on adjacent city streets. Alongside the metered entry for cars are priority bus entry ramps, but buses move in mixed traffic on all but a very small part of the system. A further innovation is the hooking of all imbedded computer sensors to a central office, where freeway traffic flows are continually monitored. Any traffic stoppage is indicated immediately by flashing lights at the point of the stoppage and a helicopter or nearby police unit is dispatched to identify the cause of the tieup. If this were not enough, along one freeway, the Santa Monica, large, scoreboard-type signs can be used to convey messages on specific traffic conditions to drivers. The signs are normally programmed to provide information on traffic flows in terms of the number of minutes to reach designated exits, but they are also used to indicate specific lane blockages, general traffic tieups, and if necessary, alternative routes.

Most urban areas already have considerable investments in freeways. Where traffic volumes have exceeded freeway capacity, it may well be more efficient to meter freeway access to increase traffic capac-

---

[39]U.S. Department of Transportation, op. cit., p. 199.
[40]Many descriptions of the Los Angeles system have appeared in local news media. One description is "Signal Slows Access to Freeway," *Los Angeles Times*, December 15, 1972, part 2, p. 8.

ity instead of building new, additional freeways or expensive rail systems. Some combination of express buses and metered freeways is probably the most efficient way to move large volumes of traffic in all but the very largest urban areas in the United States.

Taxicabs

Taxicabs are generally not thought of as a form of public transit, but they do account for more riders than all rail systems put together and collect higher net revenues than all other public transit put together.[41] Taxicab riding is on the increase—as are revenues from taxicabs. Taxis are also heavily used by the elderly, those with low incomes, and other nondrivers.

Recent analyses of taxicabs conclude that regulations designed to prevent competition with public transit have severely restricted the number of taxis and resulted in higher fare levels than would occur under less strict entry regulation.[42] The value of restricted competition to the taxi owner is indicated by the fact that the market price of a "medallion" for legal entry is often $20,000 or more. In Washington, D.C., where entry is virtually unrestricted, group riding in cabs is almost as cheap as public transit and the taxi is much more convenient. It would appear that one simple contribution to resolving urban transportation problems would be to relax restrictions on taxis and permit market competition to keep prices within reach of low-income families and the elderly. This is one area in which government regulation has probably done more harm than good for consumers.

Jitneys[43]

Jitneys are minibuses or even regular automobiles with which owner-operators develop their own routes or respond to calls for group transportation as a cab would do. Their major virtue is their flexibility to meet diverse travel demands. For example, jitney operators would find it profitable to make pickups to provide transportation to night-shift workers like nurses or cleaning personnel or to schedule regular

[41]U.S. Department of Transportation, op. cit., pp. ix, 47.

[42]Meyer, Kain, and Wohl, op. cit., pp. 353–357. For a detailed examination of regulation in a single city, see Edmund W. Kitch, Marc Isaacson, and Daniel Kasper, "The Regulation of Taxicabs in Chicago," *Journal of Law and Economics*, 14 (October 1971), pp. 285–350.

[43]General discussions of jitneys are presented in Eckert and Hilton, "The Jitneys," op. cit.

runs between public housing projects and shopping areas or medical facilities. The jitney is really nothing more than a small bus operated in whatever pattern will provide the driver with an income. It presents a mode of travel between neighborhood fixed-route bus service and individually hired taxicabs. Jitney service is sometimes approximated in cities that permit groups of riders in a cab to share fares (instead of each paying a full fare) even though the group may have multiple pickups or destinations.

Jitneys are extremely popular in many large urban cities worldwide but have been illegal in most American cities since the 1920s, when coalitions of public transit operators and cab companies joined together to get jitneys outlawed.[44] One analyst of urban transit has argued that by making jitneys illegal and not permitting taxis more flexibility, Americans have been forced to utilize private automobiles to take advantage of lower-density residential environments. If jitneys had been permitted to continue, they claim, many suburban commuters would be using them instead.[45]

Jitneys have the potential for filling a gap in the urban transit market, especially for nondrivers who need transportation other than that offered by fixed-route public transit. Jitneys may be much more appropriate for the kind of low-density trip movements that appear to be increasing within urban areas and offer at least one mode that has more potential for serving ghetto dwellers than conventional public transit or rapid rail systems.

In addition to providing improved access, jitneys would also provide employment to many relatively low-skilled persons—an objective that would also be desired for urban ghetto dwellers and others who prefer to work nontraditional hours.

Personal Rapid Transit (PRT)

Personal rapid transit has been promoted by the U.S. Department of Transportation as a major solution to the problem of improving mobility within densely populated urban areas. PRT cars would be small, usually carrying six to twelve passengers, and they would operate with electronic guidance on their own guideways. Passengers would call for a car by pressing a button (like calling for an elevator), and then they would press another button in the car to designate their destination. PRT would approach the convenience of an automobile for destinations along its routes, and it would be more comfortable and less

---

[44]Ibid.
[45]Hilton, *Federal Transit Subsidies*, p. 110.

congested. The only serious reservations appear to be cost and the problem of personal safety in unattended cars that might arise in some areas.

At present PRT represents an idea rather than a developed technology. The first PRT system was supposed to go into operation in 1972 at the University of West Virginia in Morgantown, to connect its several campuses, but it has been plagued with difficulty. Original cost estimates were approximately $18 million for a 3.6-mile system. As of 1974, $57 million had been spent and estimates were that another $50 million would be required to complete the system. It is unclear whether the system will actually be completed; the Department of Transportation has also solicited and received a $7 million bid for demolition of completed parts.[46] The City of Denver also has plans for a $1.6 billion system, but delays in technology development from the Morgantown experiment will probably lead to higher costs.[47] At present PRT remains an attractive but expensive idea.

Pricing Policies and Free Transit

Not all improvements in urban transportation depend on changes in transportation services provided. There is considerable evidence to indicate that consumers selecting their transit mode do not face prices which represent the real costs of resources used and externalities generated. Thus, it is argued, if prices can be adjusted to reflect resource use and opportunities foregone, consumers will make adjustments in their trip choices which would result in more efficient use of transportation facilities. Furthermore, if price reflected both resource use and consumer evaluation, the resulting travel patterns would provide a much better information base upon which to plan additional transit investments. Recommendations for improving the use of transportation facilities through price changes can generally be placed in three classes—congestion tolls for automobiles, peak-off-peak differential pricing for public transit, and free transit to encourage automobile drivers to switch to public transportation. We must remember, however, that demands for transit appear to be very price-inelastic, so that the actual changes in modes due to price changes may be very small. At the same time, however, small percentage changes in automobile usage or transit ridership at the peak hour can have noticeable effects on congestion levels.

[46]Andrew Wilson, "Costly People Mover Project Bogs Down," *Los Angeles Times* (June 9, 1974), part V, pp. 2–3.
[47]Hilton, op. cit., p. 44.

Congestion Tolls Tolls on automobile users have been suggested to achieve two objectives.[48] First, analysis of freeway financing indicated that peak-hour freeway users were not generating sufficient revenue through gas taxes and automobile excises to pay for the additional freeway capacity required for peak-hour movements. Thus congestion tolls on peak-hour drivers would improve the financing equity of highways by requiring peak-hour drivers to pay for the additional highway capacity necessary to serve peak-hour needs. Second, the introduction of tolls related to congestion would provide an incentive for drivers to switch to other transit modes, travel on less congested routes, or change their travel to a less congested time.

Tolls are often looked upon as an alternative to freeway metering. By this method, the toll would be raised until no more than the optimal number of drivers chose to travel by freeway. Metered access, on the other hand, forces drivers to wait for their turn to enter. The same overall traffic flows could be achieved by either approach, but it is important to recognize that the distribution of costs and benefits would be different under the different approaches. The access metering is specifically designed to provide net gains for all users. No users are excluded from using the freeway, but total travel times are reduced by increasing the number of cars able to use the freeway at any given time. Price rationing, on the other hand, may result in net welfare reductions for both users who shift to other less desired modes and for users who continue to travel by freeway, finding it the preferred mode, if the toll they have to pay is higher than the value of the marginal benefits from reduced congestion.[49] Only users who place a very high value on travel time are likely to find that the value of the time saving from reduced congestion exceeds the toll they have to pay. We believe that a majority of freeway users would find the introduction of tolls to constitute a direct reduction in their welfare.

If the introduction of tolls would work to the detriment of most users, who would gain? The major gains would be in reduced taxes (or reduced automobile-related user charges on nonfreeway or non-peak-hour drivers) on those who currently provide financing for additional peak-hour freeway capacity they do not use. However, if freeway capacities were adjusted over time to reflect financing by congestion tolls for their peak-hour capacity, the total gains would exceed total losses and highway financing would be more efficient.

[48]William S. Vickrey, "Pricing in Urban and Suburban Transport," *American Economic Review* 53 (May 1963), pp. 452–465.

[49]Martin Wohl, "Congestion Toll Pricing for Public Transport Facilities," *Highway Research Record* No. 314, (1970), pp. 21–22. Wohl concludes that all current users are net losers from the introduction of tolls. We have assumed that tolls are also used to ration access so that congestion is decreased and travel time increased. Thus some commuters may gain if travel time savings exceed the price of the toll to them.

Several problems are associated with an introduction of congestion tolls. First, there are costs of collection. These could range from
costs of toll booths on major expressways to costs of an electronic
system where signals emitted from automobiles were recorded by re-
ceivers at different locations. From the recorded signals, bills could be
calculated and sent to drivers once a month. Such a system could, at
least conceptually, be expanded to include arterial streets as well as
more limited-access expressways.[50] The savings stemming from more
efficient highway use would have to exceed collection costs for there
to be net gains from the introduction of congestion tolls. Second, in
order for prices to reflect costs of congestion, prices must be different
at different times during the day. Prices would have to be highest during the rush hours, perhaps lower immediately before and after peak
hours, and zero whenever there was no congestion during the rest of
the day. Finally, drivers would have to be aware of prices and price
differences on different routes during different times of the day. Some
analysts have indicated that monthly billing would not provide sufficient incentive for driver response to differential prices, but the evidence on the rationality of consumer choice of transit mode discussed
earlier indicates that this reservation is probably unfounded, at least
for regular journey-to-work trips.

None of the major problems of introducing congestion tolls, at
least on major freeways and expressways, appears insurmountable.
The distributional questions as to who gains and who loses by such a
policy, however, needs to be explored further. One would like to be
reasonably sure that all gains did not accrue to the wealthy and that
additional costs for lower-income commuters would not be generated.
Finally, the chances of implementing such a policy will be slight if a
majority of freeway-using commuters would be direct losers from the
program. We may view the existing subsidization of peak-hour freeway users as inequitable and inefficient, but that is not going to make
those commuters any less resistant to changes in policies which make
them worse off. At the same time the beneficiaries of congestion tolls
are likely to be very dispersed and not even aware of potential benefits.
They constitute a latent group from which little political action should
be anticipated.

While it may be difficult to achieve the introduction of congestion
tolls to raise the costs to peak-hour automobile drivers, an alternative
policy of increased parking charges or taxes for all-day parkers would
produce some of the same results. An increase in parking taxes or
prices only for all-day parkers would bear most heavily on commuters,
not on shoppers who use freeways and city streets at less congested

[50]Vickrey, op. cit., pp. 457–461.

times. The parking taxes and prices would, like congestion tolls, encourage car pooling and the use of other transportation modes. They would not be as precise as congestion tolls could be, but they would be easier to administer. Parking-place taxes are also subject to control by city or county councils rather than by more highway-oriented organizations. This would make the raising of parking prices somewhat more feasible than the imposition of congestion tolls, but higher parking prices still would not be popular with most commuters and benefits would be too diffused for any single group to be a strong advocate for them.

Peak–Off-Peak Differential Pricing for Public Transit The difference between peak-hour and off-peak transit usage is even greater than the difference between peak and off-peak highway usage.[51] Thus the high capacity of public transit systems is even more attributable to peak-hour riders than is the excess capacity of freeway systems. At the same time, it is generally the regular peak-hour commuter who receives a *reduced* transit fare, when the logic of pricing in relation to costs indicates that it is the peak-hour commuter who should pay the highest fare and the riders using the system during the rest of the day who should pay lower fares.[52] It is generally concluded that the demand for public transit is sufficiently price-inelastic and the cross-elasticity of demand with respect to price between public transit and automobiles is sufficiently low that increased commuter fares would raise the total revenues of the system. However, price reductions at off-peak hours would decrease revenue because demand-price elasticities and cross-elasticities among modes are even lower for shoppers and for travel other than the journey to work.

In addition to revenue effects, however, there would be effects on transit usage. Most peak-hour riders would continue to ride at the peak hour, but one could anticipate some shifting to other modes or times to reduce the need for peak-hour capacity. During the time of day when excess capacity exists, lower fares would encourage some additional riders. One can be sure that the shift of commuters to other modes or times will be efficient only if the prices of other modes of travel reflect all costs of the use of the alternative mode. If peak-hour freeway usage is underpriced, as previously indicated, we cannot be sure that a modal shift from public transit to automobile would lead to a net improvement. We can conclude, however, that shifts from other modes

[51]U.S. Department of Transportation, op. cit., p. 192.
[52]Wohl, "Congestion Toll Pricing for Public Transport Facilities," op. cit., p. 20.

to public transit when transit has excess capacity would represent net efficiency gains.

The basic problem with higher peak-hour pricing to reflect costs on public transit is that we have to be sure that the prices of alternative modes, especially automobile travel, also reflect their costs. Only if all transit prices simultaneously reflect opportunity costs can we be sure that improvements in the pricing of any single mode will lead to net gains.

Free Transit Concern with price relationships among modes instead of between resource costs and price on a single mode has led to recommendations for free transit. Proponents of free transit have argued that automobile usage is always underpriced to the user because of congestion and external effects such as pollution, that automobile user lobbies are too strong to obtain increased prices or taxes for automobile usage, and that therefore the way to achieve efficient usage of alternative transit modes is to reduce the cost of the alternative—public transit—to zero.[53]

Providing free public transit is recommended to attract automobile drivers to public transit and thus reduce highway congestion and pollution. It is also argued that free public transit would provide better transportation access for the poor. It the total efficiency gains from reduced automobile usage exceed the resource costs of additional free transit, free public transit would produce net efficiency gains for the society as a whole.

At least one rigorous analysis of the impact of free public transportation has been undertaken. Gerald Kraft and Thomas Domencich[54] made independent estimates of the price elasticity of demand for public transit, its potential to divert automobile commuters, the reduction in air pollution, and the costs of providing free transit. They also compared costs of free transit with alternatives for achieving better mobility for the poor.

Kraft and Domencich estimated the price elasticity of demand for public transit to be 0.19; that is, a 10 percent reduction in price would yield a 1.9 percent increase in ridership.[55] This estimate is within the range of estimates discussed earlier in the chapter. Working from this

[53]L. Leslie Waters, "Free Transit: A Way Out of Traffic Jams," in George M. Smerk (ed.), *Readings in Urban Transportation* (Bloomington, Ind.: Indiana University Press, 1968), pp. 139–147.

[54]Gerald Kraft and Thomas A. Domencich, "Free Transit," in Mathew Edel and Jerome Rothenberg (eds.), *Readings in Urban Economics* (New York: Macmillan, 1972), pp. 457–480.

[55]Ibid., p. 465.

and other estimates, they concluded that the cost of free transit nationwide for 1967 would have been $2 billion, about $1.75 billion for existing systems and an additional $250 million for capacity to handle new riders.[56] Because conditions differ in different areas, the authors then narrowed their focus to Boston and undertook a more detailed analysis of the effects of free transit. Their estimates for Boston were that 9 percent of morning peak-hour automobile drivers and 6 percent of evening peak-hour automobile drivers would be attracted to the free transit.[57] This diversion would, in turn, reduce air pollution approximately 7 percent in the morning rush hour and 4 percent in the evening rush hour—with a total reduction in air pollution for all automobile usage of 4 percent.[58] The cost of providing free transit for the Boston areas was estimated to be $75 million annually in 1967 or about $95 per household. The majority of households, however, would not use the system.[59]

Following initial estimates, Kraft and Domencich proceeded to analyze the extent to which free public transit would be helpful to low-income ghetto dwellers. Their conclusion is that the problems lie not so much in transit fares but in the fact that transit routes do not provide ghetto dwellers with access to employment opportunities. Their conclusion was that for approximately $4.3 million annually (or 6 percent of the cost of free transit), ghetto dwellers could be provided with an efficient transportation network; but that simply removing fares from the existing system would not be of much help.[60] This, of course, leaves open the question whether a $75 million annual subsidy (1967 prices) for a 9 and 6 percent reduction in automobile usage at the morning and evening peak hour respectively and a 4 percent reduction in air pollution from automobiles could not be more efficiently achieved in an alternative manner.

Additional questions were also raised about the long-run desirability of free transit. First, the removal of prices makes it impossible to obtain information that is vital to the making of investment decisions. One is then continually faced with "demands" for more service but with no evidence as to whether benefits exceed costs for that service. Second, if transit is totally subsidized, incentives for efficiency are greatly reduced. Deficits are covered by taxes, and one way to get constituents to agree to increase taxes is to promise better service only if higher taxes are forthcoming. One would not be surprised if transit management, transit unions representing employees, and or-

[56] Ibid., p. 468.
[57] Ibid., p. 474.
[58] Ibid., p. 475.
[59] Ibid., p. 469.
[60] Ibid., p. 471.

ganized commuter groups eventually were able to become the policy makers in the system, showing little general concern for nonusers and taxpayers. Third, it is unlikely that all potential transit users could ever be completely satisfied, and some rationing would have to be undertaken. This would mean that those who were most politically influential would be likely to have their preferences met first, and this might well not include good transit service to ghetto areas or for low-income riders.

A fourth issue is who would pay the subsidy. Most residents would continue to be nonusers of public transit even if it were free. Provision of free public transit would be a definite case of taxing many to subsidize a few, and there is no assurance that income redistribution effects would be progressive or even proportional. In fact, users of more expensive transit modes such as commuter rail tend to have above-average incomes, while it is lower-income individuals who ride lower-cost inner city buses if they are served by public transit at all.

Finally, what long-run effects could we anticipate from a policy of free transit? Would this mean that suburban developers could locate still further away from existing built up areas and that, after the developers' houses are sold, the new residents could "demand" their fair share of free transit services? We would expect any reduction in the price of transportation to result in the use of larger land areas and in greater use of transportation itself. The lengthened journeys to work permitted by the free transit would at the same time increase spread and total transit demands within urban areas—with the likely result that there would actually be greater automobile mileage traveled in the new, spread out system than if transportation were costly, thus encouraging more compact development. In conclusion, we might predict that the benefits from free public transit would be much fewer than its advocates have argued and that problems associated with its operation and long-run effects would be much more severe than is generally recognized. Solutions to urban transit problems are more likely to be found through other approaches.

Pricing Policies We believe there are opportunities for improving the use of urban transit facilities through pricing policies even though demands are very inelastic with respect to price changes. Initially, however, the most fruitful efforts may occur from price changes that would make the prices faced by consumers reflect real costs. This would imply policies to increase costs to peak-hour automobile commuters, perhaps through congestion tolls on major freeways or through higher taxes on parking places for all-day parkers in congested areas. At the same time it may be possible to lower transit fares for off-peak riders. We are less sure about what to do with public transit commuter fares. We know peak-hour commuter fares do not reflect the cost of resources to provide the service, and we know that many of the beneficiaries of public transit system subsidies are middle- and high-income families. At the same time, we cannot really be sure if present subsidies have brought relative prices of public transit into a relationship with automobile costs that yields an efficient modal split or whether public transit prices should be still lower if automobile prices are not raised. We do believe, however, that there is little justification for free public transit. The objectives of reducing automobile congestion and pollution and providing transportation for the poor and ghetto dwellers could be achieved more efficiently in more direct ways.

One direct method of increasing mobility for the poor is through a transportation stamps program modeled after food stamps. Coupons good for any kind of public transportation, including taxis, jitneys, and transportation arranged by any nonprofit group, could be sold for less than their face value, with price depending on the income of the purchaser. For example, in an Office of Economic Opportunity experiment in West Virginia, elderly and disabled poor may buy $24 worth of transportation coupons for from $3 to $15.[61] If a transportation subsidy were made directly to low-income individuals, then prices which would reflect the real cost of resources could be used for public transit. Transportation coupons could also be used for paying freeway tolls or higher parking prices to protect the poor from bringing the cost of automobile usage at peak hours into line with costs. Direct subsidies to the poor would provide higher benefit for the cost than would large subsidies for public transit, most of which would be used to reduce the fares paid by middle- and high-income individuals.

Other Policies   When we search for solutions to transportation problems, we generally think of direct changes in the supply side of transport systems. There are other approaches which deserve consideration, however, especially as the cost of transportation investment increases. A common approach to alleviating peak-hour capacity and congestion problems is for employers to stagger the work hours of employees. A staggering system can reduce peak-hour demands by spreading the journey-to-work traffic over a longer time period.

An extreme form of staggering will occur if many firms adopt four-day work weeks for their employees. A shift from a five-day to a four-day work week results in a 20 percent reduction in journey-to-

---

[61]"OEO to Offer Transportation Stamps to Poor," *Los Angeles Times*, (June 3, 1974), part 1, p. 10.

work trips for those employees while most likely increasing their demand for nonwork trips. Substantial shifts to four-day weeks would have a major impact on urban transportation problems. The possibility of adopting four-day work weeks also reduces the expected value of new transportation investments to accommodate peak-hour travel.

Matching Alternatives to Needs

Different kinds of public transit meet different needs most efficiently. While rail rapid transit can carry the most passengers per hour in a single corridor, its total capacity is not very important when it is recognized that in all but New York and Chicago, express buses can meet actual corridor travel requirements at equal or lower cost. In addition, when the rail systems in San Francisco and Washington, D.C., are completed, all the cities where corridor movements are heavy enough to make a rail system potentially as efficient as an express bus system will have rail systems. Corridor movements in other urban areas can be more efficiently undertaken with combinations of express buses and metered freeways. Of all the systems considered, only a few local bus experiments, jitneys (which are still illegal in most cities), and taxis present potential solutions to transit problems of the elderly, poor, and nondrivers, especially for nonwork trips. Even free transit would not help ghetto dwellers unless new routes were added to current systems.

Given the current trends in the location of economic activity, it appears that future transit systems should be oriented toward flexibility—that is, the ability to alter routes to meet changing transit demands—rather than be tied to the location of current employment and residences. If decentralization continues, there is going to be much less demand for high-capacity point-to-point systems and much more demand for low-density modes to meet a variety of origins and destinations. This, in turn, implies that we can expect continued reliance on automobiles for many of our transportation needs.

If we are going to face increased automobile usage, it would appear increasingly important that automobile users realize the real costs of automobile use. This implies that effort might best be devoted to consideration of congestion tolls, parking taxes for all-day parkers in congested areas, and even increased fuel taxes or pollution emission taxes to encourage less polluting engines. If we had greater assurance that automobile drivers realized the real costs of automobile travel, we could be much more confident in our pricing of public transit, with subsidies going only where needed, not to high-income long-distance commuters. Only by moving toward an environment where prices reflect costs can we be assured of efficient use of resources in the all-important urban transportation sector.

GOVERNMENT TRANSPORTATION PROGRAMS

Local governments have regulated or provided urban public transit in many American cities since the 1800s.[62] It was only with a 1961 amendment to the Housing Act of 1949 that federal funds became available for urban transportation other than highways. Beginning in that year, the Department of Housing and Urban Development made funds available to urban governments for the resolution of urban transit problems. Since that legislation, the Department of Transportation has assumed Housing and Urban Development's early programs, and an Urban Mass Transit Administration (UMTA) has been created with funds to help cities respond to urban transit problems in a variety of ways. Because this effort is relatively large and does make available subsidies for urban transit experiments, new equipment, new systems, training programs, and so on, the policies of the UMTA have the potential for affecting the future of urban regions. A look at the results of UMTA's experiments also provides greater knowledge of the problems and potential of alternative transit modes to resolve urban transit problems.

Objectives

UMTA began with a wide range of objectives which included all aspects of transit—from simply keeping public systems in business, financing research and development on equipment modification or subway tunneling techniques, to sponsoring management seminars.[63] It also funded many experimental programs to learn just what was necessary to persuade drivers to utilize public transit instead of their automobiles. Consistently, however, the capital grants program has absorbed over 85 percent of UMTA funds, and objectives of the capital grant program are specified pretty clearly. They include:

1 To provide mobility to those segments of the urban population which may not command the direct use of motor vehicles, specifically, the young, aged, poor, handicapped, unemployed, and "secondary workers."

[62]Many of the readings in George Smerk, op. cit., focus on governmental policies.
[63]Hilton, op. cit., provides a description and evaluation of UMTA activities.

2 To improve mobility by improving overall traffic flow and specifically by reducing travel time in peak hours.

3 To achieve land-use patterns and/or environmental conditions which effectively contribute to the physical, economic, and social well-being of urban communities. Specifically, this was an attempt to promote land-use patterns which would minimize the need for transportation facilities (which UMTA interpreted as the development of dense urban patterns like New York or San Francisco rather than diffused patterns of the Los Angeles-Houston type).[64]

The only problem identified earlier that is not specifically included in UMTA's objectives is the reduction of automobile pollution. UMTA's first two objectives relate to the transit needs of nondrivers and reductions in peak-hour congestion. UMTA was also prepared to deal with financial deficit problems by providing federal grant funds for local programs or by paying up to two-thirds of the cost of new capital equipment.

UMTA's Programs

The 1974 pattern of UMTA's expenditures is presented in Table 12-2. The largest share of funds (87 percent) is devoted to helping local transit systems to purchase capital equipment. Second in importance is research, development, and demonstration projects, which account for 8 percent of the budget. These projects, plus information gained from some technical studies (3.8 percent), have provided the most additional information about urban transportation.

Within the capital facilities program, the largest use of funds was for local government purchase of private transit systems. Between 1965 and 1973, UMTA was able to contribute from 50 to 66⅔ percent of the costs of purchasing forty-nine private systems, in most cases to keep them from going out of business. Other capital funds were devoted to the purchase of either buses or rail equipment (through 1970, grants totaling $151 million had been made for 113 bus projects and grants totaling $513 million were made for 31 rail transit projects).[65] Of all capital facilities expenditure through 1970 the amount for buses was 22 percent and the amount for rails represented 74 per-

---

[64]Ibid., p. 52.
[65]A single system may receive funds for more than one project. Each separate application and grant is a separate project.

TABLE 12-2   UMTA Expenditures

Purpose	Fiscal 1974 Funds (millions)
Capital facilities	$872.00
Technical studies	38.00
Research, development, and demonstration	80.00
Management training	.50
University research and training	2.50
Administration	7.00
Total	$1,000.00

Source: George Hilton, *Federal Transit Subsidies: The Urban Mass Transportation Assistance Program* (Washington, D.C., American Enterprise Institute, 1974), p. 51.

cent of the totals. The remaining 2 percent was for three ferryboat projects. Most of the expenditures were simply for purchasing new equipment to replace older rolling stock; for example, in 1972, about 80 percent of the transit industry's purchase of buses was subsidized with UMTA funds.[66]

What has been learned from UMTA's programs? Most of UMTA's funds have been spent to purchase capital equipment to be used in the same way buses and rail cars have always been used. UMTA did finance many innovative experiments on alternative transit modes, however, and while it would be impossible to summarize all that has been learned, some general observations have been made.[67]

Most experiments have not been successful in attracting additional transit riders from automobiles. Most new projects got 85 to 90 percent of their riders from other public transit. Among specific kinds of experiments, the bus priority or freeway flyer bus experiments appear to be the most successful at attracting drivers onto public transit and reducing congestion on urban freeways. Some of the experiments were financially solvent and others will require subsidization, but not at as high a rate as rail systems such as BART.

Another observation is that very few ghetto-oriented transit projects attracted many riders; when they did, the first thing ghetto residents who got jobs did was buy automobiles and stop riding the public transit. No ghetto-related bus experiments were financially solvent, but again the amounts of subsidy needed to sustain their opera-

[66]Hilton, op. cit., pp. 55–56.
[67]These observations come from throughout Hilton, op. cit.

tion were—with all but a few exceptions—less than the amount of subsidy higher-income BART riders will receive.

Still another observation was that new technologies have not produced any economic alternative to known systems. For a rather long time to come, we can expect to move about in autos, on buses, or on rail cars.

In addition to reinforcing existing knowledge of urban transportation, UMTA's policies themselves have had some important impacts on urban transportation. One important finding has been the degree to which capital subsidies influence local government decision making and lead to inefficient resource use. For example, when UMTA pays two-thirds of the capital cost of new buses, it becomes rational for local transit companies to use buses for much shorter periods of time. This is because as buses get older, they require higher levels of maintenance expenditure—which must be borne totally by the local authority. William Tye analyzed the effects of capital subsidies on bus replacement and concluded that unsubsidized buses were optimally used for fifteen years at 50,000 miles a year or twenty-four years at 22,000 miles per year. With a two-thirds capital subsidy, it is rational to replace 50,000-mile-a-year buses after six years and 22,000-mile-a-year buses after thirteen years. Tye estimated that $55 million of $250 million granted for new buses was wasted due to early replacement encouraged by the capital subsidy.[68]

The capital intensity bias is even more dramatic in the calculations of medium-sized urban areas when making a choice between rail and express bus systems. Rail systems, relative to bus systems, are capital-intensive but involve lower operating costs. Thus as long as UMTA is financing two-thirds of the system, it becomes desirable from a local perspective to have a rail system even if an express bus system would be much cheaper and much more efficient. It also appears that UMTA policies are strongly prorail, even though most analysts consider mass rail systems appropriate for only the largest cities. A major apparent reason for UMTA's promotion of rail systems appears to be related to the objective of promoting dense urban development. It is unlikely, however, that the construction of new rail systems in medium-sized cities like Denver, Atlanta, Seattle, or St. Louis will prevent decentralization. Decentralization has not been prevented in the larger cities with extensive rail systems, and so few people actually commute from suburbs to downtown (5 to 10 percent of the work force in most places) that rail is not predicted to have a major impact on land use other than in the immediate vicinity of the widely spaced stations.

[68]Ibid., pp. 56–59.

Legislation has been introduced to permit UMTA to go into the operating-subsidy as well as the capital-subsidy business. However, UMTA's officials are somewhat hesitant to become involved in cost-based operating subsidies because to really manage an operating subsidy program fairly, one would have to control transit pricing, service levels, collective bargaining, maintenance standards, local taxes, rents, depreciation accounting, regulation of other transit like taxis, and parking prices. If the federal government does decide to provide operating subsidies for local transit, it would be more efficient to turn to a system of special revenue sharing rather than try to administer cost based programs.

Thus far it is difficult to perceive any impact of UMTA policies on urban transportation other than to help retain traditional systems. UMTA-sponsored experiments have increased confidence in freeway flyer and express bus systems, but the inability to provide operating subsidies for local ghetto-oriented transit has meant that local governments have considered ghetto transit projects failures because they were not financially solvent while at the same time infusing massive capital subsidies into their traditional systems. The $1,330 annual subsidy a BART rider will receive would go a long way toward assisting low-income residents achieve greater accessibility. Thus we must conclude that federal government transportation policies, as expressed and implemented by UMTA, represent very traditional and even obsolete approaches to urban transportation. It is doubtful that UMTA policies will reverse trends toward decentralization and the decline in the number of trips taken on public transit.

TRANSIT SUBSIDIES AND LAND VALUES

We have noted several times that the highest transit subsidies are directed toward rail systems and especially commuter rail systems which serve high-income suburban residents who work in the downtown area of the largest central cities. A crucial question remains, however, as to whether the high-income residents receive the benefits of the subsidy or whether the availability of subsidized transit near their homes is simply capitalized into land values. This would mean that the suburbanite simply paid a higher price for his suburban location and lower transit fares; while if he had to pay higher transit fares, he would have been willing to pay much less for his house at that location. If capitalization does occur, it is unlikely that the full amount of the subsidy is capitalized into real estate values. We would expect only the difference between the cost of transit to the user and the cost of the closest alternative (probably an automobile) to be capitalized, and this amount is probably always smaller than the amount of the subsidy required to maintain the suburban commuter rail systems.

Theory tells us that transit access should affect land values because the cost of access to other land-use activities is a major determinant of land value. Thus, while we recognize that most transit subsidies go to systems serving relatively high-income riders, we cannot be sure if they or the landowners at the time of the announcement of the system are really the beneficiaries of the subsidy. In either case, we are relatively confident that transit subsidization in the United States is greater for the rich than for the poor.

TRANSPORTATION AND FUTURE URBAN DEVELOPMENT

The automobile has facilitated decentralization and dispersion, and advocates of dense, central-city oriented urban development are highly critical of the automobile and its related low-density land-use patterns. Many of these critics have argued that if only public transit had not been permitted to deteriorate or if new public transit systems (especially rail systems) were constructed, urban land use would be rechanneled toward dense rather than dispersed patterns. In other words, if there were alternatives to automobiles, automobile-related spread development would cease.

We do not believe that existing evidence on urban transportation indicates either that the existence of public transit or rail systems will prevent decentralization or that new public transit systems will reverse trends toward low-density development patterns. Instead, simple location theory would predict that any reduction in transportation costs—from the early street railways and early electric interurbans onward—will permit greater access over larger areas and hence facilitate land-intensive, or low-density, development. The only way, for example, that new suburban-downtown commuter rail systems will significantly alter land-use patterns within our urban regions is to permit downtown workers to live still further away from downtown. Once these workers live further from downtown, it is safe to predict that their shopping, recreational, school, and other nonwork trips will probably be made by automobile within the suburban area rather than by rail to downtown.

There is reason to believe, however, that new rail systems with distant station spacing will promote high-density land use immediately adjacent to the stations. These systems will provide easier access to downtown for those commuters—a declining proportion of the total—who regularly go downtown. Thus commuter mass rail systems may provide nuclei for small-area dense development in suburban areas and simultaneously contribute to the maintenance of some downtown activities. This is about all that can be expected from new suburban-oriented transit systems. The automobile and the development patterns associated with it appear to be here to stay.

SUMMARY

The development of low-cost transportation has been a prerequisite for the creation of large urban agglomerations. Prior to the development of the railway, automobile, and truck, cities were small and compact. Since the development of these modern modes, cities have grown larger and urbanization has spread far beyond the boundaries of the older central cities. As urban areas have spread, journeys to work have become dispersed and are increasingly undertaken by automobile instead of public transit. This has resulted in continual financial deficits for public transit systems, while automobile usage has led to congestion and pollution within urban areas.

Many people have viewed the decline of the central city and congestion and pollution caused by reliance on automobiles as undesirable; public policies, especially those of the Urban Mass Transit Administration, have been undertaken to reverse these trends. In spite of UMTA and its programs, however, the number of rides on public transit has continued to fall—from 8 billion in 1963 to 5.3 billion in 1972. Between 1960 and 1970, the percentage of the labor force using automobiles for the journey to work increased from 64 to 78 percent, the percentage using rail fell from 3.8 to 3.0 percent, and the number using buses fell from 8 to 5.5 percent. The number of persons needing transportation from the suburbs to the central city and back has simply continued to decline.[69]

There would appear to be no question that in the future transportation is going to have to be even more flexible in serving decentralized origins and destinations than it has been in the past. It will certainly have to be more flexible than is possible with expensive fixed rail systems. We believe there are significant gains to be made through efficient use of express buses, metered freeways, and reduced restrictions on jitneys and taxicabs. We also believe more attention must be paid to highway usage and transportation pricing, so that prices paid by consumers will reflect real costs. Only with accurate prices can consumer choices lead to efficient outcomes. Transit modes with greater flexibility and more rational pricing are more likely to serve urbanized America in the late twentieth and early twenty-first centuries

[69]Ibid., pp. 97–98.

than is either a return to subsidized railroads or continued subsidized automobile usage.

SELECTED READINGS

Downs, Anthony: "The Law of Peak-Hour Expressway Congestion," *Traffic Quarterly*, 16 (July 1962), pp. 393–409.

Eckert, Ross D., and George W. Hilton: "The Jitneys," *Journal of Law and Economics*, 15 (October 1972), pp. 293–325.

Hilton, George W.: *Federal Transit Subsidies: The Urban Mass Transportation Assistance Program* (Washington, D.C.: American Enterprise Institute, 1974).

Meyer, J. R., J. F. Kain, and M. Wohl: *The Urban Transportation Problem* (Cambridge, Mass.: Harvard, 1965).

Moses, Leon N., and Harold F. Williamson, Jr.: "Value of Time, Choice of Mode, and the Subsidy Issue in Urban Transportation," *Journal of Political Economy*, 61 (June 1963), pp. 247–264 (Bobbs-Merrill Reprint, Econ-224).

Moskowitz, Karl: "Living and Travel Patterns in Automobile-oriented Cities," in George M. Smerk (ed.), *Readings in Urban Transportation* (Bloomington, Ind.: Indiana University Press, 1968), pp. 149–162.

Quandt, Richard E. (ed.): *The Demand for Travel: Theory and Measurement* (Lexington, Mass.: Heath, 1970).

Stover, Virgil G., and John C. Glennon: "A System for Bus Rapid Transit on Urban Freeways," *Traffic Quarterly*, 22 (October 1969), pp. 465–484. U.S. Department of Transportation: *1972 National Transportation Report* (Washington, D.C.: Government Printing Office, 1972).

Wohl, Martin: "Users of Urban Transportation Services and Their Income Circumstances," *Traffic Quarterly*, 24 (January 1970), pp. 21–43.

CHAPTER **13**

THE FUTURE

In preceding analyses we have examined urbanization in the United States, location patterns and trends within urban areas, the organization and operation of the public sector, and issues surrounding housing segregation, poverty, zoning, education, the environment, and urban transportation. In this chapter we will reemphasize recent trends in the location of residences and other activities, examine the possibility of a national urban policy, and look more closely at the future potential of the public sector to permit individuals to resolve problems and achieve higher levels of well-being than is possible through market transactions alone. This final analysis will again illustrate the usefulness of location and public goods–collective action theory for public policy analysis.

TRENDS

Between 1960 and 1970 United States population growth of 13.3 percent was lower than in any previous decade except the 1930s.[1]

[1]Data is from U.S. Bureau of the Census, *1970 Census of Housing and Population, United States Summary: General Demographic Trends for Metropolitan Areas, 1960 to 1970* (Washington, D.C.: Government Printing Office, 1971).

In 1973 the birthrate was the lowest ever. These lower growth rates are consistent with long-run trends in the United States and other industrialized countries. With easier availability of birth control, legal abortions, and many younger women's interests in pursuing careers outside the home, these rates may fall still lower during the next decades.

While overall population growth is lower, 85 percent (20 million) of it occurred in metropolitan areas between 1960 and 1970 as opposed to only 15 percent in the rest of the United States. Within metropolitan areas, central cities grew by only 5 percent (3.2 million), most of which was from annexation, while the suburban areas gained 16.8 million people—growing by 28 percent. Even though these aggregate figures indicate that most population growth is suburban, a closer look is necessary to discern trends—expecially with regard to central cities.

Central cities in the Northeast and North Central states lost population, while central-city gains were concentrated in the lower-density cities of the South and West. Furthermore, central-city population growth was due almost entirely to black population increases—white population in central cities declined by 600,000 over the decade. Of the twelve largest central cities, only Los Angeles gained white population; Washington, D.C., lost 39 percent of its white population, St. Louis lost 32 percent, Detroit lost 29 percent, Cleveland lost 27 percent, Chicago lost 19 percent, and New York lost 9 percent. About half of all cities above 500,000 lost white population; white population gains were common only in cities under 500,000.

Black population growth was not confined to central cities. Rates of black population growth in suburban areas among the largest thirty SMSAs ranged up to 219 percent in San Jose, California, and high rates were achieved in larger cities as well (New York, 55.1 percent; Los Angeles, 105.2 percent; Chicago, 65.5 percent). However, because the 1960 black suburban population was relatively small, high rates of increase have served to raise the percentage of blacks in suburbs only slightly—from 4.0 to 5.1 percent in the largest twelve SMSAs, for example. There are even a few areas where either especially rapid growth of the white population or slow growth of the black population produced suburbs that had smaller percentages of black residents in 1970 than in 1960. These areas are Detroit (3.7 to 3.6 percent), Baltimore (7.0 to 6.0 percent), Atlanta (8.5 to 6.2 percent), and Kansas City (5.5 to 5.2 percent) among the thirty largest urban areas.

Population totals and changes between 1960 and 1970 by rate for inside and outside central cities in the largest twelve SMSAs are presented in Table 12-1. From examining that table, one can see that all central cities except Los Angeles and New York lost population and all suburban areas gained population over the decade. One can also identify specific changes in black and white populations. These population trends are consistent with trends toward decentralization of population and reduced densities in central cities.

The 1960s were a good decade for housing improvement. The number of dwelling units increased 17.7 percent compared to the population increase of 13.3 percent. Most housing growth was in the suburbs, but the rapid new construction and filtering of older housing did permit many housing units lacking plumbing facilities to be replaced.[2] The result was that the number of occupied units lacking plumbing fell nationally from 9,778,000 (17 percent) to 4,678,000 (7 percent) and in metropolitan areas from 9.1 to 3.5 percent. Blacks also made significant housing gains, with the percentage of families occupying units lacking plumbing falling from 41 percent to 17 percent.

Closely related to decentralization and housing improvement were rising real incomes. Current dollar GNP and per capita incomes both doubled between 1960 and 1973; in constant dollars or real purchasing power, GNP and per capita income increased 50 percent over the sa ne period. The number of individuals defined as below the poverty line also fell from 22.4 percent in 1959 to 12.6 percent of the population in 1970. For the first time since the 1940s, black incomes rose relative to white incomes (from 55 to 64 percent) during the decade— with the major relative gains occurring between 1965 and 1970.[3] These gains most likely stem from the efforts of the civil rights movement and increasing enforcement of antidiscrimination laws. If relative income gains by blacks continue, some of our most serious urban problems—those related to a combination of poverty, racial discrimination, and segregation—could be alleviated.

Changes in employment over the decade also continued to reflect long-term trends. Between 1960 and 1972, white-collar employment increased from 43.1 percent to 48.2 percent of the labor force, and service employment increased from 12.5 to 13.7 percent. Blue-collar employment fell from 36.3 percent to 34.4 percent, and agricultural employment fell from 8.1 to 3.7 percent. Data on the location of employment and economic activity is not as precise as data on population, but it appears that jobs are moving from central cities and being

[2]In 1970 the census abandoned its attempt to identify deteriorated and dilapidated substandard housing because of the difficulty of obtaining consistency from census enumerators. Thus the only time-series data available for the 1970 census (and for the future) on substandard housing is based on lack of complete plumbing for dwelling units. Ibid., p. 71.

[3]U.S. Bureau of the Census, *Statistical Abstract of the United States, 1972* (Washington, D.C.: Government Printing Office, 93d ed., 1972), pp. 315 and 317; and U.S. Bureau of the Census, *1970 Census of Housing and Population, U.S. Summary: Characteristics of the Population, Part 1, Section 1* (Washington, D.C.: Government Printing Office, 1973), pp. 1–355, 1–378.

TABLE 13-1 Population Change in Large Metropolitan Areas: 1960–1970

		TOTAL				
				Change		
		1970 Population	1960 Population	Number	Percent	1970 Population
1	New York, N.Y.	11,528,649	10,694,633	834,016	7.8	9,448,551
	Inside central city	7,867,760	7,781,984	85,776	1.1	6,023,535
	Outside central city	3,660,889	2,912,649	748,240	25.7	3,425,016
2	Los Angeles–Long Beach, Calif.	7,032,075	6,038,771	993,304	16.4	6,006,499
	Inside central cities	3,174,694	2,823,183	351,511	12.4	2,502,684
	Outside central cities	3,857,381	3,215,588	641,793	20.0	3,503,815
3	Chicago, Ill.	6,978,947	6,220,913	758,034	12.2	5,672,570
	Inside central city	3,366,957	3,550,404	−183,447	−5.2	2,207,767
	Outside central city	3,611,990	2,670,509	941,481	35.3	3,464,803
4	Philadelphia, Pa.–New Jersey	4,817,914	4,342,897	475,017	10.9	3,944,884
	Inside central city	1,948,609	2,002,512	−53,903	−2.7	1,278,717
	Outside central city	2,869,305	2,340,385	528,920	22.6	2,666,167
5	Detroit, Mich.	4,199,931	3,762,360	437,571	11.6	3,419,720
	Inside central city	1,511,482	1,670,144	−158,662	−9.5	838,877
	Outside central city	2,688,449	2,092,216	596,233	28.5	2,580,843
6	San Francisco–Oakland, Calif.	3,109,519	2,648,762	460,757	17.4	2,574,802
	Inside central cities	1,077,235	1,107,864	−30,629	−2.8	724,698
	Outside central cities	2,032,284	1,540,898	491,386	31.9	1,850,104
7	Washington, D.C.,–Maryland–Virginia	2,861,123	2,064,090	797,033	38.6	2,124,903
	Inside central city	756,510	763,956	−7,446	−1.0	209,272
	Outside central city	2,104,613	1,300,134	804,479	61.8	1,915,631
8	Boston, Mass.	2,729,776	2,586,169	143,607	5.5	2,602,741
	Inside central city	629,416	691,869	−62,453	−9.0	524,709
	Outside central city	2,100,360	1,894,300	206,060	10.9	2,078,032
9	Pittsburgh, Pa.	2,401,245	2,405,435	−4,190	−0.2	2,225,021
	Inside central city	520,117	604,332	−84,215	−13.9	412,280
	Outside central city	1,881,128	1,801,103	80,025	4.4	1,812,741
10	St. Louis, Mo.–Illinois	2,363,017	2,104,669	258,348	12.3	1,975,145
	Inside central city	622,236	750,026	−127,790	−17.0	364,992
	Outside central city	1,740,781	1,354,643	386,138	28.5	1,610,153
11	Baltimore, Md.	2,070,670	1,803,745	266,925	14.8	1,569,099
	Inside central city	905,759	939,024	−33,265	−3.5	479,837
	Outside central city	1,164,911	864,721	300,190	34.7	1,089,262
12	Cleveland, Ohio	2,064,194	1,909,483	154,711	8.1	1,721,612
	Inside central city	750,903	876,050	−125,147	−14.3	458,084
	Outside central city	1,313,291	1,033,433	279,858	27.1	1,263,528

Sources: *1970 Census of Population and Housing, General Demographic Trends in Metropolitan Areas,* 1960 to 1970, tables 10 and 11.

WHITE				BLACK					
	Change					Change		Percent of Total Population	
1960 Population	Number	Percent	1970 Population	1960 Population	Number	Percent	1970	1960
9,406,755	41,796	0.4	1,883,292	1,227,625	655,667	53.4	16.3	11.5
6,640,662	−617,127	−9.3	1,666,636	1,087,931	578,705	53.2	21.2	14.0
2,766,093	658,923	23.8	216,656	139,694	76,962	55.1	5.9	4.8
5,453,866	552,633	10.1	762,844	461,546	301,298	65.3	10.8	7.6
2,391,207	111,477	4.7	522,597	344,447	178,150	51.7	16.5	12.2
3,062,659	441,156	14.4	240,247	117,099	123,148	105.2	6.2	3.6
5,300,912	371,658	7.0	1,230,919	890,154	340,765	38.3	17.6	14.3
2,712,748	−504,981	−18.6	1,102,620	812,637	289,983	35.7	32.7	22.9
2,588,164	876,639	33.9	128,299	77,517	50,782	65.5	3.6	2.9
3,661,587	283,297	7.7	844,300	671,304	172,996	25.8	17.5	15.5
1,467,479	−188,762	−12.9	653,791	529,240	124,551	23.5	33.6	26.4
2,194,108	472,059	21.5	190,509	142,064	48.445	34.1	6.6	6.1
3.195,372	224,348	7.0	757,083	558,870	198,213	35.5	18.0	14.9
1,182,970	−344,093	−29.1	660,428	482,223	178,205	37.0	43.7	28.9
2,012,402	568,441	28.2	96,655	76,647	20,008	26.1	3.6	3.7
2,318,802	256,000	11.0	330,107	226,013	104,094	46.1	10.6	8.5
874,926	−150,228	−17.2	220,788	158,001	62,787	39.7	20.5	14.3
1,443,876	406,228	28.1	109,319	68,012	41,307	60.7	5.4	4.4
1,557,842	567,061	36.4	703,745	495,483	208,262	42.0	24.6	24.0
345,263	−135,991	−39.4	537,712	411,737	125,975	30.6	71.1	53.9
1,212,579	703,052	58.0	166,033	83,746	82,287	98.3	7.9	6.4
2,508,377	94,364	3.8	127,035	77,792	49,243	63.3	4.6	3.0
628,704	−103,995	−16.5	104,707	63,165	41,542	65.8	16.3	9.1
1,879,673	198,359	10.6	22,328	14,627	7,701	52.6	1.1	0.8
2,241,910	−16,899	−0.8	169,884	161,499	8,385	5.2	7.1	6.7
502,593	−90,313	−18.0	104,904	100,692	4,212	4.2	20.2	16.7
1,739,317	73,424	4.2	64,980	60,807	4,173	6.9	3.5	3.4
1,806,239	168,906	9.4	378,816	295,416	83,400	28.2	16.0	14.0
534,004	−169,012	−31.6	254,191	214,377	39,814	18.6	40.9	28.6
1,272,235	337,918	26.6	124,625	81,039	43,586	53.8	7.2	6.0
1,413,282	155,817	11.0	490,224	385,995	104,229	27.0	23.7	21.4
610,608	−130,771	−21.4	420,210	325,589	94,621	29.1	46.4	34.7
802,674	286,588	35.7	70,014	60,406	9,608	15.9	6.0	7.0
1,646,995	74,617	4.5	332,614	258,917	73,697	28.5	16.1	13.6
622,942	−164,858	−26.5	287,841	250,818	37,023	14.8	38.3	28.6
1,024,053	239,475	23.4	44,773	8,099	36,674	452.8	3.4	0.8

created in suburban areas as rapidly as population is decentralizing. Most central cities are encountering absolute job losses, and in none of the larger cities are job opportunities growing as fast as in the suburbs. The decentralization of employment, especially in blue-collar and low-skilled service areas, will contribute to unemployment problems for blacks unless their rate of suburbanization is increased.[4]

For the future, it is anticipated that trends exhibited during the 1960s will continue. Decentralization, rising real incomes, better housing conditions, and shifts toward white-collar and service employment have been present throughout the twentieth century. The decline in population density in central cities, especially the core area, is also a long-run trend, although absolute population decreases within central cities are relatively recent.[5] It is hard to predict the long-run strength of this latter trend, but at present there are few indications of any early reversal. It is also expected that the proportion of black residents in central cities will continue to increase, but at the same time their rate of suburbanization may also increase. This latter increase will be due to the fact that increasing quantities of post-World War II housing will come onto the market at relatively low prices as its occupants move to newer housing.

In general, these expectations generate neither great optimism—although there should be continued improvement in the well-being of low-income families and blacks—nor great pessimism. Improvments in the status of the poor and of blacks will not occur as fast as many would wish and segregation will continue to be an important issue. All the trends, however, are the outcome of both market forces and public policies. Public policies at some governmental level deal with the entire variety of urban issues from location trends through education and income redistribution. In the remainder of this chapter, our focus will be on how public policies might be modified to alleviate urban problems earlier or better.

NATIONAL POLICIES AND URBAN GROWTH

Although current trends indicate increasing affluence and more comfortable lives for most Americans, many problems remain. Many peo-

---

[4]*Statistical Abstract,* op. cit., p. 230.

[5]The densest areas of central cities have been declining in population since the middle and late 1800s. However, until recently, central cities have had net population growth because annexation and increases in outer areas of the city more than offset center decreases. By the 1960s, the area of declining density spread as far as the central city boundaries, leading to net population declines. Population declines are also beginning and will spread through the older suburban areas adjacent to central cities.

ple are concerned with the segregation of low-income people in older urban areas, others are concerned with the decline of the central city as a cultural and economic center, others are worried about the depopulation of rural areas, and still others are concerned with decentralization and urban sprawl. As one begins to explore the nature of these urban growth problems, it becomes clear that the trends in the spatial patterns are the outcome of changes in income and technology, especially in areas of transportation and communication. Furthermore, these urban spatial patterns are, in turn, closely related to problems and policies not only in highway and public transportation but also in housing finance, poverty, segregation, planning and zoning, environmental management, education, and other public goods provision.[6] Everything urban appears to be related to everything else.

Concern for urban problems and recognition of the interrelatedness of urban problems and governmental policies has generated many calls for *a* national urban policy which would guide urban and rural growth in "desired" patterns of change and development while simultaneously taking into account the interrelatedness of policies in transportation, housing, poverty, the environment, planning and zoning, and provision of other public goods and services.[7]

The Housing and Urban Development Act of 1971 provided explicit recognition of the potential desirability of a national urban policy. The act is "an act to provide for the establishment of a national urban growth policy to support 'proper' growth of states, metropolitan areas, cities, counties, and towns, with emphasis on new communities and inner city development."[8] The act itself provides for nothing except a report by the President to Congress on urban conditions every other year. It is important, however, for raising the level of awareness of the interrelatedness of urban policies and problems. As one begins to understand the nature of location choices and impacts, it becomes clear that virtually all government programs, from irrigation projects to capital subsidies for mass transit, have different spatial effects and hence influence trends of urban growth.

While virtually all government policies affect urban growth and

---

[6]As indicated in previous chapters, most public policies have facilitated or contributed to low-density suburban development. The most important are probably highway construction and housing policies. Highway construction combined with restrictive policies toward taxis and jitneys have increased mobility in suburbs and not enhanced it in central cities. The special tax treatment of owner-occupied housing and the availability of mortgage insurance through FHA has facilitated single-family home ownership and hence new construction at low densities.

[7]For discussions of national urban policies, see Daniel P. Moynihan (ed.), *Toward a National Urban Policy* (New York: Basic Books, 1972).

[8]This act is discussed in Lowdon Wingo, "Issues in a National Urban Development Strategy for the United States," *Urban Studies*, 9 (February 1972), pp. 3–27.

change, three policies have been specifically designed to influence spatial patterns of urban growth. These are the urban renewal program, designed to revitalize older central cities; a series of rural development programs designed to enhance the economic viability of rural areas and thus reduce rural-urban migration and population pressures on central cities; and proposals for new town support which would accommodate future population growth in an orderly manner. It is useful to examine the accomplishments of these policies for an indication of their potential success in channeling urban growth into desired patterns, because it is policies of these kinds that would have to provide the basis for a national urban policy if one were to be designed. Following an examination of these policies, we will proceed to indicate their implications for questions of optimal city size, optimal spatial patterns, and the relationship between residential and firm location preferences and aggregate "optimality." This examination will provide the basis for a final look at the direction public policies might take to enable citizens to improve their well-being in urban areas over the long run.

Urban Renewal[9]

Urban renewal began as part of the Housing Act of 1949. The Housing Act of 1937 had provided federal subsidies for public housing along with a requirement that for every public housing unit constructed, one substandard dwelling unit had to be destroyed. No subsidies were provided for the destruction of substandard units, however, and requirements for the destruction of substandard units were widely circumvented. Beginning in 1949, the urban renewal program permitted local governments to purchase substandard dwellings, demolish them, and sell the cleared land for new uses, with the national government paying at least two-thirds of any net losses incurred by the local government. This program was expanded in 1954. It was initially conceived as a plan to remove slums and improve the quality of housing within central cities. As indicated in Chapter 8, however, the urban renewal program has not retained a housing focus. Both congressional acts and administrative decisions have permitted the program to be turned to nonresidential development with the explicit purpose of enhancing the economic viability of downtown areas of older central cities. The result has been the destruction of many more housing units than were rebuilt in urban renewal areas. Urban renewal is also extensively used for facilitating the expansion of hospitals, museums,

[9]Issues surrounding urban renewal were presented in Chap. 8.

universities, and other desirable activities which had become surrounded by slums in older areas.

Examinations of the results of urban renewal programs indicate that they tend to reduce the supply of low-cost housing and lower the overall population densities within central cities, thus making the central city more like the denser kinds of suburban developments than its former self. Realistically, this trend in spatial patterns appears to be what is needed to make central cities competitive with other centers of economic activity, although low-income families most certainly suffer in the process. Ironically, the destruction of low-cost housing also forced the spread of low-income families into other areas and probably speeded rather than retarded the outmigration of middle- and higher-income families.

It is difficult to evaluate the real effects that urban renewal programs have had on central cities. Programs are designed by local governments and are extremely diverse. It is clear that urban renewal has not slowed and may even have speeded the exodus of residences and businesses to suburban locations; the question is whether or not the programs have provided the central area with a new, lower-density equilibrium instead of cumulative long-run decline.

Most urban renewal projects, especially early ones, were undertaken in the face of growing city populations. Thus the reduction in the housing stock brought about by urban renewal caused many negative side effects outside the renewal area. The current trends toward reduced city population and the increasing abandonment of older housing may provide an environment for more beneficial urban renewal activity, perhaps reaching the scale of new towns within the old town.

New towns within the old could involve 10,000 to 50,000 people each. Through a combination of renewal and rehabilitation, an entire area could be transformed into a renewed community. Rather than remain part of a big-city government, however, the new town would be much more attractive to residents if they had their own government through which to control public services within their area. Cities of 10,000 to 50,000 are large enough to achieve efficient production of many important face-to-face services and, through contracting and membership in larger special districts, they could be more responsive and efficient than big-city governments.

One of the attractive features of suburban location is control of one's area through relatively small political units. It may be, therefore, that if central-city locations are to become as attractive as suburban ones, political structures as well as land-use patterns may have to be altered. We would suggest that the combination of a large urban renewal rehabilitation project with a new political unit oriented toward a better response to resident's preferences would be an excellent approach to revitalizing older, deteriorating areas.

Rural Development[10]

Gallup and Harris polls have indicated that most Americans would prefer to live in a small or medium-sized town rather than in a large urban area.[11] Many others wish rural areas were more attractive so that rural-urban migration would be slowed or reversed and that present urban areas contained fewer people and were less congested. The federal government has had specific policies to promote rural growth since 1961. At that time the Area Development Program (ADP) was begun with a focus on identifying and stimulating growth in small rural centers. It was hoped that if sufficient stimulus were applied to small rural centers, they would achieve self-sustaining growth and offer jobs to rural citizens, who would then no longer need to migrate to larger cities to enhance their income prospects. The growth pole focus originally resulted in too many "centers" receiving too little stimulus, and very few self-sustaining centers were created. After the ADP was subsumed under the Economic Development Administration (EDA) in 1965, the focus turned more toward areas with high unemployment instead of rural areas per se. By the end of the 1960s and early 1970s, considerable effort was being devoted to resolving unemployment problems in cities like Oakland and Seattle, with a reduced emphasis on rural areas.

A renewed interest in rural development and the relative failure of the ADP and EDA, which were under the Department of Commerce, led to the passage of the Rural Development Act of 1972, which—through the Department of Agriculture—provides funds to improve the well-being and economic growth of rural areas. The Department of Agriculture is utilizing the funds through the land-grant college and rural extension agent network to help rural residents not involved in farming—that is, the majority of rural residents—improve life in rural areas. Whether the Rural Development Act will be more successful than previous attempts to encourage rural development remains to be seen.

The idea of small rural growth centers is an attractive one, but trends in the location of economic activity have been strongly toward urban rather than rural growth. The ranges of job opportunities for

---

[10]A good discussion of rural development is contained in Lloyd Rodwin, *Nations and Cities: A Comparison of Strategies for Urban Growth* (Boston: Houghton Mifflin, 1970), Chap. 5.

[11]*The Gallup Opinion Index*, no. 57 (March 1970), p. 21.

residents and of suppliers for businesses are extremely limited by comparison to opportunities available in urban areas. Whether rural developments can really overcome the lack of agglomeration economies associated with the large metropolitan areas remains a serious question.

New Towns[12]

New towns are an exciting idea. Everyone hopes that new cities would be more pleasant and efficient than existing cities, especially if they could arise on open space unencumbered by previous location decisions and existing capital that was too valuable to destroy. Transportation systems, housing, employment, shopping, environmental considerations, land-use relationships—all these could be planned in relation to one another from the very beginning. The National Commission on Urban Growth Policy has proposed that the national government sponsor a program of new towns that would include ten new towns of 1 million population and a hundred new towns of 100,000 population by the year 2000.[13]

There is no clear definition as to just what constitutes a new town. Most analysts define new towns as relatively self-contained cities within which most residents are also employed. New towns could either be located close to urban areas, where they are called satellite new towns, or in rural areas, where they are called rural new towns. Some writers have also referred to huge urban renewal programs containing the equivalent of a new city as new towns in town.

While close proximity of residences, employment, shipping, and cultural facilities in a self-contained small area are the objectives of new town planners, few recent new towns have been able to achieve self-containment and many developments called new towns by their developers do not plan for high degrees of self-containment in matching residents to employment opportunities. Developments providing primarily residences with employment oriented toward serving the consumption needs of residents are better called new communities than new towns.

Depending on one's choice of definitions, there have been many new towns and new communities in the United States. Washington, D.C., for example, is a prime example of a planned new town. Other new towns have been developed to serve private employment, such as

---

[12]A good discussion of new towns is contained in James A. Clapp, *New Towns and Urban Policy* (New York: Dunellen, 1971).

[13]National Committee on Urban Growth Policy, *The New City* (published for Urban America, Inc. by Praeger, New York, 1969).

Pullman, Illinois; others were designed to serve federal projects, such as Oak Ridge, Tennessee, and Richland, Washington. There were also new towns undertaken as anti-Depression projects during the 1930s. During the 1960s, a large number of new towns and new communities were proposed and several are well underway, the best known of which are Reston, Virginia; Columbia, Maryland; and Irvine, California. As many as 140 have been identified as in some stage of planning or development.[14] Relatively few of the proposed new towns are rural new towns, Lake Havasu City, Arizona, and Soul City, North Carolina being major exceptions. The others are primarily satellite new towns with close economic and commuting ties to an urban area nearby. If all new towns and new communities currently planned were to be completed by 2000, they would have a population of 5 to 6 million. This would be up to 10 percent of the population growth expected by then and nearly 2 percent of the total United States population at that time.

The developers of new towns must overcome significant problems if their projects are to be successful. First, because of the difficulty of planning a balance between employment and residence, the town must be close enough to existing urban centers so that commuting is possible. This proximity is also important for attracting first residents who are employed elsewhere. A second problem is land accumulation under single ownership for development. It is difficult to accumulate sufficient land within commuting distance of a major employment center because, as land is purchased, strategically located landowners may demand higher and higher prices as their parcels become more crucial to the final land consolidation. The high prices asked by holdouts may make land acquisition too expensive for the new town to be profitable. A third problem is the huge capital investment required and the slow payback. The heavy initial investment means that development must proceed at a rapid pace so that revenue from sales will be sufficient to provide debt service on capital. Profits come only at the end of development, perhaps fifteen to twenty years after the project is begun. A few minor errors or delays can slow down the cash flow and cause bankruptcy—as nearly happened to Reston before it was purchased by Gulf Oil.

Finally, a fourth crucial problem involves dealing with the planning and zoning restrictions of the local governments within which the development is located. Most rural zoning ordinances are not suited for the development of a new town with its apartments, townhouses, shopping, and business areas. While overall development densities are often no higher than rural zoning calls for, within a new town some

[14]Clapp, op. cit., pp. 291–298.

parts are developed to very high densities while others are left in open space. It can take considerable time to negotiate an approved plan with a rural government, and time is money for a developer who has purchased options or the land itself for future development.

Because of the high risks inherent in such projects, the National Commission on Urban Growth Policies recommended that federal assistance be made available for new town developments. Under the New Communities Act of 1968 and the Urban Growth and New Communities Act of 1970, the federal government has developed a program of new town insurance.[15] The federal insuring of new town financing should make capital available at lower interest rates and with longer payback periods, thus making private new town development much more feasible. A potential problem with the insurance program, however, is that it requires the developers to reveal their plans for the new town much earlier than would otherwise be the case. This early disclosure could encourage landowners in the new town area to hold out for higher prices from the very beginning and thus could also raise the costs of the development. If this should become a serious problem, the only approach to the development of new towns may eventually be through the use of eminent domain, as in urban renewal—although constitutional issues would surely be involved in the condemning of private property for private new town developments. With the beginning of the federal insurance program and further development of new towns initiated privately, by the early 1980s we should have enough new towns to evaluate their potential much better than at present.

Before these new towns actually arise, however, we can anticipate some consequences of their development. First, we noted in Chapter 3 that smaller towns tend to be specialized in their employment patterns, depending on a few economic activities for their economic base. Specialization may be efficient, but whenever a local economy is dependent on a limited range of activities, it may also be subject to cyclical or growth problems related to those activities rather than possessing the stability that is achieved only with a broader economic base. Second, in smaller areas, employment opportunities—including both variety and opportunities for advancement—may be limited relative to opportunities in larger urban areas. This, however, is not a problem if upwardly mobile workers are willing to move to other areas instead of being tied to a single residential location. Finally, maintaining a population balance of all income classes would require subsidization of housing for low-income individuals and that subsidization,

[15]Hugh Mields, Jr., "The Federal New Communities Program: Prospects for the Future," in Harvey S. Perloff and Neil C. Sandberg, *New Towns: Why?—And for Whom?* (New York: Praeger, 1973), pp. 81–92.

like other income redistribution programs, will probably have to have a broader financial base than just the new town or new community. Housing subsidization would be required because the cost of new housing is much higher than low-income families can afford and there is no old or filtered housing available within new towns or new communities. Heavy subsidization to enable a few low-income families to reside in new towns will also pose the question that can be asked of so many government subsidy programs like public housing: Why are a few families subsidized heavily while the majority of equally eligible families receive nothing?

We can expect a variety of new towns and new communities to be developed in the future. However, even if the government-proposed 110 new towns are completed by the year 2000, they would provide for about only 20 million people or 7 percent of the United States population at that time.[16] If, in addition, the replacement of 25 to 30 percent of existing housing is achieved, over 80 percent of all housing built between now and 2000 will still have been constructed in existing urban areas. Thus even a very large new town program will not alter current national development patterns. Furthermore, because of the additional difficulties in developing rural new towns, it is likely that most new towns will be satellites to existing urban concentrations, and thus consistent with trends in population increase in suburban areas. They would not be reversing the decline of rural areas, and—if anything—they could be expected to contribute to the further decline of older central cities as new locations for face-to-face service and management activities were created in the larger new towns. If new towns offered improved residential environments with easy access to employment and air transportation, they would provide locations for central-city-type activities that were superior to those offered by existing big cities.

Of the three urban policies—urban renewal, rural development, and new towns—new towns appear to be the most attractive to urban planners and policy makers interested in urban development. New towns would, however, continue the process of stimulating suburban, although concentrated, growth and subsidization of high- and upper-middle-income classes. They would also contribute further to the decline of rural areas and central cities; the very trends other policies such as urban renewal and rural development are supposed to overcome. Overall, we expect that new towns will provide desirable locations for some families and businesses—but that they will not have a major impact on the problems of our large urban areas.

[16]William Alonso, "What Are New Towns For?" *Urban Studies*, 7 (February 1970), pp. 37–55.

Optimal City Size and Land-Use Patterns

Underlying policies of urban renewal, rural development, new towns, and slowing urban center growth are images of ideal city size and pattern. Economists, planners, and other analysts have undertaken research to identify optimal city size and land-use patterns, and it would appear that the information generated would make a contribution to national urban policies affecting these factors.

Two approaches have dominated research on optimal city size and land-use patterns. One falls under the heading of public sector cost minimization; the other attempts to compare agglomeration economies with external costs of congestion. Each will be examined in turn.

Public Sector Cost Minimization   A large number of analyses have been made of the relationship between public sector costs and city size.[17] Concern has been devoted to identifying the city size where public sector per capita costs no longer decrease (minimum efficient size) and the size where public sector per capita costs begin to increase (maximum efficient size). Different analysts have identified different minimum efficient sizes with estimates ranging from 50,000 to 200,000. Two major problems have, however, plagued these analyses. The first is that the difficulty of measuring public outputs makes comparisons very tentative because cost differences could be a consequence of output differences as well as city size or land-use patterns. Second, different economies of scale are associated with different public goods and services. For example, the minimum size for an efficient fire station is much smaller than the minimum size for a rapid transit system or a crime laboratory.

In spite of severe empirical problems in estimating minimum and maximum efficient city sizes, the major weakness in the public sector cost-minimization approach is not its empirical base but rather its conceptual framework. Two major deficiencies are inherent in the framework. First, the public sector is only one of many sectors whose costs and benefits must be taken into account in order to determine an optimal-sized city. For example, if a larger city than the one with minimum public sector costs were sufficiently more productive to raise everyone's welfare, the larger city would be "better" than the public sector cost-minimizing one. On the other hand, if citizens enjoy residing in a city smaller than the cost-minimizing one, one cannot

[17]Good reviews of this approach are included in William Alonso, "The Economics of Urban Size," *Regional Science Association Papers,* 26 (1971), pp. 67–83; and J. F. Kain, "Urban Form and the Cost of Urban Services," Discussion Paper no. 6, Program on Regional and Urban Economics, Harvard University, 1966.

say that they would be better off in a larger city without taking into account many more factors than public sector costs.

The second major deficiency of the public sector cost-minimization approach is that the particular institutional and spatial arrangements within a city will determine what is public and what is private, and the public-private mix may be more important in empirical studies of cost-minimizing size than anything else. For example, in a large-lot area, septic tanks may serve for sewage disposal (private), while in a denser area sewers will be necessary (public). Or, in a single-family neighborhood of low density, people will travel on public streets (public), but in a very dense city people will do much of their traveling in elevators (private). Different essential functions will be handled publicly or privately in different settings, and the arbitrary movement of a function from the public to the private sector or vice-versa should not determine optimal city size.

Because of the narrow scope of public sector cost-minimization considerations and the arbitrary nature of the distinction between private and public functions, it would appear that the public sector cost-minimization approach is not a very useful one for identifying optimal city sizes.

Agglomeration Economies and External Costs Agglomeration economies and large markets are attractive for businesses, consumers, and employees. However, as indicated in the chapters on transportation and the environment, there are also external costs associated with large concentrations of people carrying out their activities in close proximity to one another. The possibility exists that at some point the benefits of agglomeration economies will be exceeded by the costs of negative externalities and that cities reaching this situation will be too large. The optimal size would be that at which the benefits from additional growth were just offset by the costs of additional growth.

The aggregative approach to optimal city size is more inclusive than the public sector cost-minimization approach, but it is so inclusive that it has not been possible to identify empirically the external costs and agglomerative benefits from city growth so that they may be compared. Attempts have been made to identify relationships between income, productivity, the cost of living, and city size, under the assumption that if there were cities where external costs exceeded agglomeration economies, real incomes and productivity would be lower in those than in smaller cities. Research along these lines does not indicate that any American cities are too large, although this conclusion is tentative because there are few large cities from which estimates can be made and conclusions inferred.[18] In addition, even if we could determine the size at which external costs exceeded agglomerative economies, that point would probably be different for each city depending on its historical land-use pattern, proximity to other densely populated areas, and technology and consumer preferences at the time of the estimate. There is no reason to expect that a single size identified as optimal would be appropriate to every circumstance.

Is Optimal City Size Meaningful?   Given the problems with both public sector cost minimization and aggregative approaches to the question of optimal city size, one may well ask whether the concept is important or useful. Certainly public sector cost minimization is an inadequate guide to identifying the size of city that would provide consumers and producers with highest welfare levels. The aggregate approach would appear more promising, but it focuses only upon identifying a maximum efficient city size, of which there may be only one in any single country. Outside the largest urban areas, one would expect to find a variety of city sizes, with each serving different market areas. The range would be from a general store, gas station, and post office in an isolated rural area to a midwestern agricultural center of 10,000, to regional centers like Seattle and St. Louis, and to national centers like New York, Chicago, and Los Angeles. The efficient size of any given place would depend on its market area, economies of scale in production for each good or service, agglomerative economies, external costs, and consumer preferences. In short, there is no optimal city size for all purposes.

An Alternative Approach to Optimal Location Patterns

As we have stressed many times, the location patterns in urban areas are the consequence of many individual choices by consumers, businessmen, and government officials, no one of whom is concerned with the eventual results of all the choices taken together. At the same time, some influence on patterns can be exercised through public policies, especially in transportation, planning, and zoning. Policy makers can also attempt to design institutions so that individual consumers and businessmen realize external costs or benefits and thus are led to decisions which are good for others as well as themselves. In earlier chapters we have stressed that the American economy and polity is

---

[18]Alonso, op. cit.

very decentralized and that criteria for normative conclusions must be based on the preferences of the individuals directly affected by specific resource allocations. This implies putting the question of optimal city size and pattern in terms of what city sizes and patterns are preferred by different kinds of firms and residents with different preferences.

An article by Alan Hahn utilizes an approach based on family and business location preferences, and this approach appears to be useful for understanding emerging spatial patterns.[19] To clarify the meaning of different spatial patterns, Hahn distinguishes two features of urban organization: density and structure. "Density" refers to the degree of *concentration* or *dispersion* of population and economic activity. "Structure" is defined in terms of a spectrum from the dominance of a *single* urban center to *multicentered* urban areas. When urban patterns are examined in terms of both characteristics simultaneously, one has a four-type classification as illustrated in Figure 13-1. In Figure 13-1, type *A* is characterized as dispersed and multicentered. This would characterize a region of urban sprawl with no dominant center of economic activity. Type *B* is concentrated and unicentered. Hahn calls this a supercity where population and economic activity are concentrated in a single place and there is a distinct break between the high-density urban area and the rural open space. A third type, *C*, is characterized as dispersed but unicentered. This type would characterize many existing urban areas where a single central city still dominates but low-density activity spreads out long distances from the center. A fourth type, *D*, is concentrated but multicentered. This would result for example, from confining development to small areas (new towns) surrounded by open space where development was not permitted.

These types represent characteristics over which there has been considerable debate and they have served as models for recommended development. For example, multicentered dispersion is viewed as a return to a rural setting with the amenities of urban living. Others have argued that high-density urban areas and elimination of sprawl are more desirable and recommend concentrated development, either unicentered or multicentered as in England, where London is surrounded by greenbelts interspersed with high-density new towns. Finally, of course, dispersed unicentered development still characterizes most American urban areas.

Using Hahn's classification of urban development patterns, we can examine which patterns would meet different residential and business location preferences. Beginning with family residential choice,

---

[19]Alan J. Hahn, "Optimal Urban Spatial Patterns: A Conceptual Framework," *Reviews in Urban Economics*, 1 (Fall 1968), pp. 51–69.

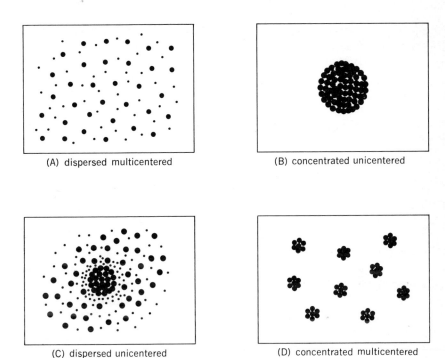

(A) dispersed multicentered

(B) concentrated unicentered

(C) dispersed unicentered

(D) concentrated multicentered

FIGURE 13-1   Patterns of Urban Development

one would expect that individuals preferring to reside in high-rise apartments with easy walking or public transit access to downtown employment and cultural life would prefer a concentrated, unicentered pattern. Multicentered concentration would be preferred by those who like apartment or townhouse living within easy walking distance of shopping and some job opportunities and easy access to open space surrounding the city but who wish to avoid the higher density and size of the large, unicentered development. New towns would appear to fit the preferences of these individuals rather well. Families preferring large-lot single-family dwellings with easy access to jobs, shopping, and open space would prefer multicentered dispersal. The dispersal would permit uncongested automobile access to a variety of uses rather than the congested access that occurs when only residences are dispersed but jobs are concentrated in a single center. Furthermore, if residences in a dispersed system were related to employment location, a shorter average journey to work would be possible than in a unicentered, dispersed pattern like that which we now have. As even this brief overview indicates, different people may well prefer different patterns of urban development.

Profit-maximizing locations also differ for different kinds of businesses. Firms requiring face-to-face interaction with a large number of diverse suppliers and purchasers, but needing little physical space for their own operations, would prefer a unicentered, concentrated pattern. For example, an advertising agency which sells its services to many larger firms but purchases supplies from many sources such as printers, photographers, modeling agencies, film studios, and market research agencies would find a location in a concentrated, unicentered area to be a superior location. At the other extreme, a manufacturing plant that moved its inputs and products by truck and used a large land area for assembly-line production would find a dispersed, multi-centered pattern superior. Different retailers would have different preferences as well. Grocery stores may fare well in multicentered areas that were either dispersed or concentrated, but sellers of fine jewelry might prefer a unicentered pattern. Different firms, like different families, would find that different patterns met their preferences most closely.

Of the four patterns presented by Hahn, the most common in America is the dispersed and unicentered, with the development of smaller centers in outlying suburban regions. The patterns most lacking are concentrated ones, although new towns such as Reston and Columbia are attempts to develop a concentrated, multicentered pattern around Washington, D.C. From a historical perspective, American land-use patterns may be in transition from the concentrated, unicentered pattern of the era before the streetcar and the automobile to a multicentered dispersal where the downtown area of the older central city becomes one node in a multicentered pattern. Within this trend, the development of concentrated new towns surrounded by greenbelts provides an alternative for families preferring smaller but concentrated locations, and urban renewal programs may improve older central cities as desirable residential and business areas for those preferring larger urban centers. Overall, if new towns and communities are developed and older central cities revitalized (although not ever again as dominant as in earlier periods) to supplement multicentered dispersal, the diverse preferences of families and firms can be accommodated in the emerging patterns—something that would not be possible within any single land-use pattern.

The existing patterns have developed in response to a large number of individual choices—not any single national policy. Even recent new towns were begun privately and prior to the national government's interest in them. Governmental policies in urban renewal and in encouraging additional new towns, however, are important, but important for expanding the range of options individuals and firms have for their location, not important for channeling growth in patterns predetermined to be desirable by any small number of central policy makers.

Within the patterns that are emerging, debate over concentration versus dispersal is still common, with predominant academic and planning thinking tending to favor more concentrated development than is occurring in most suburban areas. Concentration is favored by some because it would be possible to leave more large undeveloped areas of open space and by others because public service costs (at least for water, sewage, electricity, and roads) would be lower if empty spaces left from leapfrogging development patterns were filled from the center out as development occurred. Not all arguments favor concentration, however. Jack Lessinger, for one, has argued that while concentrated development of an area at a single point in time may appear neater and more efficient, over the long run all the buildings decline together, producing in thirty to fifty years a large, obsolete slum.[20] On the other hand, leapfrogging at any given point in time leaves open space to be filled in later, so that when the oldest buildings are deteriorating, many newer buildings are in good repair and there are greater incentives for individual building rehabilitation or demolition and rebuilding because the entire area has not fallen into disrepair. The existence of open areas for future development also provides greater flexibility for introducing new uses over time, as, for example, having space to build a new supermarket or shopping center as population densities increase to provide a sufficient market area for larger-scale businesses. Finally, by permitting scattered development, a greater supply of land is available at any one time, thus keeping its price lower than would be the case if land development were restricted to a narrow band adjacent to existing development.

Two places with extensive regulation to promote concentrated development are Hawaii and England. In Hawaii the amount of land on which development is permitted has been so limited as to result in single-family housing prices that are approximately twice as high as in the rest of the United States; consequently single-family housing ownership is too costly for most citizens. In England, zoning to obtain concentrated development has led to single-family housing densities of twelve to sixteen houses per acre (compared to two to six per acre in most of the United States). Clawson and Hall, themselves both advocates of concentrated development, conclude that the new dense British developments will deteriorate into substandard housing within twenty years because the houses and yards are too small to meet the preferences of the residents as their incomes increase.[21] It is only

[20]Jack Lessinger, "The Case for Scatteration," *Journal of the American Institute of Planners*, 28 (August 1962), pp. 159–169.

[21]Marion Clawson and Peter Hall, *Planning and Urban Growth: An Anglo-American Comparison* (Baltimore: Johns Hopkins, 1973), pp. 263–265, and 269; and Fred Bosselman and David Callies, *The Quiet Revolution in Land Use Control* (Washington, D.C.: Council on Environmental Quality, 1971), pp. 25–26.

through heavy construction of public housing in Britain that housing and land prices have been kept from rising as they have done in Hawaii.

There is insufficient evidence to indicate whether or not more concentrated land-development patterns would be superior to current suburban dispersal. We believe that our suburban development patterns have led to greater housing construction on lower-cost land than would have occurred under more concentrated patterns and that the emerging pattern of multicentered dispersal (in spite of its unsightliness to those who prefer more orderliness and regularity) meets the preferences of families and businesses much better than most urban planners and critics of suburbia have recognized. In fact, it appears that it is where public policies have been most extensively used, in restrictive zoning and building code enforcement, that the most serious problems of rising housing costs and the slow filtering of used housing to low-income residents have emerged. The market may not produce utopia, but it is uncertain that directed patterns would be superior.

A National Urban Policy?

As the interrelatedness of urban growth and urban problems has received national emphasis, there have been increasing calls for a national urban policy which would be made up of related national policies regarding urban development, transportation, housing, poverty, segregation, environmental management, intergovernmental relations, planning and zoning, and the organization of local government. As the problems become more complex, there appears to be an increasing tendency to assume that diversity and complexity equal chaos, from which only uniform national policies can bring order. With 85 percent of the population residing in urban areas, an urban policy would be equivalent to a uniform national domestic policy. This would require not only agreement on objectives and integration of policies but also an abandonment of the federal structure of government, whereby the state and over 78,000 local governments operate with considerable autonomy—but also considerable cooperation with one another. In addition, serious reservations must be maintained about the ability of any single group of decision makers to actually accumulate all the relevant knowledge of urban phenomena, to select objectives, to weigh alternative programs to achieve those objectives, to select the most efficient programs, and then to direct their implementation. Our mixed experience with past public policies does not lead us to predict great success for an even larger bureaucratic effort. To seek solutions to urban problems via national policies may well be to look in the wrong direction; but given an environment of increasing complexity and inter-relations, there is a crucial role for public or collective action.

THE ROLE OF COLLECTIVE ACTION IN FUTURE URBAN POLICY

Several important observations underlie our analysis of the potential role of collective action in an increasingly diverse and complex econ-omy and policy. While these observations were discussed in the intro-duction and repeated in the discussion of the role of collective action in Chapters 5 and 7, it is important to reiterate some of them in order to put the role of public policy in perspective.

Complexity and Diversity

The urban environment is one of increasing complexity and diversity. Accompanying this complexity and diversity are conditions of tech-nological change and rapidly expanding knowledge. Within this chang-ing and complex environment, two crucial and related issues emerge. First, the expanding knowledge widens the scope for individual choice, which in turn makes it difficult if not impossible to make accurate long-range forecasts of many crucial changes. This problem is a cir-cular one. The more we know in the sense of predicting and manipulat-ing, the greater the range of potential manipulation and hence the greater the difficulty of forecasting future consequences of individual choices. Thus the more complex and changing the environment be-comes, the greater the difficulty of forecasting and the greater reliance we must place on the capacities—of both individuals and organizations—to adjust to change. This leads us to look at governments and other decision-making structures for collective action in terms of their capac-ity to adjust to change as well as to carry out day-to-day repetitive tasks. In this regard, our findings regarding large-city bureaucracies such as New York City's school system (discussed in Chapter 10) and the lack of innovation in fire protection (discussed in Chapter 7), lead us to seriously question a structure of government in which large bureaucracies or strong monopolies are a characteristic feature.[22]

[22]Vincent Ostrom, "Order and Change amid Increasing Relative Ignorance: An Inquiry into the Relationship of Knowledge, Decision Making and Organization," (Bloomington, Ind.: Workshop in Political Theory and Policy Analysis, Indiana Univer-sity, Working Paper W73–1).

A second implication of increasing complexity and change is that the ability of any individual or group of individuals to obtain a picture of the whole problem will be increasingly reduced. As the aggregate pool of human knowledge increases, there is a correlative increase in the relative ignorance of each individual in relation to that aggregate pool of knowledge. This means that individuals may move to higher and higher levels of abstraction in attempting to relate diverse problem areas such as transportation, housing, poverty, planning and zoning, etc. Or individuals may move to increasing specialization within a single small area, knowing more and more about less and less. Within both of these kinds of specialization, scientists, academicians, and planners have biases that are very important when the relative advantages of more centralized planning and decision making relative to decentralized decision making are being considered.

Scientists, academicians, and planners are most interested in identifying regularities in relationships which help them make predictions, build theories, or identify "scientific laws."[23] There is a strong preference for scientific generalizations that are "true" regardless of time or place. In fact, it sometimes appears that this kind of scientific knowledge is the only kind worth accumulating or preserving. We do not want to negate the importance of scientific generalization, but we do believe that another kind of knowledge, which might be called time-and-place information, is also important. In fact, in a changing environment it is precisely time-and-place information that is utilized by citizens and producers to make everyday consumption, exchange, and production decisions. When a person is selecting a residence, he consults a broker who has time-and-place knowledge of the market and of specific houses for sale at that time. When one needs transportation, he wants a taxi or bus at a particular time and place. When we look at aggregate statistics on housing transactions or taxicab trips, we see only regularities over time—not the effort of individuals utilizing time-and-place information to make crucial decisions along the way. We must never lose sight of the fact that the outcomes we observe in urban growth and change, transportation, housing, poverty, planning and zoning, education, and so on are the results of many individual choices—choices where individuals selected one particular alternative which in turn led to still further choices by others. Attempting to plan or implement public policies without recognizing the complexity of this phenomenon may lead to undesired and unforeseen consequences as well as desired outcomes.

[23]F. A. Hayek, "The Uses of Knowledge in Society," *American Economic Review* 35 (September 1945), pp. 519–530.

Within this complex environment, a logical approach to public policy analysis is to focus on altering incentives for individual choice so that an individual pursuing his own ends simultaneously achieves socially desired objectives. At the same time, we must recognize that different communities of people are going to be affected differently by different incentive systems and rules and that these different groups may require the ability to make and enforce their own rules for members affected. This would imply that neighborhood-sized governments might be the proper forum for decisions on street lighting, regional governments would be the proper forum for environmental regulation, and the national government is the appropriate decision-making unit for foreign policy. We can no more expect the national government to be able to regulate garbage collection in New York City than we can expect a neighborhood government to manage trade with the U.S.S.R., and we might even conclude that New York City's government is too large to manage all garbage collection within its various boroughs. When an inappropriate forum is responsible for a program, we can expect unsupported rhetoric and gross blunders—which is what we get when the President or the Congress talk about solving the problem of ghetto unemployment or crime in the streets directly or when a city neighborhood talks about designing freeways for the entire city. Different problems affect different groups of people, and it is important to have political organizations that can help differently affected groups to resolve their common problems.

Within this framework there are two issues that require special mention. First, does the organization of the public sector in urban areas permit the participation of everyone, including minorities and average citizens who are not part of some organized interest group? Second, can we reconcile the need for the quid pro quo (something for something) transactions which are required to maintain a complex system with problems of poverty and the need to enhance equal opportunity for participation in the American economy, polity, and society?

Minority Participation

Two difficulties in organizing governments are posed by the needs to (1) create a system where one or a few groups cannot take over the system and use legal authority to advance their own interests at the expense of others and (2) assure all groups and individuals access to governments for solution of their own collective action problems. Both problems were of major concern to the drafters of the Constitution of the United States.[24] The avoidance of a potential monopoly take-over by a single faction was the single most important reason for designing a system of government that contained overlapping governments (federalism) and separation of powers within the national government. The Bill of Rights was also added to the Constitution to prevent the imposition of political externality costs on individuals. The Founding Fathers, by using an analysis similar to our approach in Chapter 5, concluded that simple governing structures were subject to monopoly takeover by single factions and thus could not be subject to constitutional law because there were no independent and competing governmental units to ensure obedience to the Constitution. The availability of small constituencies (House districts, state legislative districts, and local governments) and overlapping governments was also supposed to provide a system in which all citizens would find some political unit to respond to their needs. Furthermore, small units were designed to fall within larger units to prevent them from becoming too parochial internally. Finally, the Founding Fathers anticipated that the many governmental units would cooperate where cooperation was beneficial to each and be rivals where conflicts of interests occurred. It was the conflict or competitive element, however, which was necessary to encourage responsiveness to constituents and maintain the system of checks and balances.

These issues, which were raised directly in the drafting of the U.S. Constitution, are relevant to the organization of the public sector in metropolitan areas. In Chapter 5 we concluded that citizens in small, homogeneous groups would be able to achieve the highest level of satisfaction in their consumption of local public goods and services. We also observed that it was in big central cities, where there were no small governmental units or overlapping competing units, that dissatisfaction with local government and poor performance appeared to be highest.[25] Thus residents in large cities, especially minorities, may find little access to city government for assistance with their problems; while small suburban governments, with their homogeneous populations, meet the preferences of their citizens better. The logic of this situation would indicate that minorities within big cities would

---

[24]The arguments presenting the logic of the U.S. Constitutional structure are contained in Alexander Hamilton, John Jay, and James Madison, *The Federalist*. An analysis of the logic of *The Federalist* with special reference to contemporary work in the theory of public goods and collective action is contained in Vincent Ostrom, *The Political Theory of a Compound Republic: A Reconstruction of the Logical Foundations of American Democracy as Presented in 'The Federalist'* (Blacksburg, Va.: Center for the Study of Public Choice, 1971).

[25]For an evaluation of data bearing on these questions, in addition to that contained in Chapter 7, see Robert L. Bish and Vincent Ostrom, *Understanding Urban Government: Metropolitan Reform Reconsidered* (Washington, D.C.: American Enterprise Institute, 1973), chaps. 4–6.

benefit by having smaller governments to represent their interests and that if barriers to migration were eliminated, many central-city residents would prefer to move to suburban areas. There, suburban jurisdictions would provide a mix of goods and services that would meet their preferences better. Here a potential for conflict arises. A minority resident from a city might prefer to move to a suburban community, but the suburban community residents—because they perceive the minority's preferences as different from their own—might enact policies to exclude minorities in order to maintain their own homogeneity. Even if suburbanites feel that minorities should be permitted to reside in their communities, they may find it rational to take a free-rider attitude, hoping that other suburban communities will not be as restrictive as they are. When many suburban communities act in this manner, however, the migration of minorities—usually low-income or racial minorities—out of central cities may be restricted. This, in turn, reduces the ability of these minorities to obtain higher-quality housing, better education, and other objectives which migration from the central city to suburban areas may provide.

Our model of the public sector lets us predict the conflicts between the preferences and likely policies followed by homogeneous communities to maintain their homogeneity and the preferences of nonresidents who may differ in socioeconomic characteristics from the majority of a community within which they would like to reside. Our model, however, does not provide an unequivocal answer as to what is "fair." Is the behavior of the small community too parochial, and should it therefore be overturned by larger or different political units such as state legislatures or the courts? Or does the behavior of the small community simply represent the collective action of a group of individuals to improve their status and should it therefore be permitted? Obviously, there are different gainers and losers from alternative conclusions, and it would not be surprising if different resolutions or compromises to the issue were reached in different metropolitan areas, by different state legislatures, and by various court decisions. One can predict, however, that if minorities are minorities both within the large central city and within the metropolitan area or state as a whole, their interests are not likely to be well represented in resolution of the problems, and thus outcomes are less likely to be satisfactory to minority preferences than to the preferences of others. On the other hand, if minorities areawide or statewide are majorities in some of the political units, as would be the case if central cities had smaller political units within them, they would have a better bargaining position in regard to areawide or statewide problems. This leads us to conclude that neighborhood governments in large central cities may be important for minority participation in regional and statewide organizations as well as to improve provision of their own local public goods and services.

One area where racial minorities have been able to gain considerable access to larger political structures is in cases of racial discrimination.[26] For example, suburban community exclusion on the basis of race is unconstitutional and subject to reversal through the court system. In other areas, however, as where exclusion is based on wealth—as with zoning and land-use control (Chapter 9)—the outcome is less clear, especially when we recognize that many policies designed to enhance environmental quality have this exclusionary effect (Chapter 11).

The dilemma that arises when a small political unit acting in behalf of its constituents' interests enacts policies contrary to the interests of nonresidents is one that is always present in a complex system of government. Only through the simultaneous existence of small and large governments can we expect to have local problems cared for while areawide problems also have a forum for resolution. However, the organization of the smallest governments must be such that minorities are majorities in some of them if their interests are to be adequately taken into account in the larger forums.

Income Redistribution

Quid pro quo or something for something exchanges are necessary to achieve efficient outcomes from a complex system. Unless beneficiaries, either as individuals or as relatively small groups, see the costs of public goods and services, they will continually "demand" quantities far in excess of the costs of provision, hoping that others will bear the costs. If all individuals and groups follow this strategy, the result is a public expenditure level where costs exceed benefits, at least at the margin. Only if beneficiaries see costs can we be sure of achieving expenditure levels where marginal benefits are reasonably close to marginal costs. To achieve the adjustments in the urban public sector requires considerable complexity, including small political units, single purpose districts, user-charge financing, and earmarked taxes. Still further efficiency may be achieved by introducing service contract-

[26]The usefulness of overlapping jurisdictions for minority access to government is better illustrated by the progress blacks have made through recourse to the court system than by any other aspect of American government. Virtually every step in achieving civil rights—from *Brown v. Board of Education*, the Supreme Court case ruling against separate school systems for blacks and whites in 1954, through expanded opportunities in employment and housing and equal rights to municipal goods and services provided by state and local governments—has been achieved through court order.

ing among governmental units and between private producers and governmental units.

Within this environment there are always some political groups whose incomes are so low that through their own resources they cannot provide the level of goods and services consistent with what many citizens and representatives of other political units feel should be provided. Thus transfers of resources from wealthier individuals or groups are required. In Chapter 6 we examined why income redistribution expenditures must be financed over relatively large areas, even if direct provision by small political units of the goods or services is most efficient. The requirement for financing through relatively large units means that specific programs to achieve redistribution among individuals residing in different local political units is necessary if both the advantages of small homogeneous political units and income redistribution to enhance opportunities of low-income families are to be achieved simultaneously. Income redistribution responsibilities must be assumed by state or national governments in a complex public sector.

THE ROLE OF URBAN ECONOMICS AND POLICY ANALYSIS

To understand and be able to predict outcomes from the operation of the complex public economies of metropolitan areas is going to require considerable research by social scientists, academicians, and planners. While these specialists may not be able to prescribe solutions to particular time-and-place problems, such as how to get the garbage out of the alley behind Tenth Street or how a neighborhood's transportation problems might be resolved, specialists can produce information on programs in garbage removal and transportation that have succeeded or failed elsewhere. Program and benefit-cost analysis, as discussed in Chapter 7, can provide valuable information for public decision makers. In addition to direct problem-oriented policy research, two other kinds of research would appear to be useful to aid in resolving or ameliorating urban problems. One is the production of information on urban patterns and trends and the consequences likely to be associated with them. If urban economists and planners could develop models whereby they might predict the consequences of different decisions on zoning, codes, transportation improvements, etc., that information would be of use not only to public decision makers but would aid private investment and location decisions as well. We must remember that location decisions are made primarily by individuals in the private sector, and to the extent that their knowledge of future trends and patterns is better, we can expect more efficient private location decisions. A businessman would like to locate his factory in an area where other factories are expected to locate, and an apartment developer would like to locate away from factories in areas predicted to be developed for residences. The production of information which can serve as a base for all decision makers is itself an important and useful task which academicians and skilled planners may be best able to do.

Still a third type of research may in the long run be the most important for assisting individuals to resolve their common problems in an increasingly diverse and complex economy and polity. This is research that enables us to predict the likely consequences of different rules of political organization or different institutional structures. For example, in Chapter 7 we noted that traditional local government reformers had recommended improving the local public sector by consolidating the variety of political units that currently exist into a single areawide government. At the same time we noted that big bureaucracies running school districts were not performing well, that monopolistic fire departments did not do as well as the Rural-Metropolitan Fire Department did in serving Scottsdale, and that smaller police departments were outperforming larger departments at lower cost. This empirical evidence directly contradicted a long tradition of recommending solutions to problems by simplifying the political structure into a hierarchically ordered system. We would argue that the strongest evidence indicates that it is precisely where there are large local governments holding a virtual monopoly over their citizens—in the large central cities—where public sector failure is greatest, and that it is in the suburbs with their overlapping, duplicative, and small governments that efficiency and responsiveness are highest.[27] If our arguments are correct, the path to reform may be through permitting neighborhoods within big cities to form their own governmental units for many governmental functions, including managing neighborhood police patrols. The difficulty in dealing with questions of institutional design is simply that we do not have very much evidence as to what difference it really makes to have, for example, 3 million citizens in the city of Los Angeles served by a single city government with a small number of overlapping special districts, while the 4 million residents in the rest of the county are served by seventy-eight cities and hundreds of special authorities. We believe that more attention needs to be paid to the design of decision-making arrangements with a view to creating institutional structures within which individuals seeking to resolve their own problems come to agreeable solutions. In the past,

[27]Bish and Ostrom, op. cit., chaps. 4–6.

too little attention has been paid to how efficient and responsive small political jurisdictions are, how well areawide problems are resolved through areawide special districts or intergovernmental agreements, and how can one design income redistribution within such a complex system.

As the urban environment becomes increasingly complex and diverse, it is going to become even more important for us to understand how local governments can be organized to handle the range of collective problems that are present and are yet to come. It is impossible for anyone to understand all aspects and all interrelationships of every problem. At the same time, however, we need to improve our capacity to predict what difference different organizational structures will make if we are to have incentive systems that lead to self-correcting instead of cumulatively destructive behavior. We need to begin to understand the operation of the multitude of public agencies in the public sector as we understand the operation of the market—as a system of individuals making decisions with certain regular outcomes, not as a dichotomy between chaos and bureaucratic monopolies.

Throughout this book we have focused on predicting the consequences of different choices within different constraints. Our beginning chapters on location illustrated how the pattern and size of cities changed with changes in transportation technology. Later, we specifically introduced the institutional arrangements for dealing with public goods, externalities, and common pools. We then tried to show how the nature of the good in relation to political decision-making structures resulted in particular outcomes in the areas of housing and segregation, poverty, zoning and land-use control, education, environmental management, transportation, and—finally—in forecasting future urban spatial patterns. It is our belief that prediction must come before prescription and that prediction is the most important part of urban economics and policy analysis. For urban problems, we believe the theoretical foundations of location and public goods–collective action theory provide an extremely useful body of predictive theory from which to begin. We will be more confident when we have more empirical evidence to validate hypotheses and inferential reasoning drawn from these theories, but at present we believe these bodies of theory carry one as far as any alternatives. We are also optimistic that further development of this approach will help us to understand what differences different institutional arrangements make for permitting individuals directly involved to solve urban problems. This is a different perspective from policy analysis interpreted as designing particular programs to resolve particular problems in some particular time-and-place situation.

It is also the perspective, however, of traditional economic analysis as a body of concepts and theories which assist us to understand the operation of extremely complex systems, and the public economy of metropolitan areas needs more of this kind of analysis than it has received in the past. Urban economics, by adding public goods and collective action theory to its location and microeconomic theory bases, would appear to be well suited for this important role.

SELECTED READINGS

Alonso, William: "The Economics of Regional Size," *Regional Science Association Papers*, 26 (1971), pp. 67–83.

Clapp, James A.: *New Towns and Urban Policy* (New York: Dunellen, 1971).

Hahn, Alan J.: "Optimal Urban Spatial Patterns: A Conceptual Framework," *Reviews in Urban Economics*, 1 (Fall 1968), pp. 51–69.

Hayek, F. A.: "The Uses of Knowledge in Society," *American Economic Review*, 35 (September 1945), pp. 519–530.

Lessinger, Jack: "The Case for Scatteration," *Journal of the American Institute of Planners*, 28 (August 1962), pp. 159–169.

Ostrom, Vincent: "Order and Change amid Increasing Relative Ignorance: An Inquiry into the Relationship of Knowledge, Decision Making and Organization" (Bloomington, Ind.: Workshop in Political Theory and Policy Analysis, Indiana University, Working Paper W73–1, 1973).

Wingo, Lowdon: "Issues in a National Urban Development Strategy for the United States," *Urban Studies*, 9 (February 1972), pp. 3–27.

INDEX